An Introduction to the New Testament

THE ANCHOR YALE BIBLE REFERENCE LIBRARY
is a project of international and interfaith scope in which Protestant,
Catholic, and Jewish scholars from many countries contribute individual
volumes. The project is not sponsored by any ecclesiastical organization and is not intended to reflect any particular theological doctrine.

The series is committed to producing volumes in the tradition established half a century ago by the founders of the Anchor Bible, William
Foxwell Albright and David Noel Freedman. It aims to present the best
contemporary scholarship in a way that is accessible not only to scholars but also to the educated nonspecialist. It is committed to work of
sound philological and historical scholarship, supplemented by insight
from modern methods, such as sociological and literary criticism.

JOHN J. COLLINS
General Editor

THE ANCHOR YALE BIBLE REFERENCE LIBRARY

An Introduction to the New Testament

The Abridged Edition

RAYMOND E. BROWN, S.S.

Edited and Abridged by

MARION L. SOARDS

Yale UNIVERSITY PRESS/NEW HAVEN & LONDON

Published with assistance from the foundation established in memory
of Philip Hamilton McMillan of the Class of 1894, Yale College.

First edition published in 1997 by Doubleday, a division of Random House, Inc.
First Yale University Press impression 2010. Abridged edition 2016.
Abridgment copyright © 2016 by Yale University.
Copyright © 1997 by The Associated Sulpicians of the U.S.

Yale University Press books may be purchased in quantity for educational,
business, or promotional use. For information, please e-mail sales.press@yale.edu
(U.S. office) or sales@yaleup.co.uk (U.K. office).

Designed by Mary Valencia.
Set in Joanna MT and Scala Sans type by Newgen North America.
Printed in the United States of America.

Library of Congress Control Number: 2015949082
ISBN 978-0-300-17312-3 (paperback: alk. paper)

A catalogue record for this book is available from the British Library.

This paper meets the requirements of ANSI/NISO Z39.48-1992
(Permanence of Paper).

10 9 8 7 6 5 4 3 2

To a remarkable group of doctoral candidates
who studied at Union Theological Seminary (NYC)
in the years J. Louis Martyn and I taught New Testament
and who now teach me by their writings

Raymond E. Brown, S.S.

To my friends and colleagues who once were
doctoral students at Union Theological Seminary (NYC)
when Raymond E. Brown, S.S., and J. Louis Martyn worked
together to cultivate an uncommon environment
for work and learning

Marion L. Soards

On biblical studies:
What is the literal sense of a passage is not
always as obvious in the speeches and writings of the
ancient authors of the East, as it is in the works of our own time. For
what they wished to express is not to be determined by the rules of
grammar and philology alone, nor solely by the context; the interpreter
must, as it were, go back wholly in spirit to those remote centuries of
the East and with the aid of history, archaeology, ethnology, and other
sciences, accurately determine what modes of writing, so to
speak, the authors of that ancient period would
be likely to use, and in fact did use.

—Divino afflante Spiritu §35

—Encyclical of Pope Pious XII on
Promoting Biblical Studies, AD 1943

CONTENTS

PREFACE

GOAL OF THIS VOLUME

Though the title *An Introduction to the New Testament* would seem to explain the purpose of this volume, a number of clarifications are necessary for readers to know what is intended. Moreover, as an abridgment of Raymond E. Brown's original work, this compact version of the Foreword is meant to preserve and to re-present much of the essence of the original work for the benefit of those who may have an early interest in studying the New Testament.

First, the readership that is envisioned has implications. This book is introductory, for both readers who have become interested in the NT on their own and readers who take NT beginning courses on different levels. It aims to be a book that can give guidance the first time one reads intensively parts of the NT, and later help to consider more specific questions.

Second, this book concentrates on the New Testament, not on "Early Christianity." Why? The study of early Christianity moves into church history and so is a much wider field than biblical research. The concentration here will be on the twenty-seven books accepted as the canonical NT. Such a concentration is legitimate because these writings have had a uniquely normative place in Christian life, liturgy, creed, and spirituality. Moreover, these books exist, and in that sense are more certain than conjectural, undocumented, or sparsely documented reconstructions of early Christianity.

Third, this book concentrates on the extant text of the NT books, not on their prehistory. More scholarly attention has been devoted to the NT than to any other literature of comparable length in the world, and this attention has resulted in an uncontrollably large variety of theories about sources (not preserved) that were combined or corrected to produce the books that have come down to us. Such research is fascinating; a certain percent of it presents plausible results; but none of it is certain. For an introductory book to concentrate on nonexistent "originals" is to impose on beginning readers too much theorizing. It is far better to devote most space to what actually exists, supplying only brief guidance to the principal hypotheses about what might have been.

Nevertheless, a minor concession will be made to scholarly theorizing by treating the books in a combined logical and chronological order rather than in the order that has become canonical. A glance at the Table of Contents will show that the NT books will be studied in three groups. The first group of eight involves "the Gospels and Related Works": Mark, Matthew, Luke, Acts, John and the Johannine Epistles/Letters (since these letters comment in some ways on issues raised by the Gospel). The second group involves the thirteen Epistles/Letters that bear Paul's name, divided into two batches: the undisputed seven most likely written by Paul himself, arranged here in plausible chronological order; then the six deutero-Pauline works possibly or probably written by Pauline disciples. The third group involves a somewhat topical arrangement of six works that are hard to date: Hebrews, I Peter, James, Jude, II Peter, and Revelation.

Fourth, the primary goal is to get people to read the NT books, not simply to read about them. Accordingly only a fraction of this introduction is given over to general or topical discussions (Chapters 1–6, 15–17, 25). The rest consists of chapters devoted one by one to the books of the NT. Accordingly chapters regularly begin with a "General Analysis of the Message" designed to accompany the reading of the respective NT book. It will point out the flow of thought, elements that are characteristic of the author, and what is significant and interesting. At times this analysis will be almost a minicommentary that should help to make the NT intelligible and enjoyable. In turn, the design of the chapters on individual NT books varies according to a number of factors: the length of the book, its importance, and its difficulty. For each of the books of the NT, however, near the beginning of the chapter, a "Summary of Basic Information" offers answers (often options) for some basic questions of NT introduction: Date; From Whom (Author by Attribution; Author as Detected from Contents); From Where; To Whom; To Where; Authenticity; Unity and Integrity; and Division (Outline). At times different answers proposed for one or more of these questions will be recognized and commented on as needed.

Fifth, issues raised by the NT will receive attention throughout this book. Indeed, in most of the chapters the last subsection will take up selected issues and problems for reflection. Father Brown was a Roman Catholic (a priest who belonged to the Society of Saint Sulpice), yet he spent much of his academic life teaching other Christians (Protestant, Episcopal, Orthodox), and so the wider range of Christian practice and belief was very much his concern—as he insisted that it should be in this ecumenical era. Furthermore, as he observed, most of the main NT figures and possibly all the writers were Jews, and NT affirmations have had a major role (often devastating) in relations between Jews and Christians. The ongoing import of these statements (more benevolent, one hopes) for those relations must not be neglected. Finally, the NT has had an impact on world society and ethics beyond any religious adherence. These factors are important as one reads the NT, and, as much as possible, they will be kept in sight throughout the book.

Sixth, the book aims to be centrist, not idiosyncratic. To serve readers best this volume intends to judge what most scholars hold—even when on a particular point Brown (or the abridger) might be inclined toward a minority opinion. Inevitably, however, judgments about the majority stance are not totally free of one's own prejudices.

.⋆.

ACKNOWLEDGMENTS

Raymond Brown's full statement of acknowledgments stands in the unabridged original version of *An Introduction to the New Testament* and includes certain information about those to whom he refers. The contributions of those identified in that first version of Brown's book have deeply affected the results of abridging that magisterial volume. The names of these people bear repeating here: David Noel Freedman, John Kselman, Craig Koester, John Meier, Marion Soards, Phyllis Trible, Ronald Witherup, Cecil White, Thomas Cahill, Eric Major, Mark Fretz, and Maureen Cullen. As Brown concluded his acknowledgments, "To one and all sincere thanks."

Furthermore, at Yale University Press I would like to thank Jennifer Banks for her encouragement and guidance, Heather Gold for her assistance in the production of the manuscript of the book, and Jeffrey Schier, whose work as manuscript editor was done with diligence and understanding. My thanks also to Susan Garrett for her unflagging encouragement and support, and those students both at Louisville Presbyterian Theological Seminary in Louisville, Kentucky, and at Justo Mwale University in Lusaka, Zambia, whose enthusiasm for New Testament studies inspires the writing of books such as this one.

INTRODUCTORY
BACKGROUND MATERIAL

The NT does not stand by itself; it joins books that Christians call the OT to form the Bible. In fact, there is no Christian Bible without the interrelated parts. In traditional Christian thought the OT is Scripture, just as sacred and enduringly valid as the NT.

Although the Jews of Jesus' time had a sense of fixed sacred writings in "the Law" and "the Prophets," there was as yet no unanimity on which books constituted "the Writings." Wide general agreement fixing the contents of Sacred Scripture for the majority of Jews came only in the course of the second century AD. All the books recognized at that time were ones preserved in Hebrew or Aramaic.

From the earliest attestation, however, because Christians preached about Jesus in the Greek language, they tended to quote the Jewish Scriptures in Greek translation, chiefly the version called the Septuagint (LXX). Embracing the LXX meant having a larger OT canon than the collection of Scriptures accepted among Jews of the rabbinic period. Many centuries later in the Western church some Protestant Reformers opted for only the shorter Jewish canon, but the Roman Catholic Church (Council of Trent, 1545–63) recognized as canonical seven other books that it had used for centuries in church life—called "Apocrypha" (Protestant) and "Deuterocanonical" (Catholic). All these books were composed before Jesus' time, and probably some of them were known and quoted by NT authors (for example, John 6:35 seems to echo Sirach 24:21). Accordingly a familiarity with them is desirable whether or not they are canonical Scripture in one's tradition.

Which is the best English Bible translation to read? By way of a general answer, the most appropriate translation must be judged from one's purpose in reading. Is it public worship? Private reading? For the purpose of careful reading or study, one must recognize that translators face a challenge: either they render ambiguous texts literally and preserve ambiguity, or render freely and resolve the uncertainty. In a "free" translation, translators have already made a decision as to what they think an obscure passage means—*the translation is interpretation*. Accordingly here are a number of relatively literal translations. The value judgments are particularly in reference to the NT.

> *New Revised Standard Version* (NRSV). The *Revised Standard Version* (RSV) was an American revision (1946–52) of the *Authorized (King James) Version* (KJV, 1611) that remained faithful to its antecedent where possible. Despite the occasionally stilted Bible English ("thou" and "thee"), it was in many ways the best Bible for study purposes. The NRSV, an ecumenical reworking (1990) that has replaced it, has less Bible English and manifests sensitivity for inclusive language; the price is a certain loss of literalness. Sporadically the English translation does not express the plain sense of the original language text. A *Catholic Edition* NRSV (1993) has the Deuterocanonical Books inserted within the OT in the usual Catholic order.

> *New American Bible* (NAB). This Roman Catholic translation from the original languages (1952–70), done with Protestant cooperation, includes a revised translation of the NT (1987), which makes the NAB a serious candidate for study purposes. Its language is mildly inclusive.

> *New Jerusalem Bible* (NJB). In 1948–54 the French Dominicans of Jerusalem produced *La Sainte Bible*, a learned translation accompanied by copious (but conservative) introductions and notes. The English translation, the *Jerusalem Bible* (JB, 1966), has been

replaced by the NJB (1985), overall a significantly improved translation with better introductions.

New International Version (NIV Updated). This "update" is a revised translation of the NIV of the 1970s. It anticipates a conservative/evangelical readership. It aims at being literal, but has been the subject of controversy because of theological and translation issues. It is not a very literal rendering. As of 2014, there is no edition with Apocrypha/Deuterocanonical Books.

Revised English Bible (REB). The REB (1989) is a thorough reworking of the *New English Bible* (NEB, 1961–70) that renders texts in vigorous contemporary British English.

New American Standard Bible (NASB). The *New American Standard Bible* is an American translation (1959–71/95) in the tradition of the *American Standard Version* (ASV, 1901) that brings the ASV-inspired translation into "more current English." An "Updated" NASB (1995) is available. The NASB aspires to literalness and generally attains its goal. There is no edition with Apocrypha/Deuterocanonical Books.

Overall, according to one's purposes (study, prayer, public reading), one should choose a translation carefully. No translation is perfect, and readers can learn much from comparing them.

ABBREVIATIONS

AB	The Anchor Bible
ABRL	The Anchor Bible Reference Library
ANTC	Abingdon New Testament Commentaries
AYBRL	The Anchor Yale Bible Reference Library
BETL	Bibliotheca Ephemeridum Theologicarum Lovaniensium
BNTC	Black's New Testament Commentaries
CBQMS	Catholic Biblical Quarterly Monograph Series
CC	Continental Commentaries
DSS	Dead Sea Scrolls
GCHP	*God's Christ and His People*
GNS	Good News Studies
HUT	Hermeneutische Untersuchungen zur Theologie

JBap	John the Baptist
LEC	Library of Early Christianity
NJBC	*The New Jerome Biblical Commentary*
	References are to an article and to a section or sections
	in the article.
NT	New Testament
NTG	New Testament Guides
NTL	The New Testament Library
OT	Old Testament
RB	*Revue Biblique*
SBLDS	Society of Biblical Literature Dissertation Series
SBLSBS	Society of Biblical Literature Sources for Biblical Study
SNTSMS	Society for New Testament Studies Monograph Series
TBOB	*The Books of the Bible*
W/JK	Westminster/John Knox Press
WUNT	Wissenschaftliche Untersuchungen zum Neuen Testament

MAPS OF PALESTINE AND THE MEDITERRANEAN AREA

The NT writings about Jesus and his disciples relate a story enacted on the stage of history. Real people and real places involve geography, so that eventually readers will need to consult maps. Many "study Bibles" have an excellent series of maps. The two maps that follow here are simply a basic geographical guide. Political realities affect the boundaries drawn on geographical realities. In Palestine during the decades before and after the time of Jesus, the boundaries shifted somewhat frequently. The map of Palestine, while it supplies place names useful for all the NT stories situated in that land, shows boundaries roughly as they existed in the late 20s, that is, the time of Jesus' public ministry. In terms of physical terrain it is helpful to realize that Palestine has three principal geographical features, running parallel to one another. As one moves inward from the Mediterranean, a north-south coastal plain slopes upward to a north-south chain of mountains that runs like a spine through the center of the land. On the eastern side of those mountains, the land slopes downward to a dramatic rift-valley that (once more, north to south) contains the Sea of Galilee, the Jordan valley, and the Dead Sea. The great northwest-southeast plain of Esdraelon offers a break through the mountains and direct access from the coast to the valley.

Table 1. Chronology of people and events pertinent to the New Testament

ROMAN EMPERORS	IMPORTANT JEWISH HIGH PRIESTS	JEWISH AND ROMAN RULERS IN PALESTINE			EVENTS *Christian events italicized*
		JUDEA	GALILEE	E–NE OF GALILEE	
		Herod the Great (37–4 BC).			—*Jesus born ca. 6 BC.* —Revolts at the death of Herod the Great; Augustus divides Herod's kingdom among Herod's three sons.
Augustus (30 BC–AD 14).	Annas (Ananus I) (AD 6–15).	Archelaus, ethnarch of Judea (4 BC–AD 6). BEGINNING OF FIRST PERIOD OF ROMAN PREFECTURE Coponius (AD 6–9).	Herod Antipas, tetrarch of Galilee and Transjordan (4 BC–AD 39).	(Herod) Philip, tetrarch of Ituraea and Trachonitis (4 BC–AD 34).	—Judea made a Roman province when Archelaus is deposed (AD 6); census of Quirinius; revolt of Judas the Galilean. —No record of major violent revolts in Judea from AD 7 to 36. Rebuilding of Jerusalem Temple, begun by Herod the Great, continues.
Tiberius (AD 14–37).	Caiaphas (son-in-law of Annas) (AD 18–36).	Valerius Gratus (AD 15–26). Pontius Pilate (AD 26–36).			—Early incidents under Pilate show him as imprudent but not vicious or dishonest. —*Jesus begins his public ministry and John the Baptist is executed ca. AD 28.* —*Jesus is crucified in 30 or 33.* —Pilate's repression of the Samaritans in 36 causes Vitellius, prefect of Syria, to send him to Rome (36/37). —*Death of Stephen and conversion of Saul (Paul) ca. 36.*

Table 1. *Continued*

ROMAN EMPERORS	IMPORTANT JEWISH HIGH PRIESTS	JEWISH AND ROMAN RULERS IN PALESTINE			EVENTS *Christian events italicized*
Gaius Caligula (37–41).	Jonathan (son of Annas) (37). Theophilus (son of Annas) (37–41).	Marcellus (36–37). Marullus (37–41?).	Transferal of this region to Herod Agrippa I (39).	Transferal of this region to Herod Agrippa I (37).	—Agrippa I comes from Rome to Palestine, visits Alexandria—anti-Jewish outburst (38). —*Paul escapes from Damascus and goes to Jerusalem (39); then on to Tarsus.* —Caligula orders his statue to be set up in the Jerusalem Temple. Syrian legate Petronius stalls till Caligula's assassination.
Claudius (41–54).		END OF FIRST PERIOD OF ROMAN PREFECTURE	Transferal of Judea to Herod Agrippa I (41).		
		From 41 to 44 Herod Agrippa I rules the area once ruled by Herod the Great.			—*Execution of James, brother of John; Peter arrested under Agrippa I but escapes.* —*Paul in Tarsus (41–44).*
		SECOND PERIOD OF DIRECT ROMAN PREFECTURE OR PROCURATORIAL RULE (44–66)— AT FIRST OVER ALL PALESTINE			
		GALILEE AND JUDEA		E-NE OF GALILEE	
		Fadus (44–46). Tiberius Alexander (46–48). Cumanus (48–52).			—Fadus beheads "the prophet" Thuedas (45). —Famine under Claudius (45–48). —Tiberius Alexander crucifies two sons of Judas the Galilean. —*Paul comes to Antioch in Syria; "First Missionary Journey" (46–49).*

Emperor	Governor / Procurator	High Priest	Herodian	Events
				—Under Cumanus uprisings in Jerusalem and Samaria. —Meeting of James, Peter, and Paul in Jerusalem (49). Paul's "Second Journey" (50–52); he writes 1 Thess (51). —Agrippa II intercedes with Claudius and Cumanus is removed.
Nero (54–68).	Felix (52–60).	Ananias (47–59).	In 53 Herod Agrippa II given the realm of Ituraea and Trachonitis.	—Paul's "Third Missionary Journey" (54–58); he writes principal letters. —In Palestine under Felix hostile uprisings, including bandits (lestai), knife-wielding terrorists (Sicarii), and an Egyptian "prophet." Imprisonment of Paul in Caesarea (58–60). High priest Ananias prosecutes him. The next procurator Festus brings Paul before Herod Agrippa II; Paul is sent to Rome (60). —After the death of Festus, a Sanhedrin convoked by the high priest Ananus II condemns James, the "brother of the Lord," who is stoned to death. Ananus is removed under the next procurator. Jesus son of Ananias is seized by the Jerusalem Jewish authorities (early 60s) for warning that God would destroy the city and the Temple; he is handed over to the Romans to be put to death; but after maltreating him, Albinus releases him. Albinus and Florus are corrupt and tyrannical governors, setting the stage for revolt. —Rome burns (64); Nero persecutes Christians there; Peter and Paul put to death.
	Festus (60–62).	Ananus II (son of Annas) (62).		
	Albinus (62–64).			
	Florus (64–66).			
Galba, Otho, Vitellius (68–69). Accession of the Flavian family of Emperors.	Roman armies led by Vespasian and (after 69) by Titus struggle against revolutionaries in the First Jewish Revolt (66–70).		Herod Agrippa II remains faithful to the Romans during the Revolt.	—In May 66 Florus is forced by street battles to leave Jerusalem; mobs take over the city. Revolution throughout Galilee and Judea. Groups of Zealots (for the Law) kill Jews opposed to revolt. Supposedly Christians leave Jerusalem for Pella in the Transjordan. Josephus goes over to the Romans.
Vespasian (69–79).	Destruction of the Jerusalem Temple by the Romans (August 10, 70). ROMAN RULE		Herod Agrippa II keeps his territory till death ca. 100.	—Yohanan ben Zakkai, a teacher of the Law who escaped Jerusalem, founds the rabbinical school at Jamnia (Yavneh).

Table 1. *Continued*

EMPERORS AFTER AD 70	PALESTINE AND JUDAISM AFTER AD 70	CHRISTIANITY AFTER AD 70
Vespasian reigned till 79. *(Titus' Triumph celebrated in Rome in 71.)* Titus (79–81). Domitian (81–96).	Roman rule in Palestine. —Eleazar, grandson of Judas the Galilean, overcome at Masada in 74. In Rome Josephus writes the *War*. —Rabbinical teachers replace the high priests as leaders of Palestinian Judaism. Rabbi Gamaliel II (90–110) is a major figure. —In Rome Josephus writes the *Antiquities*.	—Many NT writings (Gospels, deuteroPaulines, Heb[?], I Pet, Jas, Jude, Rev, I–II–III John); *I Clement* (from Rome, ca. 96?). —Supposedly relatives of Jesus dominate Palestinian churches. —Under Domitian grandsons of Jude (Jesus' brother) supposedly interrogated; perhaps other local harassments of Christians.
Nerva (96–98). Trajan (98–117).	—Jewish apocalyptic (*IV Ezra*, *II Baruch*: ca. 95–120). —Jewish revolts in Egypt, Cyrene, Cyprus, Mesopotamia (115–119).	—*Didache* (after 100); Letters of Ignatius (110); *Letter of Polycarp*. —Ignatius martyred in Rome (110); Polycarp bishop in Smyrna.
Hadrian (117–138).	—Jerusalem rebuilt as Aelia Capitolina (ca. 130 on). —Second Jewish Revolt under Simon ben Kosibah (Bar Cochba—approval of Rabbi Akiba: 132–135). —After defeat Jews driven out of Jerusalem; temple to Jupiter built on Temple site.	—II Pet, *Shepherd of Hermas* (130s?), *Secret Gospel of Mark*, *Gospel of Peter*, *Protevangelium of James*. —Supposedly ca. 130 end of Jewish Christian leadership in Jerusalem, ceding to Gentile bishops. —Polycarp lives on in Smyrna.

Similarly the map of the Mediterranean area is meant to be helpful for the NT books where the story moves beyond Palestine, especially Paul's Letters, Acts, and Revelation. Yet there is no way one map can depict the constantly changing first-century Roman provincial boundaries or developing road networks. Our map attempts only a sketch combining the situation in the 50s (when Paul flourished) with the place names important at various moments in the NT period (for example, the seven cities of Revelation, marked as stars).

PALESTINE IN NEW TESTAMENT TIMES

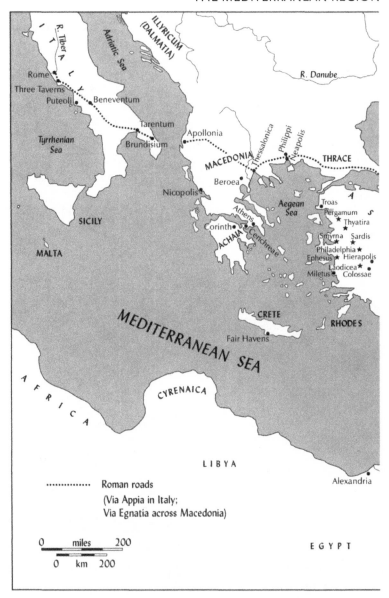

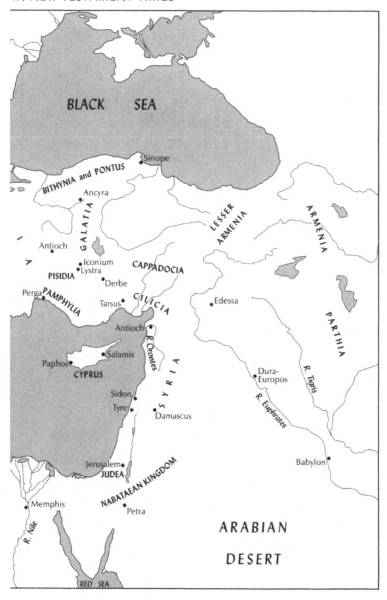

An Introduction to the New Testament

1

The Nature and Origin of the New Testament

Although the term "New Testament" evokes the idea of a body of Christian literature, that understanding is the product of a long development.

THE NATURE OF THE NEW "TESTAMENT"

Before the term "testament" (or "covenant") was applied to a set of writings, it referred to God's special dealing with human beings. We hear of a "covenant" by which God made a commitment to Noah, to Abraham, to David, promising help or blessings. In the tradition, however, the most notable covenant was that which God made with Moses and Israel (Exod 19 and 34), whereby Israel became God's special people.

Almost 600 years before Jesus' birth Jeremiah reported an oracle of the Lord: "The days are coming when I will make a new covenant with the house of Israel and the house of Judah. It will not be like the covenant that I made with their ancestors. . . . I will place my law within them and write it upon their hearts. I will be their God and they shall be my people" (Jer 31:31–33). "New" here has a connotation of "renewed" even though the renewal is "not like the covenant made with their ancestors."

All the accounts of the eucharistic words at the supper on the night before Jesus died have him relate the term "[new] covenant/testament" to his own blood. Through the death and resurrection of Jesus, therefore, Christians believed that God had renewed the covenant with a fresh dimension; and they came to understand that this time the covenant reached beyond Israel to include the Gentiles in God's people. Eventually Christian theological reflection and hostile relations between Christians and some Jews who did not accept Jesus led to the thesis that the new testament (covenant) had taken the place of the old, Mosaic covenant which had become "obsolete" (Heb 8:6; 9:15; 12:24). Of course, even then the Scriptures of Israel remained the Scriptures for Christians. Only in the second century do we have evidence of Christians using the term "New Testament" for a body of their own writings, ultimately leading to the use of the designation "Old Testament" for the Scriptures of Israel.

HOW THE FIRST CHRISTIAN BOOKS WERE
WRITTEN, PRESERVED, AND COLLECTED

Many people assume that Christians always had Bibles even as we have today. Rather, the formation of the NT, which involved the coming into being and preservation of books composed by followers of Jesus, was a complicated affair.

The Coming into Being of Books Written by Christians

By the time of Jesus Jews had become very conscious of sacred writings: the Law, the Prophets, and the other books; and these writings are what early Christians meant when they spoke of Scripture. Why were the first Christians somewhat slow in writing their own books? In the first place, Jesus did not produce a writing that contained his revelation. In turn, the first Christian generations were strongly eschatological: anticipation of the end of the world did not encourage Christians to write for future generations.

Letters. It is no accident, then, that letters were the first Christian literature of which we know. Thus in the 50s of the first century Paul produced the earliest surviving Christian documents: I Thess, Gal, Phil, Phlm, I and II Cor, and Rom. By the mid-60s death had come to the most famous of the earlier generation (that is, those who had known Jesus or who had seen the risen Jesus: see I Cor 15:3–8), for example, Peter, Paul, and James, "the brother of the Lord." The death of the first generation of Christians contributed to the production of works of more permanent nature (for example, Gospels). Letters/Epistles remained an important means of Christian communication, yet now they often had a more universal or permanent tone. Thus many scholars conclude that these later letters were written not by the first generation, but in the names of those figures to preserve their spirit and authority. In the view of many scholars, to this post-70 period belong the epistles attributed to Peter, James, and Jude, along with I, II, III John. These particular writings eventually became known as "Catholic," or "General," Epistles, that is, works addressed to the church universal.

Gospels. Literary genres other than letters also appeared of which "Gospel" is the most noteworthy. According to the common scholarly view, somewhere in the 60s or just after 70 the Gospel According to Mark was written, offering an account of Jesus' deeds and words. Experiences stemming from the decades that separated Jesus from the evangelist colored this presentation. Relevance to Christian problems determined the selection of what was preserved from the Jesus tradition.

The Gospels According to Matthew and to Luke, probably written ten to twenty years after Mark, offer much more of the Jesus tradition, especially by way of sayings (thought to be drawn from a lost collection of sayings known as Q). Still another form of the Jesus tradition found expression in the Fourth Gospel (John), written around 90–100—a form quite different from that of Mark, Matt, and Luke. Despite the local colorings of all four canonical Gospels, their overall import was to preserve for late-first-century readers (and indeed, for those of all time) a memory of Jesus that did not perish when the eyewitnesses died.

Acts; Revelation; Other Literary Genres. Another form of early Christian literature of a more permanent nature than letters is exemplified in the Acts of the Apostles, which moved the story of Christianity beyond Jerusalem and Judea to Samaria and even to the end of the earth. Such a work envisions an enduring Christianity that needs to know of its continuity with Jesus, Peter, and Paul, and to be certain that its development has not been haphazard but guided by the Spirit received from Jesus.

The Book of Revelation (also called the Apocalypse) represents still another genre in the Christian writing of the post-70 period, "apocalyptic" literature, a designation derived from a Greek noun meaning "disclosure" or "revelation." Persecution of God's people by the great world empires challenged the extent to which history is under God's control. Apocalyptic literature responds to this affront by visions that encompass what is happening in heaven and on earth at the same time. Rev gave Christians hope, nay assurance, that despite the setbacks they had suffered, God would make them victorious.

Still other forms of early Christian literature existed, concealed under the designation "letter" or "epistle." Precisely because letters were the dominant literary production of the first Christians, later works that were not letters in the ordinary sense were classified as such: I Pet, Jas, Heb, and I John. Thus in various literary genres, Christians after 70 continued to wrestle with problems and threats.

The Preservation and Acceptance of Books Written by Christians

The Christian compositions we have been discussing, most likely written between the years 50 and 150, were not only preserved but eventually deemed uniquely sacred and authoritative. They were placed on the same level as the Jewish Scriptures (the Law, Prophets, and other Writings) and evaluated as a NT alongside them (so that the Jewish Scriptures became the OT). How did this development come about? Several factors played a role.

First, apostolic origin, real or putative. The attribution either to apostles (Paul, Peter, James, Matthew, John) or to "apostolic men" (Mark, Luke) won acceptance for various NT writings. Nevertheless, apostolic origin was not an absolute criterion for either preservation or acceptance.

Many works that were rejected by church authorities as spurious or false bore the names of apostles.

Second, importance of the addressed Christian community. Those for whom the writings were intended had a role in preserving and winning acceptance for them. The traceable connections of apostles to major churches in Asia Minor, Greece, and, above all, Rome were important arguments for the inclusion of works as part of the canonical NT.

Third, conformity with the rule of faith. The importance of conformity with belief was a clear factor in the acceptance or rejection of various early Christian writings. Writings that were judged to support problematic (for example, *docetic* [Christ only seemed to be human, to suffer, and to die], *gnostic* [various religious movements emphasizing salvation from ensnarement in the material world through special revealed "knowledge"], or even *chiliastic* [belief in the coming 1,000-year reign of Christ]) teaching were typically forbidden for further church use.

These three factors scarcely do full justice to what also seems to have involved a church intuition as to what was Spirit-guided.

The Collecting of Early Christian Writings

The various literary genres just discussed had different histories of preliminary collection, and these histories throw light on the attitudes that shaped the final NT compilation.

Paul's Letters. Paul's name appears on thirteen NT letters addressed to separate communities or individuals and written over a period of some fifty years—or even longer. While writers ca. 100–120 (such as Ignatius of Antioch and the authors of I Clement and II Pet) betray knowledge of several Pauline letters, the first clear evidence of a large collection comes several decades later, with Polycarp and Marcion.

The Gospels. The church eventually accepted four Gospels composed in the period ca. 65–100, though there is no clear example of more than one Gospel being read as publicly authoritative in a given church before 150. Why four? Concentration on one Gospel could sometimes be used to support a theology rejected by the larger number of Christians. Four Gospels received ever-widening acceptance after 150.

Marcion (ca. 100–160) played a peculiar role in catalyzing the formation of the NT canon. His theological emphases sought the total rejection of the Jewish heritage. He selected a canon of Christian writings that could be interpreted as favorable to his thesis, namely, one Gospel (Luke without chaps. 1–2: the *euaggelion*) and ten Pauline letters (edited and without the Pastoral Epistles, the *apostolikon*). Reaction to Marcion's rejection of the OT and opposition to his truncated canon helped push the churches toward a larger *euaggelion* (four Gospels) and a larger *apostolikon* (at least thirteen Pauline letters); expansion of the *apostolikon* may also have meant inclusion of the Acts of the Apostles. Favoring the Twelve probably explains the inclusion of I Pet and I John. Thus, in the decades just before and after AD 200 church writers widely accepted a collection of twenty works as a NT alongside the Jewish OT.

Completing the Collection. The remaining seven works (Heb, Rev, Jas, II and III John, Jude, II Pet) were cited from the second to the fourth centuries and accepted as Scripture in some churches but not in all. Finally, however, by the late fourth century in the Greek East and Latin West there was a wide accord (not absolute) on a canon of twenty-seven works. This "ecumenical" standardization involved churches accepting from other churches books about which they had some doubts and reflected an increasing contact and communion between the East and the West.

We shall never know all the details of how the twenty-seven books were written, preserved, selected, and collected; but one fact is indisputable. Joined as the NT, they have been the single most important instrument in bringing untold millions of people from different times and places into contact with Jesus of Nazareth and the first believers who proclaimed him.

·✶·

2

How to Read the New Testament

The NT comprises different kinds of writings. Let us look in more detail at how such differences affect the way we read or interpret. The discussion brings us into a very active area in modern scholarship called *hermeneutics*, the study of interpretation, or the quest for meaning. This study employs various approaches to written documents, each called a "criticism," for example, Textual Criticism, Historical Criticism, and Source Criticism. ("Criticism" here means *careful analysis*, not the usual sense of "unfavorable judgment.")

SURVEY OF METHODS OF INTERPRETATION (HERMENEUTICS)

To be blunt, the study of different kinds of interpretation is difficult—indeed at times too difficult for beginners. Nevertheless, so many books on Scripture refer to methods of interpretation that some knowledge of the subject is essential. This subsection offers a wide-ranging, though brief, overview. We shall use the Gospels as concrete examples for surveying how various types of investigation apply. But keep in mind that the "criticisms" have a much wider application than the Gospels.

1. TEXTUAL CRITICISM. Almost 2,000 years ago evangelists wrote four Gospels in Greek. We do not have the original manuscripts (mss.) that came from the evangelists' pens, or for that matter the original of any NT work. What we do have are many handwritten copies made between 150 and 1,300 years later—for all practical purposes until the invention of printing. Many times, but mostly in minor matters, these copies do not agree among themselves because of copyists' mistakes and changes. The comparison of the diversities in these handwritten copies is called Textual Criticism.

2. HISTORICAL CRITICISM. The four evangelists were trying to convey a message about Jesus to their respective readers. That message is called the literal sense, that is, what the author literally meant to say. The detection of the literal sense is *one* aspect of Historical Criticism, which tries to comprehend the biblical text through knowledge of its historical origins, for example, persons, places, things, events, dates, sources, etc. Many times the literal sense is relatively easy to discern. Its detection is fundamental to all other forms of interpretation.

3. SOURCE CRITICISM. This is the study of the antecedents from which the NT writers drew their information. Gospel sources are a particular concern because in all likelihood the evangelists were not eyewitnesses of Jesus' life. Did the evangelists have sources from predecessors? Were these oral or written? Did one evangelist use as a basis another Gospel that had already been written? If so, what was the order of dependence (for example, Matt on Mark, or Mark on Matt)? Such questions should be studied, but priority of attention in interpretation must be given to the actual NT works, not to their largely hypothetical sources.

4. FORM CRITICISM. We do not read everything the same way. When we look through a newspaper, we read the front page with the assumption that it consists of reasonably reliable reporting; but when we turn to the advertising pages, we know we have to be much more cautious about the reliability of what is claimed. In technical language, we must determine the literary genre or "form" of what we read. The NT contains different genres, for example, Gospels, letters, and apocalypse. Yet there is a need to be more exact. This type of investigation is called Form Criticism.

Pressing beyond the general classification of whole writings, scholars have studied the genres or literary forms of components of the whole. Theoretically, each form or genre has its own characteristics, for instance, parables and miracle stories, infancy narratives and passion narratives. The more advanced classification of forms, however, is a highly technical enterprise.

One should remember that in itself the diagnosis of forms tells us nothing about the historicity of the material. Did Jesus utter this saying or parable? Did he work this miracle? Form criticism cannot answer these historical questions. Interpreters sometimes overlook this limitation, so that judgments are made based not simply on an identification of form but on a supposition about what can be historical.

5. REDACTION CRITICISM. The inclusion of individual components (miracles stories, parables, etc.) in the final product (the whole Gospel) modifies drastically their significance; and the meaning of the whole Gospel is a primary concern for those who read the NT. In the history of NT scholarship in the twentieth century, the development of Redaction Criticism, after an earlier dominance of Form Criticism, dealt with this concern. Redaction Criticism (or, better, Author Criticism) recognized that the writers creatively shaped the material they inherited. Attention thus shifted to the evangelists' interests and the work they produced. When it is possible to know with reasonable assurance the material an author used, one can diagnose theological emphases by the changes the author made in what was taken over from the source—judgments become much more speculative, however, when the reconstruction of the source is uncertain.

6. CANONICAL CRITICISM. In some ways this approach may be considered an extension of the interest in the final product evident in Redaction Criticism. Although each NT book has its own integrity, it has become Sacred Scripture only as part of the collected NT; and it has acquired new meaning from its relationship to other books in that canonical collection. Moreover, Canonical Criticism examines even a passage in the light of the whole NT or even the whole Bible wherein other books/passages offer insights.

7. STRUCTURALISM. Though Form Criticism and Redaction Criticism have literary components, these come to the fore in a number of other

approaches. Structuralism (or Semiotics) concentrates on the final form of the NT works. "Structure," which in this approach is far more than a general outline, has become a highly technical study, akin to mathematics. Often structuralists propose outlines of frightening complexity, causing nonstructuralists to wonder whether such intricacy is helpful and whether semiotic analysis produces results that could not have been obtained by commonsense exegesis.

8. NARRATIVE CRITICISM. More obviously and immediately productive is an approach that, when applied to the Gospels, would concentrate on them as stories. At first blush the terminology employed in this exegesis may seem formidable. For example, Narrative Criticism distinguishes the real author (the person who actually wrote) from the implied author (the one who can be inferred from the narrative). Yet such a distinction makes sense, and attention paid to the flow of the narrative can cast light on many exegetical problems. Too often microscopic focus on the text sees problems that exegetes can more easily explain if they appreciate a simplified narrative that takes much for granted. Narrative Criticism counters the excesses of historical investigation and helps to highlight the author's main interest.

9. RHETORICAL CRITICISM. Related to Narrative Criticism is an approach that analyzes the strategies used by the author to make what was recounted effective, for example, the discovery of suitable material to be narrated; the organized arrangement of that material; the choice of appropriate words. Rhetorical Criticism brings to light the content, structure, and style of the writing in order to discern the author's aim and what the author intends to convey. (The classification of rhetorical argumentation into judicial, deliberative, and demonstrative [epideictic] modes will be discussed in Chapter 15.)

10. SOCIAL CRITICISM studies the text as a reflection of and a response to the social and cultural settings in which it was produced. It views the text as a window into the world of competing views and voices. Different groups with different political, economic, and religious stances shaped the text to speak to their particular concerns. This important branch of NT research has contributed to a revival in historical study.

11. ADVOCACY CRITICISM is an umbrella title sometimes given to Liberationist, African American, Feminist, and related studies, because

the proponents advocate that the results be used to change today's social, political, or religious situation. This approach is defended on the grounds that the biblical writers and writings were not without their own advocacy, for example, written by men and church leaders and thus reflecting a patriarchal or ecclesiastical viewpoint. Others, however, see in this method the danger of reading into Scripture what one would like to find and of not acknowledging that the NT sociological situation may have been in fact (not simply through suppression of data) unfavorable to modern causes. Yet, by asking important questions that previous exegetes never asked, advocacy interpreters have enlightened the NT situation.

12. OVERVIEW. How can readers of the NT cope with so many different "criticisms"? *Different approaches to the text must be combined so that no "criticism" becomes the exclusive manner of interpretation.* Interpreters who employ the various forms of criticism in a complementary way will arrive at a much fuller meaning of the biblical text.

This introductory subsection has concentrated on the Gospels to illustrate the importance of various hermeneutical approaches. The different "criticisms" (Form, Redaction, Rhetorical, etc.) are applied to other NT writings as well, for example, Acts, the letters, Rev, where special issues peculiar to the individual genre arise.

THE LITERAL SENSE

Among the many (mostly complementary) "criticisms" for the interpretation of the NT, one approach in particular gave rise to modern biblical studies and remains fundamental even if controverted: Historical Criticism. In part the controversy stems from a lack of agreement on what is implied. For many people Historical Criticism has had almost an aura of pure science. Yet, since historical investigation was often combined with an antipathy toward theology, the results have appeared barren to readers looking for spiritual meaning applicable to their lives.

To an important degree, the stubborn survival of Historical Criticism has been due to its concern for something very fundamental to all other forms of interpretation (even though ardent adherents of those other "criticisms" may not agree). Historical Criticism is concerned with the commonsense observation that readers of any book of Scripture will want to know what the author of that book tried to convey. Thus, some writers choose to speak of the essential necessity of determining "the literal sense" of biblical passages (this is the approach taken in this Introduction).

The literal sense means what biblical authors intended and conveyed to their audiences by what they wrote. This sense does not exhaust the meaning of Scripture but has a fundamental relationship to meanings gained by other forms of "criticism."

By what the biblical authors wrote. The NT books were written some 1,900 years ago in Greek. From the viewpoint of language, even the most competent English translation cannot render all the nuances of the original Greek. From the viewpoint of culture and context, the authors and their audiences had a worldview very different from ours. We cannot hope to open a NT book and read it responsibly with the same ease as we read a book written in our own culture and worldview. Consequently, an intelligent effort to understand the background and outlook of the NT authors can be of great assistance.

Since they wrote in different times and different places, all the authors did not necessarily have the same background or outlook. Let us consider some examples of possible differences that affect meaning. It seems likely that most or all the NT authors were of Jewish birth. What kind of Judaism? What was their mother tongue? In what language did they know Jewish Scriptures? How much of the world had they seen and did they know? Did they write with actual knowledge, or did they write with imagination or on the basis of what they had heard?

To audiences. The writers were addressing particular audiences in the first and early second centuries. How did those audiences understand what was written? First, author's intent and audience's understanding may differ. For instance, after reflecting on the Jewish background of a NT author and the meaning he was trying to convey, we may need to ask how an audience consisting of Christians of Gentile birth who had acquired only a partial familiarity with Judaism understood what he wrote. Second, although the contents of a NT book enter into the reconstruction of both author and addressees, we have limited knowledge about the identity of the audiences addressed (with the exception of the named communities of some Pauline letters). On the level of literal sense, can one speak properly of a "meaning" of a passage when there is little chance that the original intended audience would have understood such a meaning?

Third, a particular debate centers on the extent to which the audiences of the individual NT writers understood "Scripture," that is, the sacred Jewish writings of the period before Jesus to which the evangelists frequently appealed. Would such readers have accepted as authoritative all three kinds (Law, Prophets, Writings) of the Jewish Scriptures? Would the intended audiences have caught subtle allusions? Were they aware of the OT context of the pericope? If a passage was cited, did a larger scriptural setting come to mind? Would the vocabulary in a cited Scripture passage have evoked for the readers/hearers other passages containing the same vocabulary?

Fourth, beyond being alert to the intellectual and religious background of the audience addressed, modern hermeneutics has concentrated on sociological analysis of both the author and his audience. Thus, interpreters have been made aware of differences centered on citizenship, wealth, education, and social status within the churches addressed. Diagnosis of the sociopolitical situation of the audiences generally depends on internal evidence and is a highly speculative quest.

WHAT THE BIBLICAL AUTHORS INTENDED AND CONVEYED. The two verbs are an attempt to do justice to a complex situation. The importance of "convey" is relatively obvious. The NT writers certainly knew more of the Christian tradition than they were able or chose to convey in their writings. On the level of the literal sense, exegesis that embraces what the writers did not actually convey in writing becomes very speculative.

A more delicate issue is the relationship between what the written words convey and what the writers intended. There is a span of possibilities: according to the skill of the writer, a writing may convey what the author wished, or something less, or the opposite, or something other than the author wished or foresaw.

One may well object, "How can a modern interpreter know that ancient authors intended something different from what their words convey?" Sometimes guidance can be found in the context or in other passages. Nevertheless, one should resort only rarely to such interpretation distinguishing between what was written and what was intended. The account as it now stands made sense to someone in antiquity, and so what seems contradictory to modern interpreters may not be really contradictory.

A last note on the issue of the author's intention is that we are speaking of the final or substantial author of a NT book. Discernment of the complex origins of a biblical book should enter into a diagnosis of the meaning of that book; but *Christians are committed to the authority of the canonical NT, which consists of whole books, not reconstructed sources as fascinating as they may be.*

Such insistence partially shelters NT study from a common objection, namely, that every few years scholars change their views about composition and sources and Christianity cannot be dependent on the whims of changing scholarship. In terms of this specific objection, the churches or their representatives need not (and even should not) base their preaching or practice on hypothetical, nonextant sources. Although scholars also disagree about the exegesis of texts in the extant books of the NT, that area is far less speculative than the reconstruction of sources.

3

The Text of the New Testament

The NT familiar to readers has been translated into a modern language from the ancient Greek in which the NT books were originally composed. Here only an elementary summary is presented.

MANUSCRIPT EVIDENCE FOR THE TEXT

Approximately 3,000 mss. of the Greek NT (whole or part) are preserved, copied between the second and seventeenth centuries, and 2,200 lectionary mss. from the seventh century and later. These witnesses to the text of the NT do not agree among themselves, but relatively few of the differences are significant.

Textual Families. Scholars have identified groups or families of mss. that share similar readings and peculiarities. The most commonly recognized are the following:

Alexandrian: In Alexandria mss. were copied with care by scribes who had a sophisticated appreciation of Greek.

Western: Although this group is named from the Western (North Africa, Italy, Gaul) circulation of some Greek mss. that belong to it, other mss. circulated elsewhere. The readings are often longer than Alexandrian readings.

Caesarean: The basic text in this group, dating from the early third century, was probably brought to Caesarea from Egypt. This text tradition stands between the Alexandrian and the Western.

Byzantine (or Koine): This conflated text is generally looked on as a quite late and secondary development. Yet some of its readings are ancient and go back to the church at Antioch ca. 300.

Textual Witnesses. A selection of the most important NT textual witnesses gives an idea of the diversity. Scholars distinguish three types of Greek mss.:

Papyri (abbreviated P). These are very ancient NT fragments and books of the Greek NT on papyrus; since 1890 a hundred have been discovered, dating from the second to the eighth century. Among the oldest are:

- P^{52} (ca. 135)—a small scrap with part of John 18:31–34.
- P^{46} (ca. 200 or earlier)—eighty-six codex pages with some Pauline letters and Hebrews; Caesarean.
- P^{66} (ca. 200)—heavily corrected text of much of John; Alexandrian.
- P^{75} (ca. 225)—large portions of Luke and John; Alexandrian.

Great Uncial Codices. These books, consisting of vellum or parchment pages written in block Greek letters (called uncials), were most prominent from the third to the ninth centuries. Some 300 uncial codices are known. The most important are:

- B (Codex Vaticanus; mid-fourth century)—regarded by many scholars as the best witness to the original NT text; Alexandrian.
- S or H (Codex Sinaiticus; mid-fourth century)—contains the whole NT and other noncanonical writings; Alexandrian in Gospels and Acts, elsewhere Western.
- A (Codex Alexandrinus; early fifth century)—contained the whole NT and other noncanonical writings, but pages have been lost; Byzantine in Gospels, elsewhere Alexandrian.

• D (Codex Bezae; fifth century)—contains the four canonical Gospels, III John, and Acts in Latin and Greek; the chief representative of the Western.

Minuscules. About the ninth century a cursive writing style began to supersede the uncial, and there are nearly 2,900 NT mss. in this script.

OBSERVATIONS ABOUT THE USE OF THE EVIDENCE

From this information, these observations emerge:

• Many differences among the textual families visible in the great uncial codices of the fourth and fifth centuries existed already ca. 200 as we see from the papyri and early translations. How could this be? These were holy books because of their content and origins, but there was no slavish devotion to their exact wording.
• At times a choice as to which of competing readings is more plausible cannot be decided on the ms. evidence alone because the quality of the textual witnesses may be comparable. One then has to ask which way copyists are more likely to have thought.
• By the end of the nineteenth century scholars were at work to replace Erasmus' edition of the Greek NT with new editions based on the best mss. available. Truly critical versions of the Greek NT emerged. They are all necessarily eclectic, drawing on different textual traditions as judged appropriate. Yet, no scholarly edition is the original Greek text (that is lost). Thus, none of these editions should be canonized, but scholars certainly may accept them with gratitude.

4

The Political and Social World
of New Testament Times

Most of the NT was composed in the first century AD. It is important to know the background and worldview of both the author and the audience. What was the political, social, and religious situation at that time for Jews, Gentiles, and Christians, both in Palestine and in the Roman Empire as a whole?

THE POLITICAL WORLD OF NEW TESTAMENT TIMES

In this discussion, we shall divide the first century into thirds. The first third was the period in which most of Jesus' life was lived. The second third was the period of Christian oral proclamation and of the main Pauline letters. The last third was the period of increasing Gentile dominance in the Christian communities and of the composition of most NT works (a few NT writings likely come from the early second century).

What Preceded the First Century AD

A new period of interaction between Greek lands and Palestine began in 332 BC, after Alexander the Great, King of Macedonia and

Greece, systematically conquered and established a vast empire through military victories and a program of Hellenization (the introduction of Greek culture, particularly Greek-style cities and the Greek language). The Hellenistic Age lasted from ca. 300 BC–AD 300, and during this period the Jews of the Palestine-Syria area and quickly those of Egypt became part of the amalgam of Greek and Eastern civilization known as the Hellenistic world.

After Alexander's death in 323 BC, his empire was divided among his generals. The Palestinian Jews were dominated between 323 BC and 175 BC, first by the Ptolemaic dynasty of Egypt (323–ca. 200 BC) and then by the Seleucid dynasty of Syria (ca. 200–129 BC)—although the Seleucids never had complete control over the situation after 166 BC. In 190 BC the Romans had defeated the Syrians in battle and as a result imposed a heavy war indemnity on them. In turn, the Syrians levied a significant tax increase on the Palestinian Jews. The situation became extremely grave under the rule of the unstable Antiochus IV Epiphanes (175–164), who sought to unify his subjects by requiring them to subscribe to a common Greek culture and religion, including recognition of his divinity. Antiochus retaliated against subsequent Jewish resistance by attacking Jerusalem, slaughtering the population, plundering the Temple and violating it by erecting a statue of Zeus on the Temple altar of burnt offering, and installing Syrian troops permanently in a fort (the Akra) in the city.

In 167 BC a revolt of the Jews, led by Mattathias, a priest living in Modein (northwest of Jerusalem) broke out; it continued over a period of thirty-five years, led by at least three of his five sons: Judas Maccabeus, Jonathan, Simon, as well as Eleazar and John (I Macc 2:1–5). A number of very pious Jews (the Hasideans) joined the revolt. A key Jewish victory came in 164 when Jerusalem was retaken and the site of the altar was purified and rededicated (whence "Hanukkah"). Then, some years later (in 152), Jonathan was appointed to the high priesthood. And, still later (142) the Syrian troops were finally expelled from the garrison where they had been installed. Final and complete freedom came only in 129 BC, when Rome recognized Jewish independence.

The high priest John Hyrcanus I (135/34–104 BC) ruled in an era that was regarded as a golden age for Israel, despite hostility and violence involving Samaritans. The Hasmonean/Maccabean dynasty continued after the time of John Hyrcanus I, but with significant difficulties unknown during the golden age. There was ongoing intrigue in politics and religion, and brutality was not uncommon even among the Jews themselves.

Eventually squabbling for power between two brothers, the Hasmonean heirs Aristobulus II and Hyrcanus II, opened the way for Roman intervention in Jerusalem in 63 BC. Thereafter the Romans were the rulers of the land, working through subservient high priests and kinglets.

The Romans favored the weak Hyrcanus II (63–41), but through murder and marriage an Idumean adventurer, Antipater II, initially became advisor to Hyrcanus and then, with Julius Caesar's approval, procurator in his own right. His son, Herod (the Great), maneuvered his way through the Roman civil wars after the assassination of Caesar with shifting allegiances, and by 37 BC, through brutality and expeditious marriage into the Hasmonean family, he became undisputed king of Judea with the approval of Octavian (Augustus), who enlarged Herod's domain in 31/30. Many Jews regarded Herod with contempt because of his Idumean heritage (Idumeans were forced converts to Judaism only a half century earlier). Herod's sympathies were clearly with Greco-Roman culture, and his reign included extensive and massive building projects. Herod's suspicion of perceived rivals led to the murder of even some of his own sons and his beloved Hasmonean wife Mariamne. The last years of Herod's reign were marked by virtually insane brutal cruelty. At his death some adventurers with royal pretentions forcefully sought the throne, but Rome chose three of Herod's sons to be his successors.

The First Third of the First Century AD

Although this may be considered the period of Jesus' lifetime, he was born a bit earlier, before the death of Herod the Great (4 BC). After Herod's death, Augustus split the realm among three of Herod's sons. In the two areas that most touched Jesus' life, Archelaus became ethnarch of Judea, Samaria, and Idumea, while Herod Antipas became tetrarch of Galilee and part of the Transjordan. In AD 6 Augustus deposed Archelaus, making his territory the imperial province of Judea. In the takeover the Romans conducted a tax census that produced a rebellion led by Judas the Galilean. This rebellion, when Jesus was about twelve, was the only recorded serious Jewish uprising in Palestine during Jesus' boyhood and maturity. This was not a time of violent revolution.

Such then was the Palestine of Jesus' maturity: a crafty and vain Herodian "king" in charge of Jesus' home country of Galilee and a Roman prefect controlling Jerusalem and Judea where Jesus spent his last days.

The Second Third of the First Century AD

The first period of direct Roman governance in Judea by prefects ended in AD 39/40. Herod Agrippa I, who had earlier succeeded to the territories of his uncles Philip and Herod Antipas, was a friend of the new Emperor Claudius (41–54). Accordingly he was made king over all Palestine (AD 41–44). After his death another season of Roman rule began, but the procurators were of low caliber. In the last decade of this period James "the brother of the Lord" was executed (AD 62), after a Sanhedrin hearing called by Ananus II, a high priest who was subsequently removed from office by the procurator Albinus for having acted illegally. Only two years later, after the great fire in Rome in July 64, Emperor Nero (54–68) persecuted Christians in the capital, and, according to respectable tradition, both Peter and Paul were martyred. The misrule of the Roman procurators gave rise to a major Jewish revolt against Rome (AD 66–70). Multitudinous Roman forces and the best generals were involved in suppressing the revolt. A somewhat uncertain tradition reports that the Christians in Jerusalem refused to join the revolt and withdrew across the Jordan to Pella.

The Last Third of the First Century AD

The Flavian family of emperors (Vespasian, Titus, Domitian) reigned from AD 69 to 96. Vespasian, the first, had taken command in Judea in 67 and turned around the hitherto unsuccessful Roman effort to quell the Jewish revolt. But after Nero's suicide in 68 Vespasian's attention was directed toward Rome, and in 69 the legions proclaimed him emperor. This left his son Titus as commander to press the campaign in Judea; Jerusalem was taken and the Temple destroyed in 70.

In this dynasty of emperors Domitian, Vespasian's younger son, had the longest reign (81–96). Autocratic and vengeful, in his quest to restore the purity of Roman religion he executed some who were attracted to Judaism under the charge of atheism. There is evidence that he was hostile toward Christianity as well. During the reign of the three Flavian emperors, Jerusalem declined in importance for Christians as it was outdistanced by other centers with significant Christian communities (for example, Antioch, Ephesus, and Rome). The number of Gentile Christians probably surpassed the number of Jewish Christians during this time. In the synagogues relations between Jews and believers in Jesus probably varied regionally. In certain Christian communities strong antipathy arose toward the leaders of the Jewish synagogues, bringing about a sharp distinction between the disciples of Jesus and the disciples of Moses.

Shortly after the assassination of Domitian, another dynasty of emperors arose: for our purposes, the rule of Trajan (98–117) is important. There were to be no mass persecutions. Christians were not to be hunted down. Trajan offered an ambiguous rescript indicating a certain tolerance toward Christians, but Ignatius's martyrdom (ca. 110) shows that punitive measures did reach Antioch in Asia Minor during Trajan's reign.

THE SOCIAL WORLD OF NEW TESTAMENT TIMES

The first believers in Jesus were Jews; perhaps all the authors of the NT were Jews. The memories of Jesus and the writings of his followers are filled with references to the Jewish Scriptures, feasts, institutions, and traditions. There is no doubt about the influence of Judaism on the NT. Yet, since the time of Alexander the Great the Jews had been living in a Hellenistic world and, for almost a century before Jesus' birth, in areas dominated by Roman armies. By the time of Jesus' birth a fair percentage, perhaps even a majority, of the world's Jews spoke Greek. The biblical books in Hebrew and Aramaic had been translated into

Greek, and some Deuterocanonical biblical books were composed in Greek, a number showing a popular awareness of Greek philosophical thought. Jews used coins minted by their Gentile overlords, often with images of gods. In varying ways and degrees—commerce, schools, travel—Jews were influenced by a world quite different from that of the OT. Thus in the social background of the NT, much more than Judaism must be taken into account.

Most Christian communities mentioned in the NT were in cities. There were also synagogue communities in many urban areas. In the cities the interplay of people of different backgrounds was important. Which dwellers in a city had the privilege of being citizens depended on particular circumstances. Although there was a special classification assigned to Jews in the Empire, in some cities they were granted citizenship. In general, Roman administration tried to keep peace among the different segments of the population. Perhaps because of both such a mixture of inhabitants and the considerable mobility of the people, there seems to have been a felt need "to belong," as suggested by the striking number of associations or clubs that were then in existence. In particular, those who were not citizens achieved a sense of community in these associations. Christian congregations would have addressed such circumstances.

Jews were alienated from aspects of common civic life by their religion and dietary laws, although some Jewish officials and wealthy members of society made accommodations. How far to go in participation depended on personal judgment. People who do not share common practices and beliefs are always suspect, and anti-Judaism was frequent in sections of the Empire. Nevertheless, the Jews were protected legally by privileges granted by Julius Caesar and reaffirmed by his successors. Christians, so long as they were thought of as Jews, probably received similar protection; but once most Christians were Gentiles or Jewish Christians rejected by synagogues, they no longer had a legal umbrella. Moreover, Christians were more dangerous to society than Jews. Although Jews gained some converts and sympathizers, predominantly their numbers were constituted through birth. Christians, on the other hand, aggressively converted others, while their numbers did not expand dramatically through births to Christian families. From evidence pertaining to official persecution clearly the alien behavior of Christians in regard to civic expectations was highly suspect.

Wealth/poverty and the class society found in cities of the Roman Empire created their own problems for early Christians, and both can be misunderstood in light of modern experience. There are many references in the NT to the "poor," many of whom were in fact small farmers with inadequate or barren land, or serfs on large estates; in the cities without the assistance of produce from the land the poor were somewhat worse off. Yet the situation of both groups of NT poor was economically better than that of the desperately poor of the modern world. Jesus himself, who showed affection for the poor, was a *tektōn*, that is, a "woodworker." In *Marginal Jew* J. P. Meier notes that, as a craftsman in a village Jesus might be compared to a blue-collar worker in lower-middle-class America.

As for slaves, NT translations render Greek *doulos* as both "servant" and "slave"; but those so described should not be imagined in nineteenth-century patterns of either British household servants or African slaves in America. Slavery had existed for several centuries by NT times. The status of slaves varied. Those forced to do heavy labor had a brutal existence, and at times they became restive. Yet slaves had legal rights, and under the Empire abusing or killing slaves constituted punishable crimes. Besides working in business, farming, and households, slaves could be administrators, physicians, scholars, and poets, and accumulate wealth. Christian preachers made converts among the city poor and slaves, but they also made considerable inroads among the middle class. Although there were a few wealthy Christians, the least number of converts would have been among that social class and among aristocrats.

Education is also an issue to be considered in reflecting on the NT: the education of Jesus and the preachers, and the education of the audience. There is a major dispute about the nature and extent of Jewish education in this period, stemming from differing uses of Mishnaic materials. Josephus, *Against Apion* 2.25 (#204), interprets Jewish law to order children "to be taught letters concerning the law and deeds of their forefathers." Jesus' ability to debate about Scripture suggests that he could read Hebrew (as imaged in Luke 4:16–21). The same is possible for his disciples who had their own trade or profession (fishers, tax collectors).

The pattern of Greek schooling, well established throughout the Roman Empire, consisted of an elementary school (about seven years) for teaching reading, writing, music, and athletics; then tutoring in grammar, particularly poetry; and finally (for a small number) an upper level education in rhetoric and philosophy. As regards influence on Jesus, there is little evidence that Greek schools were widespread in Palestine in NT times. The life setting of Jesus in first-century Galilee is not clear. The influence on him of culture from Hellenistic cities like Tiberias on the Sea of Galilee and Sepphoris (four miles from Nazareth) should not be exaggerated. There is no Gospel indication of Jesus' contacts with such cities. Nor do we have concrete evidence that Jesus or his Galilean disciples spoke Greek.

As for Saul/Paul, who knew Greek quite well, it is debated whether he grew up in the diaspora or in Jerusalem. If in the diaspora, he might well have had basic Greek schooling. At a center like Tarsus there were also public sources of education, for example, libraries and theaters. In general the NT writings were in Koine, or everyday spoken Greek of the period. The heavy Semitic influence on the Greek of some NT books, the colloquial character of Mark, and the grammatical mistakes of Rev might well have made these works sound crude to better educated audiences. Perhaps Paul was not simply being modest when he said that he did not preach "in words taught by human wisdom" (I Cor 2:13).

5

The Religious and Philosophical World
of New Testament Times

The Jews of this period would have had some knowledge of the non-Jewish religions of the peoples with whom they had contact; many of those peoples would have had some knowledge of Jewish religion. Often, on either side, such knowledge would have been partial, inaccurate, and even prejudiced, yet readers should be alert to the dangers of compartmentalizing. Even in Palestine, there was strong Hellenistic influence. Jewish attitudes ranged from enthusiastic participation and acculturation to ghettolike rejection.

JEWISH RELIGIOUS WORLD

The designation "Judaism" is appropriate for the period of Israelite history that began in 539 BC with the Persian release of the captives from Judah who had been held in Babylon. The Temple was rebuilt and its activities reinstituted. Yet Judaism took on a particular religious coloration from Ezra's proclamation of the Law (Neh 8:1–9:37) ca. 458/400 BC. Obedience to the Law of Moses became more and more a paramount obligation of the Jew as a corollary of accepting the one God. Eventually meetings for prayer, devout reading, meditation, and instruction known as synagogues also became an important factor in Jewish life. While up to AD 70 attitudes toward the Temple often divided Jews, internal religious divisions centered on different interpretations of the Law existed before and after AD 70.

Amidst his depiction of the Maccabean struggle under Jonathan (ca. 145 BC), Josephus wrote a famous description: "At that time there were three *haireseis* [parties, sects, schools of thought—from which 'heresies' in later usage] of the Jews which held different opinions about human affairs: the first of them was called Pharisees, the second Sadducees, the third Essenes" (*Ant.* 13.5.9; #171). In interpreting these remarks one should be careful. First, many people were without firm religious identity. Second, the differences were on a wider scale than those that might be considered purely religious. Third, knowledge of how these divisions came about is very limited. Fourth, it is difficult to know the precise coloration of the thought of each group: Josephus simplifies in trying to explain them to Roman readers.

The roots of the *Sadducees* were probably in the Zadokite Temple priesthood and its admirers. They seem to have identified with the priesthood of the Jerusalem Temple when others turned away. The Sadducees became increasingly united with the ruling Hellenized aristocracy, supposedly having little in common with the people. Yet knowledge of the Sadducees is particularly defective.

Most scholars see the *Essenes* as springing from an opposition to developments in the Temple after 152 BC. They would be Hasideans or pious ones who had joined the Maccabean revolt and who felt betrayed by Jonathan and Simon, the brothers of Judas Maccabeus, who accepted the honor of the high priesthood from the Syrian kings. What we know about the Essenes has been greatly enlarged by the discovery of scrolls or fragments of some 800 mss. near Qumran (the site of stone ruins sometimes called Khirbet Qumran) by the Dead Sea (the DSS), because in the majority view these documents stem from a settlement of Essenes at this site from ca. 150 BC to AD 70. The Qumranians (those Essenes living in community at Qumran) held that either the Spirit of Truth or the Spirit of Falsehood guides all human beings. Disdaining the Temple now presided over by those who in their judgment were wicked priests, the Qumranians formed the community of the new covenant seeking to become perfect by an extraordinarily strict practice of the Law, and awaiting an imminent messianic coming by which God would destroy all iniquity and punish their enemies.

The *Pharisees* were not a priestly movement. Their very name, which implies separation, probably results from the fact that they too ultimately became critical of and split from the Hasmonean descendants of the Maccabees who became increasingly secularized rulers. The Pharisees' approach to the written Law of Moses was marked by a theory of a second, oral Law (supposedly also derived from Moses); their interpretations were less severe than those of the Essenes and more innovative than those of the Sadducees, who remained conservatively restricted to the written Law.

Relations among these groups were at times vicious. It is worthwhile documenting some instances of the hostility so that one can place in context the religious enmity one finds in the NT. In 128 BC the high priest John Hyrcanus destroyed the sanctuary of the Samaritans on Mt. Gerizim, the central sacred site for the Samaritan religious community; a few decades later Alexander Jannaeus, Hasmonean king and high priest, massacred 6,000 Jews over a challenge (by Pharisees?) to his legal qualifications to hold the priestly office; later he crucified 800 (seemingly including Pharisees) while their wives and children were butchered before their eyes. When the Pharisees did get the upper hand during the reign of the Jewish queen Salome Alexandra, they executed and exiled their religious/political adversaries. The DSS rail against both Sadducees and Pharisees. These are but a few examples of the existing atmosphere, all of which took place before Jesus' lifetime, perhaps because strong rulers like Herod and the Romans would not tolerate such internecine religious behavior.

The Jewish revolt of AD 66–70 and the destruction of the Jerusalem Temple changed the dynamics of religious grouping. Revolutionaries were exterminated. The Sadducees lost their power base with the destruction of the Temple. The Qumran Essene settlement was destroyed. It seems (though complete clarity is lacking) that the Pharisees fed into the rabbinic movement. Nevertheless, in the post-70 period rabbinic teachers gradually won recognition by the Roman authorities as spokesmen for the Jews. In the post-70 period, when Christian writings spoke of Judaism, the censure was harsh. Local synagogues at different times in different places no longer tolerated the presence of Christians.

THE NON-JEWISH RELIGIOUS WORLD

There is no doubt that both the OT and early post-OT Judaism influenced Jesus, the early Christian preachers, and the NT writers. More debatable is the extent to which they were influenced by the non-Jewish religions and philosophies of the Greco-Roman world. If we start with Jesus himself or the early Christian preachers, we in fact do not know. Non-Jewish influence on Paul is plausible: he came from Tarsus; he wrote and spoke Greek; and he used some Greek oratorical devices in his letters. There is, however, sparse evidence of Pagan religious ideas in the letters of this man who calls himself "a Hebrew of the Hebrews."

The attempts to see the evangelists' portrayals of Jesus as influenced by Pagan "divine man" ideology are highly controverted. Scholars have not demonstrated that in a dominant way Pagan religion shaped the theology or christology of the NT. Nevertheless, the mindset of the audience that received the NT message must be taken into account. Some of the evangelized may have blended the Christian gospel into their religious and/or philosophical preconceptions.

THE GODS AND GODDESSES OF CLASSICAL MYTHOLOGY. For many this official cult of the ancient gods and goddesses did not translate into genuine religious devotion, whence the demythologizing by the philosophers, the appeal of newer Eastern and/or mystery religions, and the prevalence of divining, consulting oracles, magic, and astrology.

EMPEROR WORSHIP. Particularly in the East, there was a tendency to regard the emperor as divine. Augustus, who was hailed as divine, rejected deification during his lifetime, yet was deified after his death. Others (Caligula, Nero, Domitian) insisted on divine honors while living.

THE MYSTERY RELIGIONS involved secret religious dramas and ceremonies by which those initiated could share in the immortal life of the gods. The initiates who came from all classes were bonded into an enduring fellowship. Christian preachers would have had to compete with these cults that offered salvation without insistence on social or personal morality.

THE EASTERN RELIGIONS. The cult of Isis stemming from Egypt was popular in the empire, particularly among women. Initiates were insured life after death through a mystery rite. The cult of Mithras, restricted to men, was popular with soldiers. Mithraism involved a mediator between human beings and the god of light. The overall symbolism is the overcoming of evil and the bringing of life to the initiates, who underwent a bath in blood.

GRECO-ROMAN PHILOSOPHIES, PHILO, AND GNOSTICISM

Even though "philosophy" is a word that occurs only once in the NT (Col 2:8), Greco-Roman philosophies and combinations of them with Jewish and Pagan religious motifs also deserve attention. In various ways philosophies came much closer to monotheism than did any of the Pagan religions; and often they held up demanding codes of behavior, again much more than most of the religions.

PLATONISM. The philosophy that Plato (427–347 BC) formulated had declined by NT times; but it influenced other philosophies (and, later, the Church Fathers). The most important doctrine was that in this world people see only the insubstantial shadows cast by another world of realities where perfect truth and beauty exist. To fulfill their destiny people must escape the material world and go to their true home in that other world.

CYNICS. Behavior rather than abstract thought characterized the Cynic outlook, specifically frugality and a return to nature, rejecting (sometimes satirically) artificial conventions. Overall the Cynics showed no interest in the god/s. They took over the Socratic method of asking questions, going into the streets to ordinary people and challenging them. In particular, they engaged in the "diatribe," a pedagogical discourse characterized by conversational style, rhetorical questions, paradoxes, apostrophes, etc.

EPICUREANS. Another philosophical tradition stems from Epicurus (342–270 BC), who devalued myths and abstractions and appealed to the common people by making sensation the standard of truth—

feelings and sense perceptions are trustworthy. His philosophy was designed to free people from fears and superstitions: there is no need for religion since the movement of atoms determines events; gods have nothing to do with human existence; death is final, and there is no resurrection. Conventicles of Epicureans were bound together by friendship and care for one another.

STOICISM. This philosophy derived from Cynics the tenet that virtue is the only good. Stoicism regarded the universe as a single organism energized by a world-soul, the *logos* or divine reason that guides all things. If people live according to the guiding reason or natural law, they can remain tranquil in the face of adversity. Affections and passions are looked on as pathological states from which people can be delivered. Thus, this philosophy developed moral values and conquest of self. Stoics had a deterministic outlook on what would happen, with astrology and natural science as the tools for detecting the already fixed plan that would culminate in a great purging conflagration, before a new cycle of ages would begin.

SOPHISTS. Although there were Sophist philosophers, there was no Sophist philosophy. Sophists were teachers who made a profession of going from city to city and teaching for a fee. They emphasized material success and were able to argue for any viewpoint, true or not. At the time of the early Roman Empire a Second Sophistic wave concentrated on the practice of rhetoric, an important element in higher education.

Two other items of religious/philosophical background represent a combination of Jewish and Gentile motifs, namely, the writings of Philo and gnosticism.

PHILO (ca. 20 BC–AD 50) was a prominent Jew of Alexandria who was faithful to Jewish practice, knew the LXX, and was well equipped to translate his religious tradition in a way that a Hellenized world could understand. Philo tried to integrate philosophy with biblical principles both directly and through allegorical interpretation of the Bible. He was familiar with Aristotelianism and with Pythagorean numerical speculations; but his dominant approach reflected Platonism (especially later Middle-Platonic developments) and Stoicism. The descent of the soul into the body was explained in Platonic terms; and although Philo related the Law of Moses to the Stoic idea of rational order in nature, he rejected Stoic determinism in favor of freedom.

GNOSTICISM (from *gnōsis*, "knowledge") is a term used to describe a pattern of religious thought, often with Jewish and Christian elements, advocated by groups in the eastern section of the Roman Empire (Syria, Babylonia, Egypt). The origins of gnosticism are disputed. Our information comes from different sources. The Church Fathers wrote about these groups, explaining the gnostic systems in the course of polemicizing against them. Despite differences among gnostics, relatively common theses were that human souls or spiritual principles do not belong in this material world (which is often described as evil and ignorant), and they can be saved only by receiving the revelation that they belong in a heavenly realm of light (the plēroma, or "fullness"), where there is a hierarchy of emanations from the true God. Ascent to this realm is sometimes through baptism, sometimes through elaborate cultic rituals (often involving anointing), sometimes more through philosophical reflection. Some gnostic groups had their own hierarchy and virtually constituted a counterchurch.

6

Gospels in General; Synoptic Gospels in Particular

This chapter treats two interrelated problems: First, what kind of writing is a Gospel? Second, what are the Synoptic Gospels?

USE OF THE WORD "GOSPEL"

In NT times the word "gospel" (Greek: *euaggelion*) meant "good announcement" and referred not to a book or writing but to a proclamation or message. In non-Christian Greek *euaggelion* referred to things like news of victory in a battle and the emperor's birth. In the LXX, words related to *euaggelion* translate words from the Hebrew *bśr*, which has a similar range of proclaiming good news, especially of Israel's or of God's victory.

Whether Jesus used "gospel" is debated, but clearly his followers did, as Paul (Rom 1:3–4), Mark (1:1), and other NT authors show. For these followers "gospel" emphasized that the good news involved what God had done in Jesus.

In the second century Christians employed *euaggelion* in reference to Christian writings. The plurality of written gospels resulted in the use of distinguishing designations, so that by the end of the second century titles were prefaced to the canonical Gospels in the pattern "The Gospel according to . . ." The existence of gospels beyond the canonical is a question complicated by issues of terminology: for clarity it may be useful to keep distinct two categories: "Jesus material" (infancy and passion narratives, and collections of sayings, miracle stories, and discourses attributed to the risen Jesus); and "gospels," that is, full narratives such as we encounter in the four canonical writings (covering at least the span of public ministry/passion/resurrection, and combining miracles and sayings). Here and elsewhere in this book, except in italicized titles of works, capital "G" will be kept for the canonical gospels.

ORIGIN OF THE GOSPEL GENRE

How did the idea of writing the Gospels come about? Did it have its origin in the OT? Was it an imitation of a Greco-Roman genre? Was it a unique creative insight of Mark that Matt, Luke, and John then copied? Or was it a widespread basic pre-Marcan idea that developed naturally from early Christian preaching? Scholars tend to advocate either one or the other of those approaches.

ORIGIN IN THE OT AND JEWISH DEVELOPMENTS DERIVATIVE FROM THE OT. In the Book of Jeremiah, one has the prophet's origins, calling, life and ministry, and a type of passion narrative. By the first century AD a Jewish work, the *Lives of the Prophets* (seemingly including some Christian additions), recounts a few or many details about various prophets. Written in Greek, this work may reflect the influence of ancient biographies.

ORIGIN IN IMITATION OF SECULAR BIOGRAPHIES. Among the abundant Greco-Roman literature of the centuries immediately before and after Christ were various types of biography. Those proposed as counterparts to the Gospels, however, have divergent tonalities. Some scholars point to the "laudatory biography," where the primary concern was to show the greatness of the figure. Diversities among the proposed laudatory biographies make the definability of such a subgenre uncertain. Others consider the portrayal of "immortals" and "eternals." But the Synoptic Gospels do not present Jesus simply as a mortal who gained immortality as a reward; rather the resurrection confirms the truth of who he already was before death. And John does not present an eternal but rather a divine Word that *became* flesh and remained flesh. In fact, considerable differences exist between Greco-Roman biographies and the Gospels. Yet it is likely that many first-century hearers/readers would have thought of the Gospels almost as lives of Christ, particularly Matt and Luke, which begin with an infancy narrative.

CREATIVITY AND THE GOSPELS. How much ingenuity was required to construct a full gospel narrative about Jesus? The answer depends on the historicity of the narrative: largely fiction, or largely fact? Scholars differ considerably in this matter. On the one hand, various scholars see much of Mark, which most likely was the earliest, as being fiction. Some regard the narrative as creative reflection on the OT; some see Jesus as a wisdom teacher and judge the stories of miracles and resurrection as propaganda to make Jesus competitive as a wonder-worker; and others contend that Jesus was a magician who healed by various means and that the role of wisdom teaching was created to make him respectable. Were any of this true, much creativity would have been required to move from what some say Jesus was in fact to the very different picture of him painted in the Gospels. On the other hand, an even larger number of scholars would judge much of what Mark narrates as factual. Jesus himself would have supplied the kinds of material that ultimately went into the Gospels, no matter how much that material developed over the decades that separated him from the evangelists.

THE THREE STAGES OF GOSPEL FORMATION

(1) THE PUBLIC MINISTRY OR ACTIVITY OF JESUS OF NAZARETH (the first third of the first century AD). Jesus was active in first-century Galilee and Judea. He was a first-century Jew and belonged to his own time and place. Memories were formed around him.

(2) THE (APOSTOLIC) PREACHING ABOUT JESUS (the second third of the first century AD). Those who had seen and heard Jesus had their faith in him confirmed through postresurrectional appearances (I Cor 15:5–7). Their postresurrectional faith illumined memories of him, and so they preached with enriched significance. This was a time of preaching.

(3) THE WRITTEN GOSPELS (the last third of the first century, approximately). The era 65–100 was probably when all four canonical Gospels were written. These Gospels were attributed to two apostles, Matthew and John, and two companions of apostles, Mark (of Peter) and Luke (of Paul). Yet most scholars do not think that the evangelists were eyewitnesses of the ministry of Jesus.

The recognition that the evangelists were not eyewitnesses of Jesus' ministry is important for understanding the differences among the Gospels. Each evangelist did not write from direct memory but rather employed Jesus materials in order to portray him in a way that would speak to the spiritual needs of the community being addressed by the Gospel. The evangelists emerge as authors and as theologians, shaping and orienting Gospel material to a particular goal.

Corollaries of this approach to Gospel formation would include the following:

• The Gospels are not literal records of the ministry of Jesus. Decades of developing and adapting the Jesus tradition had intervened.
• A thesis that does not present the Gospels as literal history is sometimes interpreted to mean that they are not true accounts of Jesus. Above all, the Gospels aim to bring people to a faith in Jesus that opens them to God's rule or kingdom. Those who believe in inspiration will maintain that the Holy Spirit guided the process, and so the Gospels reflect the truth that God sent Jesus to proclaim.
• Divine providence furnished four different Gospels, not a harmonized version. Harmonization, instead of enriching, can impoverish.
• Recognizing the distinct theological orientation of each Gospel means that the Gospel pericopes should be read in the particular context of the Gospel in which they occur in order to do justice to them.

THE SYNOPTIC PROBLEM

The first three Gospels, called "Synoptic," have so much in common that there must have been some dependence of one or two on the other or on a common written source.

Statistics and terminology: Mark has 661 verses (vv.); Matt has 1,068, and Luke has 1,149. Eighty percent of Mark's vv. are reproduced in Matt, and 65 percent in Luke. The Marcan material found in both the other two is called the "Triple Tradition." The approximately 220–235 vv. (in whole or in part) of non-Marcan material that Matt and Luke have in common is called the "Double Tradition." In both instances so much of the order in which that common tradition is presented, and so much of the wording in which it is phrased are the same that dependence at the written rather than simply at the oral level has to be posited.

SOLUTIONS THAT POSIT ONE OR MORE PROTOGOSPELS. There have been many proposals that would explain the interrelationships of the Synoptic Gospels by positing a gospel that existed before they were written. These include: (1) all three Synoptic Gospels drew on a no-longer-extant Aramaic Gospel that was thought to be a full life of Christ; (2) some would invoke Papias ("Matthew arranged in order the sayings in the Hebrew [=Aramaic?] language") and contend that he was speaking not about the Matt we know but about an earlier collection (at times designated M) on which Mark drew and also canonical Matt (whether directly or through Mark); (3) other scholars judge necessary a more complex multidocument theory, including a combination of Aramaic, Greek, and oral sources and offer elaborate theories that many conclude cannot be proved right or wrong. Consequently, the scholarly majority proposes solutions based on relationships of mutual dependence among the extant Gospels.

SOLUTIONS IN WHICH MATT WAS THE FIRST GOSPEL, AND LUKE USED MATT. This hypothesis of Matthean priority, dating back to Augustine in the fourth century, is the oldest explanation. The canonical order is understood to be the order of dependence: Matt was written first, Mark severely abbreviated Matt, and then came Luke and John, with each drawing on its predecessors. In 1789 J. J. Griesbach proposed that the order was Matt, Luke, and Mark. Thus, Mark is mostly a digest of material where Matt and Luke agree. Yet, Mark omits the whole Double Tradition. Explaining Mark's treatment of Matt is the greatest difficulty in hypotheses giving Matt priority.

To some scholars, "Minor Agreements" between Luke and Matt against Mark in passages in the Triple Tradition appear to support the thesis that Luke used Matt. Yet, there are almost contradictory accounts in Luke and Matt.

SOLUTIONS BASED ON MARCAN PRIORITY. Mark was written first and both Matt and Luke drew on it. *The most common thesis posits that Matt and Luke depended on Mark and wrote independently of each other.* What they have in common and did not derive from Mark (the Double Tradition) is explained by positing Q (a reconstructed source discussed in the next subsection). This is known as the Two-Source Theory.

The basic argument for Marcan priority is that it solves more problems than any other theory. The basic argument against Marcan priority rests on the Minor Agreements mentioned in relation to the Griesbach hypothesis. Many of them can be explained, but some remain very difficult.

A realistic conclusion is that *no solution to the Synoptic Problem solves all difficulties.* If one cannot resolve all the enigmas, it is realistic to accept and work with a relatively simple solution to the Synoptic Problem that is largely satisfactory; thus, the theory of Marcan priority (as part of the Two-Source Theory) is recommended to readers. These are some points to keep in mind:

- Even when Mark was written, oral tradition about Jesus did not cease. Many think that some problems not resolved by the Two-Source Theory can be met by bringing into the picture the ongoing influence of oral tradition.
- If both Matt and Luke used Mark, their theology can at times be studied by the changes they made in Mark's report—redaction criticism.
- If one decides that Matt or Luke has added material to what was taken from Mark, that addition need not be dated later than the Marcan material.

The Griesbach Hypothesis   The Two-Source Hypothesis

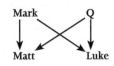

THE EXISTENCE OF "Q"

"Q" is a hypothetical source posited by most scholars to explain what was called the Double Tradition, that is, agreements (often verbatim) between Matt and Luke on material not found in Mark. ("Q" comes from the German *Quelle*, "source.") Behind the hypothesis is the plausible assumption that the Matthean evangelist did not know Luke and vice versa, and so they must have had a common source. Many cautions are necessary before Q is reconstructed. The contents are usually estimated at about 220–235 verses or parts of verses. It is, of course, possible that material found only in Matt or Luke might have existed in Q. We are not certain of the sequence of material in Q because Matt and Luke do not present it in the same order; nevertheless, most reconstructions follow the Lucan order, because scholars detect apparent thematic coherence of the Q material in Luke. Henceforth, unless otherwise specified, *references to Q material will be through Lucan versification.*

Reconstructed Q consists of sayings and some parables with an absolute minimum of narrative setting; and thus there is a strong sapiential tone. A look at the Q material helps to recognize its emphases. There is a strongly eschatological thrust: judgment is imminent, but the hour is unknown (12:39–40). Accordingly Jesus' followers are expected to live a highly moral life observing even the Law (16:17) without superficial hypocrisy (11:39–44). There is expectation of persecution and encouragement for those who bear it for the sake of the Son of Man (6:22–23).

Many would attribute to Q a low christology since in it Jesus emerges (they contend) simply as a Sophist or Cynic wisdom teacher. Yet the Q Jesus is said to be, among a number of indicators of a higher christology:

- The Son of Man who is rejected and suffers in his lifetime (7:31–35; 9:57–60).
- The Son to whom all has been given and who is known only by the Father and only he knows the Father and anyone to whom the Son chooses to reveal him (10:22).
- The Son of Man who will come in judgment (17:23–27,30,37).
- It is insufficient simply to call [the Q] Jesus Lord; one must hear his words and do them if one is to survive (6:46–49).

Table 2. Material usually allotted to Q

MATTHEW	LUKE	CONTENTS
3:7b–12	3:7–9, 16–17	JBap: warnings, promise of one to come
4:2b–11a	4:2–13	Three temptations (testings) of Jesus by the devil (different order)
5:3, 6, 4, 11–12	6:20b–23	Beatitudes (different order, wording)
5:44, 39b–40, 42	6:27–30	Love of enemies; turn other cheek; give coat; give to beggars
7:12	6:31	What you wish others to do to you, do to them
5:46–47, 45, 48	6:32–33, 35b–36	Love more than those who love you; be merciful as the Father is
7:1–2	6:37a, 38c	Judge not and be not judged; measure given is measure received
15:14, 10:24–25a	6:39–40	Can blind lead the blind; disciple not above teacher
7:3–5	6:41–42	Speck in brother's eye, log in one's own
7:16–20 (12:33–35)	6:43–45	No good tree bears bad fruit; no figs from thorns
7:21, 24–27	6:46–49	Calling me Lord and not doing; hearing my words and doing them
8:5a–10, 13	7:1–2, 6b–10	Centurion at Capernaum begs help for sick servant, marvelous faith
11:2–11	7:18–28	Disciples of JBap; message to him; praise of JBap as more than a prophet
11:16–19	7:31–35	This generation pleased by neither JBap nor Son of Man
8:19–22	9:57–60	Son of Man has nowhere to lay head; to follow him let dead bury dead
9:37–38; 10:7–16	10:2–12	Harvest plentiful, laborers few; mission instructions
11:21–23; 10:40	10:13–16	Woe to Chorazin, Bethsaida; whoever hears you, hears me

MATTHEW	LUKE	CONTENTS
11:25–27; 13:16–17	10:21–24	Thanking the Father for revealing to infants; all things given to the Son who alone knows the Father; blessed eyes that see what you see
6:9–13	11:2–4	The Lord's prayer (variant forms—Matt's longer)
7:7–11	11:9–13	Ask and it will be given; if you give good gifts, how much more the Father
12:22–30	11:14–15, 17–23	Demons cast out by Beelzebul; strong man guards his palace; not with me, against me
12:43–45	11:24–26	Unclean spirit gone out of someone returns and brings seven others, making worse
12:38–42	11:29–32	Generation seeks sign; sign of Jonah; judgment by people of Nineveh, queen of south
5:15; 6:22–23	11:33–35	Not putting lamp under bushel; eye lamp of body, if unsound, darkness
23:25–26, 23, 6–7a, 27	11:39–44	Pharisees cleanse outside of cup; woe for tithing inconsequentials, seeking first place
23:4, 29–31	11:46–48	Woe to lawyers for binding heavy burdens, building tombs of the prophets
23:34–36, 13	11:49–52	I speak/God's wisdom speaks: Will send prophets who will be persecuted; woe to lawyers
10:26–33; 12:32	12:2–10	All covered to be revealed; fear not killers of body; acknowledging me before God
10:19–20	12:11–12	Before synagogues, Holy Spirit will help
6:25–33	12:22–31	Don't be anxious about the body; consider lilies of field; Father knows what you need
6:19–21	12:33–34	No treasures on earth but in heaven

Table 2. *Continued*

MATTHEW	LUKE	CONTENTS
24:43–44, 45–51	12:39–40, 42–46	Householder and thief; faithful servant preparing for master's coming
10:34–36	12:51–53	Not come to bring peace but sword; divisions of family
16:2–3	12:54–56	Ability to interpret weather signs should enable to interpret present times
5:25–26	12:58–59	Settling before going before the magistrate
13:31–33	13:18–21	Kingdom of heaven/God: like growth of mustard seed; like leaven woman puts in meal
7:13–14, 22–23; 8:11–12	13:23–29	Narrow gate through which few will enter; householder refusing those who knock; people coming from all directions to enter kingdom of heaven/God
23:37–39	13:34–35	Jerusalem, killing the prophets, must bless him who comes in the Lord's name
22:2–10	14:16–24	Kingdom of heaven/God: a great banquet, invitees make excuses, others invited
10:37–38	14:26–27	Anyone coming must prefer me over family and must bear a cross
5:13	14:34–35	Uselessness of salt that has lost its savor
18:12–14	15:4–7	Man who leaves ninety-nine sheep to go after lost one
6:24	16:13	Cannot serve two masters
11:12–13; 5:18, 32	16:16–18	Law and prophets till JBap; not a dot of Law will pass; divorcing wife and marrying another is adultery
18:7, 15, 21–22	17:1, 3b–4	Woe to tempters; forgive brother after rebuking; Peter: how often to forgive
17:20	17:6	If you had faith like grain of mustard seed, could move mountains

MATTHEW	LUKE	CONTENTS
24:26–28	17:23–24, 37	Signs of the coming of the Son of Man
24:37–39	17:26–27, 30	As in the days of Noah, so will be the coming of the Son of Man
10:39	17:33	Whoever finds one's life will lose it; whoever loses will find it
24:40–41	17:34–35	On that night, of two, one taken and the other left
25:14–30	19:12–27	Parable of the pounds/talents
19:28	22:38, 30	Followers will sit on thrones judging the twelve tribes of Israel

Such a Jesus is far more than a wisdom teacher.

That issue leads us to a highly debatable aspect of recent Q studies: the attempt to reconstruct a Q community, its history, its theology, where it was written, and its leadership. The assumption, however, that we can attribute with *considerable accuracy* different emphases to different stages of growth in this hypothetical document presupposes an unlikely systematization in Christian life.

7

The Gospel According to Mark

The first step in considering any book of the NT is to read it through slowly and attentively. The *General Analysis* will offer brief commentary on the biblical text, attempting to bring to light inductively the distinctiveness of the writer's thought and technique.

GENERAL ANALYSIS OF THE MESSAGE

Readers can learn much about Jesus from the traditions of his parables and mighty deeds; but unless that is intimately combined with the picture of his victory through suffering, they cannot understand him or the vocation of his followers. In Mark 8, after having been consistently rejected and misunderstood despite all he has said and done, Jesus starts to proclaim the necessity of the suffering, death, and resurrection of the Son of Man in God's plan.

Part One: Ministry of Healing and Preaching in Galilee (1:1–8:26)

Mark prefaces the beginning of Jesus' public activities with JBap's proclamation. Then the first half of the Gospel describes a ministry of

SUMMARY OF BASIC INFORMATION

DATE: 60–75, most likely between 68 and 73.

AUTHOR BY TRADITIONAL (SECOND-CENTURY) ATTRIBUTION: Mark, the follower and "interpreter" of Peter, usually identified as the John Mark of Acts, whose mother had a house in Jerusalem. He accompanied Barnabas and Paul on the "First Missionary Journey" and may have helped Peter and Paul in Rome in the 60s. Some who reject this attribution allow that the author may have been an otherwise unknown Christian named Mark.

AUTHOR DETECTABLE FROM CONTENTS: A Greek-speaker, who was not an eyewitness of Jesus' ministry and made inexact statements about Palestinian geography. He drew on preshaped traditions about Jesus (oral and probably written) and addressed himself to a community that seemingly had undergone persecution and failure.

LOCALE INVOLVED: Traditionally Rome (where Christians were persecuted by Nero). Other suggestions: Syria, the northern Transjordan, the Decapolis, and Galilee.

UNITY: No major reason to think of more than one author; a few would argue for different editions to explain differences in Matt's and Luke's use of Mark.

INTEGRITY: Mark probably ended with 16:8. Mss. have appended other secondary endings recounting the appearance(s) of the risen Jesus. The "longer ending" (16:9–20) is the one most often considered canonical.

DIVISION:*

1:1–8:26: PART ONE: MINISTRY OF HEALING AND PREACHING IN GALILEE

1. Introduction by JBap; an initial day; controversy at Capernaum (1:1–3:6)
2. Jesus chooses the Twelve and trains them as disciples by parables and mighty deeds; misunderstanding among his Nazareth relatives (3:7–6:6)
3. Sending out the Twelve; feeding 5,000; walking on water; controversy; feeding 4,000; misunderstanding (6:7–8:26)

8:27–16:8 + 16:9–20: PART TWO: SUFFERING PREDICTED; DEATH IN JERUSALEM; RESURRECTION

1. Three passion predictions; Peter's confession; the transfiguration; Jesus' teaching (8:27–10:52)
2. Ministry in Jerusalem: Entry; Temple actions and encounters; eschatological discourse (11:1–13:37)
3. Anointing, Last Supper, passion, crucifixion, burial, empty tomb (14:1–16:8)
4. An ending describing resurrection appearances appended by a later copyist (16:9–20).

---

*This way of dividing Mark is designed to enable readers to follow the flow of thought, but no claim is made that the evangelist would have divided the Gospel thus (although the beginning of passion predictions in chap. 8 does seem to be an intentional major divider). In particular the distinction between units (marked numerically above) and their subunits is very hazy, for the latter could easily be elevated to units.

preaching, powerful deeds, and teaching in Galilee and its environs. Although Jesus attracts great interest, he struggles with misunderstanding and hostile rejection.

1. INTRODUCTION BY JBAP; AN INITIAL DAY;
CONTROVERSIES AT CAPERNAUM (1:1–3:6).

Mark's opening (1:1–15) presents the beginning of the gospel of Jesus Christ in the context of the ministry of JBap as the fulfillment of Mal 3:1 and Isa 40:3. In the wilderness JBap baptized with water and cried out to prepare the way of the Lord, announcing the one who will baptize with the Holy Spirit, namely, Jesus. At his baptism the Spirit descends on him like a dove and a voice from heaven speaks to him as God's beloved Son, echoing Ps 2:7 and Isa 42:1. As Satan tests Jesus and JBap is arrested the reader learns that Jesus' proclamation of the kingdom or rule of God will encounter major obstacles. Jesus begins by calling four men to be his followers (1:16–20).

In recounting the initial day of Jesus' ministry (1:21–38), Mark highlights Jesus' actions in proclaiming the kingdom: teaching with authority, exorcizing an unclean spirit, healing, and praying—all amid pressing demands. God's people must change their ways; the presence of visible evil must be opposed; and the demonic must be defeated. Paradoxically unclean spirits recognize that he is the Holy One of God, while his disciples do not understand him fully despite his teaching and powerful deeds. In 1:34 Jesus forbids demons who "knew him" to speak, whereby he seems to hide his identity as the Son of God until after his death on the cross.

The expansion of Jesus' activity (1:39–45). Jesus' ministry (preaching, exorcizing demons, healing) moves through the towns of Galilee.

Controversies at Capernaum (2:1–3:6). At this town on the Sea of Galilee, which now has become Jesus' home, Mark centers five incidents where the scribes and the Pharisees and others raise objections to his deportment. His is a higher authority and he does not fit the religious expectations of others; rather "the Son of Man is lord even of the Sabbath." Now, human beings (Pharisees and Herodians) join demons in opposition to Jesus.

2. Jesus Chooses the Twelve and Trains Them as Disciples by Parables and Mighty Deeds; Misunderstanding Among His Nazareth Relatives (3:7–6:6).

Mark begins this section with a summary (3:7–12) showing that Jesus' ministry was attracting attention from beyond Galilee. Jesus goes up to the mountain and summons the Twelve (3:13–19), whom he wants to be with him and whom he will send forth to preach. (Note that Luke 6:13–15 and Acts 1:13 present a list of the Twelve that differs slightly from that in Mark.)

In the sequence 3:20–35 we encounter an arrangement of the narrative that scholars recognize as a feature of Marcan style, an intercalation: in it Mark initiates an action, interrupts it by another scene, and then resumes the initial action, bringing it to a close. Here Jesus' relatives do not understand the developments in Jesus' life (3:20–21). Scribes come from Jerusalem (3:22–30). Both relatives and scribes misread the situation. At the end of the intercalation (3:31–35) the mother and brothers of Jesus finally arrive; but, now that the proclamation of the kingdom has begun, they have been replaced: "Whoever does the will of God is my brother, and sister, and mother." The intermediary scene (3:22–30) contains one of the Marcan Jesus' clearest statements about Satan and opposition to the kingdom of God. The unforgivable blasphemy in 3:28–30 is to attribute Jesus' works to an unclean spirit rather than to the Holy Spirit.

The next subsection (4:1–34) is a collection of parables pertinent to the kingdom of God, most of them dealing with the growth of a seed. Because they are polyvalent, the particular point of parables takes on coloration from the context in which they are uttered or placed. The only certain context is the placing of the parables in the extant Gospels—the fact that at times the context differs in Mark, Matt, and Luke exemplifies the creative use of tradition by the evangelists for their own pedagogical purposes.

Woven into the seed parables are comments and parabolic sayings about the "purpose" of the parables. In particular, Mark 4:11–12 is an offensive text if one does not understand the biblical approach to divine foresight where what has in fact happened is often presented as

God's purpose. That Jesus' purpose was not to obscure is made clear by the sayings of 4:21–23 and the summary of 4:33–34, which has Jesus speaking the word to them in parables "as they were able to understand it."

Four miraculous actions follow in 4:35–5:43. Almost half of Mark's account of Jesus' ministry (ca. 200 of 450 vv.) deals with miracles. The first-century worldview was very different from post-Enlightenment comprehension. Today many dismiss completely the historicity of the miraculous. Others accept the healings (often including the exorcisms) of Jesus as manifestations of God's mercy but reject the historicity of "nature" miracles such as the calming of the storm in 4:35–41. That distinction finds no support in an OT background where God manifests power over all creation. For Mark these stories serve to recognize Jesus' identity (4:41; 5:7,19–20), to portray his possession of power (4:39; 5:30), and to foreshadow Jesus' gift of eternal life (5:23,42).

In 6:1–6 Jesus returns to Nazareth, where his teaching in the synagogue produces skepticism. Remembering his origin, the local people discount his religious wisdom and mighty works. He encounters unbelief among those who should know him (his hometown, relatives, and household) and his power is ineffective there.

3. SENDING OUT THE TWELVE; FEEDING 5,000; WALKING ON WATER;
CONTROVERSY; FEEDING 4,000; MISUNDERSTANDING (6:7–8:26).

This section begins with the sending out of the Twelve and ends with their continued misunderstanding. This failure will lead to the second part of the Gospel, where Jesus announces his suffering and death as necessary for adequate faith.

Marcan intercalation shapes the accounts of the mission of the Twelve and Herod (6:7–33). The disciples' mission is an extension of that of Jesus, with austere conditions that make it clear that results were not effected by human means. Between the beginning (6:7–13) and the end (6:30–32) of the mission we are told that King Herod (Antipas) has killed JBap and that now he worries that Jesus may be JBap come back from the dead (6:14–29). JBap's fate foreshadows that of Jesus.

The feeding of the 5,000 and the walking on the water (6:34–52) constitute a unit in all four Gospels. Most directly we see Jesus' compassion, which as divine power feeds the hungry multitude. Yet, the story also echoes OT accounts—Elijah's feeding of 100 (II Kings 4:42–44); the manna miracle in Moses' time (Exod 16:1–36)—even as Jesus' walking on the water may echo the dry-shod crossing of the Red Sea (Exod 14:1–31). Beginning with Jesus and developing strongly in church preaching, the highlighting of parallels between Jesus' career and OT scenes became a major element in understanding God's total plan.

In the second miracle, the walking on the sea, Mark offers a type of theophany or epiphany; for the divine identity of Jesus is suggested not only by the extraordinary character of the miracle but also by Jesus' answer in 6:50, "I am" (Greek: *egō eimi*), which is given as the name of God in Exod 3:14. It is all the more poignant, then, that the disciples understood neither this miracle nor the multiplication, for their hearts were hardened (6:52). Following the paired miracles there is *a Marcan summary* (6:53–56) about the superficial enthusiasm of Galilean villagers for Jesus' many healings.

A controversy over ritual purity (7:1–23) is the next illustration of misunderstanding. Pharisees and scribes from Jerusalem criticize Jesus' disciples for not observing ritual purity (7:3–4)—a concept that Mark has to explain to his readers. The controversy leads Jesus to condemn narrow interpretations that ignore the real commandment of God for purity of heart (Jesus' attitude toward the Law may represent developments in the hard-fought struggles over kosher food in the time of the early church). In sharp contrast to the hostility of the Jewish authorities, the story of the faith of *the Syrophoenician woman* (7:24–30) raises the second major issue that sharply divided early Christians: the status of Gentiles. Jesus' response in 7:27, which is not egalitarian (children/ dogs), is offensive to some. Yet the woman's child is healed at a distance in this story (while such scandal as there is may reflect our failure to accept Jesus as a first-century Jew). If the woman's child is healed at a distance, the next miracle, *the deaf man* (7:31–37), describes an unusual amount of contact between Jesus and the afflicted, including using spittle and the Aramaic formula *Ephphatha*.

Even if in origin *the feeding of the 4,000* (8:1–9) may have been a doublet of the earlier feeding, it has strong cumulative effect in Mark as another manifestation of Jesus' stupendous power. What follows with

the disciples in the boat (8:10–21) dramatizes climactically the utter unlike-
lihood that Jesus will be accepted or understood—Pharisees seek a
sign to test him; and the disciples display no understanding despite the
two multiplications in feeding. The healing of the blind man (8:22–26) serves
as a parabolic commentary on the situation. The man gains his sight in
stages, for Jesus' first action gives him only blurry vision. This is also
the situation of the disciples despite all that Jesus has done for them
thus far. Only when Jesus acts a second time does the man see clearly,
and the next half of the Gospel will describe what Jesus must do to
make the disciples see clearly, namely, suffer, be put to death, and rise.

Part Two: Suffering Predicted; Death in Jerusalem; Resurrection (8:27–16:8 + 16:9–20)

Jesus signals a change of tone by predicting clearly his fate three
times.

1. THREE PASSION PREDICTIONS; PETER'S CONFESSION; THE TRANSFIGURATION; JESUS' TEACHING (8:27–10:52).

Part Two begins with Peter's confession of Jesus, the first passion prediction, and
its aftermath (8:27–9:1). Although Jesus was judged negatively at times
(3:21,22; 6:2–3), Peter's confession (8:27–30) comes amid more
positive evaluations of him as JBap, Elijah, and one of the prophets.
Peter goes even further by proclaiming Jesus as the Messiah, but Jesus
greets this with the same command to silence that he gave to demons
identifying him as God's Son (3:11–12). The two titles are correct in
themselves, but they have been uttered without including the necessary component of suffering. Jesus now makes that component clear
with a prediction of his own passion (8:31). Peter rejects this portrait
of the suffering Son of Man; and so Jesus categorizes his lack of understanding as worthy of Satan. Moreover, those who would follow him
will also have to suffer (8:34–37). In 8:38 Jesus warns that whoever is
ashamed of him will be judged with shame by the Son of Man when
he comes in the glory of his Father with the holy angels—a remarkable christological claim referring to the Parousia (second coming of
Christ). But does the next verse (9:1) also speak of the Parousia in
mentioning some there not tasting death before they see the kingdom

of God come with power? Or does 9:1 refer to the transfiguration which follows immediately, an interpretation that makes the "not taste death" easier?

The transfiguration (9:2–13) produces a reaction that is another example of the inadequate faith of the disciples. As the hitherto hidden glory of Jesus is made visible to three of his disciples, the heavenly voice again identifies Jesus (as at his baptism). The scene echoes the greatest OT theophany, on a mountain amidst the presence of Moses and Elijah, who encountered God on Sinai (Horeb). Awkwardly Peter proposes prolonging the experience by building three tabernacles. As they descend the mountain, Jesus charges the three disciples to silence and, then, they discuss the Son of Man, rising from the dead, and Elijah.

Mark tells *the story of the boy with a demon* (9:14–29) at unusual length. The symptoms seem typical of epilepsy, though in the Gospel worldview the evil of the illness is attributed to demon possession. Jesus is exasperated by the disciples' inability to drive out the demon: this is a faithless generation (9:19); and there is also a lack of faith implicit in the father's request for help, "If you can" (9:23). The "mute and deaf spirit" obeys Jesus' command to depart; and at the end (9:29) he tells the disciples, "This kind can come out in no other way except through prayer."

A journey through Galilee begins with Jesus' *second prediction of the passion* (9:30–32), which again the disciples do not understand. In turn, Jesus gives his disciples *varied instruction pertinent to the kingdom* (9:33–10:31).

The journey to Judea, instructing crowds, and a question of the Pharisees are the context for Jesus' teaching on marriage and divorce (10:1–12). The Pharisees cite Deut 24:1–4. But Jesus appeals to Gen 1:27; 2:24. Early Christians recognized the difficulty of Jesus' position, and the saying soon gathered comments (I Cor 7:10–11; Mark 10:12; Matt 5:31–32; 19:9; Luke 16:18) probably addressed to the situations of later hearers of the Gospel.

Jesus returns to the issue of those who enter the kingdom (10:13–31). For Jesus the kingdom of God requires only human receptivity of which a child is a good symbol (10:13–16). The question by the rich man in 10:17 asks how adults manifest receptivity. Jesus cites God's commandments enunciated in the OT, which the man says he has observed. Jesus lovingly tells him to sell his possessions and to give the proceeds to the poor. Is that a universal necessity? Jesus' remarks recognize that his demand is exceedingly difficult, impossible by human standards but not by God's. Furthermore, Jesus says that those who make great sacrifices for his sake will be rewarded; but the phrase "with persecutions" is an important realistic touch about their fate.

That realism finds expression also in *the third prediction of the passion* (10:32–34). In the moment, James and John raise the issue of *the first places in the kingdom* (10:35–45). Jesus' challenge to imitate him in drinking the cup and being baptized is symbolically a challenge to suffering. In God's kingdom service is what makes one great. "The Son of Man did not come to be served but to serve and to give his life as a ransom for many" (10:45) is a fitting summary of the spirit of this kingdom, anticipated in Isa 53:10–12.

The final scene of the journey toward Jerusalem comes in Jericho, when *Jesus heals the blind Bartimaeus* (10:46–52). With his faith affirmed, and given sight by Jesus, this liberated man follows Jesus on the way.

2. Ministry in Jerusalem: Entry; Temple Actions and Encounters; Eschatological Discourse (11:1–13:37).

The narrative gives the impression that everything described in these chaps. takes place in three days (11:1,12,20). On the first day *Jesus enters Jerusalem* (11:1–11). He sends two disciples on a mission into a village from the Mount of Olives, and all is as he foretold. He sits on the colt that they bring back (perhaps a reference to Zech 9:9); and he is acclaimed by shouts of "Hosanna," by a line from Ps 118:26, and by the people's exclamation about "the coming kingdom of our father David." Thus, Jesus is being proclaimed as a king who will restore the earthly Davidic realm—an honor but another misunderstanding. A Marcan intercalation governs actions on the next days: *cursing the fig tree, cleansing the Temple, and finding the fig tree withered* (11:12–25). Cursing the fig tree may seem irrational since, as Mark tells us, just before Passover was not the season for figs. Yet, the cursing is like a prophetic action from the OT that by its peculiarity attracts attention to the message being presented symbolically (Jer 19:1–2,10–11; Ezek 12:1–7). The withered fig tree becomes a symbol of the future punishment of the failed leadership of the chief priests and the scribes. Subsequently the withered fig tree becomes the object of a lesson by Jesus for the disciples on faith and prayer (11:22–25).

The malevolence of the authorities continues in the challenge to Jesus' authority (11:27–33). This is the first of several "trap" episodes by which Mark shows Jesus' superior wisdom when confronted by mean-spirited opponents. To the annoyance of the authorities Jesus critiques their leadership further in the parable of the wicked tenants (12:1–12). The Pharisees and Herodians lay more traps for Jesus in questions about taxes for Caesar (12:13–17) and by the Sadducees about the resurrection (12:18–27). The wide-ranging hostility to Jesus is evident. Among the questioners Mark presents one sensitive scribe who asks about the greatest commandment (12:28–34) and wins Jesus' approbation as being not far from the kingdom of God. Jesus' answer, given in the frame of the Shema (Deut 6:4) combines Deut 6:5 and Lev 19:18, two commandments that share a stress on love.

After silencing his questioners, Jesus poses his own difficult question about David's son (12:35–37), citing Ps 110:1. The denunciation of the public display of the scribes (12:38–40) provides a background for an account of genuine religious behavior, the widow's mite (12:41–44).

Most of Jesus' activity in Jerusalem thus far has been in the Temple area; after reflecting on the magnificence of the Temple buildings, seated on the Mount of Olives, he delivers the eschatological discourse (13:1–37)—the last speech of his ministry that looks to the end times. For most readers the "bottom line" taken from the discourse is that no precise timetable is given; rather, without specific knowledge of the end, Jesus' followers are to remain watchful.

3. Anointing, Last Supper, Arrest, Trials, Crucifixion, Burial, Empty Tomb (14:1–16:8).

Another Marcan intercalation occurs with Judas' treachery and the anointing of Jesus (14:1–11). The unidentified woman who does the anointing is completely anonymous. That the anointing is for burial tells the reader that the plot will succeed. The preparations for the Passover (14:12–16) supply a ritual context for Jesus' actions at the Last Supper and exemplify his ability to foretell what will happen. The Last Supper (14:17–25),

narrated briefly in Mark, provides the context for the prediction of
Judas' betrayal. The contrast is stark between Judas' giving Jesus over
and Jesus' own self-giving in the eucharistic blessing of the bread and
wine as his body and blood.

The Gethsemane section (14:26–52) begins the suffering portion of
Mark's passion narrative, as Jesus moves from the supper to the Mount
of Olives. En route Jesus predicts the disciples' flight and Peter's denials.
Jesus' isolation is dramatized in three steps as he moves from the body
of the disciples, from the chosen three, and then falls to the earth alone
to beseech the Father three times to take the cup of suffering from him.
Accepting God's will, Jesus tells the disciples that the appointed time
had come for the Son of Man to be betrayed into the hands of sinners.
Judas comes with an armed crowd from the chief priests, scribes, and
elders, and with a kiss gives Jesus over to the crowd. The disciples
flee; among them is a young man who runs away naked, symbolizing
failure.

The Jewish Trial: Jesus is condemned by a Sanhedrin and mocked while Peter denies
him (14:53–15:1). Jesus is given over to the chief priests, scribes, and
elders who meet as a Sanhedrin to determine Jesus' fate. Peter is in
the courtyard of the high priest. Mark shifts the story back to Jesus'
trial, producing contrasting scenes. Jesus courageously confesses that
he is the Son of God, while Peter curses him and denies knowing him.
Ironically, as Jesus is mocked as a false prophet, his prophecies about
his disciples are being fulfilled. The authorities do not believe that Jesus
can destroy the sanctuary or that he is the Messiah, the Son of God, but
both themes will be verified at his death.

The Roman trial: Jesus is handed over to be crucified by Pilate and mocked (15:2–
20a). The Jewish authorities give Jesus over to Pilate. Mark draws clear
parallels between the two trials: A principal figure asks a key question
in sham circumstances. Yet Jesus is condemned in each trial, spat upon
and mocked as a prophet by the Sanhedrin members and as King of the
Jews by the Roman soldiers. He is rejected by all. Pilate gives him over
to the Roman soldiers to be crucified.

The crucifixion, death, and burial (15:20b–47). Ironically only two figures
having no previous contact with him—Simon of Cyrene before the
crucifixion and Joseph of Arimathea after his death—assist Jesus. Mark

gives details of the crucifixion that are redolent of OT descriptions of the suffering just one, for example, two wine drinks (Prov 31:6–7; Ps 69:22) and the division of clothes (Ps 22:19). Mention of the third, sixth, and ninth hours indicates increasingly tragic coloring. The crucified Jesus is mocked, reviving issues from the Jewish trial; darkness comes over the land; and Jesus speaks from the cross for the only time. Mark began Jesus' passion in 14:36 with his prayer in Aramaic and Greek ("*Abba* . . . Father"); and now he closes Jesus' passion in 15:34 with another prayer citing in Aramaic and Greek Ps 22:2 ("*Elōi, Elōi, lama sabachthani* . . . My God, my God, why have you forsaken me?"). Feeling forsaken and no longer presuming to use the intimate family address, "Father," Jesus is reduced to a form of address common to all human beings, "My God." Still unanswered, Jesus dies. Yet in a stunning reversal at the moment he expires, God vindicates him in terms of the very issues raised at the Jewish trial: the veil that marked off the Temple sanctuary is torn, depriving that place of its holiness, and a Gentile recognizes a truth that the chief priest could not accept, "Truly this man was God's Son."

Women who ministered to Jesus in Galilee and followed him to Jerusalem observe his death from afar. They also observe the place of his burial and so serve as an important link between his death and the discovery of the empty tomb that reveals the resurrection. Joseph of Arimathea, a pious member of the Sanhedrin, buried Jesus in observance of the law (Deut 21:22–23).

The empty tomb and the resurrection (16:1–8). Jesus' hasty burial led the women, early on Sunday morning after the Sabbath, to buy spices to anoint him. The tomb is open and a young man, almost certainly an angel, is there, but not the body of Jesus. The decisive announcement, "He has been raised . . . he is going before you to Galilee where you will see him," represents the triumph of the Son of Man predicted three times by Jesus (8:31; 9:31; 10:34). The reaction of the women in 16:8 is astounding. Disobeying the young man's command to tell the disciples and Peter, they say nothing to anyone out of fear. Mark's theology is consistent: even a proclamation of the resurrection does not produce faith without the hearer's personal encounter with suffering and carrying the cross.

4. An Ending Describing Resurrection Appearances
Appended by a Later Copyist (16:9–20).

Most scholars believe that the Gospel originally ended with Mark 16:8. Yet some scholars contend there was a lost ending. Already in antiquity this awkwardness brought copyists to provide three different endings of Mark in an attempt to correct the abruptness of 16:8. The best attested ending is called the Marcan Appendix, or the Longer Ending. It records three appearances (to Mary Magdalene, to two disciples, and to all eleven) of the risen Jesus, his ascension into heaven, and his sitting at God's right hand.

HOW TO INTERPRET MARK

Mark has been interpreted in many ways. Part of the variety stems from different methods of interpretation. While readers may learn from these approaches, it is instructive to concentrate on particular problems that scholars have found (or created) in interpreting Mark.

Sometimes a problem is detected in the Gospel as it now stands, especially in enigmatic passages. These include: the purpose of telling parables to outsiders (4:11–12), the abrupt ending with the silence of the women (16:8), and Jesus hiding his identity as the Messiah (or Son of God) by commanding people to silence concerning his actions and identity, so that only demons recognize him (for example, 1:25,34; 3:12—cf. 1:44; 8:30).

More problems of interpretation are based on presuppositions about what preceded Mark. The sources for Mark are hypothetical. Reconstructing the theology of nonextant sources is doubly hypothetical. Then evaluating the theology of Mark on the basis of corrective changes made in proposed sources is triply hypothetical. Although many reputable NT scholars construct their analyses of Marcan thought in terms of the corrections of putative sources, the uncertainty of source reconstruction makes their analyses debatable. Nonchristological pre-Marcan stages of Christianity are purely hypothetical and run against much evidence.

Reading the Gospel for its surface impression. It may seem naïve, but for practical purposes readers being introduced to Mark should ignore the scholarly controversies related to sources. They will understand Mark better by reading on a surface level.

By the time that Mark wrote, Jesus had been preached as the Christ for several decades. To appreciate what this earliest preserved written portrayal contributed to Christian heritage, one might reflect on what would be known about Jesus if we had only Paul's letters. We would have a magnificent theology about what God has done in Christ, but Jesus would be left almost without a face. Mark gets the honor of having painted that "face" and made it part of the enduring gospel.

✦

8

The Gospel According to Matthew

While modern Gospel courses give Mark the most attention among the Synoptics, Matt stood first in the great ancient biblical codices, and its organization and clarity have historically given this Gospel priority as the Church's teaching instrument.

GENERAL ANALYSIS OF THE MESSAGE

The Matthean account of Jesus' public ministry lies between the infancy and passion/resurrection narratives. Thus, a new beginning, a new ending, and a carefully remodeled and enlarged presentation of Jesus' words and deeds during his ministry distinguish Matthew's Gospel.

Introduction: The Origin and Infancy of Jesus the Messiah (1:1–2:23)

While several interpretations are possible, the opening Greek phrase of the Gospel, *biblos geneseōs* (1:1) probably means "*the record of the generations* [= birth record] of Jesus Christ," echoing Gen 5:1.

SUMMARY OF BASIC INFORMATION

DATE: 80–90, give or take a decade.

AUTHOR BY TRADITIONAL (SECOND-CENTURY) ATTRIBUTION: Matthew, a tax-collector among the Twelve, wrote either the Gospel or a collection of the Lord's sayings in Aramaic. Some who reject this picture allow that something written by Matthew may have made its way into the present Gospel.

AUTHOR DETECTABLE FROM CONTENTS: A Greek-speaker, who knew Aramaic or Hebrew or both and was not an eyewitness of Jesus' ministry, drew on Mark and a collection of the sayings of the Lord (Q), as well as on other available traditions, oral or written. Probably a Jewish Christian.

LOCALE INVOLVED: Probably the Antioch region.

UNITY AND INTEGRITY: No major reason to think of more than one author or of any sizable additions to what he wrote.

DIVISION:

1:1–2:23: INTRODUCTION: ORIGIN AND INFANCY OF JESUS THE MESSIAH
1. The who and how of Jesus' identity (1:1–25)
2. The where and whence of Jesus' birth and destiny (2:1–23)

3:1–7:29: PART ONE: PROCLAMATION OF THE KINGDOM
1. Narrative: Ministry of JBap, baptism of Jesus, the temptations, beginning of the Galilean ministry (3:1–4:25)
2. Discourse: Sermon on the Mount (5:1–7:29)

8:1–10:42: PART TWO: MINISTRY AND MISSION IN GALILEE
1. Narrative mixed with short dialogue: Nine miracles consisting of healings, calming a storm, exorcism (8:1–9:38)
2. Discourse: Mission Sermon (10:1–42)

11:1–13:52: PART THREE: QUESTIONING OF AND OPPOSITION TO JESUS
1. Narrative setting for teaching and dialogue: Jesus and JBap, woes on disbelievers, thanksgiving for revelation, Sabbath controversies and Jesus' power, Jesus' family (11:1–12:50)
2. Discourse: Sermon in parables (13:1–52)

13:53–18:35: PART FOUR: CHRISTOLOGY AND ECCLESIOLOGY
1. Narrative mixed with much dialogue: Rejection at Nazareth, feeding the 5,000 and walking on water, controversies with the Pharisees, healings, feeding the 4,000, Peter's confession, first passion prediction, transfiguration, second passion prediction (13:53–17:27)
2. Discourse: Sermon on the church (18:1–35)

19:1–25:46: PART FIVE: JOURNEY TO AND MINISTRY IN JERUSALEM
1. Narrative mixed with much dialogue: Teaching, judgment parables, third passion prediction, entry to Jerusalem, cleansing the Temple, clashes with authorities (19:1–23:39)
2. Discourse: Eschatological Sermon (24:1–25:46)

26:1–28:20: CLIMAX: PASSION, DEATH, AND RESURRECTION
1. Conspiracy against Jesus, Last Supper (26:1–29)
2. Arrest, Jewish and Roman trials, crucifixion, death (26:30–27:56)
3. Burial, guard at the tomb, opening of tomb, bribing of the guard, resurrection appearances (27:57–28:20).

1. The Who and How of Jesus' Identity (1:1–25).

In the genealogy (1:2–17), how the fourteens are counted in 1:17 is not clear, but the overall impression is that God made precise preparations for the coming of the Messiah. The theological import of the whole genealogy is its bringing into the story of Jesus a lengthy span of Israelite history, involving the patriarchs (fourteen names), the kings (second fourteen), and the unknowns (third fourteen). Matt dramatizes Abraham and David motifs found elsewhere in the NT (Gal 3:16; Rom 1:3).

The broken pattern in 1:16 (not "Joseph begot Jesus" but "of Mary was Jesus begotten") prepares for Jesus' extraordinary conception (1:18–25). Mary conceives from the Holy Spirit—a virginal conception. This chapter tells readers who Jesus is (the Messiah, conceived from the Holy Spirit, Emmanuel or "God with us") and how that was brought about.

2. The Where and the Whence of Jesus' Birth and Destiny (2:1–23).

After the birth of Jesus, magi come to pay homage to the King of the Jews (2:1–12), and Herod the Great's plans are foiled as Joseph takes the family to Egypt and then to Nazareth (2:13–23). The magi are Gentiles guided by a star, which is a revelation in nature to those who do not have the Scriptures. The title "the King of the Jews" will reappear as Jesus is crucified, when again Gentiles recognize him while those having the Scriptures do not. Chapter 2 enlarges the OT background. Moreover, Matt weaves into his account five formula citations from the prophets, showing God's preparation for it all. The scriptural citations help chapter 2 to bring out the where of his birth and the whence or place to which his childhood brought him. The infancy narrative gives a whole OT background from the Law and the prophets for the appearance of Jesus, the kingly Messiah and the unique Son of God.

Part One: Proclamation of the Kingdom (3:1–7:29)
1. Narrative: (3:1–4:25).

Ministry of JBap, baptism of Jesus, the temptations, beginning of the Galilean ministry. Matt follows Mark's opening pattern. Jesus appears in the context of JBap's ministry in the wilderness (Matt 3:1–12). In the account of

Jesus' baptism (3:12–17), JBap objects, but Jesus answers that they are fulfilling "all righteousness." In Matt the voice from heaven speaks more openly than Mark ("You are my beloved Son"): "This is my beloved Son."

In Mark 1:12–13 Jesus was tempted in the wilderness by Satan for forty days; Matt adds a *narrative of the temptations* (4:1–11) from Q. The three temptations try to divert the proclamation of God's kingdom so that it will become a kingdom according to the standards of this world. Jesus' refusals are all phrased in quotations from Deut 6–8 (incorporating Ps 91:11–12).

Afterwards *Jesus goes to Galilee to begin his ministry and to call his first four disciples to become fishers of people* (4:12–22). Matt adds to Mark's basic story a formula citation from Isa 8:23–9:1 and draws on Mark to summarize the spread of the gospel (4:23–25).

2. DISCOURSE: SERMON ON THE MOUNT (5:1–7:29).

This is Matt's greatest composition. It weaves together Q material with uniquely Matthean passages into a harmonious masterpiece of ethical and religious teaching. Jesus teaches with divine power and authority. He teaches the beatitudes (values on which he placed priority) to the disciples who are to be *the salt of the earth and the light of the world* (5:13–16).

The ethics of the new lawgiver (5:17–48) constitutes a remarkable section, not only for the way it has shaped Christian understanding of Jesus' values but also for its implicit christology. Jesus presents God's demand for a deeper observance of the Law, that is, to be "perfect as your heavenly Father is perfect" (5:48). He also dares in six clauses to modify or correct explicitly what God said through Moses: "You have heard it said . . . but I say to you." The Matthean Jesus, speaking more confidently than any first-century rabbi (Jewish teacher), implies that he is more authoritative than Moses, and seems to legislate with all the assurance of the God of Sinai.

In 6:1–18 *Jesus reshapes the exercise of piety: almsgiving, prayer, fasting.* His warnings are not against pious practices but against ostentation. The Lord's Prayer, taken from Q, has been adapted by Matt partially along the familiar lines of synagogue prayer, for example, the reverential

"Our Father who art in heaven" (whereas the prayer in Luke 11:2–4 has only "Father"). This prayer originally had a pronounced eschatological tone.

Drawn from Q, *further instructions on behavior for the kingdom* (6:19–7:27) exhort; give assurance; state the golden rule, "Do to others what you would have them do to you" (7:12); and offer caution. Then, the formula "When Jesus finished these words" terminates the sermon, with the accompanying theme of astonishment at the authority of Jesus' teaching.

Part Two: Ministry and Mission in Galilee (8:1–10:42)
1. Narrative Mixed with Short Dialogue (8:1–9:38).

Nine miracles consisting of healings, calming a storm, exorcism, interspersed with dialogues, mostly pertaining to discipleship. Matt rejoins Mark's story line (interspersing some Q) and concentrates on Jesus' mighty deeds (miracles) effected by his word. His power to forgive sins, something that God alone can do, is challenged. More is at stake than simply the power to do mighty acts. These miracles have implications also for both discipleship and christology. Jesus justifies his behavior, using a series of maxims and metaphors, all of which indicate the startlingly different character of what he is inaugurating.

2. Discourse: Mission Sermon (10:1–42).

Composed mostly from Mark and Q, this is set in a context of sending out twelve "disciples" with authority over unclean spirits and the power to heal. Jesus is giving them the power to proclaim the kingdom (4:17; 10:7). Jesus tells them to go not to the Gentiles and the Samaritans but to "the lost sheep of the house of Israel." Then Matt (10:17–22) amplifies the eschatological dimensions of the disciples' mission by shifting material from the eschatological discourse in Mark 13:9–12 that anticipates the kind of persecution that will greet the postresurrectional apostles.

Words of encouragement assuring divine care (10:26–33) follow the prediction of persecution. Then, with its very high christology the Q passage in Matt 10:32–33 makes reaction to Jesus the basis of judgment in heaven. Matt ends the sermon noting that receiving the disciples is receiving Jesus, and receiving Jesus is receiving the God who sent him.

Part Three: Questioning of and Opposition to Jesus (11:1–13:52)

1. NARRATIVE SETTING FOR TEACHING AND DIALOGUE (11:1–12:50).

Jesus and JBap, woes on disbelievers, thanksgiving for revelation, Sabbath controversies and Jesus' power, Jesus' family. Matt's material is a combination of Mark and Q set in a loose frame of Jesus' moving among cities, fields, and a synagogue. Matt's treatment of JBap and Jesus (11:2–19) begins with John in prison hearing of the deeds of the Messiah and sending his disciples to ask Jesus whether he was "the one who is to come." Jesus' answer (11:4–6) explains that he is the kind of Messiah prophesied by Isaiah (29:18–19; 35:5–6; 61:1). Then Jesus reveals who JBap is (Matt 11:7–15): more than a prophet, he is the angelic messenger to lead Israel to the promised land (Exod 23:20), and the Elijah sent to prepare Israel for God's action (Mal 3:1,23–24). Having prepared Jesus' way, JBap became the greatest human being born before the coming of the kingdom of heaven. Yet, Jesus says that "this generation" accepted neither JBap nor himself ("the Son of Man"); a disbelieving generation cannot recognize his works.

Jesus' censuring remark leads into the *woes addressed to disbelieving cities on or near the Sea of Galilee* (11:20–24). They failed to repent in response to the mighty works that Jesus did. Yet, some have responded positively, and Jesus gives thanks to the Father. The high christology of 11:27, drawn from Q, is close to what we find in John's Gospel (3:35; 5:22,26–27; 14:9; 17:6). And the "Come to me" *invitation to the heavy-laden* (11:28–30), which Matt adds to the Q material, promises rest to those who take on the obligations of the kingdom.

Next Matt sets Jesus' teaching in a series of controversies. *Plucking grain on the Sabbath* (12:1–8) generates controversy in which Jesus ultimately declares that "the Son of Man is lord of the Sabbath." *Healing on the Sabbath* (12:9–14) occasions further friction. Jesus is aware that his adversaries plan to destroy him, so he withdraws; yet, followed by a multitude, *he heals many as the prophet predicted* (12:15–21)—see Isa 42:1–4.

A *controversy with the Pharisees over Jesus' power* (12:22–37) draws heavily from Mark 3:22–30. Jesus heals a blind and mute demoniac. The

Pharisees hostilely attribute this power over the demon to Jesus' subservience to Beelzebul. Jesus refutes the charge, warning that blasphemy against the Holy Spirit (that is, obstinately attributing to the devil the power of God) will not be forgiven. Jesus calls the Pharisees a brood of vipers whose work will condemn them on judgment day. Nevertheless, *the scribes and Pharisees request a sign* (12:38–42), but Jesus offers them only the signs of Jonah (repentance) and the queen of the South (appreciation of Solomon's wisdom). The parable of *the return of the evil spirits* (12:43–45) warns that "this evil generation" will have a final state worse than the first, because they experienced Jesus' ministry of the kingdom and took it all for granted or, worse, rejected it altogether. The unexpected arrival of Jesus' mother and brothers raises *the issue of Jesus' family* (12:46–50). Now that the kingdom is proclaimed, the disciples who do the will of the heavenly Father are brother, sister, and mother of Jesus.

2. DISCOURSE: SERMON IN PARABLES (13:1–52).

At the center of the Gospel structurally, these parables serve as commentary on the Pharisees' rejection of Jesus in the two preceding chapters. In the *parable of the sower and its interpretation* (13:1–23) Jesus emphasizes the obstacles and failures in the preaching of the kingdom. Matt 13:13 has Jesus speak to the crowds in parables "because seeing, they do not see." The citation of Isa 6:9–10 now notes the fulfillment of prophecy. The next Matthean parable, *the weeds among the wheat and its interpretation* (13:24–30,36–43), explains allegorically the mixture of good and evil and the future judgment by the Son of Man. The paired parables of *the mustard seed and the leaven* (13:31–33) illustrate the present small beginnings of the kingdom and its great future. *The purpose of the parables* (13:34–35) is glossed by a fulfillment formula citing Ps 78:2, so that part of the purpose of Jesus' parables is to fulfill the Scriptures. The paired parables of *the hidden treasure and the pearl of great price* (13:44–46) stress the great value of the kingdom and the necessity of gaining it, even if that requires selling everything else. The sermon ends with a summary parable of *the householder and the new and old treasure* (13:51–52), where the listeners who say that they have understood the parables are like trained scribes who appreciate the new (revelation of Jesus) and the old (revelation in Moses).

Part Four: Christology and Ecclesiology (13:53–18:35)
1. NARRATIVE MIXED WITH MUCH DIALOGUE (13:53–17:27).

Rejection at Nazareth, feeding the 5,000 and walking on water, controversies with the Pharisees, healings, feeding the 4,000, Peter's confession, first passion prediction, transfiguration, second passion prediction. Jesus increases his focus on the disciples. The *rejection at Nazareth* (13:53–58) helps explain his turn to them, since even his hometown people do not accept him. Next, Matt gives an account of how *Herod the tetrarch (Herod Antipas) killed JBap* (14:1–12) and was *superstitiously uneasy about Jesus.* In an attempt to get away from this Herod Jesus withdraws to a lonely place where he *feeds the 5,000 and subsequently walks on the water* (14:13–33). In a special Matthean scene Jesus invites Peter to come to him on the water, and as Peter sinks, Jesus helps him (14:28–31). Peter's actions and inadequate faith are representative of the other disciples. The end of this walking-on-the-water scene is remarkable in Matt, for in 14:33 the disciples, instead of failing to understand as in Mark 6:52, worship Jesus as "Son of God."

The boat brings Jesus and the disciples to *Gennesaret where Jesus heals all the sick* (14:34–36) and then *Pharisees and scribes from Jerusalem debate him over what defiles* (15:1–20). The attack on the Pharisees is sharp in Matt. Matt omits the comment that Jesus made all things clean (Mark 7: 19)—perhaps a problematic remark for Matt (5:17). Then, *Jesus heals the daughter of a Canaanite woman* (15:21–28), after which Matt reports that Jesus walks beside the Sea of Galilee, and goes up on a mountain, and sits down. Matt gives *a summary about the healing of many sick* (15:29–31), and then we are told of *the second multiplication of loaves, namely, for the 4,000* (15:32–39).

In Matt *hostile confrontations with the Pharisees and Sadducees* (16:1–12) follow the miracles that Jesus has been doing. The disciples' behavior brings criticism from Jesus. He warns them about the leaven (teaching) of the Pharisees and Sadducees, but they do not understand. Jesus confronts them for their lack of faith, particularly because they do not perceive the meaning of the bread miracles. Finally they do understand.

Yet Jesus' disciples have considerable faith as seen in the climactic confession of Peter at Caesarea Philippi and the first prediction of the passion (16:13–23). Beyond Mark's account (8:27–30) where Peter confessed him to be the Messiah, in Matt 16:16b–19 Peter now confesses that Jesus is the Son of the living God—a revelation from the Father in Heaven, not a matter of human reasoning. This revelation constitutes Peter an apostle, the rock on which Jesus will build his church, a church that even the gates of hell will not prevail against. In 16:19 Jesus gives Peter the keys of the kingdom, so that whatever he binds/looses on earth is bound/ loosed in heaven. There are debates about what this binding/loosing means. Matt's picture of the exaltation of Peter because of his profess- ing what God revealed to him does not cause the evangelist to elimi- nate Jesus' subsequent chastisement of Peter as Satan who thinks on a human level because he does not accept the notion of Jesus' suffering in the prediction of the passion. If anything, Matt sharpens the Marcan reproof, for 16:23 adds, "You are a scandal to me." This sobering cor- rection leads into directives to the disciples about the suffering required for discipleship (16:24–28). Encouragingly, however, the suffering of the present is contrasted with future glory.

The account of the transfiguration (17:1–13) also shows unique Matthean features. That Jesus' face shone like the sun (17:2) echoes the descrip- tion of Moses in Exod 34:29–35 and heightens the parallelism to the great theophany on Sinai. Peter himself will make the three booths. The voice from the cloud in 17:6 repeats more exactly what the voice from heaven said at Jesus' baptism (3:17) pertaining to divine sonship.

In the story of the epileptic boy (17:14–21) Matt shortens Mark's account almost by half. Matt does not deny that the boy had a demon (17:18), but he has the boy's father offer the diagnosis of epilepsy (17:15). Matt continues with the second prediction of the passion (17:22–23). There follows another special Matthean Petrine scene centered on the (Temple?) tax (17:24–27). The story adds a folklorish touch to the Gospel and por- trays Jesus as law-observant.

2. Discourse: Sermon on the Church (18:1–35).

Even if a structured church becomes the way in which the tradition and memory of Jesus are preserved, Matt recognizes the danger that any structure set up in this world tends to take its values from the other structures that surround it. This chapter is meant to insure that those values do not smother the values of Jesus.

The sermon is prefaced by the *dispute about greatness in the kingdom of heaven* (18:1–5), seemingly taken over with considerable adaptation from Mark. Both evangelists record that in Jesus' values the humble are more important than the powerful, for dependence on God is what makes one open to God's rule; and so the little child is held up as an example. The *condemnation of scandals and temptations* (18:6–9) speaks to life in a congregation. The Matthean adaptation of the Q *parable of the lost sheep* (18:10–14) further presents Jesus' values, which he phrases in an "impractical" directive that catches his eschatological outlook: "leave the ninety-nine on the mountains and go in search of the one."

The instructions on *a procedure for reproving one's "brother [and sister]," the disciples' access to heaven, and the frequency of forgiveness* (18:15–22) are clearly adapted to a church situation, as is clear from the explicit reference to "the church" (a local community). Peter asks with a tinge of legalism about the practice of forgiveness, although his offer (seven times) is quite generous. Yet, Jesus' reply is remarkable: seventy-seven indicates "no limit" (see Gen 4:24). Christian forgiveness, then, is to imitate the unlimited range of God's forgiveness. All this has a very real application in church life, where listening to the Jesus who speaks here keeps his spirit alive instead of memorializing him—"where two or three are gathered in my name, there am I in the midst of them" (18:20).

Part Five: Journey to and Ministry in Jerusalem (19:1–25:46)
1. NARRATIVE MIXED WITH MUCH DIALOGUE (19:1–23:39).

Teaching, judgment parables, third passion prediction, entry to Jerusalem, cleansing the Temple, clashes with authorities. On the road to Jerusalem, large crowds follow Jesus and he heals the sick. In Judea beyond the Jordan, Pharisees test him by asking a *question about divorce* (19:1–12) and he speaks about his standards for the kingdom. In comparison with Mark (10:1–12) the most notable Matthean feature is the addition of the exceptive phrase in 19:9: "Whoever divorces his wife *except for immorality* [*porneia*] and marries another commits adultery [verb: *moichasthai*]," an exception that also appears in Matt 5:32, but in none of the other three forms of the divorce prohibition (Luke, Mark, I Cor, though the last two have their own adaptations of Jesus' command). The exact meaning of this story in Matt is not fully decided. Much depends on the meaning of *porneia*. The consternation of the disciples at Jesus' severity is peculiar to Matt (19:10–12). In reply Jesus raises the possibility of being eunuchs (that is, totally abstinent) for the sake of the kingdom of God. Like marriage without divorce, such celibacy is an eschatological value (see Isa 56:3–5); both impose demands that this world regards as impossible.

In Matt the story of the *rejection of the children by the disciples* (19:13–15) lacks mention of Jesus' indignation at the disciples (Mark 10:14). The story of the *rich young man and its aftermath* (19:16–30) adds to the commandments of the Decalogue the demand to love one's neighbor as oneself (19:19; see Lev 19:18); yet even then one is not perfect without sacrificing all possessions to follow Jesus. Once again the severity of the eschatological demand creates consternation among the disciples. Jesus' response brings clarity, "With humanity this is impossible, but with God all things are possible." The themes of first and last and rewards govern the *parable of the workers in the vineyard* (20:1–16), which is peculiar to Matt and highlights God's sovereignty and a graciousness that is not based on what is earned.

Amidst these reflections on ultimate reward the *third prediction of the passion* (20:17–19) constitutes a paradoxical consideration of the role of suffering in the victory. The prediction precipitates misunderstanding represented by the *request for the choice places in the kingdom* (20:20–28). Matt shifts the request from the sons of Zebedee to their mother. Jesus challenges the brothers and warns the Twelve: the necessary attitude is that of service. Journeying toward Jerusalem Jesus comes to Jericho, where he performs the *healing of two blind men* (20:29–34). This is clearly Matt's variant of the Marcan healing of the blind Bartimaeus.

The *entry into Jerusalem* (21:1–9) is based on Mark with the addition in 21:4–5 of a formula citation of Isa 62:11 and Zech 9:9 stressing the meekness and peacefulness of the messianic king. The sequence of *cleansing the Temple* (21:10–17) and the *cursing and withering of the fig tree* (21:18–22) reorganizes Mark (11:12–25). Thus, on the day of his entry into Jerusalem, Jesus cleanses the Temple, heals the blind and the lame, and encounters the indignation of the chief priests and the scribes. Jesus departs the Temple and the next morning finds and curses the fig tree, which withers on the spot.

To the *challenge to Jesus' authority* (Matt 21:23–27) by the priests and the elders, answered in terms of JBap, Matt joins a series of three parables. Jesus' parables sting the authorities: chief priests (21:23,45), elders (21:23), and Pharisees (21:45)—questioning the assurance of their entry into the kingdom of God, their legitimacy, and their worthiness. The parable of the man without a wedding garment shows that none of these three parables is simply about the replacement of Israel by the church or of Jews by Gentiles—the issue is the replacement of the unworthy by those Jews and Gentiles who believe in Jesus and have worthily responded to his demands for the kingdom.

As in Mark a series of three trap questions follows: *taxes for Caesar* (22:15–22) proposed by Pharisee and Herodians; *the resurrection* (22:23–33) proposed by Sadducees; *the great commandment* (22:34–40) proposed by a Pharisee lawyer (all verses in Mark favorable to this questioner are omitted in Matt). These are followed by a riddle posed by Jesus to the Pharisees about the Messiah as *David's son* (22:41–46). To emphasize the superiority of Jesus, Matt adds observations, for example, in 22:33 about the crowd's astonishment at Jesus' teaching, and in 22:46 about none daring to ask Jesus any more questions.

Serving as a bridge to the last great discourse, *the denunciation of the scribes and Pharisees* (23:1–36) is an extraordinary Matthean construction. The hostility manifested by these authorities in the trap questions of chapter 22 is returned by Jesus' attack on their proud behavior and love for titles, and by his seven "woes" against their casuistry—woes that function almost as antitheses of the beatitudes in chapter 5. Chapter 23 ends with an *apostrophe to Jerusalem* (23:37–39), drawn from Q. Jesus has failed to persuade the city. Therefore her house (the Temple) is forsaken and desolate, and Jerusalem will not see Jesus again until she says, "Blessed is he who comes in the name of the Lord."

2. Discourse: Eschatological Sermon (24:1–25:46).

The material in 24:1–36 is taken over largely from the eschatological discourse in Mark 13, and in the rest of chapter 24 and in chapter 25 from Q and Matt's own tradition. The sequence in Matt 24 preserves the apocalyptic obscurity of Mark 13, which mixes the Gospel present time with the future. Mark had already indicated that there was no precise timetable for the final events, and the *watchfulness material in Matt 24:37–51* underlines that one cannot know when the Son of Man is coming. The judgment motif grows stronger in the Q *parable of the talents* (25:14–30). The discourse ends with material peculiar to Matt: *the enthroned Son of Man judging the sheep and the goats* (25:31–46). The Son of Man, the King, who speaks of God as "my Father," is the Son of God in the apocalyptic context of the judgment of the whole world. The admirable principle that the verdict is based on the treatment of deprived outcasts is the Matthean Jesus' last warning to his followers (the church) demanding a very different religious standard from that of scribes and Pharisees.

Climax: Passion, Death, and Resurrection (26:1–28:20)
1. CONSPIRACY AGAINST JESUS, LAST SUPPER (26:1–29).

By having Jesus predict at the very beginning that the Son of Man would be given over at this Passover (a type of fourth passion prediction), Matt emphasizes the foreknowledge of Jesus. In *Judas' disloyalty and the anointing of Jesus* (26:1–16) the sum paid to Judas is specified as thirty pieces of silver, which echoes Zech 11:12. *The preparations for Passover* (26:17–19) are briefly recounted, leading directly into *the Last Supper account* (26:20–29). Matt makes specific the identification of the one who will give Jesus over (which Mark left obscure).

2. ARREST, JEWISH AND ROMAN TRIALS, CRUCIFIXION, DEATH (26:30–27:56).

In the *Gethsemane section* (26:30–56) Matt 26:39 has only the prayer concerning the *cup*. Matt also fills out the incomplete pattern in Mark of Jesus' praying three times by supplying in 26:42 a wording for the second prayer (echoing the Lord's Prayer of 6:10). In the arrest Jesus reacts to Judas' kiss in a way that shows awareness of Judas' purposes. One of Jesus' followers cuts off the ear of the high priest's servant and Jesus comments unfavorably on such force. In 26:54 and 56 Matt stresses in typical fashion that the events fulfill the Scriptures.

The Jewish Trial: Jesus is condemned by the Sanhedrin and mocked while Peter denies him (26:57–27:1). Matt includes the name of the high priest Caiaphas and heightens the iniquity by saying that the authorities had been seeking *false* witness from the start. That two witnesses came forward and that there was a failure to designate their testimony as false (contrast Mark 14:55–60) means that for Matt Jesus did say, "I am able to destroy the sanctuary of God, and within three days I will build (it)." This assertion and the non-rejection of the title "Messiah, the Son of God" constitute the basis of the charge of blasphemy. The question "Who is it that struck you?" mocking Jesus as a prophet-Messiah (26:68) is shared by Matt and Luke against Mark. The irony of Peter's denying that he knows Jesus at the very moment when Jesus confesses to being the Messiah, the Son of God, is heightened in Matt, for that is the very title that Peter confessed in 16:16.

The Roman Trial: As Jesus is being handed over to Pilate, Judas seeks to avoid the blood-guilt; Pilate sentences Jesus who is then mocked (27:2–31a). The storyline remains the same as in Mark. Yet special Matthean material makes the account more vivid and dramatizes responsibility for Jesus' death through the imagery of "innocent blood." Almost every line of this peculiarly Matthean material echoes the OT and is perhaps taken directly from popular oral tradition. Matt 27:3–10 interrupts the beginning of the Roman trial with the brief but complex story of Judas' reaction to the condemnation of Jesus. Then the narrative returns to Jesus before Pilate. This scene and the infancy narrative share the title "King of the Jews." The Barabbas scene begins but is interrupted. Just as in Matt's infancy narrative there were dream revelations and the Gentiles were responsive when the Jewish authorities were not, so Pilate's wife receives a dream revelation that Jesus is a just man. Yet, the chief priests and elders persuade the crowd to ask for the release of Barabbas and the destruction of Jesus. Pilate washes his hands to signify that he is innocent of Jesus' blood; but finally "all the people" say, "His blood on us and our children" (27:24–25). This is not a self-curse by the Jewish people; it is a legal formula taking responsibility for the death of one considered a criminal. Matt knows what the people do not, namely, that Jesus is innocent; and he judges that the responsibility (and punishment) for the death of this just man was visited on all the Jewish people later when the Romans destroyed Jerusalem and the Temple (wherefore the reference to "children"). Nevertheless, tragically the

Matthean passage has been used to support horrendous anti-Judaism that must be repudiated.

The crucifixion and death (27:31b–56). Matt 27:36 specifies that the Roman soldiers who crucified Jesus sat and kept watch over him; thus the Roman centurion was not alone in confessing that Jesus was truly God's Son (27:54). The challenge of the Jewish authorities to the crucified Jesus (27:41–43) is lengthened to echo the Scriptures (Ps 22:9; Wisdom 2:17–18). The two drinks offered to Jesus become wine mixed with *gall* and *vinegary wine* (27:34,48) to match the gall and vinegar of Ps 69:22. The major Matthean addition, once more of a vivid, popular type, expands poetically what happened as Jesus died. Not only was the veil of the sanctuary rent from top to bottom; but the earth was shaken, the rocks were rent, the tombs were opened, and many bodies of the fallen-asleep holy ones raised, to come out and enter the holy city after Jesus' resurrection (27:51–53). This is a scriptural way of describing the last times. Human relationships to God have been changed, and the cosmos has been transformed.

3. Burial, Guard at the Tomb, Opening of the Tomb, Bribing of
the Guard, Resurrection Appearances (27:57–28:20).

Although in Mark the burial is part of the crucifixion account, Matt has reorganized the sequence to relate the burial more closely to the resurrection. *The burial account* (27:57–61) introduces Joseph of Arimathea, a rich man who was a disciple of Jesus. The story of the placing of *the guard at the tomb* (27:62–66), unique to Matt, reflects apologetics, that is, it presents an argument in defense of Christian belief meant to refute Jewish polemic against the resurrection. Matt's story of the *empty tomb* (28:1–10) is significantly different, for example, Jesus appears to the women as they run from the tomb with fear and great joy to tell the disciples that Jesus had risen. Attention turns to the *bribing of the guard* (28:11–15) by the chief priests and the lie that the disciples stole the body. The finale comes when *Jesus appears to the Eleven* (28:16–20) on a mountain in Galilee. As with resurrection appearances in Luke and John, there are typical details: doubt, reverence for Jesus, and a commission. The mountain signifies the place for the exalted Jesus' revelation with authority in heaven and on earth. The sending of the

Eleven to all nations revises the restricted sending to the lost sheep of the house of Israel and not to the Gentiles (10:5–6). The baptismal formula (Father, Son, and Holy Spirit) presumably comes from the time of Matt's church. The teaching of "all that I have commanded you" probably refers to Matt's five great discourses or even to all of Matt's Gospel. The final verse "I am with you all days until the end of the age" is an inclusion with God's revelation about Jesus through the prophet Isaiah at the beginning of the Gospel (1:23): "His name shall be called Emmanuel (which means 'God with us')."

SOURCES AND COMPOSITIONAL FEATURES

Those who accept Marcan priority and the existence of Q work with those two written sources of Matt. After considering them briefly, we shall turn to other commonly agreed-on (fascinating) compositional elements.

(a) MARK. This is Matt's principal source. The detailed common features imply that Matt had a written form of Mark before him. Overall Matt is remarkably faithful to Mark. Nevertheless, in the changes (minor in length) to what is taken over from Mark, one can detect Matthean thought and proclivities. Matt's more characteristic changes include:

- Matt writes Greek with more polish than Mark by eliminating difficult phraseology and double expressions.
- Matt omits or changes passages in Mark unfavorable to those whose subsequent careers make them worthy of respect.
- Reflecting christological sensibilities, Matt is more reverential about Jesus and avoids what might limit him or make him appear naïve or superstitious.
- Matt heightens the miraculous element found in Mark.

(b) Q SOURCE. By including Q material, Matt gives a strong emphasis to Jesus as a teacher.

(c) SPECIAL MATTHEAN MATERIAL (often called M). When one discusses material in Matt not found in Mark or Q, one enters an area that is not homogeneous and about which scholars seriously disagree. How much represents Matt's own composition/creation and how much did he draw from a source or sources known to him alone among the four evangelists?

(d) FORMULA OR FULFILLMENT CITATIONS. In some ten to fourteen instances where Matt cites the OT (Isaiah in eight of them), the scriptural passage is accompanied by the following formula (with slight variants): "All this took place to fulfill what the Lord had spoken by the prophet who said." That Jesus is to be related to the Scriptures is a commonplace in early Christianity, but this is almost a Matthean peculiarity among the Synoptic Gospels. Scholars debate whether these citations created the narrative they accompany or are appended to a narrative that already existed.

Although the evangelist did draw on previously existing written and oral material, he did not produce a collection of glued-together sources. Working with a developed christology, ecclesiology, and eschatology, he produced a highly effective narrative about Jesus that smoothly blended together what he received.

9

The Gospel According to Luke

This Gospel, the longest, is only half of the great Lucan writing. It was originally joined to Acts as part of a two-volume work that in length constitutes over one quarter of the NT—a magnificent narrative that blends together the story of Jesus and that of the early church.

GENERAL ANALYSIS OF THE MESSAGE

Among the four evangelists only Luke writes a few verses at the beginning explaining reflectively what he thinks he is about.

Prologue (1:1–4)

This is one long sentence in a style more formal than that found elsewhere in the Gospel. There are parallels in the prefaces of classical Greek historians and of Hellenistic medical and scientific treatises. There have been many writers, and now the evangelist too will write. Luke's theological goal for the dedicatee, "most excellent Theophilus," is assurance concerning the instruction that had been given him, "assurance" about its saving value, not primarily about its historicity or

SUMMARY OF BASIC INFORMATION

DATE: 85, give or take five to ten years.

AUTHOR BY TRADITIONAL (SECOND-CENTURY) ATTRIBUTION: Luke, a physician, the fellow worker and travelling companion of Paul. Less well attested: a Syrian from Antioch.

AUTHOR DETECTABLE FROM CONTENTS: An educated Greek-speaker and skilled writer who knew the Jewish Scriptures in Greek and who was not an eyewitness of Jesus' ministry. He drew on Mark and a collection of sayings of the Lord (Q), as well as some other available traditions, oral or written. Probably not raised a Jew, but perhaps a convert to Judaism before he became a Christian. Not a Palestinian.

LOCALE INVOLVED: To churches affected directly or indirectly (through others) by Paul's mission. Serious proposals center on areas in Greece or Syria.

UNITY AND INTEGRITY: Western Greek mss. lack significant passages found in other mss. Such absences are often designated Western Non-Interpolations.

DIVISION: *

1:1–4: PROLOGUE
1:5–2:52: INTRODUCTION: INFANCY AND BOYHOOD OF JESUS

1. Annunciations of conceptions of JBap and Jesus (1:5–45; 1:56)
2. The Magnificat and the other canticles (1:46–55)
3. Narratives of birth, circumcision, and naming of JBap and Jesus (1:57–2:40)
4. The boy Jesus in the Temple (2:41–52)

3:1–4:13: PREPARATION FOR THE PUBLIC MINISTRY
Preaching of JBap, baptism of Jesus, his genealogy, the temptations

4:14–9:50: MINISTRY IN GALILEE

1. Rejection at Nazareth; activities at Capernaum and on the Lake (4:14–5:16)
2. Reactions to Jesus: Controversies with the Pharisees; choice of the Twelve and preaching to the multitude on the plain (5:17–6:49)
3. Miracles and parables that illustrate Jesus' power and help to reveal his identity; mission of the Twelve (7:1–9:6)
4. Questions of Jesus' identity: Herod, feeding of the 5,000, Peter's confession, first and second passion prediction, transfiguration (9:7–50)

9:51–19:27: JOURNEY TO JERUSALEM

1. First to second mention of Jerusalem (9:51–13:21)
2. Second to third mention of Jerusalem (13:22–17:10)
3. Last stage of journey till arrival in Jerusalem (17:11–19:27)

19:28–21:38: MINISTRY IN JERUSALEM

1. Entry into Jerusalem and activities in the Temple area (19:28–21:4)
2. Eschatological discourse (21:5–38)

22:1–23:56: LAST SUPPER, PASSION, DEATH, AND BURIAL

1. Conspiracy against Jesus, Last Supper (22:1–38)
2. Prayer and arrest on the Mount of Olives, Jewish and Roman trial (22:39–23:25)

3. Way of the cross, crucifixion, burial (23:26–56)
   24:1–53: RESURRECTION APPEARANCES IN THE JERUSALEM AREA
1. At the empty tomb (24:1–12)
2. Appearance on the road to Emmaus (24:13–35)
3. Appearance in Jerusalem and ascension to heaven (24:36–53).

*Although one may divide the body of the Lucan Gospel geographically in terms of Galilee and the road to Jerusalem, further subdivision is difficult and inevitably arbitrary, since one episode runs into another. Convenience of treatment has played a large role in the subdivisions given above.

objectivity—even though that reporting has its roots in tradition stemming from the original eyewitnesses and ministers of the word.

Introduction: Infancy and Boyhood of Jesus (1:5–2:52)

The universal Gospel tradition that JBap appeared on the scene before Jesus has been applied to conception and birth, and now they are presented as relatives. Yet no doubt is left that Jesus is greater.

1. Annunciations of Conceptions of JBap and Jesus (1:5–45,56). Luke recalls Abraham and Sarah in the portrayal of Zechariah and Elizabeth. The angel Gabriel explains that God's final plan is beginning. JBap will play the role of Elijah according to Malachi (4:5–6), being sent before the coming Day of the Lord.

The annunciation of Jesus' birth catches the newness that God has begun to bring about. The angel Gabriel now comes to a virgin who is totally surprised by the idea of conception, especially conception not by human generation but by the creative Spirit of God overshadowing her. Gabriel makes a twofold proclamation about the child: First, the expectations of Israel will be fulfilled, for the child will be the Davidic Messiah. Second, the child will go far beyond those expectations, for he will be the unique Son of God in power through the Holy Spirit. The scene of the visitation (1:39–45) shows Mary, JBap in the womb, and Elizabeth rejoicing.

2. The Magnificat (1:46–55) and Other Canticles. Luke incorporates in the story canticles taken from a collection of early hymns in Greek: the Magnificat, the Benedictus (1:67–78), the Gloria in excelsis (2:13–14), and the Nunc dimittis (2:28–32). They reflect the style of Jewish hymnody and express christology indirectly, proclaiming that

God has done something decisive. Mary translates this news into a message for the lowly and the hungry and woe for the powerful and the rich. In Luke her son does the same.

3. Narratives of Birth, Circumcision, and Naming of JBap and Jesus (1:57–2:40). In these parallel episodes Luke gives extensive attention to the greater dignity of Jesus. The description of JBap's growing up and becoming strong in spirit (1:80) echoes the growth of Samson (Judg 13:24–25) and of Samuel (I Sam 2:21).

Luke's setting for the birth of Jesus, a census of the whole world, is fraught with historical problems. Theologically, this is an event on the cosmic stage, so that angels declare glory to God in heaven and peace on earth (2:14). The shepherds are Luke's counterparts to Matt's magi. Mary is the only adult who survives from the infancy narrative into the public ministry of Jesus and she still has to learn about the identity of her Son as revealed through the suffering of the ministry and the cross.

With the presentation of Jesus in the Temple (2:22–40) there are two important matching themes: (1) Jesus' parents were faithful to the Law, and (2) Simeon and Anna, representative of devout Jews waiting for the fulfillment of God's promises to Israel, accepted Jesus. The light that is to be a revelation for the Gentiles and a glory for Israel is set for the fall as well as the rise of many in Israel (2:32,34).

4. The Boy Jesus in the Temple (2:41–52). This episode seems to have come to Luke independently of the other infancy material; in 2:48–50 there is no indication of previous revelation about the identity of Jesus as God's Son or of his extraordinary conception. Yet, speaking for the first time, Jesus makes clear that God is his Father (2:49).

Preparation for the Public Ministry: Preaching of JBap,
Baptism of Jesus, His Genealogy, Temptations (3:1–4:13)

We see Luke's feel for history and his theology of world import in the subpreface (3:1–2) that he uses to mark off the beginning of the era of Jesus and the Gospel proper (probably ca. AD 29), by imperial, gubernatorial, and high priestly reigns. JBap's preaching ministry (3:1–20), which inaugurates the Jesus era, fulfills Gabriel's prediction to Zechariah in Luke 1:15b–16. The Isaian prophecy connected to JBap (Isa 40:3–5) is extended to include "all flesh shall see the salvation of God" as part of Luke's theological concern for the Gentiles. JBap's teaching emphasizes sharing goods, justice for the poor, and kind sensitivity—all this is similar to what the Lucan Jesus will emphasize. JBap preaches about the one to come (3:16–18). Luke recalls both JBap's clash with Herod the tetrarch (Herod Antipas) and his imprisonment, thus avoiding any subordination of Jesus to JBap, who is not even mentioned in the following baptismal scene.

Jesus prays (a Lucan theme) at his baptism (3:21–22) and the Holy Spirit descends in bodily form. Luke stops here to recount Jesus' genealogy (3:23–38), which mounts to Adam (preparing the way for all humanity) and even to God (3:38). In the testing/temptations (4:1–13) Jesus was "full of the Spirit," a Lucan emphasis. Only Luke specifies that the devil departed from him until an opportune time.

Ministry in Galilee (4:14–9:50)

Luke presents most of the public ministry account that he takes over from Mark, on which he imposes his own order, between 4:14–15 (Galilee) and 9:51 (Jerusalem).

1. Rejection at Nazareth; Activities at Capernaum and on the Sea (4:14–5:16). Luke begins the story with the rejection of Jesus at Nazareth (4:14–30), which takes place considerably later in Mark 6:1–6 and Matt 13:54–58. Also, this scene is much expanded beyond Mark's. This passage is used to portray Jesus as an anointed prophet and is programmatic of what his ministry will bring about. His referring to outsiders, though justified by prophetic parallels, raises the fury of the people against him, even to the point of trying to kill him. The rejection serves from the beginning to prepare readers for Jesus' ultimate fate.

Luke recounts four activities connected with Capernaum (4:31–44), the town that now becomes the operational center of Jesus' Galilean ministry. The first of twenty-one Lucan miracles is an exorcism. Then, Jesus heals Simon's mother-in-law, heals the sick, and casts out demons—who hail him as "the Son of God," though he rebukes them because they knew he was "the Christ." Compared to Mark 1:39, which has

Jesus preaching in the synagogues of all Galilee, Luke 4:44 locates the synagogues in Judea. Nevertheless, in the next verse (5:1) Jesus is still in Galilee.

The *miraculous catch of fish and the call of the disciples (5:1–11)* illustrate ingenious Lucan (re)ordering. Luke has moved the call of the first disciples from (its place in Mark) before Jesus' activity in Capernaum. He has also added to the Capernaum episodes a fishing miracle story that only he among the Synoptics records (cf. John 21:4–9). This ordering makes more intelligible why Simon and the others followed Jesus so readily.

2. Reactions to Jesus: Controversies with Pharisees; Choice of the Twelve and Preaching to the Multitude on the Plain (5:17–6:49). Drawing on Mark 2:1–3:6, Luke presents a series of *five controversies* (5:17–6:11) in which Pharisees play a role. They criticize Jesus' behavior: his claim to be able to forgive sins, his associates, his failure to have his disciples fast, their picking grain, and his own healing on the Sabbath. These controversies lead Jesus' enemies to plot against him (Luke 6:11).

Luke recounts the *choice of the Twelve, and the healing and preaching to the multitude on the plain (6:12–49)*—a parallel to Matt's Sermon on the Mount that was directed to the Twelve (Matt 5:1–2). The Lucan Sermon on the Plain is directed to all disciples. Four Lucan beatitudes open the sermon, addressing the actual poor, hungry, mournful, and hated "now." The Lucan "woes" resemble the contrasts in the Magnificat. Luke seems at times, but not consistently, to regard wealth (unless distributed to the poor) as corrupting one's relationship to God. Sharing possessions is a principal Lucan ideal.

Luke 6:27–36 enunciates Jesus' values. In comparison with Matt, there is less eschatological tone to the startling demands of the Lucan Jesus for his disciples to love those who hate and abuse them. The demands are addressed to all who would hear (6:27,47). Those who do not bear good fruit but simply say "Lord, Lord" (6:43–49) do not meet Jesus' demands.

3. Miracles and Parables That Illustrate Jesus' Power and Help to Reveal His Identity; Mission of the Twelve (7:1–9:6). The Lucan form of *the healing of the centurion's servant* in 7:1–10 has a Gentile's faith in

Jesus compared with the Jewish authorities' rejection of him. The next miracle, the raising of the son of the widow of Nain (7:11–17), is uniquely Lucan and shows Jesus' compassion and power, and gains him recognition.

Returning to Q material (Matt 11:2–19), Luke gives us a scene dealing with JBap (7:18–35) that clarifies his relationship to Jesus. The Lucan Jesus responds to JBap's disciples in part by citing Isaiah (as he did in Nazareth), and he praises JBap. The story of eating at the table of Simon the Pharisee follows, and Luke tells a beautiful story involving a penitent sinful woman who weeps over and anoints Jesus' feet (7:36–50). Is the Lucan story the same as that of the anointing of Jesus' head by a woman at the house of Simon the leper in Mark 14:3–9 and Matt 26:6–13, and that of the anointing of Jesus' feet by Mary, the sister of Martha and Lazarus, in John 12:1–8? Was the sinful woman forgiven because she loved much or did she love much because she had already been forgiven? Either meaning or both would fit Luke's stress on God's forgiveness in Christ and a loving response. After the story of this woman, Luke describes the Galilean women followers of Jesus (8:1–3), who had been cured of evil spirits and diseases. Three are named: Mary Magdalene, Joanna, wife of Chuza, Herod's steward, and Susanna; the first two will reappear at the empty tomb (24:10). Only Luke tells of their past and that they served (diakonein) the needs of Jesus and the Twelve out of their means—a picture of devoted women disciples.

Luke next recounts the parable of the sower and the seed and its explanation, interrupted by the purpose of parables (8:4–15). An array of parabolic sayings centered on the lamp, light, and hearing and heeding (8:16–18) leads into the arrival of Jesus' mother and brothers (8:19–21). Although drawn from Mark, the import is entirely changed. No unfavorable remarks occur, only praise of the mother and brothers as hearing and doing the word of God—they exemplify the good seed and fit the criterion of discipleship.

Luke now gives a sequence of four miracle-stories (8:22–56): calming the storm at sea, healing the Gerasene demoniac, resuscitating Jairus' daughter, and healing the woman with a hemorrhage. These miracles are elaborate, and the grandeur of Jesus is fully displayed as he exercises power over the sea, demons, long-lasting illness, and death itself. Luke continues with the sending out of the Twelve (9:1–6).

4. Questions of Jesus' Identity: Herod, Feeding of the 5,000, Peter's Confession, First and Second Passion Prediction, Transfiguration (9:7–50). While the Twelve are away, we are told of Herod's having beheaded JBap (9:7–9). Luke reports the "tetrarch's" curiosity about Jesus (preparing for 13:31 and 23:8). The theme of Jesus' identity is pursued in the subsequent scenes. Luke begins with the return of the Twelve Apostles and the feeding of the 5,000 (9:10–17), adapted from Mark 6:30–44. Luke leaves out a substantial section of Mark, everything from after the feeding of the 5,000 to after the feeding of the 4,000, that is, Mark 6:45–8:26.

Rejoining Mark's outline at 8:27 in that Gospel, Luke next has the threefold proposal about who Jesus is and Peter's confession (9:18–20), introduced by the typical Lucan note that Jesus was praying. Peter's confession, "the Christ of God," is greeted by Jesus' first passion prediction (9:21–22), but Luke (unlike Mark/Matt) has no misunderstanding by Peter and so, no chastisement. Rather Jesus continues by teaching about the cross and judgment (9:23–27) in a series of loosely attached sayings about discipleship. The transfiguration (9:28–36), set in the context of Jesus' praying, recognizes that glory is already present in Jesus' earthly career (9:32). Jesus speaks with Moses and Elijah about his "exodus," his departure to God through death in Jerusalem. God's voice affirms both glory and suffering in identifying Jesus as Son and Chosen One (Suffering Servant). In the following episodes (9:37–50) Luke suppresses negative dimensions regarding the disciples in the stories that he takes over from Mark.

Journey to Jerusalem (9:51–19:27)

Luke writes another subpreface to indicate major change. Jesus' time is coming, so he "sets his face" to go to Jerusalem, where he is to die. The long journey to ensue is an artificial framework for Luke's "Big Interpolation" (9:51–18:14), as he leaves Mark's outline for almost all this second half of the Gospel and inserts large blocks from Q and from his own sources (L). This section of the Gospel is most characteristically Lucan.

1. First to Second Mention of Jerusalem (9:51–13:21). Among the Gospels only Luke has the hostile encounter with a Samaritan village (9:51–56), which is the opposite of John 4:39–42. The dialogue with three would-be followers (9:57–62) highlights the absolute demand imposed by the kingdom. Earlier we saw a sending of the Twelve parallel to accounts in Mark and Matt, but only Luke has a second mission, the sending of the seventy-two (10:1–12), which seems to be created from the same Q material used for the sending of the Twelve. The need for a second sending is explained (10:2) by the size of the harvest. The proclamation that "the kingdom of God has come near" has an element of judgment in it, for it is followed by woes to the disbelieving cities (10:13–16).

Joy at the subjection of the demons marks the Lucan return of the seventy-two (10:17–20). Jesus sums up their mission in terms of the fall of Satan. Jesus thanks the Father for revelation (10:21–22) and blesses the disciples (10:23–24) chosen by the Son to receive that revelation. Next a lawyer asks about eternal life and Jesus responds about love of God and neighbor (10:25–28). The lawyer asks, "Who is my neighbor?," and Jesus responds with the Lucan parable of the good Samaritan (10:29–37). One can define only the subject of love, not the object.

The story of Martha and Mary (10:38–42) emphasizes that heeding the word of Jesus is the only important thing (cf. John 11:1–44; 12:1–8). Jesus responds with the Lord's Prayer (11:1–4) when a disciple inquires about prayer—a shorter, older, less eschatological wording than that preserved in Matt. Encouragement to prayer is inherent in the uniquely Lucan parable of the insistent friend (11:5–8), and Q material on insistence in asking (11:9–13) is added to make the point.

Abruptly in this friendly sequence, Luke shapes a controversy passage and sayings about the evil spirit (11:14–26)—both are comments on Jesus' ministry, even looking toward the passion. Peculiarly Lucan is the beatitude from the woman in the crowd (11:27–28)—anticipated by 1:42–45, and itself anticipating 23:29. In the warning signs for this generation, parabolic sayings about light, and woes to the Pharisees (11:29–12:1), there are noteworthy Lucan features: warnings, admonitions, and woes.

The exhortation to confess fearlessly (12:2–12) promises reward for anyone who proclaims the truth and warns of judgment for anyone who does not. The pericope on greed and the parable of the rich barn-builder (12:13–21) is distinctively Lucan. A strong interest in material possessions is not reconcilable with interest in God—"One's life does not depend on what one possesses" (12:15). A passage decrying cares about earthly things (12:22–34) illustrates how well off one can be without such cares. The instruction "Sell your possessions and give alms" (12:33) is very Lucan in its outlook.

Luke now changes the topic with a section on the necessity of faithful watchfulness (12:35–48). The parable that Jesus tells presents harsh images of punishment, especially for those who failed in their responsibilities—although there is some qualification for those who acted in ignorance. In eschatological language Jesus gives a frightening description of the diverse results of his ministry (12:49–53). Apparently much of this will happen soon, for Jesus expresses ire at people's inability to read the signs of the present time (12:54–56). To Q material related to settling before being judged (12:57–59), Luke adds his own examples of destruction to inculcate repentance (13:1–5). The parable of the fig tree (13:6–9) offers one more chance for the tree to bear fruit before being cut down. (Could this be a benevolent Lucan form of the cursing of the fig tree in Mark 11 and Matt 21—a miracle that became a parable?) Luke next portrays Jesus teaching in a synagogue on a Sabbath and compassionately healing a crippled woman (13:10–17), a deed that makes the ruler of the synagogue indignant, although it causes rejoicing among the people. The twin parables of the mustard seed and the leaven (13:18–21) give assurance that the kingdom will ultimately be great despite its small beginnings.

2. Second to Third Mention of Jerusalem (13:22–17:10). Luke reminds the reader that Jesus is on his way to Jerusalem. Someone asks Jesus, "Lord, will those who are saved be few?" This introduces material on exclusion from and acceptance into the kingdom (13:22–30). Then, some Pharisees report Herod's (Antipas's) homicidal hostility toward Jesus (13:31–33), to which Jesus replies by explaining the necessity of his going to Jerusalem. Jesus' thoughts about his destiny lead into the plaintive apostrophe to Jerusalem (13:34–35): as a prophet Jesus will die there, but the city itself will experience judgment/rejection.

The next three episodes are set in the home of a prominent Pharisee: the Sabbath cure of a man with dropsy, two instructions about conduct at dinner, and the parable of the great banquet (14:1–24). The cure of the man almost parallels the Sabbath healing of the woman in 13:10–17. Jesus' teaching illustrates the upside-down values of the kingdom. His eschatological perspective is explicit in the final promise of recompense at the resurrection of the just (14:14). The parable of the great banquet (14:15–24) primarily passes a judgment of rejection on the first invited guests who had priorities that they put before the invitation to the kingdom.

Luke shifts the scene by having Jesus talk about *the cost of discipleship* (14:25–35) to the great multitudes who accompanied him. The similitude of saltiness emphasizes the importance of unadulterated commitment in discipleship, for a deteriorated allegiance leaves a disciple fit for nothing.

The whole next chapter consists of *three parables: lost sheep, lost coin, lost (prodigal) son* (15:1–32). Luke has these parables directed to the Pharisees and the scribes who object to Jesus keeping company with sinners. The references to joy in heaven show that the parables give a lesson in God's loving mercy and dramatize the value of those whom others despise as lost. In the parable of the prodigal son the portrayal of the father illustrates God's remarkable love. In turn, the elder brother, resentful and jealous, expresses the Pharisees' attitude toward sinners.

Many have difficulty with the uniquely Lucan *parable of the unjust steward* (16:1–15) because it seems to commend shady business practice; but what is praised is the prudent energetic initiative of the steward, not his dishonesty. It is unclear from Luke's account whether Jesus' diverse sayings dealing with wealth begin after the parable at verse 8b, 9, or 10, but one or all of these sayings express Luke's theological perspective on the danger of the corrupting power of mishandled wealth. Noticeably in 16:14–15 Luke shifts the focus to "the Pharisees, who were lovers of money" and who justify/exalt themselves before others. A series of Q *sayings about the Law and divorce* (16:16–18) follows. Jesus recognizes JBap as marking the end of the Law and prophets, and the beginning of the preaching of the gospel (v. 16), although there is no discontinuity between the two eras, for in Jesus' teaching not even the smallest part of a letter of the Law drops out (v. 17). Perhaps to illustrate that point, the saying on divorce (v. 18) is meant to show that Jesus' prohibition of divorce (which does not agree with Deut 24:1–4) is consistent with that part of the Law in Gen 1:27 and 2:24 (although Luke does not quote the Genesis texts as do Mark 10:6–12 and Matt 19:4–9). The early church clearly wrestled with this matter: Mark 10:11–12; Matt 5:32 and 19:9; Luke 16:18; I Cor 7:10–11. The theme of the damning effects of wealth returns in the uniquely Lucan *parable of the rich man and Lazarus* (16:19–31). The different fates are based not on vice versus virtue but rather on comfort versus misery (16:25).

The topic changes as Jesus addresses his disciples with four unrelated *warnings on behavior* (17:1–10). Cautioning against scandalizing others, they stress forgiving fellow disciples, the power of faith, and the distinction between great achievement and duty.

3. Last Stage of Journey till Arrival in Jerusalem (17:11–19:27). Luke mentions Jesus' being on the way to Jerusalem, which sets the stage for the uniquely Lucan *cleansing of the ten lepers, including the thankful Samaritan* (17:11–19). Jesus is still passing between Samaria and Galilee, an artificial framework for Luke's narrative that explains the presence of a Samaritan among the lepers. Indeed, he is the sole leper to show gratitude and thus to experience salvation. Since Jesus' journey will soon end he now gives the Pharisees and then the disciples *eschatological teaching* (17:20–37), drawn from Q, L, and Luke's own composition, as an anticipation and almost doublet of the eschatological discourse of chap. 21. The teaching warns against being deceived by bogus eschatological claims on the one hand, and against thoughtless living on the other, as if there were never to be a judgment.

In face of this judgment, the uniquely Lucan *parable of the unjust judge* (18:1–8) asserts that if persistent petitioning persuades a totally amoral judge, how much more will continued, confident prayer be heard by God who vindicates the chosen ones. The theme of prayer leads into the Lucan *parable of the Pharisee and the tax-collector* (18:9–14). Beyond exhibiting God's graciousness to sinners, the story raises the issues of pride, rejection, humbleness, and justification. The emphasis on humility (18:14) leads Luke to recount Jesus' *kindness to little children* (18:15–17), who serve as a model of dependence on God (true humility) for entering the kingdom.

In turn, a ruler asks *what is necessary for eternal life*, and Jesus comments on the *obstacle offered by riches* (18:18–30). Although Luke follows Mark here, the theme is harmonious with Luke's theological perspective of selling and distributing to the poor. What Jesus himself will sacrifice is articulated in the third prediction of the passion (18:31–34). Luke hews close to Mark 10:32–34 even to the point of predicting that the Gentiles will spit upon and scourge the Son of Man—something that never happens in the Lucan passion narrative.

The healing of the blind man as Jesus comes near Jericho (18:35–43) is a variant of the healing of Bartimaeus (Mark 10:46) and of two blind men (Matt 20:29) as Jesus leaves Jericho. Luke has Jesus entering the city, perhaps because in Luke's story later the colorful scene of Zacchaeus (19:1–10) transpires there. While in Jericho Jesus is kind to a tax-collector, but beyond that the story illustrates Luke's attitude toward wealth: Zacchaeus is rich, but his encounter with Jesus liberates him from his grasp on his goods, so that he gives evidence that salvation has come to his house as he gives half his goods to the poor. This theme of the correct use of wealth continues in the peculiar parable of the pounds (19:11–27).

Ministry in Jerusalem (19:28–21:38)

Jesus arrives at Jerusalem, where his "exodus," or departure to God, will take place. Most of his activity will be centered in the Temple area, where at the end he will deliver an eschatological discourse.

1. Entry into Jerusalem and Activities in the Temple Area (19:28–21:4). The royal entry into Jerusalem (19:28–38) emphasizes the disciples' praise of Jesus as king. When the Pharisees want the disciples rebuked, Jesus reluctantly predicts the destruction of Jerusalem (19:39–44). Luke places his (less violent) picture of the cleansing of the Temple (19:45–46) on the same day on which Jesus entered Jerusalem (with Matt, unlike Mark).

Jesus now starts daily teaching in the Temple area, provoking the question of his authority (19:47–20:8). Luke describes the extreme animosity of the chief priests and the scribes toward Jesus, their frustration, and their challenge to his authority. The parable of the wicked tenants (20:9–19) serves as a critique of these authorities, as they recognize. The authorities spy on Jesus and seek to trap him with a question concerning the tribute to Caesar (20:20–26), which he deftly avoids. The Sadducees also challenge Jesus' teaching authority with their question about the resurrection (20:27–40), but the quality of his answer draws approbation even from scribes. In turn, Jesus poses his own question about David's son (20:41–44), and no answer is

given to his riddle. These confrontations end with Jesus' withering condemnation of the scribes (20:45–47). The charge that they "devour widows'
houses" leads into the story of the widow's offering (21:1–4), which comes
from Mark and has a special resonance with Luke's concerns with the
poor and giving away all that one has.

    2. Eschatological Discourse (21:5–38). Voiced admiration of
the Temple buildings elicits Jesus' prediction of the destruction of the Temple
(21:5–6); and that leads into a discourse on the last things—a theme
already expressed in eschatological exhortation (12:35–48) and eschatological teaching (17:20–37). Luke situates this discourse in the
Temple as a continuation of Jesus' daily teaching there. In the body of
the discourse (21:7–36) some maintain that 21:8–24 refers to the fate of
Jerusalem and 21:25–36 refers to the fate of the world when the Son
of Man comes. Many points in the discourse are peculiarly Lucan. Luke
21:37–38 summarizes Jesus' daily activity as a transition to the passion
narrative.

Last Supper, Passion, Death, and Burial (21:1–23:56a)

    When Luke follows Mark, he does so with substantial fidelity; but
the passion narrative is an exception. Although many scholars posit dependence on a pre-Lucan passion narrative separate from Mark, a more
plausible case can be made for Luke's dependence on Mark combined
with some special traditions. In particular, both in the passion and
resurrection accounts Luke draws on traditions that have left a trace in
John as well.

    1. Conspiracy Against Jesus, Last Supper (22:1–38). In telling
of the conspiracy against Jesus (22:1–6), Luke explains that Satan entered
into Judas (also John 13:2,27). After the temptations in the desert the
devil had left Jesus till a more opportune time (4:13); now he returns.
Also arrayed against Jesus are the chief priests and the officers of the
Temple.

    Peter and John are specified as the disciples who went ahead to
prepare for the Last Supper (22:7–38). Luke's account (twice as long as
Mark/Matt) has a more pronounced eschatological tone. Jesus' actions
are distinct. He speaks of the cup twice. The words spoken of the bread
and the (second) cup correspond to those found in Mark 14:22–24;

Matt 26:26–28; and I Cor 11:24–25. The Lucan clauses that have the body and blood given or poured out "for you" stress the soteriological thrust of Jesus' death and of the eucharist. The feast of Passover had a remembrance (*anamnēsis*) motif, but for Christians this shifted to a remembrance of Jesus.

Luke has three predictions of the disciples' fate at the Last Supper (as does John); Mark and Matt have one at the supper and two more on the way to the Mount of Olives. Jesus' other words after the supper and before the departure of the group for the Mount of Olives come from Mark, Q, and unique Lucan material. Luke's treatment of the disciples is more benevolent than Mark's, and Jesus' promise to pray for Simon (Peter) modifies the prediction of his denials and anticipates that his faith will not finally fail.

2. Prayers and Arrest on the Mount of Olives, Jewish and Roman Trials (22:39–23:25). Jesus comes out from the supper and goes to a customary place where *he prays and is arrested* (22:39–53). Luke simplifies Mark's dramatic description of the alienation of Jesus from the disciples; there is no description of Jesus' emotions and his falling on the ground. Jesus kneels to pray, only once (not three times as in Mark), and finds the disciples sleeping only once (and then "out of sorrow"). A textual problem affects 22:43–44 (the appearance of an angel to Jesus), thus raising questions about the authenticity of that incident as part of the original Lucan Passion account. If, however, the verses were written by the evangelist, they alone tell of Jesus' prayer being answered by his Father.

During the arrest Jesus' words show that he knows Judas' intention. The disciples persist in misunderstanding. They ask about striking with the sword, and Jesus tells them to desist from violence. Only in Luke's account does Jesus stop in this desperate moment to heal the ear of one who came to arrest him. Luke alone has the chief priests come to the Mount of Olives, and Jesus confronts them on account of their sinister behavior.

The *denials by Peter* (22:54–62) precede the Jewish trial, so that Jesus is present in the courtyard while Peter is denying him. The poignant moment comes when the Lord turns and looks at Peter, confirming Jesus' prophecy and recalling his promise of prayer that Peter's faith would not fail. Luke also uniquely places the Jewish mockery of Jesus (22:63–65) in the courtyard at night and has it done by those who were holding him captive. This rearrangement causes Luke to simplify the presentation of the Jewish trial (22:66–71) and to set it all in the morning. The chief priests ask Jesus about being the Messiah, and a direct answer is avoided because they would not believe; then they ask him about being the Son of God, and he answers in such a way that they conclude that they have all the evidence needed to take further action against him (compare John 10:24–25,33,36).

The Lucan account of the Roman trial (23:1–25) departs significantly from Mark. A set of charges (known to Luke's reader to be patently false) is presented to Pilate. Luke knows the pattern of Roman trials and he fits the tradition about Jesus into that pattern. Luke 23:4,14,22 dramatizes Jesus' innocence, for three times Pilate says that he finds no guilt in him (compare John 18:38; 19:4,6). Only Luke 23:6–12 reports that Pilate sent Jesus to Herod (Antipas), who questioned and mocked him, but also returned him to Pilate without finding him guilty. Pilate attempts to release Jesus, even offering the lesser penalty of whipping; but finally he gives Jesus over "to their will" (23:25). Luke avoids recording the scourging and mockery of Jesus by the Roman soldiers found in the other three Gospels.

3. Way of the Cross, Crucifixion, Burial (23:26–56). Luke elevates the way of the cross (23:26–32) beyond the transitional sentence found in the other Gospels. He mentions three parties: Simon the Cyrenaican, a great multitude of the people, and the "daughters of Jerusalem." Echoing the OT, Jesus warns the weeping daughters of Jerusalem of the fate of the city—despite the presence of some who are sympathetic.

Luke also reshapes the incidents culminating in death on the cross (23:33–46). Only in Luke does Jesus speak at the moment of crucifixion. Some manuscripts lack Jesus' words in 23:34a, "Father, forgive them, for they do not know what they do"; but the extension of forgiveness would fit the Lucan outlook admirably. Luke has Jesus mocked by a distinct threesome: the rulers, the soldiers, and one of the co-crucified. The unique scene with the other co-crucified is a masterpiece of Lucan theology. The generosity of Jesus goes far beyond what the criminal asks for. Jesus' trusting and confident final word on the cross, "Father, into your hands I place my spirit" (23:46) is quite different from the Marcan Jesus' plaintiff cry of being abandoned. All the negative signs that accompany the crucifixion in Mark are placed in Luke before Jesus dies, so that the positive, salvific results of the death stand out clearly.

To exemplify those results Luke recounts the *reaction to the death of Jesus, followed by the burial* (23:47–56). The Roman centurion joins Pilate, Herod Antipas, and the one co-crucified wrongdoer, giving testimony that Jesus was a just (or, righteous) man (*dikaios*) and did nothing wrong. The crowds express sorrow. The women followers stand at a distance looking on. They will be the connective to the future, observing the burial by a "good and righteous" Jewish leader, Joseph of Arimathea, and then later coming to the tomb, but not before observing the Sabbath.

Resurrection Appearances in the Jerusalem Area (24:1–53)

While in Mark the messenger at the tomb indicates that the risen Jesus would appear in Galilee, Luke (similar to John) concentrates his three appearance-scenes around Jerusalem.

1. At the Empty Tomb (24:1–12). Luke follows Mark 16:1–8, although he has his own traditions and greatly modifies Mark, adding clarifications (v. 3), dramatization (v. 5), and adaptations (vv. 6,9). Verse 12 is textually dubious, although 24:24 seems to make a puzzling reference to it—compare John 20:3–10.

2. Appearance on the Road to Emmaus (24:13–35). Appropriately, on a journey, the risen Jesus interpreted to two traveling companions all the Scriptures concerning himself. Still, they recognized him only when he broke bread.

3. Appearance in Jerusalem and Ascension to Heaven (24:36–53). As in John, the *first appearance to the assembled disciples* in Luke (24:36–49) is set in Jerusalem on the evening of the resurrection day. Both Luke and John (20:19–29) present these features: Jesus stands in their midst and says, "Peace be to you"; there is a reference to Jesus' wounds; and the mission given by Jesus involves forgiveness of sins and the role of the Spirit. Jesus explains the Scriptures to these disciples too—a sign that this is fundamental to any understanding of what God has done in him. He charges them to a mission proclaiming repentance and forgiveness of sins to all the nations, beginning from Jerusalem. They are to be witnesses of the things that have happened to him in fulfillment of Scripture. He promises them the Spirit: "I am sending the promise of my Father upon you."

The appearance ends with an *ascension scene* (24:50–53), when Jesus goes out to Bethany, blesses his disciples, and is carried up into heaven. Then the disciples return with joy to Jerusalem and the Temple, praising God. The Gospel began in the Temple (Zechariah), and it ends in the Temple (disciples).

SOURCES AND COMPOSITIONAL FEATURES

The evangelist acknowledges sources in the prologue to the Gospel. Here we shall deal with two written sources, Mark and Q, of which one can speak with more assurance, and then other compositional material.

MARK. The material taken from Mark constitutes about 35 percent of Luke. The majority of scholars understand that Luke had a written form of Mark before him, although some have questioned whether in all details it was identical with the form of Mark used by Matt. Luke's

Table 3. Luke's use of Mark

MATERIAL FROM MARK IN LUKE		MAJOR LUCAN INTERPOLATIONS
Mark 1:1–15	= Luke 3:1–4:15	
		4:16–30 (at Nazareth)
Mark 1:21–3:19	= Luke 4:31–44; 5:12–6:19	5:1–11 (catch of fish)
		6:20–8:3 (Little Interpolation)
Mark 4:1–6:44	= Luke 8:4–9:17	
Mark 8:27–9:40	= Luke 9:18–50	
		9:51–18:14 (Big Interpolation)
Mark 10:13–13:32	= Luke 18:15–43; 19:29–21:33	19:1–28 (Zacchaeus, parable)
Mark 14:1–16:8	= Luke 22:1–24:12	

procedure is to follow Mark and take over material in large blocks. Luke omits some Marcan material; two of the omissions are of large sections of Mark (6:45–8:26 and 9:41–10:12). Although in general Luke is quite faithful to Mark, he made changes that enable us to detect Lucan thought and proclivities.

• Luke improves Mark's Greek.

• Luke rearranges Marcan sequence to order the account more logically (although because of changes made in material received from Mark, Luke occasionally creates inconsistencies).

• Luke eliminates or changes passages in Mark unfavorable to those whose subsequent careers make them worthy of respect.

• Luke is more reverential about Jesus and avoids making him seem emotional, harsh, or weak.

• Luke stresses detachment from possessions, not only in his special material, but also in changes he makes in Mark.

• Luke eliminates Mark's transcribed Aramaic names and words.

• Luke makes Marcan information more precise, presumably for better story flow, greater effect, or clarity.

Q SOURCE. The material taken from Q constitutes just over 20 percent of Luke; it adds a strong ethical tone to the portrayal of Jesus. Luke is thought for the most part to have preserved the original order of the Q document. He inserts most Q material in two places within the Marcan sequence: a smaller body of Q material in 6:20–8:3 called the Little Interpolation, and a larger body of Q material in 9:51–18:14 called the Big Interpolation.

SPECIAL LUCAN MATERIAL (often designated L). Between one-third and 40 percent of Luke is not drawn from Mark or Q. Given the evangelist's acknowledgment of the original eyewitnesses/ministers of the word and of many who had already undertaken to compile accounts, not surprisingly scholars have posited traditions and sources peculiar to Luke. Yet, since Luke is a very capable rewriter, it is difficult to decide which material he freely composed and which he took over from already shaped traditions and sources. Moreover, where the author has taken over material, it is not easy to distinguish pre-Lucan traditions from possible pre-Lucan sources.

THE SIGNIFICANCE OF JESUS' DEATH IN LUKE-ACTS

In comparison with the writings of Mark, Paul, John, and other NT authors, some interpreters conclude that Luke-Acts lacks a concept of *atonement* to make sense of *the meaning of Jesus' death*. By pointing to Mark 10:45 ("The Son of Man . . . came to give his life as a ransom for many"), to I Cor 15:3 ("Christ died in behalf of our sins according to the Scriptures"), to John 3:14–15 ("Just as Moses lifted up the serpent in the wilderness, likewise it is necessary for the Son of Man to be lifted up, in order that the one believing in him may have eternal life"), or to similar NT texts, they make the observation that Luke-Acts has no parallel statements and thus contend that in Luke-Acts there is no saving significance associated with Jesus' death. Because of the absence of explicit language of *atonement* and *sacrifice*, which are said to be the essential NT interpretations of the meaning of Jesus' death, Luke is censured for his perceived lack of soteriological reflection on Jesus' death.

It is no matter of dispute that Luke has a distinct manner of telling and even interpreting both the story of Jesus (his life, death, resurrection, ascension) and the story of the early church, in particular about kerygmatic proclamation. But simply because Luke is not Mark or Paul, or because he does not state his soteriology in exactly their terms, his two-volume narrative is not necessarily bereft of any soteriological comprehension of Jesus' suffering and death. In fact, a few observations and examples can illustrate Luke's own sense of the saving significance of Jesus' death.

First, to fault Luke for a supposed lack of atonement theology is itself a problem. The actual language of atonement (see Lev 19:22 LXX) is rare in the NT. In fact, most interpreters refer to atonement, using the vocabulary of atonement, when the NT texts themselves use a rich variety of images and words to speak of the saving significance of Jesus' death—for example, martyr, sacrifice, scapegoat, justification, ransomed, redeemed, adoption, reconciliation, etc. There are probably no more than six uses of actual atonement terminology in the entire NT, and remarkably one of those is in Luke (Luke 18:13; Rom 3:25; Heb 2:17; 9:5; I John 2:2; 4:10). *Atonement* is but one image or metaphor among several that are used in the NT to interpret the significance of Jesus' death. Atonement has become an umbrella term, when, in fact, it is only one of the metaphors used in relation to Jesus' death. The real question is not whether Luke-Acts lacks a concept of (the?) atonement, but whether Luke's writings show an understanding of the saving significance of Jesus' death.

Second, a comparison of the three parallel Passion predictions that occur in the Synoptic Gospels finds that in the first prediction (9:22) Luke remains close to Mark; in the second prediction (9:43b–44) Luke abbreviates Mark and uses only part of Mark's version; and in the third prediction (18:31–33) Luke adds a remark about the forthcoming Passion fulfilling everything that was written by the prophets concerning the Son of Man. This Lucan addition certainly indicates that Jesus' suffering and death (and resurrection) realized purposeful divine plans that are stated elsewhere in Luke-Acts (for example, Luke 24:46–47).

Third, the account of the Last Supper in Luke (22:14–23) is distinct among the Gospels. To the words of institution, "This is my body," only Luke adds, "which is given in behalf of you." And then, with regard to the cup, Luke's wording is again distinct: "This cup is the new covenant in my blood, which is poured out in behalf of you." These eucharistic sayings in Luke articulate an understanding of the significance of the bread and the cup, which refer to the body and the blood of Jesus: they are both vicarious and sacrificial.

Fourth, at the scene of the crucifixion, the crucified Jesus speaks to one co-crucified criminal, saying, "Truly I say to you, today you will be with me in Paradise" (23:43). This comforting word promises a future (beyond crucifixion and death) that will be in Jesus' presence ("with me"), which expresses Luke's own distinct but clear conviction of the crucified Jesus' ability to save. This insight expresses neither Marcan nor Pauline theology, but it shows in Lucan language and images Jesus' authority to promise salvation, even as he is dying and even though it is an enigma.

Fifth, in 23:48 Luke writes about the assembled crowds who watched the spectacle of the crucifixion. At Jesus' death, Luke says, "When they observed the things that happened, *beating their breasts* they returned home." Earlier in the Gospel, in the parable of the Pharisee and the tax collector (18:9–14), the tax collector humbly confessed his sinfulness and asked God for mercy as "*he beat his breast*"; and Jesus comments, "This man went down to his home having been justified." The matching vocabulary in these passages is not common and may encourage viewing these parts of Luke together. If so, perhaps one may understand that the sight of the death of Jesus on the cross moved the crowds to show dramatically their own remorse (repentance?), which for Luke may mean that the cross provokes repentance that leads to forgiveness and, thus, to salvation (Acts 3:19).

Sixth, in Acts there is no set formula for "being saved" (Acts 2:40). Someone usually preaches "the word" (4:31) or "the good news" (5:42), and in some way belief (4:4) occurs, yet sometimes people repent and then they are forgiven (2:38; 3:19). At other times people appear to be forgiven and then they repent, or there is no mention of repentance at all (8:12; 10:43; 11:15–18; 13:38–39; 16:30–33; 18:8; 19:1–7), and at still other times people simply want to be or are baptized (8:36; 10:44–48). Similarly, the sermons in Acts are not set in any one pattern. There are regularly occurring features and themes, but there is no single way to say things and for things to happen. The sermons tell of Jesus' suffering, crucifixion, death, and resurrection; these items are central and essential to the proclamation. The sermons speak of the need for repentance. And, they talk about forgiveness. The blends of these themes work in a variety of ways, but in the sermons a relationship almost always exists among these themes. Luke's chief concern, however, does not appear to have been to give a cause-and-effect explanation of salvation. In all, however, Jesus' death is always somehow in the mixture.

Seventh, in Acts 20:28 Paul admonishes the elders of the church at Ephesus "to tend the church of God, which he acquired through his own blood." The seeming strangeness of the plain sense of these words led to several textual variants. However the line is read (does it say "the church of God" or "the church of the Lord"?), the last clause clearly says that God/the Lord acquired the church "through his own blood." There can be no doubt that this is a reference to Jesus' crucifixion, and just as obvious is the concept stated here explicitly that *the blood* (death on a cross) *acquired the church*. This is not far from Paul's declaration (I Cor 6:20; 7:23), "You were bought with a price," which for Paul is simply another way to say, "Christ died for us" (Rom 5:8). Luke's wording is different, but his point is much the same.

Eighth, at the end of the Gospel (24:46–47), Luke tells of the final appearance of the risen Jesus to his disciples. In the course of Jesus' teaching them the Scriptures, Jesus says, "Thus it is written: The Christ is to suffer and to rise from the dead on the third day, and repentance is to be proclaimed in his name for the forgiveness of sins to all the nations—beginning from Jerusalem—you are witnesses of these things." The statement clearly says that forgiveness of sins is to come in the name of the suffering Messiah—that is, there is a relationship between the Messiah and his suffering and the subsequent forgiveness of sins. It's not exactly I Cor 15:3, but neither is it all that different.

∴✴∵

10

The Acts of the Apostles

Luke-Acts constitutes one book in two volumes. The author gave no title to this book (nor to the Gospel); but later church writers dubbed it "Acts" (meaning "deeds"), thus implicitly comparing it to Hellenistic writings of the same name describing the career and accomplishments of famous men.

GENERAL ANALYSIS OF THE MESSAGE

In the title, the modifier "of the Apostles" is not precise. There are only two major figures: Peter (one of the Twelve Apostles) is prominent in nine or ten chaps., and Paul (who is called an apostle only twice) is prominent in seventeen chaps. The only other figure in Acts who gets lengthy treatment is Stephen, who is not designated an apostle.

Introduction: Preparing Jesus' Followers for the Spirit (1:1–26)

1. Jesus Instructs His Disciples and Ascends to Heaven (1:1–11). At the beginning in 1:1–2, *a type of subprologue* (see Luke 1:1–4), the author makes clear reference to his first volume. In this new book what

SUMMARY OF BASIC INFORMATION

DATE, AUTHOR, LOCALE: Same as for Luke (see above).

INTEGRITY: Western Greek mss. have a significant number of passages (many of them with additional information) missing from other mss.

DIVISION:

1:1–26: INTRODUCTION: PREPARING JESUS' FOLLOWERS FOR THE SPIRIT

1. Jesus instructs his disciples and ascends to heaven (1:1–11)
2. Awaiting the Spirit; replacement of Judas (1:12–26)

2:1–8:1A: MISSION IN JERUSALEM

1. The Pentecost scene; Peter's sermon (2:1–36)
2. Reception of the message; Jerusalem communal life (2:37–45)
3. Activity, preaching, and trials of the apostles (3:1–5:42)
4. The Hellenists; toleration; Stephen's trial and martyrdom (6:1–8:1a)

8:1B–12:25: MISSIONS IN SAMARIA AND JUDEA

1. Dispersal from Jerusalem; Philip and Peter in Samaria (8:1b–25)
2. Philip and the Ethiopian eunuch en route to Gaza (8:26–40)
3. Saul en route to Damascus; return to Jerusalem and Tarsus (9:1–31)
4. Peter at Lydda, Joppa, Caesarea, and back to Jerusalem (9:32–11:18)
5. Antioch; Jerusalem; Herod's persecution; Peter's departure (11:19–12:25)

13:1–15:35: MISSION OF BARNABAS AND SAUL CONVERTING GENTILES; APPROVAL AT JERUSALEM

1. Antioch church sends Barnabas and Saul: Mission to Cyprus and SE Asia Minor (13:1–14:28)
2. Jerusalem conference and approval; return to Antioch (15:1–35)

15:36–28:31: MISSION OF PAUL TO THE END OF THE EARTH

1. From Antioch through Asia Minor to Greece and return (15:36–18:22)
2. From Antioch to Ephesus and Greece, and return to Caesarea (18:23–21:14)
3. Arrest in Jerusalem; imprisonment and trials in Caesarea (21:15–26:32)
4. Journey to Rome as a prisoner (27:1–28:14a)
5. Paul at Rome (28:14b–31).

Jesus began is continued through the same Spirit working through the apostles. An oddity is that Luke 24:50–51 recounted the ascension of Jesus to heaven on Easter Sunday night from Bethany (on the Mount of Olives), but Acts 1:9–12 will recount an ascension of Jesus to heaven at least forty days later from the Mount of Olives. For the Gospel the ascension visibly terminates the activity of Jesus on earth; for Acts it will prepare the apostles to be witnesses to him to the end of the earth.

The risen Jesus appears to his disciples for forty days after his passion (1:3–7) as a preparation for the coming of the Spirit. Acts presents the preparation of the disciples for their forthcoming baptism with the Holy Spirit in a time frame that echoes Jesus' forty days and Israel's forty years in the desert.

The outline of this second volume is supplied in Acts 1:8 through a directive of Jesus to the apostles: "You will be my witnesses in Jerusalem, all Judea and Samaria, and to the end of the earth." The Acts story that begins in Jerusalem will end up in Rome, the center of an empire extending to the known ends of the earth. Then, *Jesus is taken up to heaven* (1:9–11) and two men in white robes inform the apostles that Jesus will come in the same way that he went into heaven—no time is given for his return.

2. Awaiting the Spirit; Replacing Judas (1:12–26). *Those who await the promised coming of the Spirit are listed and numbered in* 1:12–15. Those listed represent continuity with the Gospel and are witnesses to Jesus' life, ministry, and resurrection. These believers are numbered at about 120. They will act next to fill out the apostolic number left vacant by Judas.

Peter takes the initiative by recalling *how Judas lost his share in the apostolic ministry (Acts* 1:16–20). The place of Judas is filled by *the selection of Matthias (Acts* 1:21–26). Matthias is of no personal import and will never be mentioned again. Israel of old had twelve patriarchs representing twelve tribes. The story of the Israel renewed in Jesus can start with no fewer than Twelve, who are a once-for-all symbol for the whole of the renewed Israel, never to be replaced when they die (see 12:2). The choice by lots leaves the selection of Judas' replacement to God.

Mission in Jerusalem (2:1–8:1a)

1. The Pentecost Scene; Peter's Sermon (2:1–36). The Feast of Pentecost (celebrated fifty days after Passover) was a pilgrimage festival when pious Jews came to the Temple in Jerusalem. *The coming of the Spirit described in Acts* 2:1–13 occurs at this next pilgrimage feast after Jesus' death and resurrection. His Galilean followers were present at the festival. The presence of the Spirit was charismatically manifested as they began to speak in tongues, which was seen as a sign that they should proclaim publicly what God had done in Jesus.

Acts highlights the central place of Pentecost in the Christian history of salvation. Passover commemorated the deliverance from Egypt; and the "Feast of Weeks," or Pentecost (from Greek), observed the arrival of the Israelites at Sinai and God's giving the covenant (the Law). Acts 2 echoes that account and thus presents this Pentecost in Jerusalem as the renewal of God's covenant that will ultimately make even the Gentiles God's own people (28:28).

To observers the speaking in tongues of the Spirit-filled disciples looked like drunkenness. At an early level of recounting, the speech was ecstatic, whence the appearance of drunken babbling. It has been reinterpreted in Acts as speaking in other tongues or languages that are understandable. The reaction of the onlookers causes Peter to deliver the first sermon (2:14–36), which Acts presents as the fundamental proclamation of the gospel. Peter interprets the action of the Spirit as the fulfillment of the signs of the last days foretold by the OT prophet Joel. This opening affirms the basic consistency of what God has done in Jesus Christ with what the God of Israel did for and promised to the people of the covenant. Peter tells what God has done in Jesus: a brief summary of his mighty works, crucifixion, and resurrection, culminating in scriptural evidence that he was Lord and Messiah. (This concentration on christology represents a change from Jesus' own style as narrated in Luke's Gospel. The fundamental gospel became centered on the christological identity of the risen Jesus as Messiah and Son of God.)

2. Reception of the Message; Jerusalem Communal Life (2:37–45). *Acts 2:37–41 now dramatizes the fundamental acceptance of the gospel* once people believe the christological proclamation (2:36–37). Peter makes specific demands and gives a promise. The first demand is to "repent"— just as JBap preached repentance (Luke 3:3). Second, Peter demands their baptism for the forgiveness of their sins. Peter asks people to make an explicit profession of their acceptance of Jesus. As God saved Israel as *a people*, there is a collective aspect to salvation; one is saved as part of God's people. Third, baptism must be "in the name of Jesus Christ." There was a clear distinction between JBap's baptism and that in the name of Jesus Christ (18:24–19:7). Most likely "in the name of" means confessing who Jesus was—for example, Lord, Messiah,

Son of God, Son of Man. *Fourth,* Peter makes a pledge: "You shall re-ceive the gift of the Holy Spirit, for the promise is . . . to as many as the Lord God calls" (the hearers are challenged, but the priority in conversion belongs to God). The gift of the Holy Spirit will be given to all believers.

Acts 2:41 reports that about three thousand believed and were bap-tized; then it describes how they lived. *A summary in 2:42–47 lists four features in the communal life of the early believers.*

First, koinōnia ("fellowship, communion, community"). Those who believe quickly constitute a group. They had much in common, and Acts describes their voluntary sharing of goods, which shows their conviction that the last times had begun.

Second, prayers. Praying for each other was another aspect of *koinōnia,* saying prayers that they had known previously and adopting Jesus' own prayer style, visible in the Lord's Prayer.

Third, breaking bread. Early (Jewish) Christians frequently went to the Temple (2:46; 3:1; 5:12,21,42). The "breaking of bread" (the eu-charist?) would have been in addition to Temple worship. A sacral meal eaten only by those who believed in Jesus was a major manifestation of *koinōnia* and eventually helped to make Christians feel distinct from other Jews.

Fourth, teaching of the apostles. The Scriptures were authoritative for all Jews, in particular the Law and the Prophets; this would have been true for the first followers of Jesus as well. Jesus' own modifications and interpretations were remembered and became the nucleus of a special teaching.

These four characteristics of Jerusalem believers show both conti-nuity with Judaism and distinctiveness that marked off Jews who be-lieved in Jesus from other Jews. These aspects were in tension, pulling in opposite directions.

3. Activity, Preaching, and Trials of the Apostles (3:1–5:42). In the *dramatic account of the healing that takes place when Peter and John go up to the Temple* (3:1–10), the two carry on Jesus' ministry of healing through God's power to the amazement of all. The healing of a man lame from birth occurs "in the name of Jesus Christ of Nazareth" (3:6).

Peter's healing is followed by a sermon (3:11–26), which illustrates the pre-sentation of Jesus to the Jews. It amalgamates OT echoes and what God has done in Jesus. Peter's call for repentance in this sermon addresses those listening with greater specification. The Jews of Jerusalem delivered up and denied Jesus the servant of God, the Holy and Just One. Yet they acted in ignorance, as did their rulers, and accordingly they are being offered this opportunity to change. Now change of mind/heart is necessary if they are to experience the outpouring of God's grace in the sending of Jesus the Christ.

The apostolic preaching and its success (five thousand, though not most of the Jewish leaders) stirs up wrath and leads to the arrest of Peter and John (4:1–22). The priests and the Sadducees (who denied resurrection altogether) are irritated by Peter and John's proclaiming in Jesus the resurrection of the dead. A Sanhedrin meeting is convened against them. (As in the case with Jesus, Pharisees are not mentioned.) The interrogators ask about the healing, demanding, "By what name did you do this?"—which prepares for Peter's response, "By the name of Jesus Christ of Nazareth whom you crucified, whom God raised from the dead . . . There is no other name under heaven given among the human race by which we must be saved" (4:10,12).

Annoyed at the boldness of the religious proclamation of the apostles, who were not formally educated in religious matters or in the Law of Moses, the Sanhedrin authorities blusteringly cut short debate and arbitrarily order Peter and John not to speak in the name of Jesus (4:18). Peter cannot be silent about Christ. Subsequently, when released Peter and John return and report to their fellow believers what had happened—a report consisting of a triumphal prayer of praise to God (Acts 4:23–31). Then, all were filled with the Holy Spirit and continued to speak the word of God with boldness (4:31).

A summary (4:32–35) emphasizes the harmony and generosity of the koinōnia. Special mention is made of Joseph "Barnabas," who sold a field and brought the money to the apostles to contribute to the common fund. By contrast, another incident focuses on a couple, Ananias and Sapphira (5:1–11), who conspire to hold back a portion of the proceeds from goods that they had sold, claiming they were contributing everything to the common fund. Peter confronts them for their Satan-inspired lying to God/Holy Spirit. When rebuked by Peter, both drop dead. Luke reports that a great fear came upon the fellowship, which for the first time in Acts is called "the church."

The second confrontation of the apostles with the Sanhedrin (5:12–42) has many parallels with the first. Now, many signs and wonders are involved. The high priests and the Sadducees have the apostles arrested, but an angel releases them. The Sanhedrin has to have them arrested again. The high priest reprimands them for "teaching in this name." Peter expresses his defiance of the high priest with a memorable line: "We must obey God rather than human beings," and then gives a christological sermon as though he hoped to convert the Sanhedrin.

The Sanhedrin members were enraged and wanted to kill the apostles, but a famous Pharisee of the time, named Gamaliel I, intervened. Debates about the historicity of this speech (Did it happen? Did it happen as presented in Acts?) are endless. Acts to this point has not mentioned Pharisees as opposed to the followers of Jesus. And now, Gamaliel the Pharisee advocates tolerance for them. He advises, "If this work is from human beings, it will fail; if it is from God, you will not be able to overthrow it. You might even be found opposing God!" The apostles are beaten, charged not to speak in Jesus' name, and released; and tacitly the Sanhedrin adopts the policy of leaving them alone, so that "every day in the Temple and from house to house they did not cease teaching and preaching Jesus as the Christ" (5:42).

5. The Hellenists: Toleration; Stephen's Trial and Martyrdom (6:1–8:1a). After Gamaliel's speech, Acts recalls that the branch of the Jerusalem church associated with the Twelve was not persecuted. This is not to say that the Hellenist branch was not persecuted (see 8:1), but in that persecution the apostles were not bothered.

Nevertheless, removal of external threat did not mean all was well. *Acts 6:1–6 tells us about a hostile division among Jerusalem Christians.* Two groups of Jewish believers within the Jerusalem community are fighting over the common goods. One group, the Hellenists (Greek-like), were Greek-speaking and hellenized. The other group, the Hebrews, were Aramaic-speaking and more culturally Jewish. Beyond cultural difference apparently there was also a theological difference. The apostles and other Hebrew Christians have not let faith in Jesus stop them from worshipping in the Temple (2:46; 3:1; 5:12,21). But Stephen, who will become the Hellenist leader, speaks as if the Temple has no more meaning (7:48–50). The disagreement among these Jerusalem Christians has been translated into finances, so that the Hebrews are attempting to force the Hellenists to conformity by shutting off common funds from the Hellenist widows, who presumably were totally dependent on this support. To address this situation the Twelve summon the assembly of the disciples to settle the issue. They propose that the Hellenists have their own leaders and administrators of common goods.

A summary (6:7) about the spread of the word of God and the conversion of priests sets the stage for a conflict centered on Stephen (6:8–8:1a). The first-ranking among the Hellenists, Stephen stirs up opposition at a Jerusalem synagogue attended largely by foreign Jews. These opponents instigate others and concoct (false) charges that Stephen is preaching against Moses and God and against the Temple and the Law, and specifically saying that Jesus would destroy the Temple sanctuary and change Mosaic customs. In his long speech (7:2–53) in response to the Temple charge, Stephen concludes with the climactic statement: "The Most High does not dwell in houses made with hands" (7:48).

Stephen's speech surveys salvation history from Abraham to Moses (and Joshua), and then jumps to David and Solomon, before referring to the prophets and the Righteous One. Elements in the speech do not seem to reflect standard understanding of the OT. The speech ends in polemic, and Stephen enrages his hearers. He is cast out of the city and stoned to death (7:54–60). Strikingly the death of Stephen in Acts matches closely the death of Jesus in Luke: the Son of Man at the right hand of God (Luke 22:69; Acts 7:56); a prayer for forgiveness (Luke 23:34a; Acts 7:60); and the dying figure committing his spirit heavenward (Luke 23:46; Acts 7:59). Just as Jesus' death was not the end, neither is Stephen's—observing is a young man named Saul (7:58), who is later known in Acts as Paul (13:9). He consents to the death (8:1a), but in God's providence he will continue the work of Stephen as the story continues in Acts.

Mission in Samaria and Judea (8:1b–12:25)

1. Dispersal from Jerusalem; Philip and Peter in Samaria (8: 1b–25). Witness has been borne in Jerusalem culminating in the death of Stephen and the scattering of the Hellenists, who now preach in Judea and Samaria (8:1b; 9:31), not by plan but because of persecution. According to Acts 8:5 the Hellenists (Philip in particular) go to

Samaria and proclaim Christ to non-Jews. Philip is well received. Many Samaritans believe and are baptized. The Jerusalem church sends Peter and John there to pray for the Samaritans who have not yet received the Holy Spirit. The apostles lay hands on the Samaritans and they receive the Holy Spirit. While traveling back to Jerusalem Peter and John themselves preach to Samaritans (8:25).

2. Philip and the Ethiopian Eunuch En Route to Gaza (8:26–40). Philip evangelizes further in the southern part of Judea, manifesting geographical spread. The Ethiopian eunuch (probably not from modern Ethiopia), minister to the queen, is reading Isaiah. Philip interprets the prophet for the eunuch in order to explain Christ. Although Deut 23:1 rules out the admission of the castrated "to the assembly of the Lord," Philip has no hesitation about meeting the request of the eunuch to be baptized into the community of the renewed Israel.

3. Saul En Route to Damascus; Return to Jerusalem and Tarsus (9:1–30). Acts is very interested in recounting Saul's (Paul's) conversion effected by Jesus himself. The dramatic touches of the story are superb, for example, the personalizing of Saul's hostility in 9:4, "Saul, Saul, why do you persecute me?" Acts is very careful to report that Saul received the Holy Spirit (9:17), for Paul's proclamation will eventually be as potent as that of Peter and the others who received the Spirit at Pentecost. As they do, he will stress christological belief, preaching that "Jesus is the Son of God" (9:20). His great mission will be described later, after the author tells us more about Peter; the overlapping of the two figures helps to show that the same gospel is preached by both.

4. Peter at Lydda, Joppa, Caesarea, and Back to Jerusalem (9:31–11:18). With the church at peace Peter returns to the fore. Peter's cure of Aeneas at Lydda (9:32–35), with the command to rise, echoes closely Jesus' cure of the paralyzed man (Luke 5:24–26). Even more closely Peter's revivification of Tabitha at Joppa (9:36–43) resembles Jesus' action in raising the daughter of Jairus (Luke 8:49–56). Now, however, what Peter does next will start a chain of actions that will eventually take Christianity outside Judaism to Gentiles and to Rome, the representative of the end of the earth.

In 10:1–48 the author recounts how Peter is led by the Spirit to baptize Cornelius (and his household), a devout Gentile "who feared God . . . , gave alms generously to the people, and prayed continually to God." *In 11:1–18 Peter repeats what happened with a first-person report* as he defends his behavior before the Jerusalem Christians. There are heavenly revelations to both Cornelius and Peter, thus what occurs here is uniquely God's will. Two issues arise: First, were Christians bound by the Jewish rules for kosher foods? The thesis that in God's eyes all foods are ritually clean (10:15) constitutes a major break from Jewish practice. Second, did *Gentiles* have to be circumcised to receive baptism and the grace of Christ? Those who insisted that Gentiles needed to be circumcised (that is, become Jews) were maintaining that being a Jew had primacy over faith in Christ in terms of God's grace. Peter is pictured as rejecting that by word and deed in 10:34–49. Acts 10:44–48 describes the acceptance of Cornelius as a major step, accompanied by an outpouring of the Spirit manifested through speaking in tongues, comparable to Pentecost.

The radical character of what Peter has done and proclaimed is challenged in 11:2–3 by confreres in the Jerusalem church—whose objection is unclear. Peter answers this Christian "circumcision party" by telling about his visions and the coming of the Spirit upon Cornelius' household.

5. Antioch; Jerusalem; Herod's Persecution; Peter's Departure (11:19–12:25). The author picks up the Hellenists' story broken off in chap. 8, when they were scattered from Jerusalem at the time of Stephen's death. Belatedly we are told that they went also to Phoenicia, Cyprus, and Antioch, preaching at first only to Jews but then gradually to Gentiles as well. Thus, while the Jerusalem church in the person of Peter is taking the first steps toward admitting a few Gentiles, seemingly the aggressive effort to convert Gentiles began with the Hellenists, so that Antioch develops as a second great Christian center, more vibrantly involved in mission. Acts tells of many developments: the reader learns that Barnabas (see 4:32–35) brings Saul into the work of the Antioch church; that the Jewish king Herod Agrippa I persecutes the believers in Jerusalem and puts to death James, son of Zebedee, brother of John, and one of the Twelve; that in this persecution Peter is arrested but an angel releases him; that the pressure of the persecution forces Peter to leave Jerusalem for a time; and that King Herod Agrippa dies horribly, being eaten by worms.

The *stories of difficulties at Jerusalem end on a triumphal note* (12:24–25): the persecutor has fallen; God's word grows and multiplies; and Barnabas and Saul bring back John Mark to Antioch.

Missions of Barnabas and Saul Converting Gentiles;
Approval at Jerusalem (13:1–15:35)

1. Antioch Church Sends Barnabas and Saul; Mission to Cyprus and SE Asia Minor (13:1–14:28). A *short description of the church at Antioch* (13:1–3) shows that if Jerusalem has apostles (that is, the Twelve), Antioch has prophets and teachers, among whom Acts places Barnabas and Saul. Barnabas is listed first and Saul last; during the mission the order reverses to Paul and Barnabas (for example, 13:13,43).

In the context of a worship service Barnabas and Saul are commissioned through the laying on of hands by the church of Antioch for a mission. Along with John Mark, *Barnabas and Saul go to Cyprus* (13:4–12), Barnabas' home territory, where they speak in Jewish synagogues. The move from *Cyprus to Antioch of Pisidia in Asia Minor* (13:13–50) gives the author an opportunity to make what happened in Pisidian Antioch almost an exemplar of the Pauline mission. There Paul (henceforth so named) gives a synagogue sermon appealing to the OT and summarizing what God did in Jesus in a manner that is not unlike the sermons preached earlier by Peter. The sermon meets with success among "many Jews and devout proselytes," but on the following Sabbath there is hostility from "the Jews" so that Paul and Barnabas shift their appeal to the Gentiles.

The hostility continues, and Paul and Barnabas are driven from Pisidia and have to *move on to Iconium* (13:51–14:5)—"filled with joy and the Holy Spirit" (13:52). They remain there a long time and things turn out much the same; once again they have to *move on*—this time to *the Lycaonian cities of Lystra and Derbe* (14:6–21a). Paul heals a man crippled from birth (as Peter had done in 3:1–10)—and there is vivid Gentile reaction, hailing Barnabas and Paul as the gods Zeus and Hermes. Oddly, despite the display of enthusiasm, Jews from Antioch and Iconium arouse the hostility of the crowds, and Paul is stoned and left for dead (see II Cor 11:23–27). But Paul recovers and goes with Barnabas to Derbe. *The two retrace their steps through Asia Minor and then sail back to Syrian Antioch* (14:21b–28). They report to the church of Antioch: "God opened a door of faith to the Gentiles" (14:26–27).

2. Jerusalem Conference and Approval; Return to Antioch (15: 1–35).

What Paul has done does not please *the circumcision party at Jerusalem who now send people to Antioch* (15:1) to challenge the acceptance of Gentiles without circumcision. Paul's opponents cause so much trouble that *Paul and Barnabas have to go to Jerusalem* (15:2–3) to debate the issue. This *Jerusalem conference* (15:4–29) may be judged the most important meeting in the history of Christianity, for there implicitly it was decided that the following of Jesus would soon move beyond Judaism and become a separate religion reaching to the end of the earth.

We are fortunate to have two accounts of the meeting, one in Acts 15, the other in Gal 2. Some dismiss the Acts account, but each has its own optic. Acts does simplify and report less acrimony, but Paul purposefully gives a personal version of the meeting as he writes in difficult circumstances. Acts indicates that those in Jerusalem had the power of decision on the issue. Paul speaks disparagingly of the "so-called pillars" whose reputation meant nothing to him; but that very title implies that their reputation did mean something to others, and in the long run Paul could not stand alone.

The public disputation at Jerusalem is the core of the story. Four participants are involved—two predictable (on opposite sides: the circumcision advocates and Paul), one less predictable (Peter), and one unpredictable (James). Paul recounts deeds done among the Gentiles, which surely means an account of how such people had come to faith without circumcision. Peter's argument is also experiential: God had sent the Holy Spirit on the uncircumcised Cornelius. James' argument is reasoned and, as might be expected from a conservative Hebrew Christian, draws on the Scriptures: the prophets foretold that the Gentiles would come, and the Law of Moses allowed uncircumcised Gentiles to live among the people of God provided that they abstained from certain listed pollutions. Unfortunately we do not hear the arguments advanced by the circumcision party, other than the simple statement in Acts 15:5 that the Law of Moses required circumcision.

In any case, both Acts and Gal agree that Peter (and John) and James kept the koinōnia with Paul and his Gentile churches. The road was now open for free and effective evangelizing to the end of the earth. In fact that road would also lead away from Judaism.

Now *Paul and Barnabas go back to Antioch* (15:30–35), carrying a letter of clarification that circumcision was not to be required of Gentile converts. The letter required the Gentiles to abstain from four things proscribed by Lev 17–18 for aliens living among Israel: meat offered to idols; the eating of blood; the eating of strangled (nonkosher) animals; and incestuous unions (*porneia*, here with kin). This is the position that James advocated when he spoke at the Jerusalem conference (15:20). When we compare the picture to Paul's account in Gal 2:11–14[21], we realize that the history was more complicated.

Mission of Paul to the End of the Earth (15:36–28:31)

The second half of Acts now becomes almost exclusively the story of Paul, covering the years AD 50–58. After Jerusalem and Antioch he seems to be more on his own throughout what appears to have been the most creative time of his life.

1. From Antioch Through Asia Minor to Greece and Return (15:36–18:22). Acts reports *Paul's quarrel with Barnabas and Mark* (15:36–39), so that they could no longer travel together. Consequently, *Paul takes Silas as he sets out on another mission* (15:40–41), the first part of which brings him through Syria and his native Cilicia. Next *Paul revisits Lystra and Derbe* (16:1–5). That visit is the occasion of the circumcision of Timothy (the historicity of which is questioned by some who think it inconceivable that Paul would have changed his stance on circumcision even to win converts).

Paul moves on through Phyrigia and Galatia to Troas (16:6–10). In the latter site he receives a vision of a man of Macedonia pleading for help that causes him to cross over to Greece. The author of Acts sees this as a divinely inspired moment. The spread of Christian faith to Macedonia (and thus to Europe) is presented almost as manifest destiny. In v. 10 the first of several striking uses of the pronoun "we" (and "us") in parts of Acts occurs. Whether this shift in narrative style indicates the involvement of the author of Acts in the events being related is disputed. These "we" passages appear in the story here and in three additional places, often telling of travel: 16:10–17 (from Troas to Philippi, launching the early European ministry); 20:5–15 (from Philippi to Miletus after another visit to Philippi); 21:1–18 (from Miletus to Jerusalem [and James]); and 27:1–28:16 (from Caesarea to Rome, with Paul as a prisoner having made an appeal to Caesar).

The evangelizing at Philippi (16:11–40) shows us some of the best and the worst of a mission among Gentiles. Lydia, a Gentile worshiper of God, in her generous openness and support is a model for the Christian household. In contrast, the situation with the slave girl who has a spirit of divination reminds us that Paul was dealing with a crass, alien, superstitious world. The miraculous prison scene echoes prior experiences of Peter in Jerusalem and shows God's care, even advancing the missionary undertaking. The legal situation in which Paul and Silas find themselves, indicted before the magistrates for causing a riot and promoting unlawful religion, is different from the more turbulent circumstances they have faced before; here they may use their Roman citizenship for protection. Though they receive an apology, they are asked to leave the city.

At Thessalonica (17:1–9) Paul meets Jewish opposition of the kind that marred his mission in Asia Minor. Thus, *Paul goes on to Beroea* (17:10–14), where the author tells us that the Jews were nobler and less contentious. Yet the Thessalonian Jews follow, and so *Paul pushes on to Athens* (17:15–34). The author shows an appreciation of what Athens meant to Greek culture. He phrases Paul's sermon delivered there in quality Greek and has it show an awareness of the many temples and statues of the city. The clever reference to the inscription on the altar regarding an unknown god, and the philosophical and poetic quotations, offer a cultured approach to the message about Christ. The master touch may be the reaction of this cosmopolitan audience to this eloquence: some mock; others put Paul off; some believe.

Paul's stay at Corinth (18:1–18) begins with his meeting there with Priscilla (Prisca) and Aquila. They had come from Rome (probably already as Christians) and will eventually return there and be part of Paul's contacts with Rome before he ever arrives there (Rom 16:3). Again there is Jewish hostility, and Paul is brought before the tribunal of the Roman proconsul Gallio—whose time at Corinth we know to have been AD 51–52, so that we can date Paul's mission there. Gallio's unwillingness to get involved in Jewish religious issues is part of the general picture of the pre-Nero period when Rome was not hostile to Christians as such. The *return from Corinth to Antioch* (18:19–22) is compressed into a brief, confusing account.

2. From Antioch to Ephesus and Greece, and Return to Caesarea (18:23–21:14). After a while *Paul sets out from Antioch through Galatia and*

Phrygia (18:23). While he is en route, we are told of the presence at Ephesus of Apollos from Alexandria (18:24–28) and then at the beginning of Paul's stay at Ephesus (19:1–40[41]) of others, who believed in Jesus but had received only the baptism of John and knew nothing of the Holy Spirit. Paul remains at Ephesus about three years. The refrain that "the word of the Lord grew" (19:20) signals that, alongside Jerusalem and Antioch, Christianity now has another major center, Ephesus. Acts 19:21 is the first indication of Paul's ultimate plan to go to Rome via Greece and Jerusalem. A colorful account of the silversmiths' riot centered on Artemis of Ephesus (19:23–40[41]) terminates Paul's stay.

Paul travels through Macedonia to Greece (20:1–3a), that is, Corinth, where he stays three months. Then he goes back through Macedonia and Philippi (2:3b–6) to Troas where he raises the dead to life (20:7–12), as Peter raised Tabitha in Joppa (9:36–42). Hastening on to Jerusalem for Pentecost (AD 58), Paul sails along the Asia Minor coast to Miletus, bypassing Ephesus (20:13–16). At Miletus he gives an eloquent farewell sermon to the presbyters of the church of Ephesus (20:17–38). The sermon constitutes Paul's final directives to those whom he will never see again (20:25,38).

After this farewell at Miletus, the return journey to Palestine continues, bringing Paul to Tyre (21:1–6) and another dramatic farewell, and then on to Caesarea (21:7–14). At the home of Philip the Hellenist and his four daughter-prophets, the prophet Agabus comes and by symbolism forewarns Paul of imprisonment.

3. Arrest in Jerusalem; Imprisonment and Trials in Caesarea (21: 15–26:32). A climax is reached when Paul goes up to Jerusalem (21:15–17), where he is received by James and the elders (21:18–25) and reports to them his success among the Gentiles. They too report great successes among the Jews. Acts cannot disguise the negative feelings raised among the Jerusalem Christian authorities by (false) rumors about what Paul has been teaching. The ill-advised plan to have Paul show his loyalty to Judaism by purifying himself and going to the Temple (21:24) fails when fanatics start a riot, claiming that he has defiled the holy place (21:26–30) by bringing Gentiles into it. Paul is saved from the crowd only by the intervention of a Roman tribune with soldiers (21:31–40). While being arrested, Paul protests in Greek and is allowed to speak in Aramaic to the crowd.

Paul's speech of defense (22:1–21) recounts his calling and its aftermath (with variations from the original in 9:1–30—cf. 9:7 and 22:9). The *speech produces conflict* (22:22–29): the crowd reacts violently and the tribune intends to examine Paul by flogging, but he wins protection when he reveals his Roman citizenship. *The next day Paul is brought before a Sanhedrin* (22:30–23:11), where he creates controversy between Sadducees and Pharisees over the resurrection of the dead. Violent dissension arises, and the tribune has Paul removed from the melee. At night a vision of the Lord encourages Paul and informs him that he would have to testify in Rome. Paul's nephew frustrates a *Jewish plot to kill Paul* (23:12–22), and *Paul is sent to Caesarea and the Roman prefect Felix* (23:23–25). *Paul's trial before Felix* (24:1–27) has parallels to the trial of Jesus before Pilate. Accusations (false), denials, and explanations take place; but no action is taken and Paul remains in prison for two years (until the end of Felix's procuracy) because Felix hopes for a bribe (24:26).

Paul is interrogated by Festus (25:1–12), the next procurator, who ruled in AD 60–62; but he refuses to be tried in Jerusalem and appeals to Caesar. Paul's appeal is honored. *Festus passes Paul to the Herodian king Agrippa II, great-grandson of Herod the Great, to be heard* (25:13–26:32), even as Pilate sent Jesus to Herod Antipas (Luke 23:7). Paul's story is recounted a third time (26:9–20), and again a Herodian king finds the prisoner not guilty.

4. Journey to Rome as a Prisoner (27:1–28:14a). Acts now recounts a long sea journey, including a great storm and finally an arrival at Italy, landing at Puteoli. This voyage probably began in the late summer of 60 and ended in 61. Paul's survival during this adventure illustrates God's care, which is reflected in Paul's concern for others. (Some view this whole episode as unhistorical.)

5. Paul at Rome (28:14b–31). Paul's arrival after his long and treacherous sea journey is described in a portentous understatement, "And so we came to Rome" (28:14b). By this time in the early 60s, Christian communities had been in Rome for about twenty years. But in the story told in Acts, with the arrival in the capital of the great missionary, the ultimate step foreseen by the risen Jesus is fulfilled: "You will be my witnesses . . . *to the end of the earth*" (1:8). To the end Acts shows Paul appealing to the local Jews, though Paul's preaching about Jesus has no success; and the last words attributed to him in the book, despairing of a hearing from the Jews, firmly turn to the Gentiles who will listen. The summary that ends Acts speaks of Paul's preaching for two years in Rome with success.

SOURCES AND COMPOSITIONAL FEATURES

Under this heading we shall consider the various elements that make up Acts:

TRADITIONS AND/OR SOURCES. Noting how the Lucan evangelist acknowledged traditions and used sources, scholars debate the degree of the author's creativity in Acts—some defend historicity and others posit degrees of fictitiousness. Since the author indicates a consistency by dedicating both volumes of Luke-Acts to Theophilus, there is no reason to think that the tracing of everything carefully from the beginning promised by Luke 1:3 stopped with the Gospel. Accordingly, one wonders: what fonts did the evangelist have for traditions he included or developed in Acts? Did he have written or, at least, already shaped sources for Acts?

If the author was the companion of Paul in the "we" passages of Acts and/or if the tradition is accurate that the author was Luke from Antioch, the author would have met people who could have supplied certain stories in Acts. Scholars, however, suggest various explanations for the "we" passages: (1) The "we" passages are historical and the author was directly involved in the events that are recounted from the point of view of the "we" passages. (2) The use of "we" is a literary device, a recognizable convention employed by the author of Acts for the narration of travel, especially sea voyages. (3) The "we" passages come from a diary kept by one of Paul's companions and subsequently used by the author of Acts in pertinent portions of the story being told (perhaps even the author's own diary). After careful weighing of the evidence, there are still prominent scholars who defend each of these interpretations. Furthermore, fixed sources have been proposed: A Jerusalem Source (covering the apostles in Jerusalem); an Antioch Source (covering the Hellenists in Antioch); and a Pauline Source (covering Paul and his missions). There is little evidence that the author of Acts was present for much of what he narrates (except the "we" passages), and little likelihood that he invented all of it; and so he must have had at his disposal information or traditions.

But had such traditions already been shaped into sequential sources? Arguments from style are not overly convincing, for this author is capable of writing in a variety of styles, suitable for the situation or setting in the narrative. Other scholars find Lucan style and vocabulary in various sections of Acts, so that whether the author used loose traditions or fixed sources, he could have rewritten the material he took over. Nothing like the wide agreement on the Gospel's use of the sources Mark and Q exists for Acts' use of sources. Whether Acts drew on traditions or sources, a fundamental issue remains: What is the historical value of the final account?

SPEECHES. Roughly one-third of Acts consists of speeches, made principally by Peter, Stephen, Paul, and James. Instead of describing in the third person the significance of something that is happening, Acts prefers to offer a speech where one of the main characters explains that significance. Why? Some regard it as a literary device. Others understand it as a technique of ancient historiographers. Thucydides (History 1.22.1) says that although he kept as close as possible to the general sense of the words that were said, he had the speakers say what, in his view, was called for by the situation. Lucian of Samosata (How to Write History 58) advised that if someone had to be brought in to make a speech, above all his language should suit his person and subject, and then the writer of history could exercise his rhetoric and show his eloquence. Certain conservative interpreters suggest that important speeches were memorized by the speaker's disciples who were present. Others think there was no real memory so that the speeches are virtually pure Lucan creation. Still others opt for different approaches to different speeches in Acts—seeing some speeches as free compositions of the author and other speeches as working with memories preserved in the life of the early church. Whatever the derivation of the material in the speeches, above all they serve to develop the theological thrust of Acts by expressing Christian insight into God's plan of history.

SUMMARIES. In the Gospel Luke used and developed some of Mark's summaries as well as adding his own. Acts uses summary statements to portray the growth and sanctity of the community in its golden age (2:42–47), and to mark off steps in the development of the action (9:31). These transitions both enhance the readability of Acts and involve the author's knowledge of the early church, which again raises the issue of the accuracy of such knowledge.

.⊹.

11

The Gospel According to John

A better appreciation of John comes in part through understanding some significant stylistic features of the Gospel. After that discussion, the *General Analysis* will examine the present form of the Fourth Gospel, before theorizing about influences on John's thought.

STYLISTIC FEATURES

John is a Gospel where style and theology are intimately wedded.

Poetic format. Many scholars recognize a formal poetic style in a few parts of John, for example, the Prologue (1:1–18) and John 17. Some scholars perceive in the Johannine discourses a uniquely solemn semi-poetic pattern marked by rhythm.

Misunderstanding. Jesus, the Word become flesh, must use earthly words to convey his message of what is "true" or "real" (heavenly). Thus, he uses figurative/metaphorical language that in dialogue is understood by his conversation partner in a merely material manner, which allows Jesus to explain his thought more thoroughly and thereby to unfold his doctrine (for example, 2:19–21).

SUMMARY OF BASIC INFORMATION

DATE: 80–110. Those who think that the Gospel was redacted (edited) by another hand after the main writer composed it may place the body of the Gospel in the 90s and the additions of the redactor ca. 100–110, about the same time as III John.

TRADITIONAL (SECOND-CENTURY) ATTRIBUTION: To John, son of Zebedee, one of the Twelve.

AUTHOR DETECTABLE FROM THE CONTENTS: One who regards himself in the tradition of the disciple whom Jesus loved. If one posits a redactor, he too may have been in the same tradition. Plausibly there was a school of Johannine writing disciples.

PLACE OF WRITING: Traditionally and plausibly the Ephesus area, but some opt for Syria.

UNITY: Some think sources (collections of "signs"; collection of discourses; passion narrative) were combined; others think of a process of several editions. In either case, plausibly the body of the Gospel was completed by one writer, and a redactor later made additions (chap. 21; perhaps 1:1–18); but no text of the Gospel has been preserved without these "additions."

INTEGRITY: The story of the woman caught in adultery (7:53–8:11) is an insertion missing from many mss.

DIVISION:

1:1–18: PROLOGUE: AN INTRODUCTION TO AND SUMMARY OF THE CAREER OF THE INCARNATE WORD

1:19–12:50: PART ONE: THE BOOK OF SIGNS: THE WORD REVEALS HIMSELF TO THE WORLD AND TO HIS OWN, BUT THEY DO NOT ACCEPT HIM.

1. Initial days of the revelation of Jesus to his disciples under different titles (1:19–2:11).

2. First to second Cana miracle; themes of replacement and of reactions to Jesus (chaps. 2–4): changing water to wine, cleansing the Temple, Nicodemus, the Samaritan woman at the well, healing the royal official's son.

3. Old Testament feasts and their replacement; themes of life and light (chaps. 5–10):
   Sabbath—Jesus, the new Moses, replaces the Sabbath ordinance to rest (5:1–47);
   Passover—the Bread of Life (revelatory wisdom and the eucharist) replaces the manna (6:1–71);
   Tabernacles—the Source of living water and the Light of the world, replaces the water and light ceremonies (7:1–10:21);
   Dedication—Jesus is consecrated in place of the Temple altar (10:22–42).

4. The raising of Lazarus and its aftermath (chaps. 11–12): Lazarus raised to life, Jesus condemned to death by the Sanhedrin, Lazarus's sister Mary anoints Jesus for burial, entry to Jerusalem, the end of the public ministry and the coming of the hour signaled by the arrival of Gentiles.

**13:1–20:31: PART TWO: THE BOOK OF GLORY: TO THOSE WHO
ACCEPT HIM, THE WORD SHOWS HIS GLORY BY RETURNING TO
THE FATHER IN DEATH, RESURRECTION, AND ASCENSION. FULLY
GLORIFIED, HE COMMUNICATES THE SPIRIT OF LIFE.**

1. The Last Supper and Jesus' Last Discourse (chaps. 13–17):
   (a) The Last Supper (chap. 13): the meal, washing of the feet, Judas'
   betrayal, introduction to discourse (love commandment, Peter's
   denials foretold);
   (b) Jesus' Last Discourse (chaps. 14–17):
   Division One (chap. 14): Jesus' departure, divine indwelling, the
   Paraclete;
   Division Two (chaps. 15–16): vine and branches, the world's hatred, witness by the Paraclete, repeated themes of Division One;
   Division Three (chap. 17): the "Priestly" Prayer.
2. Jesus' passion and death (chaps. 18–19): arrest, inquiry before Annas
   with Peter's denials, trial before Pilate, crucifixion, death, and burial.
3. The resurrection (20:1–29): four scenes in Jerusalem (two at the tomb,
   two inside a room).
   Gospel Conclusion (20:30–31): Statement of purpose in writing.

**21:1–25: EPILOGUE: GALILEAN RESURRECTION
APPEARANCES; SECOND CONCLUSION.**

Twofold meanings. Sometimes a double meaning can be found in what
Jesus says. (a) He may use ambiguous words or terms—the dialogue partner takes one meaning, while Jesus means another (*anōthen*
in 3:3,7—"again" or "from above"). (b) The author frequently intends the reader to see several layers of meaning in the same metaphor
("Lamb of God" in 1:29,36—apocalyptic lamb, paschal lamb, and suffering servant who went like a lamb to slaughter).

Irony. Sometimes the opponents of Jesus make statements about him
that they intend to be derogatory, sarcastic, or incredulous. By way
of irony, however, these statements are often true in a sense that the
speakers do not realize (3:2; 7:35; 11:50).

Inclusions. The careful structure of the Gospel is indicated by certain
techniques. An inclusion means that John mentions a detail (or makes
an allusion) at the end of a section that matches a similar detail at the
beginning of the section (2:11 with 4:54; 11:4 with 11:40).

Parentheses or footnotes. Frequently John supplies parenthetical notes,
explaining Semitic terms or names (for example, "Messiah" in 1:41),

offering background information (for example, 2:9), and even supplying theological perspectives (for example, 2:21–22—temple/body).

GENERAL ANALYSIS OF THE MESSAGE

The Gospel is carefully arranged to illustrate themes chosen by the
evangelist.

Prologue (1:1–18)

Serving as a preface to the Gospel, the Prologue is a hymn that
encapsulates John's view of Christ. A divine being (God's Word, the
light, and God's only Son) comes into the world and becomes flesh.
Although rejected by his own, he empowers all who do accept him
to become God's children—a gift reflecting God's enduring love that
outdoes the loving gift of the Law through Moses. The background of
this description of the Word descending into the world and the even-
tual return of the Son to the Father's side lies in the mythological OT
picture of personified Wisdom (Sirach 24 and Wisdom 9) who was
with God at the creation of the world and came to dwell with human
beings when the Law was revealed to Moses.

Part One: The Book of Signs (1:19–12:50)

This part of the Gospel shows Jesus bringing different types of people to believe in him while at the same time provoking many among
"the Jews" to hostility. [It is important to note that the evangelist may be a
Jew by birth; yet most often he uses this expression, "the Jews," with a
hostile tone for those of Jewish birth who distrust or reject Jesus and/
or his followers. "The Jews" include Jewish authorities but cannot be
confined to them. The generalizing term may be an attempt to portray
the Jewish opponents in the synagogue of John's time—opponents
who are persecuting John's community (16:2) even as Jewish opponents in Jesus' time were remembered as persecuting him. Consequently, most often "the Jews" seem to be a disliked group separate
from the followers of Jesus; and Jesus at times speaks as a non-Jew (or,
at least, not as one of those "Jews"): "written in your Law" (10:34);
"in their Law" (15:25); "as I said to the Jews" (13:33).] At the end of the

Book of Signs (12:39–40) the Gospel quotes Isa 6:10 to the effect that God has blinded their eyes and hardened their hearts that they might not see.

1. Initial Days of the Revelation of Jesus to His Disciples Under Different Titles (1:19–2:11). In a pattern of separate days (1:29,35,43; 2:1) John shows a gradual recognition of who Jesus is. Christological titles abound: the Lamb of God, God's chosen one/Son, teacher, Messiah, the one described in the Mosaic Law and the prophets, the Son of God, the King of Israel—and Jesus refers to himself as the Son of Man.

The quantity of christological titles appearing here, while scattered in the other Gospels, almost makes it seem that the evangelist is portraying as elementary the christological tradition known to other Gospels and beginning his Gospel at a stage where the others end. In this opening chap. followers become disciples—then, in a consistent pattern disciples go out to proclaim Jesus to others with a christological perception deepened through that very action.

2. First to Second Cana Miracle (chaps. 2–4). The Cana scene is "the first of his signs" (2:11). The theme of replacement runs through Jesus' actions and words in the three chapters of this section.

In the initial Cana miracle (2:1–11), which John calls a sign, Jesus replaces the water prescribed for Jewish purification by wine so good that the headwaiter wonders why the best has been kept until last. (The mother of Jesus who appears here will reappear at the foot of the cross, where her incorporation into discipleship will be completed [19:25–27]).

In Jerusalem near Passover, the next subsection (2:13–22) treats Jesus' attitude toward the Temple. There are parallels to two Synoptic scenes: the cleansing of the Temple (Mark 11:15–19,27–28 and par.) and the false witnesses at the Sanhedrin trial on the night before the crucifixion, who testified that Jesus said he would destroy the Temple (Mark 14:58; Matt 26:61). In John the scenes are combined and placed early in the ministry. There are two peculiar Johannine theological emphases. The antagonism of "the Jews" from the beginning shows the utter incompatibility between Jesus and his own who do not receive him (1:11); also in John's interpretation the Temple is Jesus' body, "destroyed" by "the Jews" but raised up by Jesus, so that the Jerusalem Temple has been replaced by the body of Jesus as the true holy place.

The Nicodemus scene (3:1–21) is the first of the important Johannine dialogues. Nicodemus comes "at night," because he does not yet belong to the light, and acknowledges Jesus as a "teacher who has come from God" (divinely inspired), whereas Jesus has actually come from God. Thus Nicodemus is a representative of an inadequate faith. The dialogue becomes a monologue (he appears twice more: 7:50–52; 19:39–42). In 3:15–21 Jesus proclaims the basic Johannine theology of salvific incarnation: he is God's Son come into the world bringing God's own life, so that everyone who believes in him has eternal life.

JBap's final witness to Jesus (3:22–30), resuming 1:15,19–34, is in the context of Jesus' own baptizing. Here, JBap once more clarifies just who he is not and the greatness of the one for whom he has prepared.

Jesus goes from Judea toward Galilee in 4:1–3, and on the way he stops in Samaria at the well of Shechem/Sychar. The dialogue with the Samaritan woman and its aftermath (4:4–42) is the first full example of Johannine dramatic ability. Jesus speaks of water. The Samaritan woman understands only natural water, but Jesus is referring to his divine revelation and to the Holy Spirit who will be given as living water to those who accept that revelation. Further conversation produces further misunderstanding. The woman seeks to change the subject, ultimately shifting the focus to the distant future when the Messiah comes; but Jesus will not let her escape. His "I am (he)" confronts her with a current demand for faith. Indeed, the "I am" (Greek, egō eimi) formula that Jesus uses here and throughout the Gospel seems to echo Isa 43:10 LXX and other OT texts where "I am" occurs as the name of God. In turn, the woman goes off to the village and through her the villagers come to believe when they encounter Jesus (4:40–42). Their expression of faith reflects Johannine theology that all must come into personal contact with Jesus.

The second sign at Cana (4:43–54) terminates this subdivision. The transitional 4:43–45 sets up a contrast between the inadequate faith (based on miracles) of the Galileans and the faith in Jesus' word illustrated by the royal official in this story of the healing of his son. This prepares for a key saying in the next subdivision that the Son grants life to whomever he wishes (5:21).

3. OT Feasts and Their Replacement (chaps. 5–10). The theme
of life that will be developed in chaps. 5–7 will yield to the theme of
light in chaps. 8–10—both of them motifs anticipated in the Prologue.
A more dominant motif, however, is the sequence of Jewish feasts that
move through this subdivision (Sabbath, Passover, Tabernacles, Dedication), and on each something Jesus does or says to some extent replaces a significant aspect of the feast.

On the Sabbath Jesus heals and thus gives life, leading to a hostile dialogue (5:1–47).
Jesus cures a lame man who has been waiting to be healed at the pool
of Bethesda. Jesus' instruction to take up the mat does violate the Sabbath law. His explanation to "the Jews" is that God continues to work
on the Sabbath. God is Jesus' Father and the Father has given the Son
power over life and death. "The Jews" recognize that Jesus "was speaking of God as his Father, thus making himself God's equal" (5:18).
Thus, in John a lethal antipathy toward Jesus appears early and consistently, and a claim to divinity comes through clearly.

At Passover time Jesus multiplies the loaves and fish and gives a discourse on the Bread
of Life (6:1–71). There are two Synoptic accounts of the feeding, and
John's account shares certain details with each of them. The marvelous supply of food and Jesus' walking on the water may echo Moses'
miracles in the Exodus, even as the murmuring of 6:41 matches similar action of Israel in the desert. Jesus makes clear that he did not come
simply to satisfy earthly hunger but to give bread that would nourish
people for eternal life. A discourse follows that tells how this would be
done. First, one must believe in the Son to have eternal life. Second, one
must feed on his flesh and blood to have eternal life. Here (6:51), the
language is evocative of the eucharist. John (6:60–61,66) reports that
certain disciples complained of this "hard saying" and that "many of
his disciples broke away and would not accompany him any more."

The next Jewish feast, Tabernacles (Tents, Booths), seems to cover 7:1 to 10:21,
before the mention of the feast of Dedication in 10:22. Themes of
water and light played prominently during this feast. Jesus' dialogue
with "the Jews" (7:16–36) recalls previous hostility over violating the
Mosaic Law and involves the questioning of Jesus' authority. The Jewish authorities seek to arrest him, but that goes nowhere at this point
(7:32). Jesus announces that from within himself shall flow rivers of

living water, that is, the Spirit that would be received when he was glorified. Again there is a desire to arrest him (7:43–44), which brings Nicodemus back, defending Jesus but still not professing that he is a believer (7:50–52).

In the continuation in 8:12–59 Jesus proclaims himself to be "the light of the world," the replacement for the light theme of the feast. In sharp exchanges Jesus both gives defensive testimony against Jewish charges (for example, suggestions of his illegitimacy [8:41]), and asserts that the devil is the father of his opponents (8:44). The scene ends with one of the most awesome statements attributed to Jesus in the NT, "Before Abraham even came into existence, I AM" (8:58), which brings about an attempt to stone Jesus.

Chap. 9, describing how the man born blind came to see, is the masterpiece of Johannine dramatic narrative. Evidently the Tabernacles feast has kept Jesus in Jerusalem. The blind man, having washed in the waters of Siloam (interpreted as "the sent one," a Johannine designation for Jesus), exemplifies one who is enlightened on the first encounter, but comes to see who Jesus really is only later, after undergoing trials and being cast out of the synagogue (9:34): "the man called Jesus" (9:11); "he is a prophet" (9:17); ["Christ" (9:22)]; "he is from God" (9:33); "Lord" (9:38)—and "the Son of Man" (9:35). This Johannine drama could be a double-exposure: memories of Jesus during his ministry upon which later experiences of his followers have been superimposed.

In the narrative sequence the metaphorical discourse on the good shepherd (10:1–21) is directed to the Pharisees whom Jesus accused of being blind in 9:40–41. This and the description of the vine in 15: 1–17 are the closest that John comes to the parables so common in the Synoptics.

The next Jewish feast is Dedication (Hanukkah: 10:22–42), celebrating the dedication of the altar and the reconstruction of the Jerusalem Temple by the Maccabees (164 BC) after several years of desecration under Syrian rulers. This festal theme is replaced when in the Temple portico Jesus claims to be the one whom the Father consecrated and sent into the world (10:36). Questions about Jesus' identity as Messiah lead to his explicitly saying in several ways that he is God's Son, which is judged to be blasphemy by "the Jews," so that they attempt to arrest him, but he goes back across the Jordan to where the story began in 1:28, and where the witness of JBap still echoes (10:40–42).

4. The Raising of Lazarus and Its Aftermath (chaps. 11–12). *Jesus gives life to Lazarus* (11:1–44), thus performing the greatest of his signs. Paradoxically the gift of life leads to the decision of the Sanhedrin that Jesus must die (11:45–53), a decision that will bring about his glorious return to the Father. In the dialogue preceding the raising of Lazarus, Jesus leads Martha to a deeper faith. Jesus is the resurrection, but he also is the life, so that whoever believes in him will never die. Lazarus' being raised is but a sign, for he will die again. Jesus comes to give an eternal life impervious to death.

A Sanhedrin session (11:45–53) is provoked by the size of Jesus' follow-ing and the fear that the Romans might intervene to the detriment of the nation and the Temple. Caiaphas, high priest that year, spoke in a way that proved, ironically, to be prophetic: "Don't you realize that it is more to your advantage to have one man die in behalf of the people than to have the whole nation destroyed." Jesus' fate is sealed by the Sanhedrin who plan to kill him, and *the intermediary verses* (11:54–57) *prepare for the arrest at Passover.*

At Bethany six days before Passover, Mary, the sister of Lazarus, anoints Jesus' feet (12:1–11). The story has the motif of preparing Jesus for burial. In the scene on the next day when Jesus triumphantly enters Jerusalem (12:12–19), only John mentions palm branches. Jesus finds a young donkey to ride, thus pointing to the king promised in Zechariah who is to bring peace and salvation (Zech 9:9–10).

The end of the public ministry is signaled by the arrival of Gentiles (12:20–50), which causes Jesus to exclaim, "The hour has come" and to speak of a grain of wheat that dies in order to bear much fruit. The atmosphere resembles that of Jesus' prayer in Gethsemane on the night before he dies, in Mark 14:34–36. In both, Jesus' soul is troubled/sorrowful. In Mark he prays to the Father that the hour might pass from him; in John he refuses to pray to the Father that he might be saved from the hour since this is why he came—different reactions mirroring what would later be called the humanity and divinity of Jesus.

Part Two: The Book of Glory (13:1–20:31)

The theme of chaps. 13–20 is enunciated in 13:1 with the announcement that Jesus was aware that the hour had come for him to pass from this world to the Father, showing to the very end his love for his own who were in this world. Thus, this "Book" illustrates the theme of the Prologue (1:12–13): "But all those who did accept him he empowered to become God's children," that is, a new "his own" consisting of "those who believe in his name," not those who were his own people by birth.

1. The Last Supper and Jesus' Last Discourse (chaps. 13–17). In John, Jesus' discourse at supper on the night before he dies is much longer than in the Synoptics. Initially in the account of the Last Supper (chap. 13), John's narrative has parallels to Synoptic material where at table Jesus talks about Judas and warns (there or afterwards) that Simon Peter will deny him three times. Yet in place of Jesus' words over the bread and wine, John has the washing of the disciples' feet. Unique to John is the presence of "the disciple whom Jesus loved." Mentioned only in the Book of Glory, he is close to Jesus and contrasted with Peter.

After Judas has gone out Jesus speaks, issuing his new commandment: "As I have loved you, so you too must love one another." This is "new" not because the OT was lacking in love, but because of two peculiarly Christian modifications: The love is empowered and modeled on the way Jesus manifested love for the disciples, and it is a love to be extended to one's fellow Christian disciples.

In the body of Jesus' Last Discourse (chaps. 14–17) he speaks to "his own" as he contemplates his departure. In form and content the Discourse resembles a "testament" or farewell speech where a speaker announces his imminent departure, often producing sorrow; he recalls his past life, words, and deeds, urging the addressees to emulate and even surpass these, to keep the commandments, and to keep unity among themselves.

Division One of the Last Discourse (chap. 14). Stressing his departure, Jesus consoles his disciples by promising to return to take them to himself so that they may be with him. Some of his most striking statements come in these sections (for example, "I am the way and the truth and the life" and "Whoever has seen me has seen the Father . . . I am in the Father and the Father is in me").

Jesus also speaks of the Spirit as the Paraclete. Just as Jesus received everything from the Father and while on earth is the way to know the Father in heaven, so when Jesus goes to heaven, the Paraclete who receives everything from Jesus is the way to know Jesus. The Paraclete, however, does not become incarnate but dwells in all who love Jesus and keep his commandments and is with them forever. The Paraclete is in a hostile relationship to the world and serves as a teacher explaining the implications of what Jesus said.

Division Two of the Last Discourse (chaps. 15–16). That three chapters of Discourse follow 14:31c is surprising and has led some interpreters to suggest that a later editor inserted discourse material into the original work of the evangelist. Be that as it may, what follows here focuses on the subsections of the present Gospel.

15:1–17: The vine and the branches. Alongside the shepherd imagery of chap. 10, this is the other significant instance of Johannine parabolic/allegorical language. In the OT Israel is frequently pictured as God's vine or vineyard. Here Jesus portrays himself as the vine of the New Israel.

15:18–16:4a: The world's hatred; witness by the Paraclete. In contrast with Jesus' stress on love, he speaks of how the world hates him and those whom he has chosen out of the world.

16:4b–33: Themes resembling those of Division One (chap. 14). Jesus reiterates what he said at the beginning of the Discourse, although whereas earlier the Father was said to give or send the Paraclete (14:16,26), now Jesus is said to send him (16:7)—an illustration of Jesus' claim that the Father and he are one (10:30).

Division Three of the Last Discourse (chap. 17). This sublime conclusion to the Last Discourse is often evaluated as the "Priestly" Prayer of Jesus, the one who consecrated himself for those whom he would send into the world (17:18–19). First (17:1–8), Jesus prays for glorification so that the Son may glorify the Father properly. Second (17:9–19), Jesus prays for those whom the Father has given him. Third (17:20–26),

Jesus prays for those who believe in him through the words of the disciples.

2. Jesus' Passion and Death (chaps. 18–19). Here John is closer to the overall Synoptic outline than elsewhere.

Arrest in the garden across the Kidron (18:1–12). The Synoptics refer to Gethsemane and/or the Mount of Olives, but John speaks of Jesus crossing the Kidron valley to a garden. This scene centers on the arrest, with Jesus eager to drink the cup the Father has given him. Jesus goes out to meet Judas; and when he identifies himself to the arresting party with the words "I am," the Jewish police and Roman soldiers fall back to the ground.

Interrogation by Annas; Peter's denials (18:13–27). The four Gospels have Jesus delivered to the high priest's palace for interrogation—along with accounts of abuse/mockery of Jesus and of Peter's three denials. There is no Sanhedrin session in John (cf. 11:45–53), and although Caiaphas is mentioned, Annas conducts the inquiry. Peter's denials are introduced by the presence of another disciple who is unnamed and said to be known to the high priest.

Trial before Pilate (18:28–19:16). All the Gospels have Jesus led from the high priest to be tried by the Roman governor Pilate. In the Synoptics Jesus barely speaks to Pilate, but in John this trial is a developed drama with conversations and brief speeches. Only John explains that Jesus was brought to Pilate because "the Jews" were not permitted to put anyone to death. Jesus' challenge to Pilate concerning the truth (18:37) transforms the scene into the trial of Pontius Pilate before Jesus, over whom he has no real power (19:11). Although Pilate yields to the demand for the death penalty, ultimately "the Jews" insist, "We do not have a king other than the Emperor" (19:15).

Crucifixion, death, and burial (19:17–42). John is more dramatic than the Synoptics, making major theological episodes out of details in the tradition. All four Gospels mention the charge "King of the Jews," but in John this becomes the occasion for Pilate's finally acknowledging the truth about Jesus, proclaiming it in the style of an imperial inscription in three languages. John develops details to show the fulfillment of the Scripture and that Jesus remained in charge. In John the Galilean women do not stand at a distance; they are near the cross while Jesus is still alive. Two figures whose names John never gives us are present: the mother of Jesus and the disciple whom Jesus loved. Jesus brings them into a mother-son relationship, thus constituting a community of disciples who are mother and brother to him—the community that preserved this Gospel. With this the Johannine Jesus is able to say his final word from the cross, "It is completed," and to hand over his Spirit (19:30). The piercing of Jesus' side fulfills both 7:37–39, that from within Jesus would flow living water symbolic of the Spirit, and (since his bones were not broken as with the paschal lamb) 1:29, that he was the Lamb of God. Peculiar to John is the reappearance of Nicodemus, who together with Joseph from Arimathea publicly gives an honorable burial to Jesus.

3. Four Scenes in Jerusalem and Faith in the Risen Jesus (20:1–29). John 20 places all the appearances of the risen Jesus in Jerusalem, with no indication of appearances to take place in Galilee. The arrangement here reflects John's love for personal encounter with Jesus.

At the tomb (20:1–18). Mary Magdalene's coming to the tomb, finding it empty, and reporting this to Simon Peter and the Beloved Disciple are preparations for two scenes at the tomb. The *first scene* (20:3–10) has Simon Peter and the Beloved Disciple run to the tomb. Both enter and see the burial wrapping and head cloth, but only the Beloved Disciple believes. Peter was the first of the Twelve to see the risen Lord, but the Beloved Disciple was the first full believer. The *second scene* (20:11–18) has Mary Magdalene return to the tomb, where two angels are now present. Neither what they say nor the sudden appearance of Jesus (whom she mistakes for the gardener) causes her to believe. That happens when Jesus calls her by name. Mary is sent to proclaim all this to the disciples, who are now called Jesus' brothers because as a result of the resurrection/ascension his Father is their Father.

Inside a room (20:19–29). The *first scene* (20:19–25) takes place on Easter Sunday night in a place where the doors are locked for fear of "the Jews." Jesus appears to the disciples and extends peace to them. He gives them a mission that continues his own. He breathes on them and gives them the Holy Spirit with power over sin, continuing his own power over sin. The appearance scenes in the other Gospels always include an element of disbelief on the part of the Eleven, but John more dramatically embodies it in Thomas, who vocalizes a determined incredulity (vv. 24–25). The *second scene* (20:26–29) is set in the same place a week later, with Thomas present. Although the proof offered Thomas presents a tangibly corporeal image of the risen Jesus, one should note that Thomas is not said to have touched Jesus. Ironically, the one who embodied disbelief now utters the highest christological confession in the Gospels, "My Lord and My God"—an inclusion with the Prologue's "The Word was God." In response, Jesus blesses all future generations who will believe in him without having seen (20:29), thus showing an awareness of the Gospel audience for whom John had been writing throughout.

4. Gospel Conclusion (20:30–31). *Statement of purpose in writing.* In selecting material to be included in the Gospel, John pursues a goal of having people believe in Jesus as the Messiah, the Son of God, in order that by possessing this belief they may have eternal life in his name. This statement is true to the constant emphases of the Gospel, but also warns against a literalist interpretation of John as if the main purpose were to report eyewitness testimony.

Epilogue (21:1–25)

Although the Gospel concludes with chap. 20, there is another chapter of resurrection appearances containing two scenes (in Galilee) and another conclusion.

The *first scene* (21:1–14) involves fishing. The disciples do not recognize the risen Jesus. In a scene similar to Luke 5:4–11 the risen Jesus engineers a miraculous catch of fish. The Beloved Disciple displays his greater perceptiveness by being the first to recognize the Lord. Simon Peter is impetuous, though subsequently he alone hauls in the net of 153 fish. The food Jesus provides may be eucharistic, with emphasis on his risen presence at meals.

The *second scene* (21:15–23) shifts symbolism abruptly, moving from fish to sheep. Probably this represents a second stage in Peter's image: missionary apostle (fisherman), and now a model for pastoral care (shepherd). The story may reflect a late Johannine concession to church structure, for chap. 10 portrayed Jesus as the sole shepherd. But, the qualifications remain faithful to Johannine idealism: Peter's shepherding flows from his love for Jesus; and Peter must be willing to lay down his life for the sheep. The appearance of the Beloved Disciple challenges the unity of the scene, but the contrast between him and Peter is typically Johannine. Here, Peter may symbolize apostolic authority, but the Beloved Disciple may last until Jesus returns. The concern expressed in 21:23 suggests that the Beloved Disciple is now dead.

The conclusion in 21:24–25 identifies the Beloved Disciple as the witness behind the Gospel and certifies the truth of his testimony. It also reminds us that the whole Jesus cannot be captured in the pages of any book, even a book such as the Fourth Gospel!

INFLUENCES ON JOHANNINE THOUGHT

John is often characterized as a Hellenistic Gospel, the product of Greek philosophical thought, or of combinations of philosophy and religion, or of the Pagan mystery religions. An intermediary proposal was that the works of the Jewish philosopher Philo (before AD 50) served as a channel of such thought, particularly in relation to "the Word." Another group of scholars has stressed the relationship of John to (incipient) Gnosticism. Still another proposal would see parallels between John and the later Mandaean writings (with their syncretistic mixture of Jewish lore and Gnostic myth). In substance all these theories agree that the Johannine idiom of language and thought did not stem from the Palestinian world of Jesus of Nazareth.

A very different approach would see the basic origins of Johannine Christianity within that Palestinian world with all its Jewish diversity—a world that had been influenced by Hellenism but where reflection on the heritage of Israel was the primary catalyst. That heritage would be judged not simply from the books of the Law and the Prophets, but also from the protocanonical and deuterocanonical Wisdom Literature, and from apocryphal and intertestamental literature. In particular, the enrichment supplied by the DSS comes into the picture. The resemblance in vocabulary and thought between the DSS and John should banish the idea that the Johannine tradition could not have developed on Palestinian soil. There is, however, no evidence for a direct familiarity of John with the DSS; rather there is the possibility of indirect acquaintance with a type of thought and expression current at Qumran, and perhaps in a wider area. If Qumran exemplifies a wider range of thought, Jesus could well have been familiar with its vocabulary and ideas.

THE WRITING OF THE JOHANNINE GOSPEL

The Johannine Gospel is the result of a complex history and process of composition. Recognizing and appreciating its characteristics provide insights that facilitate understanding the distinctive theological perspective of this remarkable writing.

Stage One: As with all the Gospels, the Gospel of John had its origins in the ministry and teaching of Jesus, witnessed to by a disciple. The Gospel refers to this particular follower of Jesus as the Beloved Disciple. He is not likely a named disciple in the other Gospels. His testimony, however, is foundational for the formation and ongoing existence of the early Christian group referred to as the Johannine Community.

Stage Two: For several decades Jesus was proclaimed in the postresurrectional context of a particular Christian community. At this stage the Beloved Disciple, not one of the Twelve, but a disciple and a witness to the life and ministry of Jesus, played a crucial role. The bulk of this lengthy period (several decades) would have been marked by the oral transmission of the tradition of the Beloved Disciple. There may have been something written toward the end of this stage.

Stage Three: There are two moments in this final stage. The first is the creative writing of a remarkable storyteller, the evangelist. This person is not the Beloved Disciple, but one who faithfully, and indeed brilliantly, receives the tradition of the Beloved Disciple and communicates it through a coherent theologically motivated story. He is the author of the bulk of the Gospel. It seems probable that the evangelist did retouch his own work, especially as an adaptation of the gospel to meet new problems. However that may be, finally the redactor (see the treatment of the narrative of the Gospel above) produced the Gospel as we now have it. This figure is responsible for such features as the Prologue (1:1–18) and the Epilogue (21:1–25), and for shifting the position of certain blocks of material within the evangelist's story. The redactor did not, however, despite past claims about the development of the Gospel, introduce material on traditional eschatology and Sacraments to correct a more radically realized and existentialist reading of the Jesus story. The redactor is in deep sympathy with the evangelist, who, in his own turn, has brilliantly rendered the traditions passed on by the Beloved Disciple into narrative forms that produced the Gospel.

✦

12

First Epistle (Letter) of John

In style and vocabulary there are so many similarities between I John and John that no one can doubt that they are at least from the same tradition. Indeed, I John makes most sense if understood as written in a period following the appearance of the Gospel, for the clear concern with the conflict between Johannine Christian Jews and other synagogue Jews who did not believe in Jesus (those who are called "the Jews" in the Gospel) was no longer a major issue. Rather a division among Johannine Christians themselves has now occurred, sparked by different views of Jesus. One group held that his actions set a moral standard to be followed; the other contended that simply believing in the Word was all that mattered, and what Christians did had no more importance than what Jesus did.

GENERAL ANALYSIS OF THE MESSAGE

After the General Analysis the major issues regarding Composition will be discussed.

SUMMARY OF BASIC INFORMATION

DATE: Most likely after the Gospel according to John; thus ca. AD 100.

TO: Christians of the Johannine community who had undergone a schism.

AUTHENTICITY: Certainly by a writer in the Johannine tradition, probably not by the one responsible for most of the Gospel.

UNITY: Great majority of scholars think of unified composition; Bultmann's thesis of combined sources has little following.

INTEGRITY: The "Johannine Comma" or additional Trinitarian material in 5:6–8 is a third–fourth-century Latin theological gloss; otherwise no additions.

FORMAL DIVISION:

1:1–4: Prologue

1:5–3:10: Part One: God is light and we must walk in light

3:11–5:12: Part Two: Walk as the children of the God who has loved us in Christ

5:13–21: Conclusion.

Prologue (1:1–4)

This resembles a primitive sketch of the Prologue to the Fourth Gospel, without the clarity found in the Gospel. The "beginning" in 1:1 refers to the start of Jesus' ministry. "The word of life" that was made known ("word" here is less personalized than in John) constitutes the "message" of I John 1:5; 3:11, which enables the readers to participate in divine life, and thus to have fellowship with the living God.

Part One: God Is Light and We Must Walk in Light (1:5–3:10)

The message of I John opens (1:5–7) by reiterating the Johannine view of a world divided into light and darkness (see John 3:19–21), with God as the light of the just. Walking in light and acting in truth guarantee fellowship with one another and "with him," for the blood of Jesus cleanses from sin. I John 1:8–2:2 turns to the false propagandists who refuse to acknowledge their wrongdoing as sin. True Christians acknowledge or publicly confess their sins and have a Paraclete with the Father, "Jesus Christ the just one."

"Children," "fathers," and "young people" address Johannine Christians to praise and encourage them in their struggle against the Evil One. An impassioned denunciation of the world (2:15–17) follows. I John 2:18–23 sees this struggle already going on in the opposition to the author and the true

Johannine Christians offered by the false teachers (who are the anti-christs) and their followers.

I John 2:28–3:3 deals with the theme of the appearance of Christ, emphasiz-ing the idea of union with God and Jesus. An even bolder concept is advanced in I John 3:4–10:We are children of God because God's seed begot us (cf. John 1:12–13).

Part Two: Walk as the Children of the God of Love (3:11–5:12)

In 3:11–18 the writer proclaims the message as love. Then, echoing John 14:15,21; 15:12,17, the necessity of keeping the commandments, specifically of loving, is inculcated in I John 3:19–24.

I John 4:1–6 invokes a test: "by their fruits you shall know them"—to discern false prophets. There is a Spirit of God and a spirit of the antichrist, and every Spirit-led person who acknowledges Jesus Christ come in the flesh belongs to God. More practically, "Anyone who knows God listens to us" helps distinguish the spirit of truth from the spirit of deceit.

Abruptly 4:7–21 returns to the theme of love for one another, proclaiming, "God is love." We know this not because of our initiative of know-ing God, but because God took the initiative of sending the only Son into the world so that we might have life and that sins might be expiated.

The close interconnection of Johannine motifs is illustrated by the treatment of faith, love, and commandments in 5:1–5. Previously we heard that sinlessness and righteousness were marks of those begotten by God (3:9–10); now we are told that everyone who believes that Jesus is the Christ is begotten by God and will conquer the world—a victory won by belief in Jesus, the Son of God, who came by the water and the blood (an emphasis on his humanity and death).

Conclusion: 5:13–21

The epistolary writer clarifies his purpose: "That you may know that you possess this eternal life—you who believe in the name of the Son of God" (I John 5:13).

The guarantee of knowing God and the truth is the recognition that the Son of God has come. Most likely "He is the true God and eternal life" (5:20) refers to Jesus, so that I John ends as did John (20:28), with a clear affirmation of the divinity of Christ.

COMPOSITION

AUTHOR. Traditionally it was assumed that the same writer composed John and the three Epistles (or Letters) of John. The similarities between I John and John are numerous; yet there are surprising differences:

- The Prologue of I John does not emphasize the incarnation of the personified Word, as does the Prologue of John.
- I John assigns to God features that the Gospel assigns to Jesus, for example, in I John 1:5 God is light (cf. John 8:12; 9:5).
- There is less epistolary emphasis on the Spirit as a person. Christ is the Paraclete in I John 2:1.
- Final eschatology is stronger in I John than in John. The Parousia is the moment of accountability for Christian life (I John 2:28–3:3).
- The Dead Sea Scroll parallels (especially vocabulary) are even closer in I John than in John.

Some of these differences may reflect the author's claim to be presenting the gospel as it was "from the beginning" (I John 1:1; 3:11). Overall they suggest that the same person may not have written the Epistles and the Gospel.

DATING AND OCCASION FOR WRITING. While a date cannot be determined precisely, I John was known by Polycarp and Justin—thus existing before AD 150. In turn, in the situation behind the writing of the Epistles, "the antichrists" would seduce the writer's adherents on several issues:

Faith. The secessionists deny the full import of Jesus as the Christ, the Son of God (2:22–23). Presumably the denial means that they negated the importance of the human career of Jesus, especially the bloody death of Jesus as an act of love and expiation (1:7; 2:2; 4:10; 5:6).

Morals. They boast of being in communion with God and knowing God while walking in darkness and not keeping the commandments (1:6; 2:4); indeed, they will not recognize that they have sinned

(1:8,10; 3:4–6). If they denied the importance of what God's Son did in the flesh after the incarnation, perhaps they denied the importance of what they did in the flesh after becoming children of God through belief.

Spirit. Seemingly the secessionist leaders claim to be teachers and prophets, led by the Spirit. The author disclaims the need for teachers (2:27) and warns against false prophets (4:1).

GENRE AND STRUCTURE. Scholars disagree about both issues. As for genre, I John has none of the features of a letter. Plausibly it is a written exhortation interpreting the Fourth Gospel in light of secessionist propaganda. As for structure, the author offers no clear indication of plan. Some favor a tripartite division (Prologue, Three Parts, Epilogue). But others prefer a bipartite division, wherein "This is the gospel" (1:5; 3:11) marks off two main Parts of the Epistle: Part One (1:5–3:10) defines the gospel as "God is light" and stresses the obligation of walking in the light; and Part Two (3:11–5:12) defines the gospel as "We should love one another" and holds up Jesus as the example of love for one's Christian brother and sister.

13

Second Letter of John

II and III John are almost parade examples of brief ancient letters.

THE BACKGROUND

II and III John are alike in their letter format. Both describe the writer as "the presbyter." II John has similarities of content to I John, especially in vv. 5–7: the commandment to love one another (I John 2:7–8); and condemnation of "many deceivers gone out into the world, not confessing Jesus Christ come in the flesh" (I John 2:18–19). Most scholars think that the presbyter composed all three works.

II John is sent to a Johannine community, where no secessionists have gone. The presbyter instructs that community not to let such false teachers into "the house."

GENERAL ANALYSIS OF THE MESSAGE

Opening Formula (vv. 1–3). The Sender and Addressee sections are succinctly phrased: "The presbyter to an Elect Lady and her children." The

SUMMARY OF BASIC INFORMATION

DATE: About the same time as I John, thus ca. AD 100.

TO: Christians of a Johannine community threatened by the advent of schismatic missionaries.

AUTHENTICITY: By a writer in the Johannine traditions, who wrote III John as well and probably I John.

UNITY AND INTEGRITY: Not seriously disputed.

FORMAL DIVISION:

    A. Opening Formula: 1–3

    B. Body: 4–12

        4: Transitional expression of joy

        5–12: Message

    C. Concluding Formula: 13.

---

customary Greeting "grace, mercy, peace" is followed by the Johannine addition of "truth" and "love."

Transitional expression of joy (v. 4). In epistolary format a statement of joy is often transitional to the Body of the letter.

Message (vv. 5–12). The insistence in 5–6 on the commandment of love and the necessity of walking in the commandment echoes the main ethical thrusts of I John. The christological thrust of I John echoes the insistence in II John 7 of acknowledging the coming of Jesus Christ in the flesh as what differentiates those whom the presbyter acknowledges as beloved children from the antichrist deceivers. These adversaries are described in v. 9 as "progressive" (literally, "going ahead and not remaining in the teaching of Christ"). I and II John contend that the presbyter's christology and ethics represent what was from the beginning. Differences are crucial, for whoever has the wrong teaching does not have God!

The presbyter closes with an explanation of the brevity of the letter, and a stated hope to visit soon; both are epistolary conventions and not veiled threats. The presbyter anticipates the joy of a personal meeting.

Concluding Formula (v. 13). The presbyter sends the greetings of the children of a sister church, that is, other Christians in his (?) church.

PRESBYTERS

What does the writer of II John mean by the designation "presbyter"? We see that he speaks authoritatively to other Johannine Christians and that he sends out missionaries. One gets the impression that "the presbyter" has prestige but not judicial authority. How does this picture fit into what we know about "presbyters" from elsewhere? At least five different early Christian usages have been offered as parallels:

- An elderly man of dignity and importance.
- Church officials (many also designated *episkopos*—"bishop" or "overseer") who in groups administered local churches in the late 1st century.
- One of the Twelve Apostles.
- A companion of Jesus who was not one of the Twelve.
- A disciple of the disciples of Jesus and thus a second-generation figure.

It is the last category that would best fit the use of "presbyter" in II and III John.

.⋆.

14

Third Letter of John

The shortest book in the NT and very similar to II John in format, style, authorship, and length, III John is, nevertheless, quite unlike I and II John in subject matter. There is no critique of moral indifference or christological error, only of complicated church relationships that involve rival authority.

THE BACKGROUND

In one community a certain Diotrephes has kept out traveling missionaries, including those from the presbyter. His refusal of hospitality causes the presbyter to write III John to Gaius, seemingly a wealthy person in a neighboring community. Gaius has been providing hospitality, and the presbyter wants him to take over larger responsibility for helping the missionaries, particularly the well-known Demetrius.

GENERAL ANALYSIS OF THE MESSAGE

Opening Formula (vv. 1–2). The Sender and Addressee section (v. 1) is the briefest in the NT, but close to the secular letters of the time. A

SUMMARY OF BASIC INFORMATION

DATE: Perhaps after I and II John, reflecting attempts to deal with the situation described in those writings; III John may be related to the pastoral development in John 21 and thus written shortly after AD 100.

TO: Gaius, a Johannine Christian friendly to the presbyter, because Diotrephes, who has taken over leadership (in a neighboring community), is not friendly.

AUTHENTICITY: By a writer in the Johannine tradition, who wrote II John as well and probably I John.

UNITY AND INTEGRITY: Not seriously disputed.

FORMAL DIVISION:
   A. Opening Formula: 1–2
   B. Body: 3–14
       3–4: Transitional expression of joy
       5–14: Message
   C. Concluding Formula: 15.

health wish (v. 2) is also a feature of the Opening of secular letters, but the presbyter extends his concern to Gaius' spiritual welfare—a connection of soul and body.

Transitional expression of joy (vv. 3–4). The joy that Gaius is walking in the truth is more than conventional. Testimony has been borne to Gaius by "brothers" who have come to the presbyter, who himself seems aware of the situation(s).

Message (vv. 5–14). The "brothers" of vv. 5–6, among whom Gaius has a reputation of being hospitable, are coming from the presbyter's community to that in which Gaius lives; and Gaius is asked to help them farther on their way. We get a picture here of early preachers of Christ who depend on the assistance of generous local Christians. In vv. 9–10 a much more complicated situation is suddenly revealed; for a certain Diotrephes, "who likes to be first," in the church has ignored the presbyter's letter. The presbyter insists that Diotrephes is spreading evil nonsense about him, refusing to receive "the brothers," hindering those who wish to do so, and expelling them from church! Apparently the presbyter did not have the authority to act against Diotrephes. Rather he writes to Gaius endorsing a figure named Demetrius, for whom this letter serves as a recommendation.

Concluding Formula (v. 15). III John has "the beloved here" (i.e., in the presbyter's church) send greetings to Gaius and to the beloved there, "each by name."

DIAGNOSIS OF THE SITUATION

Ironically the only work in the Johannine corpus to give the personal names of Johannine Christians (Gaius, Diotrephes, Demetrius) is imprecise as to how these are related to one another and the presbyter. We cannot be sure of all the reasons for the antagonism between the presbyter and Diotrephes; but the letter seems to make the most sense if both figures were opposed to the secessionist missionaries. If we assume that the presbyter wrote I John as well, he thought that there was no need for human teachers. Diotrephes may have judged all this too vague, since the secessionists claimed that they had the spirit, making it impossible for people to know who was speaking the truth. Diotrephes would have decided that authoritative human teachers were needed. He took on that role for his local church. In the presbyter's outlook Diotrephes was arrogant in departing from the principle that Jesus was the model shepherd and all other (human) shepherds were thieves and bandits (John 10). In Diotrephes' outlook the presbyter was naïve and impractical.

·✦·

15

Classification and Format of New Testament Letters

Of the twenty-seven books of the NT, half have Paul's name attached, all of them in letter form. That is explicable, in part, because the early Christians thought that Christ would return soon, and so only "immediate literature" that dealt with existing problems was of import. Yet letters continued to be written even when more permanent literature (Gospels, Acts) had begun to be produced. Twenty-one of the twenty-seven NT books are called "Letters" or "Epistles"—by comparison none of the OT books carries that designation.

In the canonical order accepted in modern Bibles, all the NT letters come after the Acts of the Apostles. The thirteen letters/epistles that bear Paul's name come first. They are divided into two smaller collections: nine addressed to communities at geographical places (Rom, I–II Cor, Gal, Eph, Phil, Col, I–II Thess) and four addressed to individuals (I–II Tim, Titus, Phlm). Each collection is arranged basically in descending order of length. Hebrews, long associated with Paul, follows; and then come the so-called Catholic Epistles associated with James, Peter, John, and Jude.

CLASSIFICATIONS

For many, "letter" and "epistle" are interchangeable, but in the early twentieth century A. Deissmann, who was a major influence in the study of Greek papyri letters for NT background, made a distinction: "Epistle" was an artistic literary exercise for publication, while "letter" was a nonliterary means of communicating information. This distinction may not account fully for the complexity of the actual Greek writings, but according to its straightforward criterion all or most of the Pauline writings, along with II–III John, might be classified as "Letters"; whereas Hebrews and perhaps I–II Pet, James, I John, and Jude would be "Epistles." Not all scholars accept this distinction.

Today, however, almost all scholars recognize that ancient rhetorical handbooks show a wide range of Greco-Roman letter types. Indeed, one author lists forty-one types of letters. In the following chaps. works that are clearly "Letters" will be entitled in that way. In the instance of I John, Eph, Heb, Jas, Jude, and II Pet, both "Letter" and "Epistle" appear in the title of the respective Chapter, placing first the designation that does more justice to the work.

Letters could be written in different ways, sometimes by the sender's own hand and sometimes dictated. In the latter case some scribes were mere recording secretaries, while others had more authority to formulate, almost as co-authors. As for Paul, we do not know how literally he would have supplied wording to scribes (were they secretaries or co-authors?).

The NT letters, particularly the Pauline letters, were meant to be read aloud in order to persuade. Like speeches, they can be judged as rhetoric. Aristotle (*Ars rhetorica* 1.3; §1358b) distinguished three modes of argumentation: (1) Judicial/forensic (found in the law courts); (2) Deliberative/hortatory (found in public or political assemblies debating about the future); (3) Demonstrative/epideictic (found in speeches given at public celebrations).

Yet, there is no way to be sure that Paul would have been aware of the classic analyses of rhetoric and/or would have been consciously following them. The extent to which disputes about precise rhetorical classification are important for interpretation is not always clear.

FORMAT

The Hellenistic world has left us many Greek and Latin letters of literary quality, as well as papyrus fragments of thousands of letters from Egypt. Letters tend to follow a set format, and one who lacks knowledge of that format can seriously misinterpret a letter. Generally four parts of the letter are distinguished: (1) Opening Formula; (2) Thanksgiving; (3) Body or Message; (4) Concluding Formula.

(1) Opening Formula (*Praescriptio*)

The Opening Formula of the Greco-Roman letter consisted of three basic elements (sender, addressee, greeting), although sometimes another element extends the greeting.

Sender (Superscriptio). This involves the personal name of the author, sometimes further identified with a title to establish the author's authority—for example, "Paul, a servant of Christ Jesus."

Addressee (Adscriptio). The simplest form is a personal name; but most NT letters address communities in stated regions. In the few early Christian letters written to individuals, further identification is supplied—for example, "to Philemon our beloved fellow worker."

Greeting (Salutatio). Occasionally this was omitted. Jewish letters of the period tend to replace "greetings" (Greek *chairein* = Latin *ave*, "hail") with "peace" (Greek *eirēnē*, reflecting Hebrew *shālôm*). Similarly typical NT letters employed a combination of two or three nouns, like "grace, peace, mercy, love," characterized as coming from God the Father (and Jesus Christ).

Remembrance or Health Wish. In the Greco-Roman personal letter, the greeting was often expanded by a remembrance or a health wish as the sender prayed for the health of the addressee and gave assurance of the sender's own health. While lacking remembrances and health wishes, most NT letters expand one or the other element in the Opening Formula by attaching the high status and privileges of Christians—for example, Gal expands the greeting: "Grace and peace from the Lord Jesus Christ who gave himself for our sins . . ."

(2) Thanksgiving

In Hellenistic letters a statement wherein the sender gives thanks to the gods for specified reasons often follows the Opening Formula. A different pattern appears in the Pauline Thanksgiving. The specified reason for the thanks is not some act of divine intervention but the faithfulness of the congregation addressed, and the supplication is for the continuance of such fidelity. Often some of the main themes of the Body of the letter are briefly anticipated in the Thanksgiving.

(3) Body or Message

The Body of a letter is sometimes defined as what comes between the Opening Formula (+ Thanksgiving) and the Concluding Formula. Increasingly, discrete sections are being recognized in the Body, especially in the transitional sentences at the beginning (Body-Opening) and the end (Body-Closing).

(4) Concluding Formula

Two brief conventional expressions mark the end of a Greco-Roman letter, namely, a wish for good health and a word of farewell. In the Roman period an expression of greetings became customary as a third feature. The Pauline letters never conclude with either the health wish or the farewell. Paul does have greetings from the co-workers who are with him to people whom he knows at the community addressed.

Besides greetings, Paul's Concluding Formula sometimes contains a doxology to God and a benediction of the recipients. In four of the Pauline letters (I Thess, I–II Cor, Rom) and in I Pet the greeting is to be done with "a holy kiss." Evidently the Christian community adopted the kiss as a sign of fellowship; it was holy because it was exchanged among the saints, that is, the members of the Christian community. At times Paul takes care to include a line stating that he is writing with his own hand, which suggests that the rest of the letter was physically penned by another, and may imply that Paul has checked the whole so that it could justifiably be sent in his own name.

·✦·

16

General Issues in Paul's Life and Thought

Next to Jesus Paul has been the most influential figure in the history of Christianity. The range of Paul's letters to particular communities, plus the depth of his thought and the passion of his involvement, have meant that since his letters became part of the NT, no Christian has been unaffected by what he has written. Whether or not they know Paul's works well, all Christians have become Paul's children in the faith.

THE LIFE OF PAUL

There are two sources for his life: his own letters and the account of his career in Acts (beginning with 7:58). There are three views of how to relate these sources. First, virtually complete trust in Acts. Such confidence in Acts was typical of almost all older attempts to write an account of the life of Paul. These lives were constructed in what is now referred to as the traditional manner of putting together Paul's story. They fit and adapt information from the letters into the Acts framework. Second, great distrust of Acts. The pendulum swung to the

Table 4. Paul's activities in the Letters and Acts

PAULINE LETTERS	ACTS
Conversion near Damascus (implied in Gal 1:17c)	Damascus (9:1–22)
To Arabia (Gal 1:17b)	
Return to Damascus (1:17c): 3 yrs.	
Flight from Damascus (II Cor 11:32–33)	Flight from Damascus (9:23–25)
To Jerusalem (Gal 1:18–20)	To Jerusalem (9:26–29)
"The regions of Syria and Cilicia" (Gal 1:21–22)	Caesarea and Tarsus (9:30)
	Antioch (11:26a)
	(Jerusalem [11:29–30; 12:25])
	Mission I: Antioch (13:1–4a)
	Seleucia, Salamis, Cyprus (13:4b–12)
Churches evangelized before Macedonian Philippi (Phil 4:15)	South Galatia (13:13–14:25)
	Antioch (14:26–28)
"Once again during 14 years I went up to Jerusalem" (for "Council," Gal 2:1)	Jerusalem (15:1–12)
Antioch Incident (Gal 2:11–14)	Antioch (15:35); **Mission II**
	Syria and Cilicia (15:41)
	South Galatia (16:1–5)
Galatia (I Cor 16:1) evangelized for the first time (Gal 4:13)	Phrygia and North Galatia (16:6)
	Mysia and Troas (16:7–10)
Philippi (I Thess 2:2 [= Macedonia, II Cor 11:9])	Philippi (16:11–40)
Thessalonica (I Thess 2:2; cf. 3:6; Phil 4:15–16)	Amphipolis, Apollonia, Thessalonica (17:1–9)
	Beroea (17:10–14)
Athens (I Thess 3:1; cf. 2:17–18)	Athens (17:15–34)
Corinth evangelized (cf. I Cor 1:19; 11:7–9)	Corinth for eighteen months (18:1–18a)
Timothy arrives in Corinth (I Thess 3:6), probably accompanied by Silvanus (I Thess 1:1)	Silas and Timothy come from Macedonia (18:5)
	Paul leaves from Cenchreae (18:18b)
	Leaves Priscilla and Aquila at Ephesus (18:19–21)

Table 4. *Continued*

PAULINE LETTERS	ACTS
Apollos (in Ephesus) urged by Paul to go to Corinth (I Cor 16:12)	Apollos dispatched to Achaia by Priscilla and Aquila (18:17)
	Paul to Caesarea Maritima (18:22a)
	Paul to Jerusalem (18:22b)
	In Antioch for a certain amount of time (18:22c)
Northern Galatia, second visit (Gal 4:13)	**Mission III:** North Galatia and Phrygia (18:23)
Ephesus (I Cor 16:1–8)	Ephesus for three yrs. or two yrs., three mos. (19:1–20:1; cf. 20:31)
Visit of Chloe's people, along with Stephanas et al., to Paul in Ephesus (I Cor 1:11; 16:17), bringing letter (7:1)	
Paul imprisoned (? cf. I Cor 15:32; II Cor 1:8)	
Timothy sent to Corinth (I Cor 4:17; 16:10)	
Paul's second "painful" visit to Corinth (II Cor 13:2); return to Ephesus	
Titus sent to Corinth with letter "written in tears" (II Cor 2:13)	
(Paul's plans to visit Macedonia, Corinth, and Jerusalem/Judea, I Cor 16:3–8; cf. II Cor 1:15–16)	(Paul's plans to visit Macedonia, Achaia, Jerusalem, Rome, 19:21)
Ministry in Troas (II Cor 2:12)	
To Macedonia (II Cor 2:13; 7:5; 9:2b–4); arrival of Titus (II Cor 7:6)	Macedonia (20:1b)
Titus sent on ahead to Corinth (II Cor 7:16–17), with part of II Cor	
Illyricum (Rom 15:19)?	
Achaia (Rom 15:26; 16:1); Paul's third visit to Corinth (II Cor 13:1)	three mos. in Greece (Achaia) (20:2–3)
	Paul starts to return to Syria (20:3), but goes via Macedonia and Philippi (20:3b–6a)

PAULINE LETTERS	ACTS
(Plans to visit Jerusalem, Rome, Spain [Rom 15:22–27])	Troas (20:6b–12) Miletus (20:15c–38) Tyre, Ptolemais, Caesarea (21:7–14) Jerusalem (21:15–23:30) Caesarea (23:31–26:32) Journey to Rome (27:1–28:14) Rome (28:15–31)

opposite extreme. Skepticism about the historical value of what Acts reports about Paul leads some scholars to abandon Acts or to correct it as almost constantly contradicting the letters. Third, a mediate stance of various inclinations uses Paul's letters as a primary source and cautiously supplements from Acts, not hastening to declare apparent differences contradictory.

No doubt, Acts has offered a theological interpretation of Paul, adapting his role to fit an overall view of the spread of Christianity. Nevertheless, there is simply too much correspondence between Acts and autobiographical remarks in Paul's letters to ignore that the author knew a great number of facts about Paul.

Birth and Upbringing

Paul was probably born ca. 5–10, during the reign of Emperor Augustus. Acts 7:58 calls him a "young man," and Phlm 9 (written after AD 55) refers to him as an "old man." It is not clear, however, how literally one ought to take the remark in Philemon. Diaspora Jews of the period often had two names, one a Greek or a Roman name and the other Semitic—thus, "Paul," a Roman name, and "Saul," a Jewish name, appropriate for one from the tribe of Benjamin. Acts tells us that he was a citizen of Tarsus, capital of Cilicia, where there was a considerable Jewish colony. It further identifies Paul as a Roman citizen by birth.

Probably most scholars maintain that Paul was reared and educated at Tarsus. He wrote good Greek, had basic Hellenistic rhetorical skills, quoted from the Scriptures in Greek, and knew Deuterocanonical Books composed or preserved in Greek. Paul learned a trade that Acts 18:3 defines as tent making, a skilled craft with skins involving tasks such as leatherwork and making tents and awnings. As a tradesman he would have been among the lower social classes, but a step higher than a freedman. Supporting himself for the sake of the gospel was a point of pride for Paul in his missionary travels since it meant that he did not have to beg money from those whom he evangelized.

Paul would have known something about the religion(s) of the Gentiles. He may have known something of popular philosophies. On a simpler level he would have known how ordinary Gentiles lived and worked. Clearly Paul understood the major role of the household in the Greco-Roman culture.

Paul also was, however, an educated Jew, as his thorough knowledge of Judaism and the Jewish Scriptures indicates. The claim in Acts 22:3 that Paul was brought up in Jerusalem and educated by Gamaliel I the Elder, who flourished in Jerusalem ca. AD 20–50, probably needs qualification. His letters do not suggest that he had seen Jesus during the public ministry or at the crucifixion, and so implicitly cast doubt on his continuous presence in Jerusalem in the years AD 26–30/33. Nevertheless, Paul says he was zealous for the traditions of the ancestors and advanced in Judaism beyond many of his own age (Gal 1:14).

Belief in Jesus and Immediate Aftermath

Paul says that he persecuted the church of God violently and tried to destroy it (Gal 1:13). Why did Paul persecute the followers of Jesus? E. P. Sanders (*Paul* [1991], 8–9) argues that the persecution was due to Paul's zeal, not to his being a very observant Pharisee. But, making a connection between the clauses of Phil 3:5–6, "According to the Law a Pharisee, according to zeal a persecutor of the church, according to righteousness based on the Law blameless," others suspect that Paul saw the followers of Jesus proclaiming a message contrary to the Pharisee interpretation of the Law. More precisely, was Paul's hostility toward these people related to their confessing as the God-approved Messiah one who had been condemned by the Jewish authorities (and the Law itself—Gal 3:13) as a blasphemer?

After a period of persecuting, according to both Gal 1:13–17 and Acts 9:1–9, Paul received a divine revelation in which he encountered Jesus and after which he came to stay in Damascus. Paul never speaks of a conversion, but of a calling or commission. Yet he did have a change or reversal of values, as he reconsidered the import of the Mosaic Law in the light of what God had done in Jesus. In I Cor 9:1 Paul says he *saw* Jesus (also 15:8); but in none of the three accounts of the experience in Acts does that happen (yet see 9:27), even though he does see light. (Moreover, the three accounts of Paul's "conversion" do not agree in detail—an indication that Luke's information was limited, or he felt free in his dramatization of the tradition.)

Theologically the encounter with the risen Jesus revealed to Paul that the scandal of the cross was not the end of the story of Jesus. Both in Acts (26:17 = Jesus speaks) and Galatians (1:16 = Paul reports) one finds that Paul was directed to "the Gentiles." This raises the question whether from the first moment of his encounter with the risen Jesus Paul knew of his mission to the Gentiles. Interpreters differ on this matter, reading Galatians and Acts, and even parts of Acts, differently.

The discussion to follow draws on what is known as the Traditional Pauline Chronology both because it is the one readers will most often encounter, and because it seems more reasonable to most scholars. Table 5 includes the proposed Revisionist dates for information and a comparison with the Traditional Chronology. For the sake of completion, following is a simple outline of Paul's life that is favored by some Pauline scholars. Presented in 1950 by John Knox, it is probably the best known sketch of Paul's career from his letters alone. It draws on the autobiographical remarks in Paul's letters exclusively without trying to factor in the account in Acts. It also does not attempt to assign dates to particular events, because of the limited information in Paul's statements.

I. Conversion in Damascus—Gal 1:15–17
II. Three years or more, spent largely or entirely in Syria and Arabia—Gal 1:17–18
III. First visit to Jerusalem after the conversion ("acquaintance"), and departure for Syria and Cilicia—Gal 1:18–21

Table 5. Pauline chronology

TRADITIONAL	EVENT	REVISIONIST
AD 36	Conversion to Christ	AD 30/34
39	Visit to Jerusalem after Damascus	33/37
40–44 44–45	In Cilicia At Antioch	after 37
46–49	(First) Missionary Journey, beginning in Antioch, to Cyprus and southern Asia Minor, returning to Antioch	after 37
see below	(Second) Missionary Journey, beginning in Antioch, through southern Asia Minor to N. Galatia, Macedonia, Corinth (I Thess), return to Jerusalem and Antioch	39–41/43 (41–43)
49	Jerusalem conference	47/51
50–52 (51–52)	(Second) Missionary Journey, beginning in Antioch, through southern Asia Minor to N. Galatia, Macedonia, Corinth (I Thess), return to Jerusalem and Antioch	see above
54–58 (54–57) (summer 57) (57/58)	(Third) Missionary Journey, beginning from Antioch through N. Galatia to Ephesus; three-year stay there—imprisoned? (Gal, Phil, Phlm, I Cor) Paul goes through Macedonia toward Corinth (II Cor, Gal?), winters at Corinth (Rom), returns to Jerusalem	indistinct from second (48/55) (after 54)
58–60 60–61	Arrested in Jerusalem; imprisoned two years in Caesarea (Phil?) Sent to Rome; long sea journey	52–55 or 56–58
61–63	Prisoner in Rome for two years (Phil? Phlm?)	
after summer 64	Death in Rome under Nero	

IV. Fourteen years, presumably passed in activity as an apostle—
   Gal 2:1

V. Second visit to Jerusalem ("conference")—Gal 2:1–10

VI. Activity in churches of Galatia, Asia, Macedonia, and Greece,
   especially in connection with raising the offering for the
   poor at Jerusalem—Gal 1:10; 1 Cor 16:1–4 (also 2 Cor 8–9);
   Rom 15:25–32

VII. Final visit to Jerusalem ("offering") (1 Cor 16:4;
   Rom 15:25–32)

Missionary Journey; the Jerusalem Meeting; the Antioch Aftermath

According to Acts 13:3–14:28 a missionary journey from Antioch
in Syria took Barnabas, Paul, and John Mark to Cyprus, then to the Asia
Minor cities of Perga (and, after John Mark departed), Pisidian Antioch, Iconium, Lystra, and Derbe, and back to Antioch in Syria (ca. AD
49). Having met opposition in synagogues, Paul addressed himself to
Gentiles among whom the gospel was well received.

According to Acts, there were others before Paul who made converts among the Gentiles (without insistence on circumcision). But
apparently Paul's innovation was to have formed entire communities
of Gentile Christians with little or no attachment to Judaism. What did
this portend for the future of Christianity? A meeting was held in Jerusalem ca. 49 to answer that question (Gal 2:1–10 and Acts 15:1–29).
Although there are differences between the two accounts, they agree
that Paul, James "the brother of the Lord," and Peter/Cephas were involved, and that there was a group opposed to Paul that insisted that
the Gentiles should be circumcised. In Acts Peter and James agree that
circumcision could not be demanded. Gal 2:9 reports that James, Cephas, and John recognized the grace and apostolate bestowed on Paul
and extended to him and Barnabas the right hand of fellowship. This
decision, however, did not settle all problems.

Were the Gentiles bound by other parts of the Mosaic Law, especially
the food purity laws? How were Jewish Christians who kept these laws
to relate to Gentile Christians who did not? In Antioch a major dispute
occurred: Peter, who had been eating with the Gentiles, backed down
when men came from James with an objection. To Paul this attempt

to compel the Gentiles to live like Jews violated the truth of the gospel! (Acts seems confused about this whole episode.) Paul (Gal 2:13) reports that at Antioch Barnabas too sided with the men from James. Subsequently (Gal 2 and Acts 15) Paul and Barnabas parted unhappily so that Paul left Antioch with Silas immediately afterward. Most scholars conclude that Paul lost this battle, which may explain why Antioch no longer features prominently as the home base of Paul's missionary activity. In his journeys he is now much more on his own.

Further Missionary Journeys

Acts 15:40–21:15 can be taken as Luke's illustration of Paul's wider-ranging enterprise after the Jerusalem decision opened the Gentile world to belief in Jesus without circumcision (AD 50–58). Now Paul returned to sites in SE Asia Minor evangelized during his earlier missioning. Then going north (for the first time) to Galatia and Phrygia, he crossed over to Macedonia (Europe) from Troas, clearly under divine guidance. His travels brought him to Philippi, Thessalonica, Beroea, Athens, and Corinth. Paul stayed in Corinth for eighteen months. His first preserved letter, **I Thessalonians,** was written from Corinth at this time. In Corinth Paul met Prisca (Priscilla) and Aquila, who worked with him there and then moved on with him to Ephesus before returning to Rome (whence earlier they had been expelled by Emperor Claudius [Acts 18:2]). In Corinth Paul was haled before the Roman proconsul. Acts 18:18b–22 has Paul depart shortly thereafter from Cenchreae, the port of Corinth, touch down at Ephesus and Caesarea, and then go up to greet the church at Jerusalem.

Later, after spending time at Syrian Antioch, he went again through Galatia and Phrygia to the important Roman city of Ephesus, where he stayed three years (54–57). Many scholars suspect that Paul may have been imprisoned at Ephesus. If so, he may have written the letters to the **Philippians** and to **Philemon** while in prison there (if not there, later in Caesarea or Rome). More generally agreed is that while in Ephesus he wrote to the **Galatians** and to the church at Corinth, where there were troubles (a lost letter [I Cor 5:9]; **I Corinthians** [16:8]; a tearful letter [II Cor 2:3–4: lost?]).

Sometime after Pentecost (57) Paul left Ephesus for Troas, a principal port city of northwest Asia Minor; but not finding Titus, whom he had sent to straighten out things in Corinth, he crossed to Macedonia (II Cor 2:12–13), where he met Titus, who was bearing the good news that a reconciliation had been effected. Paul then wrote (perhaps in [two] stages) what is now **II Corinthians.** He went on to Corinth, where he spent three months and gathered receipts from a collection for the Jerusalem Christians, taken up in various churches he had evangelized. He would bring these funds to Jerusalem on his planned journey. At Corinth Paul also composed **Romans,** stating that he intended to visit there on his way to Spain, after taking the collection to Jerusalem (15:24–26).

According to Acts 20:2–17 (spring 58) Paul set out from Corinth for Jerusalem. Despite having been warned of impending danger, when Paul arrived at Caesarea he displayed a determination to complete his mission. In fact, prior to embarking for Jerusalem Paul had asked for prayers, that he might "be delivered from the disobedient in Judea" (Rom 15:30–31).

Paul Arrested in Jerusalem; Imprisoned
in Caesarea; Taken to Rome; Death

Most of the last half-dozen years of Paul's life (ca. 58–64) is recounted in Acts 21:15–28:31—years marked by suffering, four of them by imprisonment. Only in passing does Acts 24:17 mention that Paul brought money to Jerusalem. A meeting, rather tense beneath surface politeness, took place between Paul and James (the brother of the Lord and head of the Jerusalem church) in which Paul was told to behave like a pious, practicing Jew while in Jerusalem. Nevertheless, his presence in the Temple court precipitated a riot so that a Roman tribune had to intervene to save him. Further conflict caused the tribune to take him to Caesarea to be judged by the Roman governor Felix, before whom he defended himself. Felix was looking for a bribe, however, and he put off judgment and left Paul in prison for two years. The next Roman procurator, Festus, took office and Paul's case was taken up once more. Festus heard the case, and before a verdict was rendered

Paul appealed to Caesar for a hearing. Later Festus invited King Herod Agrippa II to hear Paul. Although neither ruler found Paul guilty, he was sent to Rome because of his appeal to the Emperor.

Paul had a hazardous, seemingly disastrous sea journey before arriving at Rome. Paul stayed there two years under house arrest. The sentiment of Paul with which Acts closes the story (ca. 63)—that the Jews will never hear whereas the Gentiles will—is scarcely that expressed by Paul himself in Rom 11:25–26, namely, that when the Gentiles have come in, all Israel will be saved. Neither the letters nor Acts tell us of his death; but a good tradition reports that he was martyred under Nero (EH 2.25.4–8), either about the same time as Peter (AD 64) or somewhat later (67). Tradition has Paul buried on the Via Ostiensis, a spot commemorated by the basilica of St. Paul outside the Walls.

✳

17

An Appreciation of Paul

The preceding two chapters offer general information that will enable readers to appreciate the Pauline letters as they are discussed individually. In addition this chapter affords a different kind of introduction, that is, one centered on appreciating this man who did more than anyone else in his time to lead people to see what Jesus Christ meant for the world.

IMAGES OF PAUL

What image does Paul evoke? Most artistic portrayals of Paul are imaginative re-creations of dramatic moments in Acts. Paul's own words do not seem to have fed the artistic fancy. Yet his writing is the most autobiographical in the NT. In particular, one passage creates indelible images:

> Often near death; five times I have received thirty-nine lashes from
> Jews; three times I have been beaten with rods; once I was stoned;
> three times I have been shipwrecked; a night and a day I passed on the

watery deep; on frequent journeys; in dangers from rivers; in dangers
from bandits; in dangers from (my own) kind; in dangers from Gentiles; in dangers in the city; in dangers in the wilderness; in dangers
on the sea; in dangers from false brethren; in toil and hardship; many
times without sleep; in hunger and thirst; many times not eating; cold
and not clothed; and besides other things there is on me the daily
pressure constituted by anxiety for the churches. Who is weak and I am
not weak? Who is made to stumble into sin, and I am not indignant?
(II Cor 11:23–29)

Paul was an itinerant artisan who would have had to struggle with
all aspects of life. Here was a Jew with a knapsack on his back who
trudged the Roman roads hoping to challenge the world in the name
of a crucified criminal before whom, he proclaimed, every knee in
the heaven, on earth, and under the earth had to bend. Both Acts and
Paul's letters portray struggle and hostility. Paul himself testifies to the
fact that his strife was not over when he brought people to believe
in Christ. Even among other Christians, Paul encountered significant
problems for his ongoing ministry.

PAUL'S MOTIVATION

Why did Paul subject himself to all this "grief"? Before a dramatic
moment in the mid-30s of the first century AD Paul had been at peace
with his upbringing, with himself, and with his God. What brought
about a drastic change whereby all this became so much "dross"?
Acts 9:3–8 and Gal 1:12,16 offer a partial answer: God was pleased
to reveal "His Son" Jesus Christ to Paul. In the revelation Paul, who
already knew the love shown by God to his Israelite ancestors, discovered love that went beyond his previous imagination: "The love
of Christ impels us once we come to the conviction that one died for
all" (II Cor 5:14).

And how can people know the love of Christ unless they hear about
it? The mission to the Gentiles who would otherwise not hear is not
for Paul an abstraction, but an inevitable translation into action of the
overflowing love that he experienced. If the love of God was manifested in the self-giving of Christ, how could the love of Christ be
shown to others except in the same way?

PAUL'S LIVING HERITAGE

A major component in appreciating Paul is the heritage he left:

THOSE WHOM PAUL BROUGHT TO CHRIST. As explained in Chapter 15, Paul was following his heart as well as letter-form when he gave thanks for the faithfulness of those who had been chosen to experience God's love in Christ even as he had. Paul was their father in Christ Jesus (I Thess 2:11); he was in labor like a mother until Christ was formed in them (Gal 4:19); and as gentle with them as a nursing mother (I Thess 2:7). They were his brothers and sisters, his partners in the gospel (Phil 1:7). At times Paul could be harsh. Yet despite his failures, the enduring love of his converts and their gratitude for what he revealed of Christ were a major tribute to his apostleship.

PAUL'S LETTERS. No other follower of Jesus in NT times left behind a written testimony comparable to that of Paul. In the whole library of Christianity it is hard to match his impassioned eloquence: "I died to the Law that I might live for God. I have been crucified with Christ; it is no longer I who live, but Christ who lives in me" (Gal 2:19–20). That eloquence has been a key factor in the ongoing appreciation of Paul by audiences in places and times that he would have never envisioned.

PAUL'S DISCIPLES AND THEIR WRITINGS. Paul was a man of great intensity and a wide range of emotions. He must also have been a man capable of engendering deep friendship: Timothy, Titus, Silvanus, Prisca (Priscilla), Aquila, Onesimus, and Phoebe are but a few of Paul's loyal friends.

Beyond those and other named disciples and companions, a lasting appreciation of Paul stems from the pens of those who themselves remained anonymous while writing about him or in his name. *The author of Acts* (Luke?) has often been criticized for not fully understanding Paul's theology. We should not overlook, however, the extraordinary tribute he paid by devoting to Paul half the book's lengthy description of the spread of Christianity. Paul's own writings may be remarkably autobiographical, but the biography in Acts contributed enormously to his image.

Apparently a half-dozen pseudonymous deutero-Pauline authors found the apostle, even after his death, an enduring authority to speak to the churches in the last third of the first century. For instance, *II Thessalonians* shows Paul facing the great evil of the end-time. Even more impressively the author of *Colossians* developed with new depth Pauline themes of christology, ecclesiology, and eschatology. *Ephesians*, although close to Col, was probably the contribution of another admirer, the most talented of the Pauline writing disciples, who succinctly summarized Paul's theology in Eph 2:8: "For by grace you have been saved through faith; and this is not your own doing, it is the gift of God." *The Pastoral Letters* (Titus, I–II Tim) have sometimes been dismissed as unworthy of the Pauline corpus because of their pedestrian concern with church structure, diatribes against heretical dangers, and downgrading of women. Yet the very concern that caused these letters to be called "Pastoral" is faithful to Paul.

The ultimate gift of Paul is to have preached a gospel that had enormous power in itself and therefore could not be chained or silenced even when its proponents were. Readers who keep in mind *the apostle whose preaching unchained the gospel* will not allow the Pauline message to be buried beneath details as we now consider the thirteen NT writings that bear Paul's name.

·✳·

18

First Letter to the Thessalonians

As the oldest preserved Christian writing, this document has a special significance even outside the Pauline corpus. Within the corpus I Thess has at times been neglected because it does not treat the great Pauline theme of justification by faith apart from the works of the Law. Yet can our evaluation of the importance of a Pauline letter be independent of the relation of the letter to the life-situation in and for which it was composed? Moreover, perhaps he was not yet honed by the Galatian crisis that brought "justification" to the fore in his thought?

THE BACKGROUND

Paul, with Silas and Timothy (and the "we companion" of Acts 16), had crossed over from the province of Asia (Asia Minor, or present-day Turkey) to Macedonia (Europe, present-day northern Greece) ca. 50. His first preaching was at Philippi, where he "suffered and was shamefully treated" (I Thess 2:2). In turn, Paul and his companions came to Thessalonica, where he proclaimed the gospel. How long he stayed

SUMMARY OF BASIC INFORMATION

DATE: The oldest preserved Christian document: 50 or 51 in the Traditional Chronology, during Paul's (Second Missionary) journey, undertaken after the meeting in Jerusalem (or 41–43 in the Revisionist Chronology,* before the Jerusalem meeting).

FROM: Corinth within a few months of Paul's preaching at Thessalonica.

TO: The Christians at Thessalonica, probably of mixed Gentile and Jewish origin.

AUTHENTICITY: Not seriously doubted today.

UNITY: That two letters have been combined to make up I Thess has been suggested by a small number of respected scholars, but unity is overwhelmingly asserted.

INTEGRITY: The Pauline authorship of 2:13–16 is strongly affirmed by the majority. A few look on 5:1–11 as an addition to the letter.

FORMAL DIVISION:
   A. Opening Formula: 1:1
   B. Thanksgiving: 1:2–5 or 1:2–10; or a longer Thanksgiving 1:2–3:13, subdivided into first (1:2–2:12) and second (2:13–3:13)
   C. Body: 2:1–3:13 (or 1:6–3:13): Pauline indicative (relationship to Thessalonians)
      4:1–5:22: Pauline imperative (instructions, exhortations)
   D. Concluding Formula: 5:23–28

DIVISION ACCORDING TO CONTENTS:
1:1–10: Address/greeting and Thanksgiving
2:1–12: Paul's behavior at Thessalonica
2:13–16: Further Thanksgiving about the reception of the gospel
2:17–3:13: Timothy's mission and Paul's present relationship to the Thessalonian church
4:1–12: Ethical admonitions and exhortations
4:13–5:11: Instructions about the Parousia
5:12–22: Instructions about church life
5:23–28: Concluding blessing, greeting (with a kiss).

*For the two Chronologies see Table 5 in Chapter 16 above.

---

there is uncertain, although Acts 17:2 mentions three consecutive Sabbaths at the synagogue, and afterward indicates a ministry centered around the house of Jason (17:5–9), followed by a hasty departure. Besides preaching, Paul (I Thess 2:9) recalls that he had labored and toiled, slaving night and day, so that he would not be a financial burden; and in Phil 4:16 he remembers that the Philippians sent money to him at Thessalonica several times—a description that suggests more than a few weeks' stay.

Thessalonica was a city with a Jewish community but marked by a multiplicity of cults, reflecting the mixture of population. The letter that Paul writes (1:9) implies that his converts were Gentiles, and (4:1) that they were largely working class. Although Paul preached first in the synagogue, he attracted many God-fearers and Gentiles. In I Thess 2:2 he speaks of "great opposition" at Thessalonica, which caused him to flee the city with Silas. It is not unlikely that the opposition that Paul faced from both Gentiles and Jews continued after he left and afflicted his converts.

GENERAL ANALYSIS OF THE MESSAGE

Because Paul's thought shifts back and forth in the letter, readers will benefit by quickly scanning through I Thess to get a surface impression of the contents, and then they may find useful this analysis that highlights the main issues.

Clearly Paul cared for the Thessalonians. He addresses them as his "brothers" (= brothers and sisters) some fourteen times—proportionate to the letter's length this is an intense usage. Sometimes Paul benevolently flatters his addressees, but one gets a sense that he was genuinely relieved when Timothy returned to him at Corinth with the good news that the Thessalonian Christians had not been unsettled by affliction (3:3) and were holding firm in the Lord (3:6–8), spreading the faith in Christ by making the word of the Lord ring out elsewhere in Macedonia and Greece (Achaia; 1:7–8; see 4:10). Thus Paul is able to write this gentle letter in which there is encouragement to do more but little expressed reproof or major new instructions. Indeed, throughout most of it, using oratorical style, Paul is able to appeal to what the Thessalonians already know. A major exception is 4:13–5:11, where he teaches something new.

First, why in much of the letter does Paul remind the Thessalonians of things they already know? On the simplest level, any community that consisted largely of Gentiles converted after a relatively brief missionary visit by Paul had made an enormous change in accepting belief in the one God of Israel who was also the Father of Jesus Christ; and so reinforcement by recalling what had been preached would be appropriate.

Moreover, he reminds his readers of his behavior as a preacher at Thessalonica in I Thess 2:1–13. Does Paul need to remind the Thessalonians that he himself underwent suffering when he preached there (2:2) because he is being accused of cowardice in having fled the city and left others to face the results of his preaching (Acts 17:9–10)? Was this reminder provoked by charges made against him by those afflicting the church there? Was he being compared to the stereotype of the crude and avaricious wandering Cynic philosopher peddling his message?

Second, why in 4:13–5:11, instead of reminding the Thessalonians of what they already know, does Paul indicate that they need further precision? Paul had a strongly apocalyptic or eschatological understanding of what God had done in Christ: the death and resurrection of Jesus marked the change of times, so that all were now living in the end-time. This was a message of hope for all who believed; and Paul had taught the Thessalonians about the ultimate fulfillment of that hope, namely, Christ's second coming (1:10; 4:16–17). As they underwent affliction and suffering, this expectation supplied strength. No time or date can be attached to all this; indeed, it will come suddenly, so that they should be careful to stay wide awake and sober (5:11). Notice that Paul is not interested in the details of the Parousia as such; his pastoral concern is to calm any disturbance in the community he had evangelized.

DID PAUL WRITE I THESS 2:13–16?

Is 2:13–16 an original part of I Thess written by Paul, or was it added by a later editor? It refers to "the Jews who killed the Lord Jesus" and generalizes about them in hostile terms. If written by Paul, who certainly had been in Jerusalem in the 30s, it constitutes a very early, major refutation of the revisionist theory that the Romans were almost exclusively responsible for Jesus' death. *Arguments against Pauline authorship of I Thess 2:13–16 include:* (a) It constitutes a second Thanksgiving in the letter; (b) The statement that certain Judean Jews "are the enemies of the whole human race" resembles Pagan polemic; (c) The statement that the Jews "are filling up their sins" and divine "wrath has finally overtaken them" contradicts Rom 11:25–26 that "all Israel will be saved." *Arguments for Pauline authorship of I Thess 2:13–16:* (a) All mss. contain it; (b) Paul speaks hostilely of "Jews" as persecutors in II Cor 11:24, and he is not incapable of polemic hyperbole; (c) In Rom (2:5; 3:5–6; 4:15; 11:25) Paul speaks of the wrath of God against Jews, so that the hope of their ultimate salvation does not prevent portrayal of divine disfavor.

In Paul's thought the jealous Jews at Thessalonica who harassed both him and those who came to believe in Jesus would represent what Rom 11:25 calls the part of Israel upon whom "hardening" (= the "wrath" of I Thess) had come. If before Paul arrived, Jews who observed the Law had attracted some God-fearing Gentiles and prominent women (Acts 17:4), understandably they might have been infuriated when their converts went over to Paul's proclamation of the Messiah in which Law observance was not required.

✦

19

Letter to the Galatians

In some ways this has been considered the most Pauline of the Pauline writings, the one in which anger has caused Paul to say what he really thinks. Paul discards diplomacy in challenging the Galatians. Not surprisingly, Christian innovators or reformers have appealed to Gal's vigorous language and imagery. For instance, Luther called it his "pet epistle," for he found in Paul's rejection of justification by the works of the Law support for his rejection of salvation by good works. Others, however, have been embarrassed by the crudeness of the polemic and the lack of nuance about the Jewish heritage. One thing is certain: no one can fault the Paul of Gal for making theology dull.

THE BACKGROUND

In the years before AD 55 Paul had proclaimed the gospel to Gentiles who now constituted the churches of Galatia. Although his stay among them was brought about or affected by a "weakness of the flesh" (4:13), the Galatians were more than kind during Paul's affliction and treated him as an angel of God. Seemingly they saw him work

SUMMARY OF BASIC INFORMATION

DATE: 54–55 from Ephesus is more likely than 57 from Macedonia (Traditional Chronology; see Table 5 in Chapter 16 above for Revisionist Chronology).

TO: Churches around Ancyra in ethnic Galatian territory, i.e., north-central section of the province of Galatia in Asia Minor (evangelized in 50 and 54), or, less likely, to churches at Antioch, Lystra, and Derbe in the south of the province (evangelized in 47–48 and 50).

AUTHENTICITY, UNITY, AND INTEGRITY: Not seriously disputed.

FORMAL DIVISION:
  A. Opening Formula: 1:1–5
  B. Thanksgiving: None
  C. Body: 1:6–6:10
  D. Concluding Formula: 6:11–18

  DIVISION ACCORDING TO CONTENTS (AND RHETORICAL ANALYSIS):
1:1–10: Introduction:
  1:1–5: Opening Formula (already defensive in describing apostleship and what Christ has done)
  1:6–10: Exordium or introduction (astonishment in place of Thanksgiving), describing the issue, the adversaries, and the seriousness of the case (by anathemas)
1:11–2:14: Paul narrates his preaching career to defend his thesis about his gospel stated in 1:11–12
2:15–21: Debate with opponents, contrasting his gospel with theirs; justified by faith in Christ, not by observing the Law; Christians live by faith
3:1–4:31: Proofs for justification by faith not by Law: six arguments drawn from the past experiences of the Galatians and from Scripture, particularly centered on Abraham
5:1–6:10: Ethical exhortation (paraenesis) for them to preserve their freedom, and walk according to the Spirit
6:11–18: Conclusion: authenticating postscript in Paul's own hand (as distinct from scribe who took dictation); recapitulation of attitude toward circumcision; benediction.

---

miracles (3:5). This memory sharpens his outrage that the Galatians now (4:16) evaluate him as an enemy who somehow cheated them in his preaching about Christ. How had this come about?

After Paul left Galatia, Christians of Jewish origin (6:13) had come, probably from Jerusalem, preaching another gospel (1:7), that is, an understanding of what God had done in Christ different from Paul's. In subsequent Christian history a sense of the sacredness of NT Scripture and respect for Paul as the great apostle have naturally led Christians to a conviction that his gospel was true to Christ and that of his adversaries was not. Nevertheless, since there is no convincing reason for thinking that "the preachers," as they may be called, were fools or dishonest, I shall seek to show why their gospel, so far as it can be reconstructed, sounded plausible.

A key factor in the preachers' proclamation was an insistence on circumcision and observing the calendrical feasts (4:10). As the preachers explained, the one true God had blessed all the nations of the world in Abraham who believed in God (Gen 15:6) and then, as part of the covenant, gave Abraham the commandment of circumcision (Gen 17:10) and the heavenly calendar. Through the preachers the work of Jesus the Messiah was now being extended to the Gentiles, who can be fully included in the covenant if they are circumcised in imitation of Abraham and do the works of the Law.

Yet had not Paul already brought the gospel to the Gentile believers in Galatia? No! In order to make quick converts Paul had preached a truncated gospel that did not tell them that sharing in the Abraham covenant depended on circumcision. Paul had left them without the guidance of the Law, prey to the desires of the flesh; and that is why sin was still rampant among them. This was a persuasive message, especially if the preachers pointed out that Paul was a latecomer to the gospel; that he had not known Jesus as the real apostles had; that Jesus, who was circumcised himself, had never exempted anyone from circumcision; and that the real apostles at Jerusalem kept the feasts and the food laws. How could Paul answer the preachers and win back the Galatians to recognize that he had preached the truth? (As we turn to analyze the letter he wrote, we should keep in mind that controversy with the preachers shapes his expression and phrasing. Too often Paul's "theology" of justification, faith, and freedom is abstracted from Gal without recognizing the apologetic shaping.)

GENERAL ANALYSIS OF THE MESSAGE

In the Opening Formula (1:1–5), Paul designates himself as an apostle, a status stemming not from human beings but from Jesus Christ (1:1—and from God: 1:15). Atypically, he does not explicitly name a co-sender as he addresses himself "to the churches of Galatia," that is, a group of communities in the Galatian region or in the larger province of Galatia. Paul is the target of the attack in Galatia, and his response is marked by anger that does not allow for a Thanksgiving.

The Body opens with a type of *exordium or introduction* (1:6–10) that, with a biting tone of disappointed astonishment, quickly lays out the issue, the adversaries, and the seriousness of the case: there is no other gospel than the one proclaimed by Paul to the Galatians in the grace of Christ; cursed are those who preach something different. Then, using the rhetorical pattern of court defenses, Paul writes in letter form *an apologia* (1:11–2:21), polemical in tone but employing a sequence of rhetorical devices. To appreciate the points made by Paul, one should keep in mind the claims of the preachers as reconstructed in the *Background* above. Paul's main thesis is that the gospel he proclaims came through divine revelation and not from human beings (1:11–12). As a paradigm of that, Paul relates the story of his call and preaching, touching down on key points, for example: the initial divine revelation and commission; no dependence on the Jerusalem apostles; the challenge to him from the party insisting on circumcision for the Gentiles; the agreement reached between him and the Jerusalem authorities rejecting the challenge; and the acknowledgment that he was entrusted with the gospel and apostolate to the uncircumcised (1:13–2:10). Then, in 2:11–14, describing those of the circumcision party who afterward came to Antioch from Jerusalem claiming to represent James, Paul is suggesting that they were the progenitors of those who came to Galatia; for he blends his defense of the gospel at Antioch against the earlier adversaries into a type of dialogue with the Jewish Christian preachers in Galatia (2:15–21).

Paul next piles up *six arguments from experience and Scripture to convince the foolish Galatians who have allowed themselves to be bewitched* (3:1–4:31)—arguments now simplified. First (3:1–5): The Galatians received the Spirit without observing works of the Law. Second (3:6–14): Against the preachers' insistence on the circumcision of Abraham (Gen 17:10,14) he cites God's promise that in Abraham all the nations would be blessed (Gen 12:3)—a promise independent of circumcision. Third (3:15–25): A will that has been ratified cannot be annulled by a later addition. The Law came 430 years after the promises to Abraham. The Law was but a prison warden until Christ came. Fourth (3:26–4:11): The

Galatians, who were slaves to the elemental spirits of the universe, have been redeemed by God's Son and adopted as God's children; why do they want again to become slaves, this time to the demands of the Law? Fifth (4:12–20): The Galatians treated Paul like an angel; how can he have become their enemy? Sixth (4:21–31): Paul takes up the Hagar/Sarah story (Gen 16–21) in an allegorical interpretive fashion. Hagar, the slave woman, does not represent the descendance of the Gentiles but the present, earthly Jerusalem (the church there?) and the enslaving covenant of the Law given on Mt. Sinai; Sarah, the free woman, represents the heavenly Jerusalem and the covenant of God's promise to Abraham—she is the mother of all who have been made free in Christ.

After the argument Paul finishes the Body of Gal with *a passionate exhortation* (5:1–6:10) against the preachers and a warning that the Law will not help the Galatians against the works of the flesh (contrasted with the fruit of the Spirit in 5:19–26). In 5:6, "In Christ Jesus neither circumcision nor uncircumcision has any force, but faith working through love," Paul makes it clear that he does not consider circumcision something evil but rather something that has no power to bring justification to the Gentiles. Paul thought of faith as something that had to find expression in love manifested in the life of the believer. (He would see God at work in both the faith and the love, with neither being simply human reactions.) "The law of Christ" is not the Law of Sinai but the obligation to bear one another's burdens (6:2).

Then, Paul stops the scribe and writes the *Conclusion* (6:11–18) against circumcision with his own hand in big letters, so that the Galatians cannot miss the point. In "the Israel of God" it makes no difference whether one is circumcised. As for the preachers, "From now on let no one make more trouble for me, for I bear the marks of Jesus on my body." What Paul has suffered as an apostle is more important than the marks of his circumcision!

THE "FAITH [PISTIS] OF CHRIST" (2:16, ETC.)

A major discussion has centered on what Paul means when he speaks of being justified or of justification, not from the works of the Law but from/through the *faith of* (Jesus) *Christ* (2:16; 3:22; also Rom

3:22,26; Phil 3:9). The construction "from/through faith of Christ" (*ek/dia pisteōs Christou*) can be understood as an objective genitive—that is, the Christian's faith in Christ, or as a subjective genitive, that is, the faith possessed or manifested by Christ. The debate also affects the simpler and more common expression "from faith" (*ek pisteōs*). Both interpretations require comment.

Faith in Christ is probably the more common interpretation and may be supported by Gal 3:26, which uses the preposition "in." In that interpretation, however, although faith in what God has done in Christ, especially through the crucifixion and resurrection, can be seen as a response that brings about justification, one needs to emphasize that God also generates the response—a divine grace given to believe, responding to the divine grace manifested in Christ. The faith of Christ is sometimes understood as his fidelity to God's plan, a fidelity that brought about justification. Some find that interpretation weak and prefer to think of the faith manifested by Jesus in going to crucifixion without visible divine support. J. Louis Martyn contends that Gal 2:20–21 shows that Christ's faith is Christ's faithful death. Still others combine the two approaches and suggest that Christ's faith manifested in his death is given to his followers through faith in Christ.

∗

20

Letter to the Philippians

In some ways this is the most attractive Pauline letter, reflecting more patently than any other the warm affection of the apostle for his brothers and sisters in Christ. It contains one of the best-known and -loved NT descriptions of the graciousness of Christ: one who emptied himself and took on the form of a servant, even unto death on a cross. Nevertheless, Phil involves several much-debated interpretive issues: Where was Paul? When did he write? Is the letter a unity, or is it two or three originally distinct letters?

THE BACKGROUND

Paul had crossed over by sea with Silas and Timothy from the Province of Asia (Asia Minor, or present-day Turkey) to Macedonia (Europe, present-day northern Greece) in AD 50–51. They landed at the port of Neapolis, where the great Roman highway across Macedonia, the Via Egnatia, had an access coming down to the sea from Philippi, which is about nine miles inland. This site was a major Roman city. Here

SUMMARY OF BASIC INFORMATION

DATE: Ca. 56 if from Ephesus. (Or 61–63 from Rome, or 58–60 from Caesarea.)

TO: The Christians at Philippi, a Roman colony (Acts 17:12) where army veterans were allotted property after battles in the civil wars (42 BC), and like Thessalonica (farther west) an important commercial city on the Via Egnatia. Evangelized by Paul ca. AD 50 on his "Second Missionary Journey" (see Table 5 in Chapter 16 above for Revisionist Chronology).

AUTHENTICITY: Not seriously disputed.

UNITY: Scholarship about evenly divided: that two or three letters have been combined to make up Philippians is widely suggested, but a respectable case can be made for unity.

INTEGRITY: Today no major theory of interpolations. In the past, proposed interpolations for theological reasons: "bishops and deacons" (1:1), or the christological hymn (2:6–11).

FORMAL DIVISION (OF EXISTING, UNIFIED LETTER):
A. Opening Formula: 1:1–2
B. Thanksgiving: 1:3–11
C. Body: 1:12–4:20: From Paul's prison situation: Christ-mindedness exhortations, warning against false teachers, gratitude to the Philippians
D. Concluding Formula: 4:21–23

DIVISION ACCORDING TO CONTENTS:
1:1–11: Address/greeting and Thanksgiving
1:12–26: Paul's situation in prison and attitude toward death
1:27–2:16: Exhortation based on example of Christ (christological hymn)
2:17–3:1a: Paul's interest in the Philippians and planned missions to them
3:1b–4:1: Warning against false teachers; Paul's own behavior (a separate letter?)
4:2–9: Exhortation to Euodia and Syntyche: unity, joy, higher things
4:10–20: Paul's situation and the Philippians' generous gifts
4:21–23: Concluding greeting, blessing.

Paul proclaimed the gospel and founded his first church in Europe (Acts 16:11–15; Phil 4:15).

Reading Acts 16 one gets the impression of a relatively brief stay and some success among Jews and Gentiles, despite civic harassment. At the beginning (16:13–15), by a stream outside the city gate, Lydia, a merchant woman from Thyatira who was attracted to Judaism ("a worshiper of God"), was baptized with her household and offered her house for Paul to stay. This story seems to reflect accurately social realities in Philippi, especially the prominent position played by women. Some confirmation may be supplied in Phil 4:2 by Paul's mentioning two women, Euodia and Syntyche, who were in some disagreement but who had been his evangelistic coworkers there. Their names and those of Epaphroditus and Clement (2:25; 4:3) suggest that there was a high percentage of Gentiles among the Philippian Christians.

More conversions at Philippi are recorded in Acts 16:16–40. The fact that Paul had driven out a spirit from a fortune-telling slave girl caused the owners to haul him and Silas before the local magistrates as troublesome Jews. They were stripped, beaten, and imprisoned. When an earthquake jarred open the prison doors, Paul and Silas refused to escape—a gesture that led to the conversion of the jailer and his household. Eventually the magistrates apologized for mishandling Roman citizens but asked them to depart, and so they set out west along the Via Egnatia for Thessalonica.

GENERAL ANALYSIS OF THE MESSAGE

The analysis of most of the Pauline letters moves sequentially, following the traditional letter format, but here, because Paul's thought shifts back and forth, readers may want to scan the letter quickly to get a surface impression of the contents, and then turn to this analysis that highlights the main issues.

Those converted at Philippi by Paul entered into a unique partnership with him (1:5) that lasted until this very moment when he was writing from prison. Their sending Epaphroditus to Paul had been a new attestation to this fidelity; and now, because of concern over that valuable co-worker's health, Paul has sent him back (4:18; 2:25–26). A strong bond of friendship colors this letter that expresses Paul's gratitude and keeps the Philippians informed; indeed the human attraction of Paul the man is revealed in their loyalty. One cannot dismiss simply as letter-form his emotional words to the Philippians, written in a context that had brought him face to face with the possibility of his own death: "I hold you in my heart" (1:7); "With God as my witness, I yearn for all of you with the affection of Christ Jesus" (1:8). Besides the strong attestation of gratitude and friendship, which may be considered the main motivation for the letter, there are important indications about Paul's outlook from prison and the situation at Philippi that need to be considered.

PAUL'S OUTLOOK FROM PRISON: The letter reflects thoughts forced on Paul by his imprisonment for preaching the gospel. First, he is not despondent despite what he is suffering. His imprisonment advances the gospel since clearly he is suffering for Christ (1:12–13; 3:8); and others have been emboldened by his example to preach without fear (1:14), though some are doing that in a spirit of rivalry in order to outdo Paul (1:15), and he shows contempt for such competitiveness (Phil 1:18). The preachers do not matter; the only thing that matters is that Christ is preached.

Second, reflection on death is brought on by Paul's current situation. Earlier in I Thess 4:17, Paul used the language of: "We who are alive" at the coming of Christ. If that is not just an editorial "we," Paul expected to survive till the Parousia. But in Phil 1:20–26 he wrestles with the possibility of dying (also II Cor 5:1–10), trying to decide whether the immediate access to Christ provided by death is better than the continued ministry of proclaiming Christ.

THE SITUATION AT PHILIPPI: Paul wants the Philippian Christians to be blameless, shining as lights amid a crooked and perverse generation and holding fast to the word of life, so that he will know that he has not run in vain (Phil 2:14–16). Paul wishes to hear that they stand firm in one spirit, striving with one mind (2:2,5). Yet there are some who are troubling the Philippian church. At least three distinct attitudes are reprimanded in the text:

First, there is internal dissension in Philippi among those, like Euodia and Syntyche, who had labored side by side with Paul (4:2–3). The cause of the dissension is not clear, but against conceit and pushing one's own interests Paul holds up Christ as an example of self-giving service in the christological hymn of 2:5–11.

Second, apart from the different-minded persons who had worked with Paul, there is an external opposition to the Philippian Christians that causes them to suffer (1:28–29). Seemingly this involves people complaining about the strange teachings of the Christians because it does not acknowledge the gods, and appealing to the local authorities to arrest or to expel them (1:30). Nothing can be done about such injustice, but God will overcome.

Third, there are the workers of evil (3:2–3) whom Paul calls dogs, and whom the Philippians should look out for. They mutilate the flesh, seemingly by circumcision; and believers in Jesus who worship in the spirit should put no faith in such emphasis on the flesh. Paul can refute these adversaries by describing his own impeccable Jewish credentials—even though he counts all that as loss when compared to the supreme gain of knowing Christ Jesus the Lord (3:4–11). Some think that this Philippian passage is a general warning in case such people show up; for, if they were already at work in Philippi, Paul would have devoted more of the letter to them. Or else they may be just beginning to appear in small numbers in Philippi. (What complicates the further diagnosis of the adversaries in this third group is the tendency of scholars to interpret other parts of chap. 3 as referring to them.)

Do Paul's remarks in 3:12 and 3:18–19 refer to (actual?) distinguishable adversaries who were different from those mentioned in 3:2–3? Our inability to answer this question cautions against complicating the clearer condemnation in 3:2–3 of adversaries who would try to emphasize circumcision and confuse the Philippians. Since most of what Paul says about himself and his outlook in chap. 3 would have its value no matter who and how distinct the adversaries were, a decision about them is not essential to reading Phil intelligently.

HYMNS IN NT LETTERS AND THE
CHRISTOLOGICAL HYMN OF 2:5–11

HYMNS IN NT LETTERS. Although there are references to Christians singing "psalms and hymns and spiritual songs," the NT does not contain a book of hymns. Rather first-century Christian canticles and hymns seem to be incorporated into larger writings of another genre— for example, gospel, letter, apocalyptic vision—and detectable only by scholarly investigation. Most often nothing in the context states that a hymn is being introduced and quoted. Among the criteria proposed for detecting a hymn are the following:

- Worship milieu, for example, Eph 5:14.
- Introductory formulae, for example, I Tim 3:16; or in christological hymns a clause introduced by a relative pronoun, "The one who . . ." (Phil 2:6), extended by causal connectives.

• Rhythmic style, parallel patterns, lines or strophes of equal length, for example, the series of six aorist passive verbs in I Tim 3:16.
• Vocabulary or syntax different from that customarily used by the author—if the author did not compose the hymn.
• Often characteristic of the hymns is a high christology, for example, John 1:1; Col 1:16; Phil 2:9—including themes of creation, struggle against evil and restoration, resurrection, exaltation, enthronement.
• The redactional addition of explanatory clauses/phrases to traditional hymns relates them more directly to the author's theme, for example, "even death on a cross" (Phil 2:8c).

The detection of hymns is an inexact "science." Thus there are debates about the individual hymns—where they end, or how they are to be divided, or which lines are original.

THE CHRISTOLOGICAL HYMN OF 2:5–11. These issues are worth mentioning:

• Most think that Paul wrote but did not create these lines.
• The structure of the hymn is debated.
• Proposals about the background of the hymn include both pagan and OT/Jewish literature. A relation to the OT figure of personified Wisdom is clear; other proposed references are not.
• Also debated is whether the hymn was originally composed in Greek or in Aramaic.
• Dispute about the precise focus of the christology is centered on 2:6–7: does the hymn posit an incarnation of a divine figure, or is Christ the human who was in the image of God but, by humbly choosing to go lower, ultimately was exalted by being given the divine name (2:9–11).
• Although the hymn is christological, it exhorts the addressees for their own salvation to follow the exalted Christ.

UNITY: ONE LETTER OR TWO OR THREE?

Many scholars view Phil as a composite of two or more original Pauline letters. While the unity of many of Paul's letters has been called into question, only II Cor and Phil remain debated today. The reasons for understanding Phil as a combination of prior writings include:

in the mid-second century Polycarp (*Philippians* 3:2) referred to Paul's "letters" to the Philippians; in Phil 3:1b Paul himself says, "To write the same things to you again is no trouble to me," perhaps referring to another earlier letter; at the end of chap. 2 (vv. 23–30) Paul discusses his travel plans, which he usually does toward a letter's conclusion; in turn, at 3:1a Paul uses the word "finally" as if he were about to close the letter, but two more chaps. follow; why is it that Paul mentions sending Epaphroditus back before he refers to Epaphroditus's arrival with gifts from the Philippians for Paul?; some argue that 3:1b–4:3 are an insertion and that 3:1a and 4:4 fit together uniquely well; still others have more complicated understandings of the pieces that would have been used to construct canonical Phil. Some scholars see two original letters and still more discern three. Nevertheless, while Paul does switch back and forth in Phil., there are not two or three distinct Opening and Concluding Formulas. The logic of the arrangement of segments of the letter into its current form as a composite is far from clear. Moreover, there are rare Pauline words and a community of ideas shared by the proposed two or three letters. This debate, probably never to be resolved, need not be of great concern to one who simply wishes to read the letter.

21

Letter to Philemon

Even those who contend that he did not write Col, a letter that has the same setting and many of the same dramatis personae as Phlm (and that is considered in its own right below), do not seriously dispute that Paul wrote this letter.

THE BACKGROUND

This is the shortest of the Pauline letters (335 words), and in format closest to the pattern of ordinary Hellenistic letters. It is not simply a letter from one individual to another asking a favor. Paul, a prisoner, who sacrificed his freedom for Christ, writes to the head of a Christian house-church to ask for another's freedom; and in every line just beneath the surface is the basic challenge brought to the societal rank of master and slave by the changed relationship introduced by the gospel.

The specific slavery situation dealt with in Phlm is unfortunately not spelled out. Some scholars suggest that Philemon was a well-to-do Christian, Apphia was his wife, and Archippus was close to him.

SUMMARY OF BASIC INFORMATION

DATE: ca. 55 if from Ephesus; 58–60 if from Caesarea (unlikely); 61–63 if from Rome.

TO: Philemon, with Apphia, Archippus, and the church at Philemon's house.

AUTHENTICITY, UNITY, AND INTEGRITY: Not seriously disputed.

FORMAL DIVISION:
- A. Opening Formula: 1–3
- B. Thanksgiving: 4–7
- C. Body: 8–22 (21–22 can be considered a Body-Closing or part of the Conclusion)
- D. Concluding Formula: 23–25.

DIVISION ACCORDING TO CONTENTS (AND RHETORICAL STRUCTURE):

1–3: Address, greeting

4–7: Thanksgiving serving as an *exordium* to gain Philemon's good will by praise

8–16: Appeal offering motives to Philemon on behalf of Onesimus (*confirmation*)

17–22: Reiteration and expansion of appeal (*peroration*)

23–25: Concluding greetings, blessing.

Philemon's home served as the meeting place of a house-church. Paul's actual, personal relationship to Philemon is not entirely clear. Onesimus was Philemon's slave who seemingly ran away (some contend that Onesimus was simply out of town on business and that things went poorly, so he was fearful of returning home). Somehow, Paul had (recently) converted him. In any case the fact that Paul was responsible for the new life shared by both Philemon and Onesimus underlies this message designed to work out the effects of that theological reality on the social plane.

GENERAL ANALYSIS OF THE MESSAGE

The letter, designed to persuade, is astute, with almost every verse hinting at something more than is stated. In vv. 4–7, which constitute a *captatio benevolentiae* (an opening seeking goodwill), Paul flatters (not necessarily insincerely) by reporting what he has heard about Philemon's Christian love and faith. Then in v. 8 Philemon is given an oblique reminder of Paul's apostolic authority to command; yet by Paul's preference this letter is an appeal concerning Onesimus, Paul's child in Christ. Onesimus was useful to Paul in prison and Paul would have liked to keep him as a co-worker, but Paul will do nothing without Philemon's consent. Consequently he is sending Onesimus back with the wish that Philemon will accept him no longer as a slave but as a beloved brother. Paul asks for much: not simply that Onesimus escape any punishment, not simply that Onesimus be freed, but that Onesimus be moved to the plane of the Christian relationship: "Receive him as you would receive me" (v. 17). The request is a dramatic example of Paul's way of thinking in fidelity to the change of values brought about by Christ. Paul writes in his own hand a promise to pay back anything owed; but by emphasizing that he is one to whom Philemon owes his Christian life, Paul makes any demand for repayment virtually impossible. Paul expresses his confidence in both Philemon's "obedience" (to Paul or to God?) and Philemon's doing more than asked. Some interpret the "more" as a hint that Philemon should release Onesimus, who is his Christian brother. Paul promises a visit (to see the situation?) and sends final greetings.

SOCIAL IMPORT OF PAUL'S VIEW OF SLAVERY

Paul had an apocalyptic approach to reality in which the death and resurrection of Christ marked the changing of the times. Precisely because Christ is coming back soon, structures that do not represent gospel values can be allowed to stand provided that they can be bypassed to enable Christ to be preached. It will not be for long. The implications of the gospel for slavery are clear for Paul: in Christ Jesus "there is neither slave nor free" (Gal 3:28); all are of equal value. Yet to overturn the massive Roman societal institution of slavery is not a feasible accomplishment in the very limited time before Christ comes. Obviously on the worldly level slaves will seek to gain freedom; but if one is a slave at the time of being called and physical freedom is unobtainable, that situation is not of essential importance. "In whatever state each was called, there let that person remain with God" (I Cor 7:21–22).

To some interpreters Phlm reflects a welcome, stronger Pauline position on slavery, one that would eventually move sensitive Christians as a whole to reject it. Here we see that when Paul can hope for cooperation, he challenges a Christian slave owner to defy certain conventions;

and from a theological viewpoint to recognize in Onesimus a beloved brother and thus acknowledge his Christian transformation.

To other interpreters, Phlm represents a lack of nerve. Despite his implicit encouragement to release Onesimus, Paul does not tell Philemon explicitly that keeping another human being as a slave factually denies that Christ has changed values. Indeed Paul's not having condemned slavery explicitly has been used by some as proof that the institution is not evil in itself. The question was not asked whether Paul's partial toleration was not so fundamentally determined by his apocalyptic outlook that it could not serve as a guide once the expectation of the second coming was moved to the indefinite future.

22

First Letter to the Corinthians

Paul's known contacts with Corinth lasted nearly a decade, and there is more Pauline correspondence to that city than to any other place. Attempts to live according to the gospel in the multiethnic and cross-cultural society at Corinth raised issues still encountered in multiethnic, multiracial, and cross-cultural societies today.

THE BACKGROUND

The mainland of Greece (Achaia) is connected to the large Peloponnesus peninsula to the south by a narrow, four-mile-wide isthmus. On a plateau controlling the isthmus was the city of Corinth. This spot had been settled for more than 4,000 years when the city effectively came to an end through defeat by the Romans in 146 BC. The replacement city to which Paul came in AD 50/51–52 had been founded a century before (44 BC) by Julius Caesar as a Roman colony. With its strategic placement Corinth attracted a cosmopolitan population, and many of them soon became wealthy. The site thrived as a manufacturing (bronze

SUMMARY OF BASIC INFORMATION

DATE: Late 56 or very early 57 from Ephesus (or 54/55 in the Revisionist Chronology).

TO: Mixed church of Jews and Gentiles at Corinth converted by Paul in 50/51–52 (or 42–43).

AUTHENTICITY: Not seriously disputed.

UNITY: Some see two or more separate letters interwoven, but unity is favored by an increasing majority, even if the one letter was composed in disjunctive stages as information and a letter came to Paul from Corinth.

INTEGRITY: No widely agreed-on major interpolations, although there is some debate about 14:34–35 and chap. 13; a lost letter preceded (I Cor 5:9).

FORMAL DIVISION:

    A. Opening Formula: 1:1–3
    B. Thanksgiving: 1:4–9
    C. Body: 1:10–16:18
    D. Concluding Formula: 16:19–24.

DIVISION ACCORDING TO CONTENTS:

1:1–9: Address/greetings and Thanksgiving, reminding Corinthians of their spiritual gifts

1:10–4:21: Part I: The factions

5:1–11:34: Part II: Problems of behavior (incest, lawsuits, sexual behavior, marriage, food, eucharist, liturgy); what Paul has heard and questions put to him

12:1–14:40: Part III: Problems of charisms and the response of love

15:1–58: Part IV: The resurrection of Christ and of the Christians

16:1–18: The collection, Paul's travel plans, commendations of people

16:19–24: Greetings; Paul's own hand; "Our Lord, come."

---

and terra cotta) and commercial center. Indeed, under Augustus it became the capital city of the province of Achaia.

Although Latin may have been the first language of the Roman colony, inscriptions show wide use of Greek, the language of commerce. Temples honored the standard Greek deities. The Egyptian cult of Isis and Serapis is attested. Homage was given to the emperors. There was a large first-century AD Jewish colony with its own officials and internal management.

Greek Corinth acquired an overblown reputation (partly through slander) for sexual license. Whatever was true of Greek Corinth, Roman Corinth simply had all the problems of a rough, relatively new boomtown adjacent to two seaports. Yet it also had advantages from Paul's point of view. A craftsman like Paul could find work and be self-supporting there. Because of the many who came and went, he would not be rejected as an outsider or even a resident alien; and the seed of the gospel that he sowed in Corinth might well be carried far and disseminated by those whom he evangelized.

AD 50/51–52. Acts 18 tells of Paul's residence in Corinth for eighteen months.

AD 54–57. From Corinth Paul eventually came to dwell in Ephesus for about three years.

Ca. AD 56. While staying in Ephesus (54–57) Paul got reports about Corinth from "those of Chloe" (I Cor 1:11). We know nothing of Chloe. About the same time or shortly afterward at Ephesus, Paul received a letter from the Corinthians (I Cor 7:1), perhaps in reply to his earlier (now lost) letter and apparently brought by Stephanas, Fortunatus, and Achaicus (16:17–18), who probably added their own reports. Paul then wrote I Cor from Ephesus. He refers to the letter from Corinth and seemingly answers questions that the Corinthians had raised.

GENERAL ANALYSIS OF THE MESSAGE

THE OPENING FORMULA (1:1–3) joins Sosthenes to Paul as co-sender. Seemingly this is the same man, now a Christian, who earlier was the ruler of the Corinthian synagogue and was beaten before the *bēma* when Gallio refused to judge Paul (Acts 18:17). In the first nine verses, including the Thanksgiving (1:4–9), Paul mentions (Jesus) Christ nine times, an emphasis befitting Paul's coming correction of Corinthian factionalism by insisting that they were baptized in the name of Christ and of no other. He also gives thanks that the Corinthians have been given grace enriching them in speech and knowledge and that they were not lacking in any charism—an ironic touch since he will have to castigate them in the letter about their pretended wisdom and their fights over charisms. Paul's letter shows that the situation in Corinth was complicated, but since he does not deal separately with groups of the Corinthians whom he mentions, but integrates his directions to them with his answers to questions that the Corinthians posed in their letter to him, it may be best to understand that the array of issues are facets of the same general problem.

PART I OF THE BODY OF THE LETTER (1:10–4:21). Almost four chapters are addressed to the problem of divisions or factions that exist at Corinth, about which members of Chloe's household have informed Paul. As a result of the coming of other missionaries (especially Apollos), but probably without an incentive from the missionaries themselves, there were now conflicting loyalties among the Corinthian Christians who declared preferences: "'I belong to Paul,' or 'I belong to Apollos,' or 'I belong to Cephas [Peter],' or 'I belong to Christ'" (I Cor 1:12). Paul's response may surprise us: All the preachers are only servants (3:5). "Is Christ divided? Was Paul crucified for you? Or were you baptized in the name of Paul?" (1:13). "Whether Paul, or Apollos, or Cephas . . . you belong to Christ, and Christ belongs to God" (3:22–23).

In choosing a particular preacher, like Apollos, some Corinthians may have been opting for what sounded like greater wisdom, whereas Paul had preached a foolishness really wiser than human wisdom, namely, Christ and him crucified (1:18–25). Paul laid down a solid foundation, indeed, the only possible foundation, Jesus Christ; and on the day of final judgment everything else that is insubstantial will be shown up and burned off (3:10–15). In a highly rhetorical manner Paul contrasts "us apostles" (4:9) to the proud Corinthians. "Here we are, fools for Christ, while you are so wise in Christ . . ." (4:10–13). This letter is a warning from a father to his children. "Shall I come to you with a rod, or with love in a spirit of gentleness?" (4:17–21).

PART II OF THE BODY OF THE LETTER (5:1–11:34). Next Paul turns to various problems of Christian behavior among the Corinthians. Apparently chaps. 5–6 involve things he has heard about Corinthian Christian practice. The first instance addressed by Paul (5:1–5) involves a man and his stepmother. Apparently, from Paul's perspective, there are inappropriate relations between them. Paul is furious over the situation, but he is equally irate with the church's attitude toward it: "And you are proud." Paul's outrage may betray his Jewish roots, but he bases his argument on the observation that such behavior was not tolerated even among Gentiles. His main concern is not the immorality of the world outside the community but sinfulness within the community that might leaven it harmfully (5:6–13). Inappropriate pride in the circumstances is symptomatic of sinful corruption in the congregation.

Paul's Jewish distrust of the standards of the pagan world is reflected in his insistence that disputes are to be settled by having fellow Christians act as judges rather than going before Gentile courts (6:1–8) and in his list of vices of which the Corinthian Christians were formerly guilty (6:9–11). In 6:12 we hear a slogan in circulation at Corinth: "For me everything is permissible." Paul qualifies it by insisting that not everything is helpful and that none of our choices must produce mastery over us.

In chap. 7 Paul begins to answer questions posed to him by the Corinthians. The first involves the statement "It is good for a man not to touch a woman." Paul does not encourage abstention from sex within marriage because it could create temptations and effect injustice. He encourages marriage for those who cannot exercise control, even though "I would like everyone to be as I am myself"—single (widower or never married?) and practicing abstinence (7:2–9).

To those already married Paul repeats the Lord's ruling against divorce and remarriage (7:10–11), but then adds a ruling of his own that permits separation when one of the partners is not a Christian and will not live in peace with the believer (7:12–16). In 7:17–40 Paul shows the extent to which his thinking is apocalyptic: he would have all people (circumcised Jew, uncircumcised Gentile, slave, celibate, married, widow) stay in the state in which they were when called to Christ because the time has become limited.

In chap. 8 Paul answers questions about food sacrificed to the gods and then offered in the marketplace. Since there are no gods other than the one God, it is quite irrelevant that food has been offered to gods. Yet pastorally Paul is concerned about weak converts whose understanding is imperfect. One must be careful not to scandalize weak believers. Knowledge, even correct knowledge, can puff up the self, but love builds up others and thus puts constraints on self-serving behavior. (The notion of pastoral limitations on one's rights can be an important challenge to a generation that constantly speaks of rights but not of responsibilities.)

In *chap.* 9 Paul gives an impassioned defense of his rights as an apostle. Following chap. 8 Paul uses himself as an example of foregoing one's "rights" for the sake of (service to) others. Moreover, it is not insecurity about his status that has caused him to pass over his rights as an apostle. Rather he supported himself and preached the gospel free of charge lest a request for support give the wrong impression that he was preaching for money. Indeed Paul presents the gospel free of charge as his own contribution to the ministry of evangelization.

Chaps. 10–11 deal with more problems at Corinth, predominantly those affecting community worship. Paul warns the Corinthians by using examples from the testing of Israel in the desert that "were written as a lesson to us on whom the ends of the ages have come." In 10:2,14–22 Paul writes of baptism and of the eucharistic cup of blessing that is a sharing in the blood of Christ and bread-breaking that is a sharing in the body of Christ (10:16). He makes it clear that through baptism and the eucharist God delivers and sustains Christians, yet he also shows that such exalted help does not exempt them from divine judgment. Interrupting the issue of the eucharist, 11:1–16 supplies directions for community "liturgical behavior": a man must pray or prophesy with head bared, while a woman must have her head covered. The basis offered for this demand may not have been deemed fully probative even by Paul himself, for at the end (11:16) he resorts to citing the authority of his own custom and those of the churches.

Then in 11:17–34 Paul returns to the eucharist and the meal in which it was set, bluntly expressing his displeasure with Corinthian behavior. Seemingly some have a meal that precedes the special bread-breaking and cup blessing, while others are excluded and go hungry. Perhaps this echoes a social situation where social status informs arrangement of believers into groups—the wealthy dine while the poor go without. That is not Paul's notion of the church of God (11:22); either all should eat together, or they should eat first at home (11:33–34). The whole purpose of the sacred breaking of the bread is *koinōnia* (10:16), not division of the community. Indeed, Paul contends that judgment is already falling on the Corinthians, for some have died and many are sick (11:30).

PART III OF THE BODY OF THE LETTER (12:1–14:40). *Chaps. 12 and 14* deal with the spiritual gifts or charisms given in abundance to the Corinthian Christians, while *chap. 13*, sometimes called a hymn to love, appears as an interruption corrective of any acquisitiveness about charisms. These chaps. have received so much attention that the brief focus here is on just one aspect of what is implied by the picture Paul has painted. Because 12:28 lists apostles, prophets, and teachers as the first charisms, most often the Corinthian community is thought to have been administered by charismatics—that is, those who were recognized to have been given one of those charisms by the Spirit. Yet we know relatively little of how functions were divided and should note that a special charism of "administration" is mentioned in 12:28. (Eph 4:11 lists apostles, prophets, evangelists, pastors, and teachers—suggesting that order and function may not have been exact or uniform.) The idea that in the 50s all the Pauline churches were administered charismatically is risky because of both the lack of information in most of the other letters written at this time, and the reference to bishops and deacons at Philippi (Phil 1:1). Finally, in 14:34–35, immediately after a description of prophecy, women are excluded from speaking in churches; yet 11:5 allows women to pray or prophesy with their head covered. (Some would argue that 14:34–35 is a later interpolation by someone else into Paul's letter.)

PART IV OF THE BODY OF THE LETTER (15:1–58). Here Paul describes the gospel in terms of the resurrection of Jesus and then draws implications from that for the resurrection of Christians. Some Corinthian Christians have been saying that there is no resurrection of the dead (15:12). In 15:1–11 Paul reminds them of the common tradition that Jesus rose from the dead and appeared to Cephas, the Twelve, 500, James, all the apostles, and finally Paul himself—a tradition totally conformed to the Scriptures and solidly attested: "Whether, then, it was I or they, thus we preach and thus you believed" (15:11). Basing himself on what happened to Christ, Paul contends that all the dead are to be raised (15:12–19), that the resurrection is future (15:20–34), and bodily (15:35–50). There is an eschatological order: first, Christ; then, at his return, those who belong to Christ; then, at the end, when he has destroyed every dominion, authority, and power, and has subjected all the enemies (with death as the last enemy), Christ hands over the kingdom to the Father. Finally, the Son himself will be subjected to God, who put all things under him so that God may be all in all (15:23–28). Resurrection is not an abstract issue for Paul; rather, the hope of being raised explains his willingness to suffer (15:30–34).

In 15:35–58 Paul concentrates on another objection raised at Corinth to the resurrection of the dead: With what kind of body? Paul gives a subtle answer: a transformed body, as different as the grown plant is from the seed—a body imperishable, not perishable; powerful, not weak; spiritual, not physical; in the image of heavenly origin, not from the dust of the earth. At the end, whether alive or dead, we shall all be changed and clothed with the imperishable and immortal (15:51–54).

BODY CLOSING (16:1–18) AND CONCLUDING FORMULA (16:19–24). The closing of I Cor gives instructions for how the Corinthians are to take up the collection for Jerusalem and outlines Paul's plans. The concluding greetings are warm, but with pen in hand Paul acts as a judge, cursing anyone at Corinth who does not love the Lord (16:22). Still, his last words are positive, extending love to all and uttering a prayer in Jesus' mother tongue (Aramaic *Máráná' thā'*: "Our Lord, come").

THOSE CRITICIZED BY PAUL AT CORINTH

In chaps. 1–4 Paul corrects factionalism among the Corinthians, not by addressing each group separately but by criticizing the whole community of Christians for allowing themselves to be split up into the three or four groups. There is no evidence that Paul blamed the missionaries whose names designate the factions (Paul, Apollos, Cephas) for encouraging such factionalism, and there is little evidence that these ideas criticized by Paul came from abroad to Corinth.

The words *sophia* ("wisdom") and *sophos* ("wise") occur over twenty-five times in chaps. 1–3, as the wisdom of God (which others consider foolishness) is contrasted with human wisdom. The criticism of Jews and Greeks, both of whom reject the Christ who was the wisdom of God, shows that Paul is not criticizing any one view of human wisdom. While in chaps. 1–4 the word *gnōsis* ("knowledge") occurs only in 1:5, a considerable number of scholars contend that Paul was criticizing a gnostic movement at Corinth. For evidence they sometimes turn to the later chapters of I Cor, for example, "We all possess knowledge" (8:1) and the discussion of knowledge in 8:7–11—see also 13:2,8; 14:6. Some point to the denial of the resurrection of the dead (15:12,29) as possible evidence of a gnostic influence, and Paul's remark about saying "Jesus be cursed" (12:3) is also thought to indicate gnostic tendencies. Nevertheless, efforts at identifying a gnostic movement at Corinth, of which Paul is critical, falter on the evidence present in the letter when it is compared with the second-century Gnostic systems that claimed a special revealed knowledge about how recipients possessed a spark of the divine and could escape from the material world.

This leads us into the problem of evaluating a number of slogans in I Cor. "All things are permissible for me" (6:12; 10:23); "Food is meant for the stomach, and the stomach for food" (6:13); "Avoid immorality; every other sin that a person may commit is outside the body" (6:18); "It is good for a man not to touch a woman" (7:1). Paul correctively modifies these slogans, and so those whom he would admonish at Corinth are using them. His modifications raise two possibilities: these statements were coined either by Paul himself (but are now misused) or by Paul's adversaries (which seems more likely since these slogans do not occur in Paul's other letters). In either case, one could posit their use in a system of thought whereby superior knowledge leads a group toward libertinism on the principle that the body is unimportant, both as to what one does in the body and to what happens after death.

Other points in Paul's critique may have nothing to do with a profound theological stance (lawsuits, head coverings); they may reflect nothing more than Corinthian social mores. Although one may suspect that his repeated remarks about the inappropriateness of "boasting" (kauchasthai), which remarkably are amplified threefold in II Cor, may identify an activity that itself indicates an attitude capable of generating many forms of destructive behaviors. Nevertheless, appeals to II Cor for clarification of I Cor seek to explain the obscure through the equally obscure, since the actual appearance and temperament of the II Cor opponents are not overly clear.

·✱·

23

Second Letter to the Corinthians

Although there is no doubt that Paul wrote II Cor, transitions from one part of the letter to the other have been judged so abrupt that many scholars would chop it up into once-independent pieces. Nevertheless, it may well be the most oratorically persuasive of all Paul's writings, for in the various hypothetically independent pieces he has left unforgettable passages. Perhaps no other letter of Paul evokes so vividly the image of a suffering and rejected apostle, misunderstood by his fellow Christians.

THE BACKGROUND

Paul wrote I Cor in late 56 or very early AD 57. Thereafter Timothy came to Corinth (Acts 19:21–22; I Cor 4:17–19; 16:10–11). He found the situation bad. Many conclude that this was the result of the arrival of the false apostles described in II Cor 11:12–15, who were hostile to Paul. Timothy went to Ephesus to report the situation. This emergency caused Paul to depart Ephesus in order to pay what turned out to be a "painful visit" to Corinth (II Cor 2:1). The visit was a failure. He had

SUMMARY OF BASIC INFORMATION

DATE: Late summer/early autumn 57 from Macedonia (55/56 in the Revisionist Chronology).

TO: The church already addressed in I Cor, and to Christians in the whole province of Achaia.

AUTHENTICITY: Not seriously disputed.

UNITY: Most scholars think that several (two to five) letters have been combined.

INTEGRITY: 6:14–7:1 is thought by some to be a non-Pauline interpolation.

FORMAL DIVISION (of existing letter):
   A. Opening Formula: 1:1–2
   B. Thanksgiving: 1:3–11
   C. Body: 1:12–13:10
   D. Concluding Formula: 13:11–13.*

DIVISION ACCORDING TO CONTENTS:

1:1–11: Address/greeting and Thanksgiving, stressing Paul's sufferings
1:12–7:16: Part I: Paul's relations to the Corinthian Christians
   (a) 1:12–2:13: His deferred visit and the "tearful" letter
   (b) 2:14–7:16: His ministry (interruption: 6:14–7:1)
8:1–9:15: Part II: Collection for the church in Jerusalem
10:1–13:10: Part III: Paul's response to challenges to his apostolic authority
13:11–13: Concluding greetings, blessings.

---

*The RSV divides Greek 13:12 into two verses, so that the final verse (13:13) becomes 13:14.

threatened to come "with a rod" in I Cor 4:21; yet according to II Cor 10:1,10b he was perceived as weak and ineffective when face to face with the Corinthians. Apparently someone confronted him publicly and undermined his authority with the community (II Cor 2:5–11; 7:12). Paul left Corinth planning to return quickly, without stopping on the way back to visit the Macedonian churches.

Either before or after Paul returned to Ephesus, he changed his mind about going back to Corinth directly, realizing it would be another painful visit (II Cor 2:1); and instead he wrote a letter "with many tears" (2:3–4; 7:8–9—now lost). There may have been some severity in the letter, but it was meant to let them know his love. Encouraged by Paul's hope (7:14), Titus carried the letter. Anxious about the outcome, Paul departed Ephesus, going north to the port of Troas and crossing over by sea to Macedonia (II Cor 2:12–13). Meanwhile, Titus had been well treated at Corinth (II Cor 7:15); indeed, he was even able to begin collecting money for Paul to bring to Jerusalem (8:6); and he brought that joyful news to Paul in Macedonia (7:5–7,13b). Paul's "tearful" letter had caused sorrow. The Corinthians had repented and expressed concern for the grief they had caused Paul. Indeed, they were anxious to prove themselves innocent (7:7–13). In immediate response Paul wrote II Cor, which was carried by Titus (and two others) as part of a continued mission to raise money for Jerusalem (8:6,16–24). Paul himself went on to Corinth (his third visit; 12:14; 13:1–2), where he spent the winter of 57–58 before taking the collection to Jerusalem. There is no clear evidence that he ever returned to Corinth.

GENERAL ANALYSIS OF THE MESSAGE

OPENING FORMULA (1:1–2) AND THANKSGIVING (1:3–11). Paul changes the address from that of I Cor 1:2 (to the church of God in Corinth and saints everywhere) to include specifically the Christians "in the whole of Achaia." In 1:3–11 Paul speaks of the trials he suffered in Ephesus—an experience that highlighted his own afflictions and Christ's comfort and also served as background for his recent dealings with Corinth.

PART I OF THE BODY OF THE LETTER (1:12–7:16) discusses those dealings with the Corinthians, both narrating them and looking back at them theologically. In 1:12–2:13 he concentrates on his change of plans after the painful visit he had paid and explains that instead of exposing them to another harrowing confrontation, he wrote a letter "with many tears" to change their minds, so that when he did come it might be a joyful experience. From 2:5–11 we learn that the problem during the painful visit had centered on an obstreperous individual. In response to Paul's "tearful" letter the Corinthians have disciplined this person, but now Paul urges mercy and forgiveness.

In 2:14–7:16 Paul relates his ministry on a larger scale to the Corinthian crisis. That crisis wrings out of Paul passages of remarkable oratorical power—for example, 5:16–21 describing what God has done in Christ. Stressing that he is no peddler of God's word (2:17), Paul insists that he, unlike the others, should need no letter of recommendation to the Corinthians—they themselves are his letter (3:1–3). Paul then launches into the superiority of a ministry involving the Spirit over a ministry engraved on stone that brought death (3:4–11). He further mentions Moses' veil, declaring that when one turns to Christ, the veil is taken away because the Lord who spoke to Moses is now present in the Spirit (3:12–18). The power in Paul's ministry is really God's, for even though this treasure (apostolic evangelization) is in an "earthen vessel," it has not been crushed despite the fragility of the container (4:7–12): Paul has been sustained despite the hardships he has suffered.

In 4:16–5:10 in a series of contrasts (inner/outer; seen/not seen; naked/clothed) Paul explains why he does not lose heart. Paul's life draws nourishment from the unseen, as he lives in the tension of the "already" and the "not yet." In 5:14 Paul's "The love of Christ compels us" is a magnificent summary of his devotion. His declaration that God "gave us the ministry of reconciliation . . . so we are ambassadors for Christ" (5:18–20) describes movingly the vocation that Paul would share with them. In a stirring account of his life (6:4–10), Paul bares his soul to the Corinthians with a challenge for them to open their hearts to him (6:11–13).

Shifting to dualistic contradictions (6:14–7:1—righteousness/wickedness, etc.), Paul admonishes the Corinthians to holiness of living, using a patchwork of elements of various biblical texts (called "testimonia").

PART II OF THE BODY OF THE LETTER (8:1–9:15) treats Paul's collection for the church in Jerusalem. He holds up to them the example of the Macedonian Christians (8:1–5), as well as that of Jesus Christ himself, "who, though he was rich, for your sake became poor, that you might become rich by his poverty" (8:9). Paul is sending Titus to arrange the collection. With him will go two unnamed figures. The collection for Jerusalem is also the subject of chap. 9, which seems to speak specifically to Achaia.

PART III OF THE BODY OF THE LETTER (10:1–13:10) abruptly turns more pessimistic as Paul indicates uncertainty about his reception when he comes the third time. Indeed, he threatens to be as severe when he comes as he has been in his writing, presumably including his "tearful" letter (10:2,6,11; 13:2). Nevertheless, Paul wants to stress that the authority given him by the Lord is for building up, not for pulling down (10:8; 13:10). There have been would-be "super-apostles"

(11:5; 12:11) undermining Paul at Corinth; but as far as he is concerned, they are masqueraders and false apostles (11:13–15) who in the end will be punished. From his soul there rings out a cry of confidence in the power of Christ: "When I am weak, then I am strong" (12:10). Although 12:12 lists signs, wonders, and miracles as "signs of an apostle" that Paul had wrought among the Corinthians, clearly the times he was imprisoned, flogged, lashed, stoned, shipwrecked, imperiled, hungry, thirsty, and stripped naked are more important to him as an expression of his apostolic concern for all the churches (11:23–29).

THE CONCLUDING FORMULA (13:11–13) serves as Paul's final exhortation to the Corinthians in the missive as it now stands: "Mend your ways, heed my appeal, think alike, live in peace." Was he successful? Neither Acts nor Rom 16:1,21–23 gives any indication of internal Christian conflict during Paul's third visit. Paul's triadic blessing in 13:13, including God and Jesus and the Holy Spirit (the fullest benediction that Paul composed), has served Christians in liturgy even to this day as a model invocation.

THE OPPONENTS OR FALSE APOSTLES IN II COR 10–13

Paul refers to "super-apostles" (11:5 and 12:11) and to "false apostles" (11:13). Granted the thesis that only one set of "apostles" is described throughout 10–13, what are their characteristics? Reading through the chapters with that question in mind, one may create a portrait not only from what Paul says in direct critique but also from his self-defense. They seem to have "come" recently to Corinth. They are of Jewish stock but have rhetorical skills; they preach Jesus and what passes for a gospel. They boast of extraordinary powers and experiences, and the fact that they ask for support makes the Corinthians feel important. Interestingly, Paul concentrates his attacks on their flashy pretensions and attitudes more than on their doctrine, and he does so largely in a style of one-upmanship. If they are Hebrews and Israelites and servants of Christ, so is he (11:21–23). If the super-apostles talk about their powers, Paul too worked signs, wonders, and miracles when he was at Corinth (12:11–12). If they talk about their experiences, fourteen years ago he was taken up to third heaven and heard things he cannot utter (12:1–5). They have to build on his foundation, boasting about what really are others' labors; but he builds on no one else's (10:15; I Cor 3:10). More than any other point of comparison, can they match his record of suffering and being persecuted for Christ (II Cor 11:23–29)?

The picture of the false apostles can be enlarged and confirmed by recognizing that Paul had them in mind at times earlier in II Cor (3:1–6:13). They evidently arrived at Corinth with letters of recommendation from other Christians; Paul needs none, for his Corinthian converts are his letter (3:1–3). These "apostles" charged for their gospel (2:17) and they boasted about what they had seen (5:12). Is Paul's defense of his suffering and life-threatening predicaments (4:7–5:10; 6:4–10) an indication that the false apostles were invoking these as a sign of his failure? Is Paul's insistence that God's treasure is held in earthen vessels an indication that the false apostles thought the power belonged to them rather than to God (4:7)?

Overall, however, beyond the theological implications of the false apostles' claims about themselves, no clear doctrinal fallacy emerges from II Cor 3–7; 10–13. We may have to be content that those designated "apostles" were vainglorious about their own marvelous gifts of the Spirit and preached a victorious Christ with little emphasis on his suffering or Christian imitation of those sufferings.

ONE LETTER OR A COMPILATION OF SEVERAL LETTERS?

While the analysis of the letter just presented moved through the letter in the sequence in which it is preserved, the unity of II Cor is the subject of ongoing discussion. First, many who evaluate II Cor as a unity note that there is only one Opening Formula (1:1–2) and one Concluding Formula (13:11–13). If once-independent letters have been truncated, at least one cannot posit a simple gluing together of documents. Second, the shift of tone in II Cor from the generally optimistic chaps. 1–9 to the more pessimistic 10–13 is sharp; a majority of scholars would argue for independent origins of at least those two components. Some would have chaps. 1–9 written before 10–13, while others contend 10–13 preceded 1–9. Beyond that, II Cor 6:14–7:1 has the air of a self-contained unit, and chaps. 8 and 9 seem to involve a certain duplication in referring to the collection. Third, accordingly some would find five letters in II Cor. In this hypothesis every discrete subject in II Cor has been interpreted as a separate letter. Moreover, the problem of sequence may be added to the problem of these once-independent units. For instance, Soards (*Apostle* 88), following Bornkamm and D. Georgi, would argue that II Cor 8 was written first and sent with Titus, who brought back news of troubles at Corinth. Then Paul wrote II Cor 2:14–7:4, a letter that failed. Next Paul visited Corinth; and when that failed, he wrote the "tearful letter" consisting of II Cor 10–13. Titus brought back news that this time Paul had succeeded; and so he wrote II Cor 1:1–2:13 and 7:5–16. Finally he wrote II Cor 9. To the obvious question of why any editor reorganized this material in the existing order, some would resort to positing stupidity.

What is at the root of these and a dozen other theories? An important factor in judging unity is whether the breaks from one section of II Cor to another are so sharp that they cannot be interpreted as a shift of focus within the same missive. Although at times even those who affirm the unity of II Cor, in explaining the abruptness or difficulty of several of the letter's transitions, are obliged to argue that Paul was interrupted several times with surprising news as he dictated the letter.

The discernible parts of II Cor have different concerns, tones, and modes of expression. Recognizing these distinctions is important for understanding this multifaceted and complicated writing, no matter what theory of its composition one may hold.

24

Letter to the Romans

Longer than any other NT letter, more reflective in its outlook than any other undisputed Pauline writing, Rom has been the most studied of the apostle's writings—indisputably Paul's theological chef d'oeuvre. This letter has played a major role in the development of theology and is the most important of Paul's letters.

THE BACKGROUND

There are two important introductory issues: the situation in Paul's life that served as the context of the letter, and the history of the Roman community that received it. The first is relatively easy to discern. Items in Rom 16:1–2,23 (Phoebe, Cenchreae, Gaius) indicate that Paul wrote to Rome from Corinth (57/58), whence he was about to take a collection to Jerusalem (15:26–33).

The second issue involves the recipients of the letter, a debated matter. Some insist Paul knew little about the Roman church. But if (another debated matter) chap. 16 belongs to Rom and Paul knew and

SUMMARY OF BASIC INFORMATION

DATE: In the winter of 57/58 from Corinth (55/56 in the Revisionist Chronology).
TO: God's beloved in Rome, where Paul had never been but had friends.
AUTHENTICITY: Not seriously disputed.
UNITY: A very small minority posits the joining of two separate letters; a larger minority maintains that chap. 16 was added later.
INTEGRITY: Besides chap. 16 (or the doxology in 16:25–27), a few have rejected chap. 9–11 as not truly Pauline.
FORMAL DIVISION:
  A. Opening Formula: 1:1–7
  B. Thanksgiving: 1:8–10
  C. Body: 1:11–15:13
  D. Concluding Formulas (15:14–16:23) plus Doxology (16:25–27).
                  DIVISION ACCORDING TO CONTENTS:
1:1–15: Address/greeting, Thanksgiving, and Proem about Paul's wish to come to Rome
1:16–11:36: Doctrinal Section:
  Part I: 1:16–4:25: Uprightness of God revealed through the gospel
    1:18–3:20: God's wrath and the sins of Gentiles and Jews
    3:21–4:25: Justification by faith apart from the Law
  Part II: 5:1–8:39: God's salvation for those justified by faith
  Part III: 9:1–11:36: God's promises to Israel
12:1–15:13 Hortatory Section:
  Part I: 12:1–13:14: Authoritative advice for Christian living
  Part II: 14:1–15:13: The strong owe love to the weak
15:14–33: Paul's travel plans and a blessing
16:1–23: Recommendation for Phoebe and greetings to people at Rome
16:25–27: Concluding doxology

---

greeted twenty-six people in Rome, presumably he knew something about the Roman church.

Accordingly, Paul's letter in 57/58 implies the Christian community had been in existence for a considerable period of time, since he had been wishing "for many years" to visit (15:23). Thus it seems that the Roman Christian community must have existed by the early 50s. Indeed, Suetonius (*Claudius* 25.4) states that Claudius "expelled Jews from Rome because of their constant disturbances impelled by Chrestus [*impulsore Chresto*]," which many scholars believe is a garbled remembrance of "Christ." Strikingly, Acts 18:1–3 reports that when Paul came to Corinth (ca. 50) he found lodging with Aquila and Priscilla, a Jewish couple who had recently come from Italy "because Claudius had ordered all the Jews to leave Rome." Apparently they came from Rome as Jews who already believed in Jesus. This expulsion may have meant that by AD 49 the Christian mission had been in Rome long enough to cause serious friction in the synagogues. If so, very likely Christianity had reached Rome by the early 40s.

GENERAL ANALYSIS OF THE MESSAGE

THE OPENING FORMULA (1:1–7), THE THANKSGIVING (1:8–10), and a PROEM (1:11–15) that serves as Body-Opening may be treated together. While Paul did not use the expression "the church of God that is in Rome" or "the churches of Rome" to address the Roman community he could scarcely call a group that he did not consider a church "the beloved of God in Rome called to be holy" (Rom 1:7). (He also did not use "church" at the beginning of Phil.)

In the salutation Paul uses only his own name—no co-sender— and states that he is "an apostle set apart for the gospel of God" (1:1), which is "The gospel concerning God's Son who was born/begotten of the seed of David according to the flesh, designated Son of God in power according to the Spirit of holiness by the resurrection from the dead" (1:3–4). Critical scholarship recognizes that here Paul is not using language of his own coinage but offering a Jewish Christian formulation of the gospel—presumably because such a formulation would be known to the Roman Christians and acceptable to them. What he preaches agrees with the preaching of those who evangelized the Romans. Thus, he and the Romans can be encouraged by each other's faith (1:12). In the transition to the Body of the letter (1:10–15) Paul relates his future plan to come to Rome.

DOCTRINAL SECTION OF THE BODY: PART I (1:16–4:25): *The uprightness/ righteousness [dikaiosynē] of God revealed through the gospel.* Paul continues into the main section of his letter by stressing that the gospel is the power of God for the salvation of all who believe, first for the Jew, then for the Greek. (Notice the theological sequence, which would be effective against any who claimed that Paul devalued Jewish believers.) A central theme of Rom is that "the righteousness of God" is now revealed, namely, a manifestation of that quality whereby in judgment

God acquits people of their sins through faith. What was the relation of people to God before the coming of the gospel of Christ? Turning first to the Gentiles (1:18–23), Paul wishes to explain that a gracious God was knowable from the time of creation. In terms of Jewish standard values, in the pagan world the divine image was obscured through idolatry, which was expressed in lust and depraved conduct. Then, in 2:1 Paul speaks to an imagined Jewish listener, who might be passing judgment on what Paul has condemned and yet, despite this superior stance, be doing the same things. God does not show favoritism: Jews will be judged according to the Law; then, Gentiles will be judged according to nature and what is written in their hearts and consciences (2:5–16).

In a remarkable section (2:17–24) Paul taunts the proud claims of Jewish superiority. All human beings are guilty before God. Well, then, what is the advantage of circumcised Jews? Paul answers: To the Jews were given God's own words of promise, and God is faithful. Through faith of/in Jesus Christ, the righteousness of God justifies without distinction Jew and Greek. God's integrity is vindicated: God is not unfair, for the sins of all have been expiated by Christ's blood. No one has the right to boast, since God has graciously justified the circumcised and the uncircumcised in the same way, by faith apart from deeds/works of the Law (3:27–31).

In chap. 4 Paul reaches back to the first book of the Law and cites Abraham to show that God has worked consistently, for Abraham's righteousness came by faith, not by the Law (Gen 12,15,17). The Jews of Paul's time would have looked to Abraham as their forebear, but for Paul he is "father of us all" who share his faith (4:16). The story of the righteousness attributed to Abraham was written for those who believe in the One who raised from the dead Jesus our Lord, "who was given over for our transgressions and raised for our justification" (4:25).

DOCTRINAL SECTION OF THE BODY: PART II (5:1–8:39): *Reconciliation to God in Christ and Its Benefits.* If people are justified by faith and have peace with God through Christ, they also experience God's grace. This brings many benefits: peace with God, hope of sharing God's glory, and an outpouring of God's love (5:1–5). The description of how Christ's death accomplished justification, salvation, and reconciliation (5:6–11) contains one of the great NT explanations of what is involved in divine love: a willingness to die for sinners who do not deserve such graciousness. Paul now compares what has been accomplished through Christ with the state of all human beings stemming from Adam: grace and life compared to sin and death. As Adam led to condemnation for all, so Christ led to justification and life for all. This passage (5:12–21) gave rise to the theology of original sin.

In 6:1–11 Paul introduces baptism. Our old self was crucified with Christ; we were baptized into his death, a death to sin, and buried with him, so that as he was raised from the dead we too might walk in newness of life. But Sin (personified by Paul) remains an active force, and 6:12–23 warns against being enslaved by Sin.

In chap. 7, Paul returns to the issue of the Mosaic Law. The basic principle is that Christ's death has annulled the binding power of the Law. The "I" monologue that runs through 7:7–25 is among the most dramatic of Paul's rhetorical passages in Rom: "I do not understand what I do. I do not do what I wish, but I do the very thing I hate . . ." This impassioned speech has had many interpretations, but a parallel from DSS (1QS 11:9–15) confirms that Paul is describing sinful humanity from a Jewish viewpoint, and for Paul deliverance comes from a gracious God through faith in Jesus Christ. Here in part is this text from the DSS document referred to as The Community Rule:

> As for me, I belong to wicked humanity, to the assembly of unjust
> flesh. My iniquities, transgressions, and sins, together with the wicked-
> ness of my heart, belong to the assembly of worms and of those walk-
> ing in darkness. No human being has a course or determines his own
> steps, for judgment is with God alone. . . . As for me, if I stumble, the
> grace of God is my eternal salvation. If I fall because of the sin of the
> flesh, my judgment shall be according to the righteousness of God that
> remains forever.

How is our new life to be lived? In chap. 8 Paul's answer is that we are to live not according to the flesh but according to the Spirit of God, who raised Christ from the dead. We become children of God, heirs of God and co-heirs of Christ in a relationship with God through the Spirit of him who was uniquely God's Son. Moreover, the earth was cursed because of Adam's sin (Gen 3:17–19; 5:29). As part of his contrast between Adam and Christ, Paul (Rom 8:18–23) speaks also of Christ's healing effect on all material creation. As we hope and wait with endurance, the Spirit intercedes for us with sighs that cannot be spoken (8:24–27). Both justification and glorification are part of the purpose of God predestined from the beginning (8:28–30). In 8:31–39 Paul ends this section of Rom with one of the most eloquent statements in all Christian writing: "If God is for us, who is against us? . . . I am convinced that neither death nor life, nor angels nor principalities, nor present things nor future, nor any powers . . . will be able to separate us from the love of God in Christ Jesus our Lord."

DOCTRINAL SECTION OF THE BODY: PART III (9:1–11:36): *How is one to understand God's dealings with Israel concerning belief/unbelief in the Christ?* How is it that the Israelites (Jews), who received the promises through the Law and the Prophets, rejected Christ? How does God's purpose of election continue? Paul writes chapters so surprising that some scholars (beginning already in the second century with Marcion, who rejected the God of the OT as an inferior deity and not the Heavenly Father of Jesus Christ) have deemed them to be foreign to the letter and contradictory. Paul would be willing to be cut off from Christ and be damned for the sake of his Jewish kinsmen! Giving the lie to all who say that he denigrates Judaism, he lists with pride the marvelous Israelite privileges (9:4–5).

Paul explains that the word of God has not failed. God cannot be asked to account for the choices made. Israel failed because it sought righteousness by deeds, not by faith; and to compound the error, despite its zeal, it has not recognized that God has manifested righteousness to those who believe in Christ and that, in fact, Christ is the end of the Law (9:30–10:4). "If you profess with your lips that 'Jesus is Lord' and believe in your heart that God has raised him from the dead, you will be saved" (10:9). In this "you" (singular) there is no distinction between Jew and Greek (10:12).

In 10:14–21 Paul offers Israel little excuse. "Has God then rejected His people?" (11:1). In an indignant negative response to the question rhetorically posed, Paul speaks as an Israelite, a descendant of Abraham, who has been chosen by grace. He cites an example from Israel's history where the majority failed, but God preserved a remnant

(11:2–10). In fact, Paul foresees that everything will work out well (11:11–32). Israel's stumbling and partial hardening of heart have been providential in allowing salvation to come to the Gentiles. Then because of the Gentile experience of salvation Israel will become jealous, and all Israel will be saved. Gentile believers should not boast; they earlier and Israel now have been disobedient, and God is showing mercy to all.

HORTATORY SECTION OF THE BODY: PART I (12:1–13:14): *Authoritative advice for Christian Living.* Beginning in 12:3, Paul echoes ideas that he also expressed in I Cor: one body, many members, different gifts/charisms, among which are prophecy and teaching, and an emphasis on love.

The directive to be subject to governing authorities (13:1–7) is particularly appropriate in a letter to the capital. Paul's admonition is theologically based, not merely practical. Strikingly, in 13:8–10 Paul is in harmony with the Jesus tradition, writing, "The one who loves the other has fulfilled the Law" and, then, contending that the commandments are summed up in "You shall love your neighbor as yourself" (Lev 19:18).

HORTATORY SECTION OF THE BODY: PART II (14:1–15:13): *The strong owe love to the weak.* We are not certain of the origin of the language of "strong" and "weak" that appears here. The "strong" are convinced they can eat anything and need not treat any days as special; the "weak" are cautious about eating and observe certain holy days. The issue probably reflects observances stemming from the purity and cultic demands of the Mosaic Law. The "strong" regard those demands as irrelevant, the "weak" ("weak in faith"; 14:1) think they are obligatory. The matter, however, is not simply Gentile vs. Jew, with Gentile indicating "the strong" and Jew indicating "the weak." Any controversy being indicated is about religious practices, not ethnicity (or race). Both groups would have included Jews and Gentiles.

Paul is concerned that the two groups should not judge or despise each other (14:3–4,10,13). If the Roman Christians, "strong" or "weak," have heard that Paul does not oblige his Gentile Christian converts to observe the Mosaic Law, then, they are learning that he would never countenance that this freedom be used to divide a community. Identifying himself with the "strong," Paul warns them that it is better not to eat meat or drink wine if it causes the brother or sister to trip or stumble (14:21). Christ did not please himself (15:3) but became a servant of the circumcision to show God's fidelity, confirming the promises made to the patriarchs, so that the Gentiles may glorify God's mercy (15:8–9a).

FIRST CONCLUDING SECTION (15:14–33): *Paul's future plans.* Paul explains his dealings with the Romans. His preaching the gospel is a liturgical service so that the Gentiles might become an acceptable sacrifice to God (15:16). In executing that service Paul has gone from Jerusalem to Illyricum (western Greece). Now he hopes to push farther west, through Rome, whose Christians he has desired for many years to visit, to preach the gospel where Christ has not been named, namely, Spain (15:14–24). But first he must bring to the Jerusalem poor the money he has collected, and that journey worries him. Paul wants the Romans to help him on his journey by praying for him (15:25–33).

SECOND CONCLUDING SECTION (16:1–27): *Greetings to Roman friends.* First, Phoebe, a woman deacon of the church at Cenchreae a few miles from where Paul is writing and a great help to him, is going to Rome (perhaps carrying this letter); she should be received well. Second, there are various people already in Rome who know Paul, and he proceeds to greet twenty-six of them in 16:3–16. Paul's references to groups suggest that the Roman community consisted of a number of small house-churches. (Among those greeted by Paul are "Andronicus and Junia/Junias," who are "outstanding among the apostles" [16:7]. Inscriptions indicate that Junia/Junias is most likely a woman's name [Junia]. This identity would mean that Paul could apply the term "apostle" to a woman.)

The letter ends (16:21–23) with Paul including greetings from other Christians in Corinth. The doxology in 16:25–27 is missing from many mss. and may well be an early copyist's or editor's liturgical addition for public reading in church.

JUSTIFICATION/UPRIGHTNESS/RIGHTEOUSNESS/JUSTICE

This key idea in Pauline thought and in Rom is expressed in a number of terms: the verb *dikaioun;* the nouns *dikaiosynē, dikaiōsis;* and the adjective *dikaios.* The noun *dikaiosynē* can be translated in English as "righteousness" or "justification," depending on the context. Paul speaks of the "righteousness of God" (*dikaiosynē theou*), but how is the genitive to be interpreted? In times past it has been understood as a possessive genitive, an attribute of God's being, a divine virtue, almost equivalent to "the righteous God." Today, two other understandings have major support. The phrase can be taken as a possessive genitive, describing an active attribute of God, the justifying activity of God—for example, Rom 3:25–26, which speaks of God's forbearance "as proof of God's righteousness at the present time: that He Himself is righteous and justifies the person who has faith in Jesus." Or, the phrase can be understood as a genitive of source or origin, describing the state of uprightness communicated to human beings as a gift from or by God—for example, Phil 3:9: "not having my own righteousness which is from the Law but that which is through the faith of/in Christ, the righteousness from [ek] God that depends on faith."

There is a legal background in the root of the word, as if people were being brought before God for judgment and God is acquitting them and thus manifesting divine graciousness. In this just and merciful divine judgment there is also a sense of God asserting authority and power, triumphing over the forces that would mislead people, setting things right, and saving the world. Although such a notion of the righteousness of God, often in other terminology, was a reality for OT Israel, for Paul there was in Jesus a greater, eschatological manifestation of God's dikaiosynē, extended to all.

"Justification" is also used by Paul to describe an effect worked in those who believe what God has done in Christ. Since God acquitted people in judgment, they were now justified. This acquitting took place not because people were innocent but because, although they were sinners, the truly innocent Jesus was himself made sin for the sake of others (II Cor 5:21). For Paul this justification or righteousness took the place of the righteousness under the Law (Phil 3:6) and was a grace or gift received through faith (Rom 3:24–25). A major scholarly debate is centered on whether for Paul God simply declares people upright by a type of judicial sentence (forensic or declarative justification) or actually changes people and makes them upright (causative or factitive justification). Yet, is a sharp distinction possible since God's justifying declaration has an element of power that is also causative? Can people be reconciled without being transformed?

::: center
✦
:::

25

Pseudonymity and the Deutero-Pauline Writings

Before entering the problematic terrain of deutero-Pauline letters, that is, those that bear Paul's name but possibly were not written by him, it is good to consider the difficult concept of pseudepigraphy (literally, but often misleading, "false writing") or pseudonymity ("false name")—terminology employed in biblical discussions with special nuance.

PSEUDONYMOUS COMPOSITION IN GENERAL

Normally, for us, "author" means not simply the one responsible for the ideas contained in a work but the one who actually drafted its wording. Ancients were often not that precise and by "author" may have meant only the authority behind a work.

In NT research some who first proposed that letters attributed to Paul were really pseudonymous hinted that the purpose might be fraudulent. That connotation has largely disappeared. Today what is being suggested is that one of the Pauline "school" of disciples wrote a letter in Paul's name because he wanted it to preserve Paul's teachings, and to be received authoritatively as what Paul would say to the situation addressed. Attribution of the letter to Paul in those circumstances would be treating Paul as the author in the sense of the authority behind the letter that was intended as an extension of his thought.

Justification for positing this type of pseudepigraphy is found in the OT: books of the Law were attributed to Moses; the Psalms were attributed to David; the book of Wisdom was attributed to Solomon; prophets wrote in Isaiah's name and their compositions were included in the Book of Isaiah; and Apocalypses invoked the names of Daniel, Baruch, Enoch, and Ezra. In the centuries just before and after Jesus' time pseudepigraphy seems to have been particularly frequent in Jewish works of apocalyptic and nonapocalyptic nature.

Moreover, without a doubt, outside the canonical NT there are pseudonymous letters written in Paul's name, letters such as *Laodiceans* or *III Corinthians* (and others). These are writings that, for many obvious reasons, no one accepts as authentic Pauline letters. Thus, the question is not whether there are pseudonymous Pauline letters—there are—but whether there are any pseudonymous Pauline letters in the canonical NT.

PROBLEMS ABOUT PSEUDONYMITY

True as all that may be, when one posits the pseudonymous character of NT works, difficulties remain that should not be overlooked. OT examples of pseudonymity are not really parallel to works written within a few years of Paul's life. How soon/long after Paul's death could someone write in his name? How are canonical pseudonymous works different from apocrypha that were rejected by the church as noncanonical?

Is the audience (church) addressed to be taken as historical? Did the audience who first received a pseudonymous letter know that it was actually written by another in Paul's name? Would the letter's authority have been diminished if that were known?

Did the writer think that such knowledge made any difference? Would the later church have accepted these letters into the canon had it known they were pseudonymous? What difference does a decision on the question of pseudepigraphy make in how this letter/epistle is understood?

What are the criteria for determining genuineness and pseudonymity? They include internal data, format, style, vocabulary, and thought/theology. In looking at certain of Paul's undisputed letters, we have seen some problems with these criteria: uncertainly about the role of a scribe; perceived logic of arrangement of contents; and implications of the use of unique vocabulary that requires interpretation of the sense of its use. But, we can test such matters more practically on the documents themselves.

.∵✦∴.

26

Second Letter to the Thessalonians

There is considerable dispute whether Paul wrote II Thess. After the General Analysis, a subsection will be devoted to: The Authorship and Purpose of II Thess.

GENERAL ANALYSIS OF THE MESSAGE

Just as in I Thess, the Opening Formula (1:1–2) lists "Paul, Silvanus, and Timothy," even if Paul is the one who communicates. The Thanksgiving (1:3–10) praises the faith and love of the Thessalonians, as well as their steadfastness in the suffering imposed on them. The Prayer reported in 1:11–12 is for God to make them worthy of their calling.

As he begins the Indicative Section of the Body (2:1–17), Paul does not want the Thessalonians overly excited by "spirit or word," or any letter alleged to be from him about the immediacy of "the day of the Lord" (2:1–2). They can relax because the apocalyptic signs that must precede the coming of that day have not yet occurred (2:3–12), although the mystery of lawlessness is already at work (2:7). Paul then

SUMMARY OF BASIC INFORMATION

DATE: If by Paul, probably ca. AD 51/52, shortly after I Thess. If pseudonymous, probably late first century, when increased apocalyptic fervor was manifest.

FROM: If by Paul, probably from Corinth, like I Thess. If pseudonymous, there is no way to know.

TO: If by Paul, to Thessalonica. If pseudonymous, perhaps the same; yet the address to the Thessalonians may simply have been borrowed from I Thess.

AUTHENTICITY: Scholars are almost evenly divided on whether Paul wrote it, although the view that he did not seems to be gaining ground even among moderates.

UNITY: Queried by very few.

INTEGRITY: No major advocacy of interpolations.

FORMAL DIVISION:
  A. Opening Formula: 1:1–2
  B. Thanksgiving: 1:3–10, plus Prayer: 1:11–12
  C. Body: 2:1–17: Pauline indicative (instructions)
    3:1–16: Pauline imperative (paraenesis and exhortations)
  D. Concluding Formula: 3:17–18.

DIVISION ACCORDING TO CONTENTS:

1:1–2: Greeting

1:3–12: Thanksgiving for Thessalonians' faith and love that will save them at the Parousia when their persecutors will be punished; continued prayer for them

2:1–12: Instruction on signs that precede the Parousia

2:13–17: Thanksgiving and instructions on God's choosing them for salvation

3:1–5: Paul requests prayer and prays for them

3:6–15: Ethical admonitions and exhortations (against idleness and disobedience)

3:16–18: Concluding blessing, greeting.

---

writes a second thanksgiving and admonishes the Thessalonians to hold firm the traditions they were taught (2:13–17).

In 3:1–2, in transition to the Imperative Section of the Body (3:1–16), Paul requests a corresponding prayer "for us . . . that we may be delivered" from evil men. The Lord will strengthen the Thessalonians and protect them from the evil one, and Paul is confident of their faithfulness and obedience (3:1–5). Then Paul enunciates a special command (3:6–13) that addresses a problem that derives from false expectations about the day of the Lord: some have become idle, probably because they thought the day of the Lord had come. That is not imitating Paul, who during his stay among them, precisely in order to set an example, worked night and day. Consequently, "If anyone does not want to work, let that person not eat" (3:10). Paul warns against those who pay no heed to his directions, yet says that such a person is a "brother" and is not to be regarded as an enemy.

In the Concluding Formula (3:17–18) Paul switches from "we" to "I," as he sends a greeting with his own hand.

THE AUTHORSHIP AND PURPOSE OF II THESSALONIANS

II Thess is a bit more than one-half the length of I Thess; and close resemblances between I and II Thess have been estimated to affect about one-third of II Thess. The *similarity of format* between the two letters is striking—greater than between any other two genuine letters: they have the same Opening Formulas; a double Thanksgiving; and the same last verse. Furthermore, II Thess 3:8 repeats almost verbatim I Thess 2:9 about Paul's labor and toil night and day. Why would Paul copy himself in this almost mechanical way?

Style and vocabulary arguments are invoked. Remarkable similarities and dissimilarities in vocabulary characterize the two letters. Overall II Thess is more formal and less personal than I Thess.

Internal indications of the time of composition are seen in the reference to the temple of God in II Thess 2:4, which some believe shows that the Jerusalem Temple was still standing, so that the work was written before AD 70. Others suggest that the divine temple is being interpreted symbolically as in Rev 21:22, and any date is possible.

The closeness of II Thess to post-Pauline works is invoked as an argument for pseudonymity. Scholars point to similarities in thought to the Pastorals and Rev.

The purpose of II Thess is cited as a major argument on both sides of the debate about genuineness and pseudonymity:

If Paul wrote this letter, perhaps in I Thess he had focused too much attention on the Parousia and intensified an expectation of its immediacy. Paul now writes a second letter to reassure the Thessalonians that there have to be some apocalyptic signs before the day of the Lord.

If Paul did not write II Thess, in some ways interpretation becomes more complex. It could not have been written too late, since Marcion and

Polycarp knew it before the mid-second century. Some scholars would see II Thess as not being clearly related to I Thess and its issues, but rather addressing a completely different situation; others see continuity with some of the themes of I Thess.

It is possible to see II Thess in the same light as Rev. Perhaps a writer who knew I Thess 5:1–2 containing Paul's cautions about the times and seasons and the coming of the day of the Lord like a thief in the night decided to write a letter patterned on it. Paul would speak again in the midst of heated apocalyptic expectations. Otherwise, how can this insistence that noticeable signs must come before the day of the Lord (II Thess 2:3–5) be reconciled with I Thess 5:2, "The day of the Lord will come like a thief in the night"?

Although in considering the arguments for and against Paul's writing II Thess the current tide of scholarship has turned against writing by Paul himself, it is difficult to conclude with confidence. But, false confidence is not an asset in interpretation, for biblical studies are not helped by being certain about the uncertain.

.⋅✶⋅.

27

Letter to the Colossians

In its vision of Christ, of his body the church, and of the mystery of God hidden for ages, Col is truly majestic, and certainly a worthy representative of the Pauline heritage. That evaluation should not be forgotten amid the major scholarly debate about whether the letter was written by Paul himself. After the Background, the General Analysis will reflect on what is actually communicated in Col, and then, because of their significance and complexity, two topics, the *Christological hymn* (1:15–20) and the *False teaching* (2:8–23), are treated in subsections.

THE BACKGROUND

About 110 miles east from Ephesus, along a major trade route, lies the Lycus River valley, in which were *Laodicea, Hierapolis, and Colossae*. In Roman times Laodicea had become the most important and Colossae the least important of these three cities. Their population would have been largely Phrygian (descendants of an ancient kingdom in west-central Asia Minor) and Greek, but Jewish families from Babylon had been resettled there just after 200 BC. By Paul's time the Jewish

SUMMARY OF BASIC INFORMATION

DATE: If by Paul (or by Timothy while Paul was still alive or had just died), 61–63 (or slightly later) from Rome, or 54–56 from Ephesus. If pseudonymous (about 60 percent of critical scholarship), in the 80s from Ephesus.

TO: The Christians at Colossae, in the Lycus River valley in Phrygia in the province of Asia, not evangelized by Paul but by Epaphras, who has informed Paul about the church and its problems.

AUTHENTICITY: A modest probability favors composition by a disciple of Paul close to certain aspects of his thought (perhaps part of a "school" at Ephesus) who drew on Phlm.

UNITY AND INTEGRITY: Not seriously debated. Probably in 1:15–20 an extant hymn has been adapted.

FORMAL DIVISION:
  A. Opening Formula: 1:1–2
  B. Thanksgiving: 1:3–8
  C. Body: 1:9–2:23: Pauline indicative (instructions)
      3:1–4:6: Pauline imperative (paraenesis and exhortations)
  D. Greetings and Concluding Formula: 4:7–18.

DIVISION ACCORDING TO CONTENTS:
1:1–2: Opening Formula
1:3–23: Proem consisting of Thanksgiving (1:3–8), Prayer (1:9–11), Praise of Christ's Lordship including a hymn (1:12–23)
1:24–2:5: Apostolic office and preaching the mystery revealed by God
2:6–23: Christ's Lordship vs. human ordinances
3:1–4:6: Practice: Vices, virtues, household code
4:7–17: Greetings and messages
4:18: Paul's own hand; blessing.

---

population in the Laodicea area seems to have been more than 10,000 and (from a later written Jewish reference) quite Hellenized.

Evidently the churches in the three cities had close relations. Paul mentions Epaphras, who has worked hard in all three (Col 4:12–13). This area had not been evangelized by Paul and had never seen his face (Col 2:1). Yet given that Paul feels free to instruct the Colossians and address them with a sense of pastoral responsibility (1:9, 24; 2:1–2), it is likely that a Pauline mission had proclaimed Christ in the Lycus valley, perhaps sent out when Paul was in Ephesus in AD 54–57. Such an intermediate connection of Paul with their being evangelized is supported by the fact that Epaphras, a Gentile and one of their own who had taught them the truth, was now with Paul (1:6–7; 4:12–13).

Paul is imprisoned (4:3,10), and so communicates with Colossae by this letter to be carried by Tychicus, accompanied by Onesimus (4:7–9). Thus, though absent in the flesh, Paul can be with them in spirit (2:5).

GENERAL ANALYSIS OF THE MESSAGE

THE OPENING FORMULA (1:1–2) lists Timothy as co-sender, as in 2 Cor; Phil; I and II Thess; and Phlm. In the THANKSGIVING (1:3–8), Paul shows knowledge of the situation at Colossae gained through Epaphras and is pleased by it, writing words of encouragement. One gets the impression that the addressees, in Paul's judgment, have received the gospel well and it is bearing fruit among them.

Paul moves smoothly into the INDICATIVE SECTION OF THE BODY (1:9–2:23) by explaining that he wants to deepen their sense of the gospel's completeness by appealing to what they know of Christ in whom all the fullness of God was pleased to dwell. He does this through a famous christological hymn (1:15–20—see the following subsection). Paul wants the Colossians to understand Christ fully as the mystery of God in whom are hidden all the treasures of wisdom and knowledge (2:2–3).

The reason for this emphasis is the danger presented by false teaching (2:8–23) that threatens the Lycus valley Christians, who by implication were Gentiles. What can be discerned about this false teaching from Paul's critique is sketchy and uncertain. Far more important is what Col emphasizes positively. Implicitly countering the teaching is profound knowledge through the gospel, "the word of truth" (1:5). No elements of the universe have any power over the Colossians because Christians have been delivered from the power of darkness and transferred to the kingdom of God's beloved Son (1:13). Indeed, all the principalities and powers were created through God's Son, and all things whether on earth or in heaven were reconciled through him; he is preeminent over all (1:16,18,20). Believers in him do not need to worry about food or drink (2:16), for Christ through his death will present them holy and without blemish before God (1:22). Feasts, new moon, and Sabbath were only shadows of things to come; the substance belongs to Christ (2:17).

In the Imperative Section of the Body (3:1–4:6) Paul's message turns from christology to how Christians should live. It is not clear that his commands are directly influenced by reaction to the false teachers. Having been raised with Christ, the Colossians should be thinking about what is above; for when Christ appears, they will appear with him in glory (3:1–4). Col first gives two lists of five vices each to be avoided and then a list of five virtues to be exhibited by those who have put on a new self in Christ (3:5–17). Finally, in a household instruction (a summary list of attitudes and actions appropriate to persons in various pairings in ancient household situations, often called a "household code"), the author speaks more specifically to various members of the Christian household (wives, husbands, children, slaves, masters), showing how the mystery of God revealed in Christ affects every aspect of day-to-day life (3:18–4:1). The remarks do not necessarily imply social equality—as becomes apparent when the list in Col 3:11 (that is similar to Gal 3:28) is followed by these instructions embodying the social inequalities of a patriarchal structure.

The Greetings and Concluding Formula (4:7–18) mention eight to ten people alluded to in Phlm. That parallelism is very important for considering the authorship and setting of Col.

THE CHRISTOLOGICAL HYMN (1:15–20)

A key element in Colossians' presentation of Christ is a poetic passage describing his role in creation and reconciliation, a passage commonly regarded as a hymn. This hymn has been the subject of extensive study, which has raised these points:

• Most think that the writer of the letter used an already existing Christian hymn familiar to the Colossians and perhaps to the whole Lycus valley to correct false teaching.
• The structure of the hymn is debated. Yet despite differences among them regarding 17–18a, the proposed divisions are alike in recognizing that within the hymn to God's beloved Son the most visible parallelism is between the descriptions in 15–16a, "who is the image of the invisible God, the firstborn of all creation, for in him all things were created," and 18b–19, "who is the beginning,

the firstborn from the dead . . . for in him all the fullness has been pleased to dwell."
• How exalted is the christology centered on the parallelism of the firstborn? If Jesus was raised from the dead first before all others, was he the first to be created? Answering no, many see the reference to the uniqueness of the Son, a firstborn who existed before all creation (as in John 1:1–18). Yet the closest and most commonly accepted background for 1:15–16a is the OT picture of personified female Wisdom, the image of God's goodness (Wisdom 7:26) who worked with God in establishing all things (Prov 3:19)—that Wisdom was created by God at the beginning (Prov 8:22; Sirach 24:9).
• Besides personified Wisdom other backgrounds for the hymn have been suggested. These include: (1) a pre-Christian text dealing with the gnostic redeemer myth of a primal man who breaks into the sphere of death to lead out those who belong to him; (2) the Jewish Day of Atonement (Yom Kippur) when the Creator is reconciled to the people of God; and (3) the Jewish New Year (Rosh Hashanah). While some of the language of the hymn echoes Hellenistic Jewish descriptions of Wisdom, it also has parallels in Platonic, Hermetic, and Philonic terminology. Consequently, its christology is very different from that of the syncretistic false teachers attacked in Col; yet it is phrased in a language not too distant from theirs.
• The hymn's emphasis on all things being created in God's Son (1:16) underlines the superiority of Christ over the principalities and the powers. Special attention has also been paid to the plērōma ("fullness") in 1:19: "For in him all the fullness was pleased to dwell." In both second-century gnosticism, as articulated by the influential gnostic theologian Valentinus, and in the Hermetic corpus (Egyptian-Greek wisdom texts of disputed date), the language of the plērōma ("fullness") was used in relation to God, but not in the sense of what is meant in Col, where 2:9 ("all the plērōma of deity" in Christ bodily) interprets 1:19. By divine election God in all fullness dwells in Christ. That is why through him all things can be reconciled to God (1:20a).

THE FALSE TEACHING (2:8–23)

The teaching that presents a danger at Colossae has to be reconstructed mirror-wise from the letter's hostile polemic against it (that is, comments in Colossians are taken to reflect the reality to which they refer, so that it may be reconstructed from the perceived reflections), and that makes the tone and content of the teaching hard to evaluate. By way of TONE, clearly the situation at Colossae is not like that recounted in Gal or that at Philippi. Indeed, we cannot be certain that the Christians at Colossae were aware of their peril; and some of the description might be purely potential (2:8).

By way of CONTENT, we may begin by noting that the cities of the Lycus River valley constituted an area where religious observances reflected a mixture of native Phrygian cults, Eastern imports (Isis, an Egyptian goddess whose cult spread throughout the Hellenistic world; Mithras, originally a Persian god), Greco-Roman deities, and Judaism with its insistence on one God. In the description of the teaching that threatened the Christians at Colossae, elements that seem related to Judaism are described: circumcision (not made by hand!), food and drink, and observing a feast, a new moon, or Sabbaths. Nevertheless, the false teaching assumed by Col appears to be coherent and more complex than an attempt to persuade the Colossian Christian Gentiles to observe the Mosaic Law for salvation.

In 2:8 Paul would have the recipients beware of being seduced by an empty deceitful "philosophy" that is according to human tradition. The statement is vague, and there are several possibilities, both Hellenistic and Jewish. Col 2:8 goes on to describe the error as putting emphasis on the "elements" (*stoicheia*) of the world/universe. These could be the elements that constitute everything (earth, fire, water, air), but in Hellenistic times the term also referred to cosmic rulers or spirits that dominated the world, including heavenly bodies that astrologically controlled human affairs. Col's hostile references to "principalities" and "powers" (2:15), and to abasement and the "worship of angels" (2:18), point in that direction. Might extremes of asceticism be in mind in reference to "food and drink" (2:16)—an asceticism that manifested obedience to the elemental spirits, the principalities, and the powers?

Combining these elements, many would describe the false teachers at Colossae as Jewish Christian syncretists in whose "philosophy" were combined (hellenized) Jewish, Christian, and pagan elements in a cosmic pattern that people must follow in life. This syncretism could incorporate believers in Christ under the proviso that they rated him as subordinate to the angelic principalities and powers. After all, Christ was flesh while the principalities are spirits.

Two other factors are sometimes detected in the teaching. First, some would describe the teaching rejected by Col as gnosticism because of references to visions, to being inflated by the bodily mind, to the gratification of the flesh, and to the elemental spirits if they are understood as emanations of God. Yet there is no direct reference to "knowledge" in the critique of the teachers. Unfortunately our information about incipient gnosticism in the first century is very limited, so that identifying the teaching as gnostic because of the vague features just mentioned amounts to elucidating the unknown by the less known.

Second, in the positive sections Col speaks of the divine mystery (mystērion) hidden from past ages but now revealed in Christ—the knowledge of which has been shared with the Colossians. Some would find in that an implicit critique of the false teachers as adherents of a mystery religion. That the false teachers had some mystery religion connections or used mystery religion language is possible. Paul's own use of mystērion stems from apocalyptic Judaism and is certainly not dependent on his having been exposed to mystery religions.

If these observations leave a picture filled with uncertainties, that is an honest estimate of the state of our knowledge of the teaching. At this distance in time and place we may not be able to decipher all the elements that went into the syncretism attacked in Col or identify the end-product with precision. What is truly probable is that the opponents had combined belief in Christ with Jewish and pagan ideas to shape a hierarchical system of heavenly beings in which Christ was subordinated to angelic powers to whom worship was due.

∴✦∴

28

Epistle (Letter) to the Ephesians

Among the Pauline writings only Rom can match Eph as a candidate for exercising the most influence on Christian thought and spirituality. Indeed Eph, which has been called the "crown of Paulinism," is more attractive to many because it spares them the complex argumentation of Rom. Especially appealing to an ecumenical age is the magnificent Eph view of the church universal and of unity among Christians. A fair estimate might be that *at the present moment about eighty percent of critical scholarship holds that Paul did not write Eph.* Yet, there have been major defenses of Pauline authorship up to the present.

Nevertheless, arguments against actual Pauline authorship focus on the following: the apparent lack of a specific address (1:1); the seeming impersonal character of the writing (1:15; 3:2–13; 6:21–24); remarkable vocabulary and syntax by comparison with undisputed letters (1:3–10; 2:1–7); an apparently later historical situation: the Jew/Gentile conflict is resolved (2:11–22); theological developments and shifts are noticeable in christology (1:15–23; 2:20–22), ecclesiology (3:10,20–21), eschatology (2:5–6, 7), and the status of Church

SUMMARY OF BASIC INFORMATION

DATE: If by Paul, in the 60s. If pseudonymous (about 80 percent of critical scholarship), in the 90s.

TO: Pauline Christians (probably as imaged in western Asia Minor).

AUTHENTICITY: Probably by a disciple of Paul (perhaps part of a "school" at Ephesus) who drew on Col and some of the undisputed Pauline letters.

UNITY: Not seriously disputed.

INTEGRITY: "In Ephesus" probably added in 1:1; otherwise not seriously debated.

FORMAL DIVISION:
   A. Opening Formula: 1:1–2
   B. Thanksgiving: 1:3–23
   C. Body: 2:1–3:21: Pauline indicative (instructions)
      4:1–6:20: Pauline imperative (paraenesis and exhortations)
   D. Concluding Formula: 6:21–24.

DIVISION ACCORDING TO CONTENTS:

1:1–2: Greeting to all the saints

1:3–3:21: "Indicative" or doctrinal section

1:3–23: *Doxology* praising God for what has been done for "us" in Jesus Christ (1:3–14) and intercessory *prayer* that "you" (recipients) may know this (1:15–23)

2:1–3:13: Exposition of saving, unifying, revealing activity of God

3:14–21: Further intercessory *prayer* (for "you") and *doxology* ("us")

4:1–6:20: "Imperative" or paraenetic section

4:1–5:20: Exhortations concerning unity, pastoral ministry, two ways of life (dualism), walking as children of the light, no works of darkness

5:21–6:9: Household code

6:10–20: Armor in struggle against evil powers, especially prayer

6:21–22: Mission of Tychicus

6:23–24: Blessing.

---

members (2:4–7) and leaders (2:20; 3:5; 4:11–14). Moreover, there are marked parallels to Colossians; for example, 6:21–22 agrees almost exactly with Col 4:7, and overall seventy-three of the one hundred and fifty-five verses in Eph have verbal parallels to lines in Col.

After the General Analysis treats the basic message of the letter, a subsection considers: the Ecclesiology of Eph and "Early Catholicism."

GENERAL ANALYSIS OF THE MESSAGE

Paul is a prisoner for the Lord, and Tychicus is being sent to tell the recipients about him. Otherwise there is no story in Eph, recounting

Paul's past dealings with the audience or any details about them. Those addressed in the Opening Formula (1:1–2), "The saints who are also faithful in Christ Jesus," could be any Christians, although the mention of Tychicus (see Col 4:7–8) probably means that the Christian communities in western Asia Minor are the ones known to the writer.

In 1:3–14, the first part of the Thanksgiving (1:3–23), using the quasiliturgical language found in Jewish blessings, Paul celebrates the role of Christ and the Christians in God's plan to unite in Christ all things in heaven and on earth. In this mystery of God's will, before creation, God destined Christians to "sonship" in Jesus Christ in whom they have redemption, forgiveness, and grace. They have heard the gospel of salvation. Then (1:15–23) Paul acknowledges thankfully the faith and love of the recipients and prays for their growth in Christ. And all this is for the church, his body, a goal of God's plan, which involves the whole of creation.

The INDICATIVE SECTION OF THE BODY (2:1–3:21) begins by explaining how this plan, manifesting the richness of God's mercy and love, has converted sinners into saints, the spiritually dead into the spiritually alive, now saved by grace through faith, which is the gift of God (2:1–10). Furthermore, 2:11–22 lyrically describes how God's grace reached out to the Gentiles, so that those who were once far off have been brought near. The dividing wall of hostility has been broken down, Israel and the Gentiles are one, fellow citizens in the household of God built on a foundation of the apostles and prophets with Christ as the cornerstone (2:20). Paul explains that God had made him, the least of all of the saints, a minister of the gospel to the Gentiles. Indeed, through the church the wisdom of God was now being made known to the heavenly powers. Paul offers his prayers (3:13–19), so that his audience may be filled with all the fullness (plērōma) of God. Paul finishes this part of the letter with a doxology (3:20–21).

The IMPERATIVE OR PARAENETIC SECTION OF THE BODY (4:1–6:20) explicates the implications of this great plan of God with thirty-six verbs in the imperative. In 1:4 Paul said that God chose "us" in Christ before the foundation of the world to be holy and without blemish in the divine presence. In 4:1 he leads into directives for living a life worthy of God's calling. Paul spells out seven manifestations of oneness in the

Christian life (4:4–6) and tells how the ascended Christ poured forth a diversity of gifts to equip Christians for building up the body of Christ: apostles, prophets, evangelists, pastors, and teachers (4:7–12). Such gifts help "the saints" to grow up into Christ the head of the body (4:13–16).

Since Gentiles and Jews have been made one by Christ's work, Paul instructs this new human being not to live according to the old pattern of life. Paul sees two contrasting ways of "walking," corresponding to light/darkness, the devil/the Holy Spirit, truth/falsehood. This dualism produces children of light and sons of disobedience (5:6–20), the wise and the unwise. Rather than carousing, Christians are to sing and make melody to the Lord.

Eph 5:21–6:9 specifies the way of Christian life in terms of a *household code* (a summary list of attitudes and actions appropriate to persons in various pairings in ancient household situations) for *wives*/husbands, *children*/fathers, *slaves*/masters. The overall pattern is the same as in the household code of Col 3:18–4:1; but the Eph code is a third longer than that of Col, and there are interesting differences. Eph (5:21) begins with an instruction to be subject to one another out of reverence for Christ; and, of course, that affects husbands to wives, as well as wives to husbands. Thus the opening of this code modifies more radically the established order than did the code of Col. The lyric language of 5:25–27 brings Christ and the church into the relationship of husband and wife, so that respectively the subjection and the love are given a uniquely Christian stamp. The obligation of the husband to love is treated more extensively than the obligation of the wife to be subject, and both are rooted in God's initial plan for union in marriage (5:31 = Gen 2:24). The children/fathers instruction is also fortified with an OT motif. The Eph change in the slave/master relationship is largely in the master section: not only should the master be impartial in treating the slave as in Col; he should forbear threatening—with the reminder that Christ is the master of the master. The radical thrust of the gospel is putting pressure on those who have authority and power.

Employing the figurative language of armor and weapons, a final exhortation concerns the ongoing battle with the principalities and powers (Eph 6:10–20). Now we discover that realized eschatology (God's promises fulfilled in Jesus Christ are now a lasting legacy in time) has not entirely replaced future eschatology (ahead lies a day of final reckoning and fulfillment of God's purposes), for the divine struggle with the powers and the rulers of the present darkness continues. Paul asks for prayers for himself, describing himself as "an ambassador in chains" (6:20), that he might declare the gospel boldly.

In the Concluding Formula (6:21–24) minimal greetings refer to one companion, Tychicus, who is being sent to the addressees as in Col 4:7–8.

ECCLESIOLOGY OF EPHESIANS AND EARLY CATHOLICISM

In Eph the Jew/Gentile struggles seem past, and Paul's mission is triumphing. The Paul of Eph has been given an understanding, not only of the redemption accomplished by the crucifixion/resurrection, but also of the full plan of God where everything in heaven and earth is subject to an exalted Christ and united with him. This is visible in the church, Christ's masterpiece, since Jews and Gentiles, without losing their own identity, have been made one in the church. There is no need to emphasize the second coming because so much has already been accomplished in Christ (in the church).

Eph's exaltation of the church goes beyond the already high estimation in Col. Even though Col had a universal concept of "church," half of its four uses of *ekklēsia* were to local church (4:15,16); there is no such local reference in the nine uses in Eph. These are all in the singular and designate the universal church. As in Col 1:18,24, the church is Christ's body and he is the head (Eph 1:22; 5:23). Yet in Eph the church has a cosmic role. According to 1:21–23 Christ has been made head over all things "for the church." Glory is given to God in the church (3:20). Christ loved the church and gave himself over for her (5:25)—that is different from the idea that Christ died for sinners (Rom 5:6,8) or for all (II Cor 5:14–15). Christ's goal was to sanctify the church, cleansing her by the washing of water and the word, rendering her without spot or blemish. He continues to nourish and cherish her (Eph 5:23–32).

This, then, is a convenient moment to mention briefly the issue of "Early Catholicism," which the ecclesiology of Eph is thought to

Table 6. Comparing Ephesians and Colossians

TOPIC	EPH	COL
(1) Redemption, forgiveness	1:7	1:14, 20
(2) The all-inclusive Christ	1:10	1:20
(3) Intercession for the readers	1:15–17	1:3–4, 9
(4) Riches of a glorious inheritance	1:18	1:27 (hope of glory)
(5) Christ's dominion	1:21–22	1:16–18
(6) You he made alive	2:5	2:13
(7) Aliens brought near	2:12–13	1:21–22
(8) Abolishing the commandments	2:15	2:14
(9) Paul the prisoner	3:1	1:24
(10) Divine mystery made known to Paul	3:2–3	1:25–26
(11) Paul, minister of universal gospel	3:7	1:23, 25
(12) Paul to make known the mystery to all	3:8–9	1:27
(13) Lead a life worthy of your calling	4:1	1:10
(14) With all lowliness, meekness, patience, forbearing one another	4:2	3:12–13
(15) Christ unites members of church	4:15–16	2:19
(16) Put off old nature and put on new nature	4:22–32	3:5–10, 12
(17) No immorality among you	5:3–6	3:5–9
(18) Walk wisely and make the most of the time	5:15	4:5
(19) Sing songs, hymns, and spiritual songs, giving thanks to God	5:19–20	3:16–17
(20) Tables of household duties for husbands, wives, children, parents, slaves, and masters	5:21–6:9	3:18–4:1
(21) Paul the prisoner exhorts persistence in prayer	6:18–20	4:2–3
(22) Tychicus sent to inform church about Paul and to encourage them	6:21–22	4:7–8

exemplify. The term designates the initial stages of high ecclesiology, sacramentalism, hierarchy, ordination, and dogma—in short the beginning of the distinctive features of *Catholic* Christianity. Some have suggested that there was no early Catholicism in the NT, but that it began in the second century under the influence of the Greek spirit that distorted the pristine evangelical character of Christianity. But others have contended that there is "Early Catholicism" in the NT itself, although these developments were not necessarily normative for Christianity. Thus, recourse was taken by some to the principle of "the canon within the canon," since they held that Christians must distinguish the real Spirit within the NT.

There is an arbitrariness in this type of judgment, for it asserts the right to reject those voices in the NT with which one does not agree. All Christians/churches tend to give more weight to some parts of the NT than to other parts. Yet one must recognize that there are important differences among the NT books on issues such as ecclesiology, sacramentalism, and church structure. A church (or a Christian) may make a theological decision to give preference to one view over another. Yet an awareness of what is said in the NT on the other side of an issue can modify some of the exaggerated or objectionable features of one's own position. Repeating the NT passages that support one's views may give reassurance, but listening to the scriptural voices on the opposing side enables the NT to act as a conscience.

29

Pastoral Letter: To Titus

After some observations on the *"Pastoral" Letters in general*, this chapter and the next two (30, 31) will treat them in the order Titus, I Tim, II Tim. As we shall see, there is a major debate about whether Paul wrote them. But first they will be discussed at face value. The issue of authorship will be examined in the next chap. in a subsection after the General Analysis of the Message of I Tim.

In the treatment of Titus, after Background and General Analysis, a subsection will deal with Presbyter/bishops.

THE PASTORAL LETTERS IN GENERAL: TITLE, INTERRELATIONSHIP

The Title. Many refer to the three as "Epistles." Yet they have the letter format. As for "Pastoral," that designation has been applied to them since the early eighteenth century in recognition of their central concern—the care of evangelized communities after the missionaries had moved on. Titus and I Tim focus on church structure or order, that is, the appointment of officials to administer the Christian community;

SUMMARY OF BASIC INFORMATION

DATE: If by Paul, ca. AD 65. If pseudonymous (80 to 90 percent of critical scholarship), toward the end of the first century, or (less probably) early second century.

TO: Titus in Crete (newly founded churches?) from a Paul depicted as recently departed from there and now in coastal Asia Minor (Ephesus?) or western Greece (Macedonia?), on his way to Nicopolis.

AUTHENTICITY: Probably written by a disciple of Paul or a sympathetic commentator on the Pauline heritage several decades after the apostle's death.

UNITY AND INTEGRITY: Not seriously disputed.

FORMAL DIVISION:
    A. Opening Formula: 1:1–4
    B. Thanksgiving: None
    C. Body: 1:5–3:11
    D. Concluding Formula: 3:12–15.

DIVISION ACCORDING TO CONTENTS:

1:1–4: Address/greetings to Titus
1:5–9: Church structure and the appointment of presbyter/bishops
1:10–16: False teaching that threatens the community
2:1–3:11: Community behavior and belief:
        2:1–10: Household code
        2:11–3:11: What Christ has done and its implications
        3:12–15: Concluding greetings and blessing.

and often such figures are designated "pastors." More than any other letters attributed to Paul, these three (Titus, I Tim, and II Tim) are profitably considered together and in relation to one another.

Interrelation from the Viewpoint of Order: Overall they are very homogeneous in style and atmosphere, but treating the three as a group may blind an interpreter to individual differences, especially those of II Tim. Some scholars identify different modes of rhetoric in the letters, while others notice that the letters have different atmospheres, for example, problems and purposes. Notably, the Pastorals do not give detailed directives on how the church order is to function.

The canonical order (I–II Tim, Titus) is simply an arrangement by descending length, and any order of composition is possible. Yet there is a certain appropriateness in the order Titus (less developed church structure), I Tim (more developed church structure), II Tim

(Paul dying). This order is attested in the Muratorian Fragment (late second century) and Ambrosiaster (fourth century) and is probably the oldest.

THE BACKGROUND (OF TITUS)

In the NT Titus (never mentioned in Acts!) is described as having been converted by Paul and brought to the Jerusalem meeting in AD 49 (Gal 2:1–3) to demonstrate how genuine a Christian an uncircumcised Gentile could be. In the crisis between Paul and the church at Corinth (after Paul's "painful visit"), Titus carried the letter written "with many tears" from Ephesus to Corinth. He was successful in effecting a diplomatic reconciliation (II Cor 2:1; 7:6–16). He was later sent to Corinth to gather the collection that Paul would bring to Jerusalem in 58 (II Cor 8:6,16,23). The present letter assumes that Paul has been on Crete with Titus and has left him there to order anything still undone, specifically to appoint presbyters in every Christian community (Titus 1:5). Paul's whereabouts when writing this letter is not stated.

Most scholars who accept Paul as the writer of Titus, or at least the accuracy of the details given in Titus, posit a "second career" for the apostle in the mid-60s during which he was released following his two-year captivity in Rome (AD 61–63) and went back east—to Crete, Ephesus, and Nicopolis. II Tim is brought into this theory to posit a terminus of Paul's second career in another Roman captivity and execution there in 65–67.

GENERAL ANALYSIS OF THE MESSAGE

After a comment about the Opening Formula, this section organizes the message in the Body of Titus under three headings: church structure, false teaching, and community relations and belief.

OPENING FORMULA (1:1–4). This is both long and formal; indeed only Rom is noticeably longer. Since a major concern is to preserve the faith of Christians on Crete, Paul is shown as insisting that one of the duties of an apostle is to be concerned with the faith of God's elect.

Body (1:5–9): *First theme: Church structure or order.* The letter tells us that Paul had not established a fixed structure on Crete, and so he is now entrusting that task to Titus. Such order is a concern because of the danger presented by false teachers. While Titus mentions only the appointment of presbyter/bishops (not deacons as in I Tim), the qualifications demanded of these figures were to guarantee leadership faithful to Paul's teaching and thus protect the faithful from undesirable innovations.

Body (1:10–16): *Second theme: False teaching.* Titus attacks a pressing danger. The description of the teachers, however, is phrased polemically. Thus, it is hard to diagnose the teaching from the remarks describing the moral failure(s) of these teachers.

Christians of Jewish ancestry come under fire in Titus 1:10–16, and although there are references to "those from the circumcision," "Jewish myths," and concern with "pure" and "defiled," it is not clear at what these comments aim. Some suggest that the author was facing a Jewish/Gnostic syncretistic false teaching, but the vagueness of what is described warns us how uncertain is any judgment.

Body (2:1–3:11): *Third theme: Community relations and belief.* The first section (2:1–10) is a household code similar to those in Col 3:18–4:1 and Eph 5:21–6:9. The pattern here is less regular: older men/older women, younger women/younger men/slaves. The issue is not the relationship of the older men to the older women, but the general edifying comportment of both and their training of younger counterparts. Yet when women (2:4–5) and slaves (2:9) are told to be submissive, Titus comes close to Col and Eph. The demand for sober, dignified behavior is traced to sound doctrine (2:10).

In 2:11–3:11, with a proselytizing interest the author gives pastoral instructions based on what Christ has done. Above all, he wants the Cretan Christians to be models (Titus 2:7) to attract others to the faith. This involves submitting to authorities, being courteous to outsiders, and avoiding inner-Christian dissensions and quarrels (3:1–2,9–10).

Concluding Formula (3:12–15). The final greeting mentions Artemas, Tychicus, Zenas, and Apollos and envisions a wider audience than Titus.

PRESBYTER/BISHOPS IN THE PASTORALS

Although scholars are not in total agreement about what is envisaged, here are likelihoods:

- In each community there were to be appointed presbyters. Normally, as the designation *presbyteroi* (literally "old ones," whence "elders") indicates, these would be older, experienced men of the community, and they would have two major functions. First, seemingly as a group, they were to give the community directions, for example, by guiding policy decisions and supervising finances. Second, they were to exercise pastoral care for individual Christians in matters of belief and moral practice.
- In the Pastorals, "overseer, bishop" (*episkopos*) is another title for the *presbyteros* (whence "presbyter/bishop"), particularly in the function of pastoral care of individuals. We may speak of presbyter/bishops in the communities envisioned by Titus and I Tim with reasonable confidence that there was an overseeing group rather than a solitary overseer/bishop—the latter being a development attested only later. It is clear from I Tim 5:17 that not every presbyter exercised the same kind of pastoral overseeing, for only some preached and taught.
- Before appointment, the qualifications of potential presbyter/bishops were to be examined carefully. Presumably if a person met the qualifications and was appointed presbyter/bishop, that appointment would have been regarded as taking place under the guidance of the Spirit, but that is never said; and so the Pastorals' structure is often contrasted with charismatic leadership.

To probe that contrast: Titus 1:6–9 and I Tim 3:1–7 list the qualities and qualifications expected of the presbyter/bishop. Four categories may be distinguished: (a) Negative descriptions of disqualifying behavior or attitudes: not arrogant . . . not loving money. (b) Positive descriptions of desired virtues and abilities: faultless . . . dignified. (c) Life-situation to be expected of a public figure who would be setting a standard for the community: married only once . . . not a recent convert. (d) Skills related to the work to be done: a good reputation with outsiders . . . an adept teacher (of sound doctrine).

The qualifying virtues described in (a) and (b) are sometimes called institutional: they would result in the selection of presbyter/bishops whom a congregation could like, admire, and live with. The qualifications do not have a dynamic thrust and would not be inclined to produce leaders who change the world. The demands in (c) distance the Pastorals from a charismatic approach to ministry. A person with remarkable leadership abilities would not be eligible to be a presbyter/bishop if certain conditions were not met.

• In 1:5 Titus is told to appoint presbyters on Crete, but how will a continuity of presbyters be preserved once he departs? Was there a designating action that might have been considered an ordination? From later church history and Jewish practices, one may strongly suspect that, at the time the Pastorals were written, presbyters were installed by the laying on of hands. Yet, once again, we may doubt that there was as yet uniformity in the Christian churches.

.✦.

30

Pastoral Letter: The First to Timothy

There are two letters of Paul in the NT canon to this disciple, but neither shows an awareness of the existence of the other. "First" means only that it is longer than the shorter one, called "second." The subject matter of I Tim resembles that of Titus; but nothing in either missive shows awareness of the other, nor do we know which of the three Pastorals was written first. After the Background and the General Analysis, a subsection will be devoted to Implications of Pseudepigraphy for the Pastorals.

THE BACKGROUND

Some biographical details about Timothy, drawn from Acts and the rest of the Pauline corpus, can be useful since they may have shaped the writer's image of the recipient. Timothy lived at Lystra in SE Asia Minor and presumably was converted as a result of Paul's evangelizing there ca. AD 46. Timothy joined him as a traveling missionary ca. 50 and remained at his service as a faithful helper through Paul's subsequent career. According to Acts 16:1–3, although Timothy's father

SUMMARY OF BASIC INFORMATION

DATE: If by Paul, ca. AD 65. If pseudonymous (80 to 90 percent of critical scholarship), toward the end of the first century, or (less probably) early second century.

TO: Timothy in Ephesus (with the possibility that Ephesus may represent churches already in existence for quite a while) from a Paul depicted as recently departed from there and now in Macedonia.

AUTHENTICITY: Probably written by a disciple of Paul or sympathetic commentator on the Pauline heritage several decades after the apostle's death.

UNITY AND INTEGRITY: Not seriously disputed.

FORMAL DIVISION:
    A. Opening Formula: 1:1–2
    B. Thanksgiving: None
    C. Body: 1:3–6:19
    D. Concluding Formula: 6:20–21.

DIVISION ACCORDING TO CONTENTS:
1:1–2: Address/greetings to Timothy
1:3–11: Warning against false teachers
1:12–20: Paul's own career and charge to Timothy
2:1–15: Ordering of public worship (especially for men and women)
3:1–16: Instructions for bishop and deacons
4:1–5: Correction of false teaching
4:6–5:2: Encouragement for Timothy to teach
5:3–6:2: Instructions for widows, presbyters, and slaves
6:3–10: Warning against false teachers and love of money
6:11–21a: Charge to Timothy
6:21b: Concluding blessing.

was a Gentile, his mother was a Jewish Christian; and so Paul had him circumcised lest Jews be scandalized. Then, during 50–52 Timothy accompanied Paul through Phrygia and Galatia and over to Europe (Philippi, Thessalonica, and Beroea). After departing Thessalonica, Paul sent him back to strengthen the Thessalonians, and he rejoined Paul in Corinth bringing good news (I Thess 3:6). He aided Paul in evangelizing Corinth (II Cor 1:19); but we lose track of him for years. During Paul's stay in Ephesus in 54–57 Timothy was with him at least part of the time. Paul sent him from Ephesus into Macedonia (I Cor 4:17; 16:10) and eventually to Corinth. Things were not going well, and so Timothy returned to Paul in Ephesus to report. Probably Timothy was with Paul when the apostle finally left Ephesus in the summer of 57; for when Titus brought good news from Corinth, Paul and Timothy sent II Cor from Macedonia. Timothy spent the winter of 57–58 with Paul in Corinth, during the time when Rom was sent. Acts has him with Paul at the beginning of the journey from Corinth to Jerusalem before Pentecost of 58; he went on ahead and awaited Paul in Troas. That is the last mention of Timothy in Acts.

Timothy's name was listed as co-author of I Thess, Phil, Phlm, and II Cor. It is also joined to Paul's in Col 1:1, which some view as authentically Pauline, so that Timothy is often thought to have been with Paul in the Roman imprisonment of 61–63; but that is far from certain. Through the years Paul wrote warm evaluations of Timothy. Among other things Paul speaks of him as his brother; God's servant in the gospel of Christ; a son to Paul in service to the gospel ("I have no one like him"); one who looks not after his own interests, but after Christ's; his beloved and faithful child who is not to be despised as he does the work of the Lord.

How does the biographical information in I Tim fit into this picture? In its attitude toward Timothy I Tim (and II Tim) is very close to the undisputed Pauline letters: Timothy is a beloved son to Paul and a servant to God—he is an example, not to be despised. Beyond this I Tim describes Timothy as a youth (4:12) who has a gift (4:14) and who is subject to frequent illness (5:23). At the time of writing he was at Ephesus, left there by Paul, who had gone to Macedonia (1:3) and hoped to return to Ephesus soon (3:14–15). This information does not fit into the career of Paul and Timothy just recounted, derived from Acts and the undisputed Pauline letters.

GENERAL ANALYSIS OF THE MESSAGE

As with Titus, some posit a "second career" of Paul. After captivity in Rome (61–63) he returned to Ephesus, and then sometime in the mid-60s he went to Macedonia, from where he wrote to Timothy. Here, the message in the Body is studied under three headings: church structure, false teaching, and community relations and belief.

OPENING FORMULA (1:1–2). The apostle identifies himself as commissioned by God our Savior and Christ Jesus our hope.

BODY (3:1–13; 5:3–22a): *Theme of church structure or order.* The treatment of structure at Ephesus is spread over two strangely unconnected segments, the first describing the bishop and deacons, the second describing widows and presbyters. Most qualifications stipulated in Titus 1:5–9 for the combined presbyter/bishops who are the teachers of the community are stipulated in I Tim 3:1–7 for bishops. In all likelihood those bishops were presbyters; but since only certain presbyters were involved in preaching and teaching (5:17), probably not all presbyters were bishops.

Alongside the presbyter/bishops at Ephesus there are deacons (3:8–13) who are to have similar qualifications: respectable, not given to too much wine, not pursuing dishonest gain, married only once, managing their children and household well. The root verb *diakonein* suggests service; and deacons may have rendered service more menial than that provided by presbyter/bishops. Probably there are also women deacons (3:11) for whom qualifications are listed: respectable, temperate, trustworthy. Presumably they rendered the same kinds of service supplied by the men deacons, but some *speculate* that women deacons performed duties for women (and men for men).

Widows (5:3–16) constitute another group at Ephesus. They had fixed community status, but it is not clear that they should be described as holding office or constituting an order. Not all widows were alike. The special, or "true," widows must be sixty years old, have been married only once (thus committed to remaining single), not have children or grandchildren to be cared for, have brought up their children well, and be well known for good deeds. These women would be without personal wealth (5:5,16), and so the church provides for them from common goods. In the church they pray night and day, extend hospitality even in menial tasks, and help those in need. We have no idea how this role differs from that of the deacons.

What is peculiar in Paul's description is the clearly hostile tone toward widows who should not be enrolled among the special group of widows. He fears that the younger among them might even be "merry widows," indulging themselves, gadding about, gossiping, and even looking for another husband. In the long run, then, Paul judges it better that young widows remarry and have children rather than give scandal.

BODY (1:3–20; 3:14–4:10; 6:3–5): *Theme of false (and true) teaching.* False teaching is described in several places in I Tim, and we cannot be sure that the same danger is always in mind. There is much polemic in the description, making it difficult to know what precisely was the basic error. Timothy, despite his youth, has had prophecies made about him, has followed sound doctrine, and is capable of being a good minister of Christ (1:18–19) in counteracting the false teachers. Alongside an indication of the Jewish background of the opponents who would be teachers of the Law (1:7), there is an unclear reference to their devotion to myths and genealogies. Some of the criticized issues are more specific, but there is no certain background for the problems; nevertheless, proposals include Jewish apocrypha, Jewish gnosticism, or a combination of the two, and common Cynic philosophy.

BODY (2:1–15; 4:11–5:2; 5:22b–6:2; 6:6–19): *Theme of community relations and belief.* This is harder to delineate in I Tim than it was in Titus because part of it is woven into the condemnation of false teaching, for example, 1:8–11. As in Titus 2:1–10 there is a *household code* but in a scattered form. Thus, in I Tim 5:1–2 there are instructions about the interrelations of various members of the community; in 2:8–15 men and women are told how to behave during worship; in 6:1–2 slaves receive an admonition about showing respect to masters; and in 2:1–2 prayer is inculcated for those in authority.

The instructions for men and women in worship are disproportionately corrective of women. Normally these verses are read as a general attitude toward women, which today is heard as extremist in limiting women's roles. Yet there has been support recently for another way of interpreting this passage against the background of the letter's attack on false teaching. That these women were wealthy (2:9) and that they had the leisure to flit about (5:6,13) may mean that they were targets for the message being propagated by the false teachers, who themselves were seeking monetary gain (6:5). Thus, not women in general but wealthy women who became the spokespersons of the error to

which they had been enticed would have been the object of the prohibition of teaching and holding authority (2:12). These women may
have been spreading the error.

Beyond the household code one may notice a particular distrust of
wealth in 6:5–10,17–19, including the famous "The love of money is
the root of all evils" (6:10). A notable number of *hymnic passages* support
the writer's moral instructions, the most famous of which is 3:16,
where in six short poetic lines the mystery of religion/godliness (*euse-
beia*) is praised in terms of what happened to Christ. Hymnic elements
have also been diagnosed in 6:7–8 and 6:15–16. The latter is a blessing
that would have been seen as giving to Christ titles that might elsewhere be claimed by the emperor. In 2:4–5 Jesus has become part of
a monotheistic creedal statement of "truth": "There is one God; there
is one mediator between God and human beings, Christ Jesus himself
human."

In the Concluding Formula (6:20–21) one does not find the greetings that terminate most Pauline letters, but only a passionate plea to
Timothy.

WHO WROTE TITUS AND I TIMOTHY?

There is enough evidence now to consider this issue, and because
II Tim is partially a different problem it will be left till the next chapter. Paul is the apparent author, even supplying details about his travels. For reasons to be given below, that has been challenged for the
past 200 years. Suggested alternatives include: (1) A close Pauline
disciple carrying out Paul's designs; (2) a sympathetic commentator
on the Pauline heritage writing later to strengthen churches against
gnosticism; (3) non-Pauline attempts to correct the apostle's heritage
in troubled times when he is being invoked in dangerous ways (by
Marcion or apocryphal *Acts*)—that is, the Pastorals would have been
written to domesticate the memory of Paul; or (4) forgeries, as part
of a design to deceive the readers. Scholars evaluate the authenticity of
these letters by using different factors—which are rarely unambiguous
and can produce confusion. Resolving with great assurance who wrote
the Pastorals, and when, does not respect the evidence.

First, the language of the Pastorals is distinct when compared with Paul's undisputed usage. Vocabulary and syntax (use of particles, conjunctions, and adverbs) differs notably from Paul's other letters. The style of the Pastorals is less Hebraic and more colorless and monotonous (longer sentences, less variety of words and style). Statistics about language can be misused in such arguments, but here the statistics do create a doubt about Pauline writing.

Second, comparison of theology and ethics between undisputed Pauline writings and the Pastorals produces a similar report to that about language. Familiar Pauline terms (law, faith, righteousness) appear but with a slightly different nuance.

Third, the data about Paul's ministry and whereabouts cannot be fitted into what we know of Paul's life before the Roman imprisonment of 61–63. If historical, the information in the Pastorals demands the positing of a "second career" in the mid-60s. *Terminus a quo*: Titus and I Tim could not have been written before 64–66.

Fourth, some who place the Pastorals late in the second century observe that they are missing from Marcion's canon (ca. 150). Tertullian (*Adversus Marcion* 5.21) contends that Marcion knew and rejected them. Furthermore, Polycarp, *Philippians* 4:1, is close to I Tim (5:3–6; 6:7, 10); most judge that Polycarp's letter (AD 120–130) has been influenced by the Pastorals. *Terminus ante quem*: the external evidence slightly favors the Pastorals having been written before AD 125.

Fifth, the false teaching being criticized is often judged to be a Judaizing gnosticism that developed later than in Paul's lifetime. But there is insufficient evidence in the Pastorals to suggest that any one of the great gnostic systems of the second century was the target of criticism.

Sixth, it is argued that the church structure envisioned in the Pastorals goes beyond Paul's lifetime. Granted, no undisputed letter mentions presbyters, but church structure is not the subject of those letters. Moreover, Phil 1:1 mentions bishops (or "overseers") and deacons. There is insufficient information given about these figures to form a completely clear picture of the situation(s).

Seventh, Titus mentions the appointment of presbyter/bishops, and I Tim supposes the existence in Ephesus of presbyter/bishops and deacons. This bipartite structure is not far from that of *Didache* 15:1 (ca. AD 100?), which speaks of bishops and deacons, and that of I *Clement* 42:4,5; 44:4–5; 54:2 (AD 96), which refers to presbyter/bishops and deacons. It is distinct from the tripartite structure urged by Ignatius in most letters (ca. 110), namely, one bishop, presbyters, and deacons. While a linear progression is surely too simple a picture, in such development the Pastorals would be placed in time before Ignatius's writings.

Eighth, in atmosphere and vocabulary the Pastorals are very close to Luke-Acts. Some have even proposed that the same person wrote them. Several items in Acts are paralleled in the Pastorals: Paul's sufferings and travels in Acts 13–14 are similar to II Tim 3:11; and Paul gives a farewell address in II Tim 3:10–4:8 through Timothy to the church at Ephesus, and in Acts 20:18–35 the farewell is directed to the presbyter/bishops of Ephesus. The most plausible dating of Luke-Acts is the 80s.

Ninth, I Tim implies the existence of a certain type of false teaching at Ephesus. Neither the letter to the angel of the church in Ephesus in Rev 2:1–7 (probably written in the 90s) nor Ignatius's *Ephesians* (ca. 110) describes a similar heresy. Was it stamped out by I Tim, which at face value was written to Ephesus before those two letters? Or did the heresy develop after those two letters, so that I Tim was written after them?

Tenth, more than the undisputed letters of Paul, the Pastorals contain a large amount of biographical material. Drawing on pseudepigraphical writings attributed to other personalities in antiquity, some scholars have concluded that such personal details are meant to impress readers and to give an appearance of genuineness to the writings. The details given in the Pastorals would require some knowledge of other Pauline letters and Acts; but would these works have been easily available before AD 100?

Eleventh, for those of a literalist perspective, pseudepigraphical authorship of the Pastorals is unacceptable; even more it is impossible. For some others not of a literalist persuasion, pseudepigraphy in itself is not an obstacle to an affirmation of inspiration or to an understanding of divine communication through such writings.

IMPLICATIONS OF PSEUDEPIGRAPHY FOR THE PASTORALS

If one accepts pseudepigraphical authorship, virtually every issue pertinent to the letters has to be rethought. No one can pretend to give definitive answers to the questions that now arise, but readers should know the issues.

Authority of the Pastorals? The authority of the historical Paul as an interpreter of Jesus Christ is based on God's call and the revelation given to him, as well as on his response to God's grace by self-sacrificing fidelity to the apostolic mission. If the writer of the Pastorals is a disciple several times removed from the historical Paul, do his instructions have the same force as those of the historical Paul? The answer to that question may well reflect one's acceptance of inspiration and biblical authority.

Composition as a Group? Did the pseudepigraphical writer compose the letters separately as a problem arose in real places, for example, Crete, Ephesus, and Rome (where Paul died)? That would be the easiest solution; otherwise one seemingly has to posit a master design of remarkable complexity.

Historicity of the Travels? More radically one has to ask whether there is any historicity at all in the "second career" of Paul. Either the writer knew details about Paul not preserved elsewhere, or there was a fictional embellishment (on the grounds that imaginative settings are often part of pseudepigraphy).

Historicity of the Geographical Addressees? We have to ask whether surface directions of the Pastorals (Titus/Crete, Timothy/Ephesus [I Tim], and probably Timothy/Asia Minor [II Tim]) are authentic. Or were sites from the Pauline mission mentioned to illustrate types of Christian churches—Crete, churches being newly formed; and Ephesus, churches long in existence?

Historicity of the Personal Addressees? If a pseudepigraphical Paul has become an authoritative model voice giving instructions to churches beyond his time, what about Titus and Timothy? Were they still on the scene, or were they dead and these letters written to regions where they had served in order to continue the work? Or were the names simply chosen from Pauline history and used paradigmatically to address church leaders and churches decades later? If so, the Pastorals are in effect doubly pseudonymous: historically not written by Paul, and not addressed to Timothy and Titus.

Historicity of Places of Composition? While Titus does not specify the place from which it was written, either Ephesus or Macedonia is likely; I Tim indicates Macedonia; II Tim indicates Rome. How accurate/actual are these points of origin?

31

Pastoral Letter: The Second to Timothy

Nothing in this letter conveys an awareness of previous Pastoral Letters having been written to Timothy or Titus. Therefore we have no direct indication that II Tim was written after Titus or I Tim. Although stylistically it is very similar to them, it is not concerned with church structure, which for them is a central issue.

After discussion of *Possibilities about the Pastorals* and the *General Analysis*, a subsection will be devoted to *Inspired Scripture* (3:15–16).

II TIMOTHY AND POSSIBILITIES ABOUT THE PASTORALS

Paul's life situation pictured in Titus and I Tim could not be fitted into his "original career" known from Acts and the undisputed Pauline letters. Consequently in each case scholars posit a "second career" (actual or fictional) for Paul after his being released from the Roman captivity of 61–63. That career would have included a ministry alongside Titus on Crete, a return to Ephesus (where he left Timothy in charge), and then a departure to Macedonia. Most contend that what II Tim

SUMMARY OF BASIC INFORMATION

DATE: Written either *first* or *last* of the Pastorals. If by Paul, perhaps through a secretary, ca. 64 or shortly after (if written *first*) or 66–67 (if *last*). If pseudonymous (80 to 90 percent of critical scholarship), in the late 60s shortly after Paul's death (if written *first*) or decades later, most likely toward the end of the first century (if *last*).

TO: Timothy (in Troas? In Ephesus?) from a Paul depicted as imprisoned and dying in Rome.

AUTHENTICITY: Probably written by a disciple of Paul or a sympathetic commentator on the Pauline heritage (either soon after Paul's death with historical memories, or decades later with largely fictional biographical content). Yet it has a better chance of being authentically Pauline than do the other Pastorals.

UNITY AND INTEGRITY: Not seriously disputed.

FORMAL DIVISION:
A. Opening Formula: 1:1–2
B. Thanksgiving: 1:3–5
C. Body: 1:6–4:18
D. Concluding Formula: 4:19–22.

DIVISION ACCORDING TO CONTENTS:

1:1–5: Address/greetings to Timothy; recollection of his family background
1:6–18: Encouragement to Timothy from Paul in prison, feeling himself abandoned
2:1–13: Instruction on faithful preaching of the gospel, ending in a poetic saying
2:14–3:9: Examples of true teaching vs. false teaching
3:10–4:8: Final encouragement to Timothy based on the example of a Paul about to die
4:9–18: Practical charges to come and be wary; Paul's situation
4:19–22: Concluding greetings and benediction.

---

tells us about Paul and Timothy also cannot be fit into the "original career"; and so they look on it as an ending to the "second career" in which (actually or fictionally) ca. 65 Paul was once more imprisoned in Rome (II Tim 1:16–17) and wrote II Tim just before he died in 66–67.

A serious minority, however, argues that II Tim can be fit into Paul's career described in Acts—with the assumption that after the two years of relatively easy detention in Rome Paul was subjected to harsher jailing that led to his death ca. 64. II Tim would have been written in a context just before Paul's death without any "second career" leading to a second imprisonment ca. 65. How do the data of II Tim fit into that minority hypothesis? There is no convincing objection to this minority proposal, and so II Tim must be read without any presuppositions about how it is related to the other Pastorals. Then, there are four serious possibilities:

(1) All three Pastorals are genuinely by Paul (Titus, I–II Tim during a "second career" ca. 65–67), culminating in a second Roman imprisonment.

(2) II Tim is genuinely by Paul, written ca. 64 at the end of his one, prolonged Roman imprisonment that led to his death. Titus and I Tim are pseudonymous, partly in imitation of II Tim. A "second career" was created.

(3) All three Pastorals are pseudonymous, but II Tim was written not long after Paul's death as a farewell testament by someone who knew Paul's last days, so that the biographical detail is largely historical. Titus and I Tim were written later, partly in imitation of II Tim. A "second career" was created.

(4) All three Pastorals are pseudonymous and written in the order Titus, I–II Tim, most likely toward the end of the first century. A "second career" was shaped for Paul with a second Roman imprisonment, so that he might speak final words about problematic issues troubling the areas addressed.

Although the majority of scholars favors a variant of (4), in my judgment (3) best meets some of the problems related to the authorship of Titus and I Tim, and the implications of pseudepigraphy.

This discussion of somewhat technical issues should not be allowed to obscure the power of this letter read simply as it is presented: an eloquently passionate appeal of the greatest Christian apostle that his work continue beyond his death through generations of disciples. He may be chained; but the gospel he has proclaimed, which is the word of God, cannot be chained (2:9). If Paul has contributed enormously to making the love of Christ (in both senses) real to Christians, in no small way II Tim has contributed to making Paul loved.

GENERAL ANALYSIS OF THE MESSAGE

THE OPENING FORMULA (1:1–2) resembles that of I Tim but designates
Paul an apostle by "the will" of God, rather than by "the command" of
God. By speaking of God's will rather than of God's command, II Tim
more closely approaches the normal pattern of the undisputed letters
(I Cor 1:1; II Cor 1:1). Similarly closer to authentic Pauline practice is
the presence of a THANKSGIVING (1:3–5), a feature lacking in I Tim. Its
concentration on Timothy illustrates the very personal character that
distinguishes II Tim from the other Pastorals. Timothy's Jewish mother
and grandmother are remembered here without the slightest hint that
belief in Christ constituted a conflict with Judaism.

THE BODY (1:6–4:18) of II Tim is about 20 percent shorter than that
of I Tim, and the contents are less scattered. It takes Timothy's personal-
ity and situation into account and reflects Paul's loneliness and suffering in prison as death approaches. In II Tim Paul is intensely personal
and enthusiastically encouraging. With death so specifically envisaged
in II Tim 4:7–8, Paul can still give eloquent confident testimony: "I
have fought the good fight; I have finished the race; I have kept the
faith henceforth there is laid up for me the crown of righteousness."
The letter fits well the literary genre of last-testamentary discourses or
farewell speeches in the Bible. The tone of Paul's message is apparent:
"Proclaim the word, be persistent in season and out of season, convince,
reprimand, exhort in all patience and teaching" (4:2). The problem of
false teaching is part of the farewell discourse's foreseen danger. In one
instance the false teaching is described quite specifically: the teaching
being given is that the resurrection has past already (2:17–18). But,
more, the description of the falsity is ambiguous (3:1–9).

The Body Ending in 4:9–18, with its directions to Timothy and its
account of Paul's situation, leads into the greetings of the CONCLUDING
FORMULA (4:19–22).

INSPIRED SCRIPTURE (3:15–16)

This passage contains the famous words: "All/every Scripture
[is] inspired by God and useful for teaching, for reproof, for correction, and for training in righteousness." Grammatically the distributive

"every" is the more likely translation, i.e., "every passage of Scripture" with a reference back to the "sacred writings" known to Timothy from his childhood (3:15). There is no doubt that "Scripture" designates all or most of the books we call the OT; only by later church teaching can it be applied to the NT, which in its full form (as now accepted in Western Christianity) did not come into general acceptance for another 200 or more years. No verb "is" appears in the Greek; and so this could be a qualified statement, viz., "Every Scripture that is inspired by God is also useful . . . " No matter how one translates the verse, the primary emphasis indicated by the context is less on the inspiration of all Scripture passages than on the utility of inspired Scripture for continuing what Timothy has learned from his childhood in order to teach and correct and thus to counteract evil impostors.

A somewhat similar description is found in II Pet 1:20–21 in reference to the prophecies of Scripture: "Not ever is prophecy brought forth by human will; rather people who were carried along by the Holy Spirit spoke from God." The texts in II Tim and II Pet are very important in the development of a Christian belief in the inspiration of the Scriptures (OT and NT).

32

Letter (Epistle) to the Hebrews

By all standards this is one of the most impressive works in the NT. Consciously rhetorical, carefully constructed, ably written in quality Greek, and passionately appreciative of Christ, Heb offers an exceptional number of unforgettable insights that have shaped subsequent Christianity.

Yet in other ways Heb is a conundrum. The treatment of the Pauline letters usually began with a subsection entitled Background, but Heb says virtually nothing specific about any of these issues, and almost all information pertinent to background must come from an analysis of the argumentation advanced by the author. The *General Analysis* follows the design of the "Division According to Contents" in the Summary Page and is simply a convenient way of highlighting some of the main ideas. The subsection following the Analysis treats *By Whom/Where/When*.

GENERAL ANALYSIS OF THE MESSAGE

In the eschatological context of the last days, the INTRODUCTION (1:1–3) immediately affirms the superiority of Christ over all that

SUMMARY OF BASIC INFORMATION

DATE: 60s or more likely 80s.

FROM: Not specified; greetings extended from "those from Italy."

TO: Addresses not identified but, based on content, to Christians who are attracted by the values of the Jewish cult; surmises would place them at Jerusalem or Rome, with the latter more likely.

AUTHENTICITY: Author not identified; later church attribution to Paul now abandoned.

UNITY AND INTEGRITY: Not seriously disputed.

FORMAL DIVISION (Vanhoye's proposal):

    A. 1:5–2:18: The name superior to the angels (Eschatology)
    B. 3:1–5:10: Jesus faithful and compassionate (Ecclesiology)
    C. 5:11–10:39: The central exposition (Sacrifice)
    D. 11:1–12:13: Faith and endurance (Ecclesiological paraenesis)
    E. 12:14–13:19: The peaceful fruit of justice (Eschatology)

DIVISION ACCORDING TO CONTENTS:

1:1–3: Introduction
1:4–4:13: Superiority of Jesus as God's Son
    1:4–2:18: Over the angels
    3:1–4:13: Over Moses
4:14–7:28: Superiority of Jesus' priesthood
8:1–10:18: Superiority of Jesus' sacrifice and his ministry in the heavenly tabernacle inaugurating a new covenant
10:19–12:29: Faith and endurance: availing oneself of Jesus' priestly work
    10:19–39: Exhortation to profit from the sacrifice of Jesus
    11:1–40: OT examples of faith
    12:1–13: The example of Jesus' suffering and the Lord's discipline
    12:14–29: Warning against disobedience through OT examples
    13:1–19: Injunctions about practice
    13:20–25: Conclusion: blessing and greetings.

has gone before in Israel. The main contrast is between two divine revelations: one by the prophets and the other by the preexistent Son through whom God created the world and who has now spoken to believers. The description, in language that may be drawn from a hymn, shows that the writer is interpreting Christ against the background of the OT portrayal of divine Wisdom. Going beyond the Wisdom pattern, however, the interpretation depicts the Son as a real person who made purification for sins; and that accomplishment is intimately related to the Son taking his seat at the right hand of Majesty.

SUPERIORITY OF JESUS AS GOD'S SON (1:4–4:13). This extraordinarily "high" christology is now worked out in the Son's superiority over the angels and over Moses. *Superiority over the angels* (1:4–2:18) is worked out through a chain or catena of seven OT quotations in 1:5–14 that match the designations of the Son in the introductory description of 1:1–3. The superangelic status of Christ the Son is sublime exaltation indeed. Employing the words of Ps 45:7–8, the writer has God address to Jesus words never addressed to an angel: "Your throne, O God, is forever and ever . . . therefore (O) God, your God has anointed you with the oil of gladness"—one of the important NT texts where Jesus is called God.

As frequently in Heb, the description (doctrinal) section leads into a moral exhortation (2:1–4): if the message of the Law declared by angels was valid, how can we escape if we neglect the great salvation declared by the Lord Jesus and "attested to us by those who heard"? One finds introduced in 2:5–18 an outlook that colors the christology of Heb, viz., combining lowliness and exaltation. Using Ps 8:5–7 the author points out that God's Son, who was for a while made lower than the angels, now has everything subject to him. Christ tasted death for every human being; and God has brought many to glory through Jesus, the pioneer of their salvation made perfect through suffering (2:10). In his role as pioneer the Son partook of the flesh and blood of the children of God, and was made like his brothers and sisters in every respect, so that he might become a merciful and faithful high priest to make expiation for the sins of the people.

Superiority over Moses (3:1–4:13) is exemplified in 3:1–6 by the greater glory of the builder over the house building, of the son over the servant in a household. "The apostle and high priest of our confession" is another example of the magnificent titles given to Jesus. In 3:7–4:13 the writer turns to exhortations based on Scripture, but now centered on the exodus of Israel. The Israelites who were disobedient failed to enter God's rest in the Holy Land. Similarly present hardship is a testing for those who believe in Jesus, as Heb 4:12 makes explicit in describing the word of God: "For the word of God is living and active, sharper than any two-edged sword, piercing to the division of soul and of spirit, of joints and of marrow, and discerning the thoughts and intentions of the heart." (Here, "the word of God" is not the Bible; it designates Jesus.)

SUPERIORITY OF JESUS' PRIESTHOOD (4:14–7:28). The opening verse states the dominant theme: "We have a great high priest who has passed through the heavens, Jesus the Son of God." Although Heb and John share the notion of an incarnation, we do not find in John a description of the reality of Jesus' humanity comparable to that offered by this section of Heb. A high priest who is able to sympathize with our weaknesses, Jesus was tested in every way as we are, yet without sin (4:15). Jesus learned obedience despite his being God's Son.

Apostasy from Christ is a concern of the writer, who warns that there is no repentance after being enlightened (that is, baptized). God is faithful to promises, and that serves as a guarantee for the effectiveness of Jesus' intercession in the inner heavenly shrine as a high priest according to the order of Melchizedek (6:13–20). To understand the argument in Hebrews about the mysticism that surrounded Melchizedek as a heavenly figure, little more is needed than the OT and the rules of contemporary exegesis (that is, the failure to mention Melchizedek's ancestry permits one to argue as if he had no father or mother). Above all, according to the order of Melchizedek, a priest is eternal (Ps 110:4). When he offered himself, this holy, blameless, undefiled high priest, separated from sinners and exalted above the heavens, effected a sacrifice that is once for all (7:26–27).

SUPERIORITY OF JESUS' SACRIFICIAL MINISTRY AND OF THE HEAVENLY TABERNACLE, INAUGURATING A NEW COVENANT (8:1–10:18). The idea that Jesus is a high priest before God leads to the notion of a heavenly tabernacle. Exod 25:9,40; 26:30, etc., describe how God showed Moses the heavenly model according to which the earthly tabernacle was built. In Heb 8:2–7 this antecedent may be influenced by a Platonic scheme of reality in which the heavenly tabernacle set up by God is true, while the earthly tabernacle is a copy or shadow. The levitical priests who serve this shadow sanctuary have a ministry inferior to that of Christ. Heb 8:8–13 (see also 8:6), picking up the language of new covenant from Jer 31:31–34, makes it clear that the first covenant made with Moses is now old, obsolete, and passing away.

In chap. 9 the writer presents a prolonged comparison between Jesus' death and the ritual of the Day of Atonement (Yom Kippur) carried out in the transportable sacred edifice of Israel's desert wanderings, the Tabernacle or Tent. The fact that both he (9:5) and Paul (Rom 3:25) appeal to the image of the *hilastērion*, the place of expiation where the blood of the sacrifices was sprinkled to wipe out sins, suggests a wider awareness that Jesus' death could be compared to levitical sacrifices (sacrifices prescribed in the OT book of Leviticus). What is unique to Heb is Jesus going once for all into the heavenly sanctuary with his own blood, thus ratifying the new covenant in the presence of God "on our behalf" (9:24); and he will appear a second time to save those who are eagerly waiting for him (9:28).

The superiority of the sacrifice of Jesus is that God prefers obedience to a multiplicity of sacrifices. The obedience of Jesus' sacrifice has made perfect forever those who are being given a share in Jesus' own consecration; their sins are forgiven, and so there is no longer a need for offerings for sin.

FAITH AND ENDURANCE: AVAILING ONESELF OF JESUS' PRIESTLY WORK (10:19–12:29). Through the way opened by Jesus, those whom the writer calls "brothers" should enter the Holy Place by Jesus' blood with faith, hope, and love, meeting together as a community (10:19–25). If they sin deliberately, there is no longer a sacrifice for sins, but horrible punishment: "It is a fearful thing to fall into the hands of the living God" (10:26–31). Yet there is no reason for discouragement. In times past they suffered joyfully. Now again they need endurance and faith in order to save their souls (10:32–39). In 11:40 the writer gives a famous description of faith ("The assurance [or reality] of things hoped for, the conviction [or evidence] of things not seen") and a long list of OT figures who had that kind of faith or faithfulness. At the end (11:39–40), faithful to his contrast between the old and the new, he points out that all these people of faith did not receive what had been promised, for "God had foreseen something better for us, so that without us they should not be made perfect."

FINAL EXHORTATIONS (13:1–19). Containing Heb's only detailed concrete ethical injunctions, this is the area in which Heb comes closest to Pauline style. After some imperatives on the issues of community life characteristic in NT works, Heb 13:7 appeals to the faith of past leaders in the history of the community who preached the gospel. One can appeal to the past because "Jesus is the same yesterday, today, and forever" (13:8)—another unforgettable example of the eloquence of the writer. But the writer also appeals for obedience to the present leaders who watch over the readers' souls (13:17) and solicits prayers for himself (13:18–19).

CONCLUSION (13:20–25). The exhortation closes with a blessing invoked through "the God of peace who brought again from the dead our Lord Jesus, the great shepherd of the sheep" (13:20). Amid the greetings, the references to Timothy, who has been released, and to those from Italy are some of the very few clues in Heb as to the place of origin and destination.

BY WHOM, FROM WHERE, AND WHEN?

BY WHOM? Some refer to Heb as pseudonymous; but "anonymous" is more accurate since no claim is made within the work about its writer. Yet by the end of the second century some were attributing Heb to Paul. Reflecting Alexandrian tradition, Beatty Papyrus II (P[46]), our earliest preserved text of the Pauline letters places Heb after Rom. In official late-fourth and early-fifth century canonical lists, Heb was counted within the fourteen Pauline letters. Gradually Paul's name was introduced into the title, appearing both in the Vulgate (and subsequent translation drawn from it) and the KJV. The attribution to Paul came from noticing: (a) The appearance of the name of "brother Timothy" in 13:23. (b) The benediction and greetings in 13:20–24 (and, to a lesser extent, the ethical imperatives of chaps. 12–13) resemble a Pauline ending. (c) Hab 2:3–4, cited in Heb 10:37–38, is used by Paul in Gal 3:11; Rom 1:17 (though Heb does not relate the passage to justification by faith, not works). (d) Elements in the phrasing and theology of Heb have parallels in works bearing Paul's name (though differences exist in all the parallels).

The evidence against Paul's writing Heb is overwhelming. In its style, common expressions, major theological themes, and outlook, Heb is very different from Paul's letters. Perhaps above all, Paul denied receiving his gospel from any other human being—God revealed the

Son to him (Gal 1:11–12); Heb writes that the message was declared first by the Lord "and attested to us by those who heard it"
(Heb 2:3).

Despite the evidence (or lack thereof) some have made suggestions
for authorship of Heb. Origen left anonymous the actual author, while
others made specific guesses: for example, Tertullian suggested Barnabas; some posited either Luke or Clement of Rome; Luther attributed
it to Apollos; and still others have suggested either Priscilla, Aquila,
Silas, or Philip. The suggestion by J. M. Ford that Mary, the mother of
Jesus, is responsible for the content of Heb may qualify for the prize
for dubious ingenuity.

FROM WHERE? The dubious thesis that Heb was written from Alexandria would be of little service in any case, for we know nothing of
the origins of the Christian church in Alexandria. The argumentation
in Heb based on the Jewish liturgy and priesthood has made Jerusalem
or Palestine a more prominent candidate. Parallels have been found
between the attitude of Stephen, the Hellenist leader at Jerusalem
(Acts 6:8–53,56,59–60), and the writer of Heb—although according
to Acts 8:4 and 11:19, the Hellenists functioned mostly outside Jerusalem and even Palestine. The greetings extended to the readers from
"those who come from Italy" (Heb 13:24) remind some of the presence of Roman Jews at Jerusalem on Pentecost. Nevertheless, theories
about the place whence Heb was sent are almost as much a guess as are
theories about the writer.

WHEN? This question is partially related to the answer to the previous questions. At the lower end of the spectrum, the writer of Heb
does not belong to the first generation of Christians since apparently
he is dependent on those who heard the Lord (2:3). At the upper end,
a limit is set by I Clement 36:1–5 (probably written in the late 90s, but
not later than 120), which echoes Heb 1:3–5,7,13. Thus the most frequent range suggested for writing Heb is AD 60 to 90, with scholars
divided over whether it should be dated before (60s) or after (80s)
the destruction of the Jerusalem Temple. More information about the
writer or even Timothy's release would likely add to the accuracy of
attempts to determine the dating.

The strong emphasis on the replacement of the Jewish feasts, sacri-fices, priesthood, and earthly place of worship is support for a dating in the 80s—indeed the first or old covenant is being replaced by the new (8:7–8,13). Similarly it was in the last third of the century that the custom of using "God" for Jesus became more prominent. Finally, one must recognize that an argument for dating that draws on com-parative theology is very weak, since "advanced" theological insights did not all come at the same time in every place.

⚹

33

First Letter of Peter

Since Eusebius in the fourth century, seven writings have been known as the Catholic or General Epistles, a designation that (at least in Eastern Christianity) was deemed appropriate for works addressed to the church universal, namely Jas, I–II Pet, I–II–III John, and Jude. The question of pseudepigraphy is an issue for several of these writings.

Here we begin with a writing attributed to Peter, the most important first-century follower of Jesus. I Pet is one of the most attractive and pastorally rich writings in the NT.

After the *Background* and the *General Analysis* of I Pet, a subsection will treat I Pet 3:19 and 4:6 and the descent of Christ into hell.

THE BACKGROUND

Simon, who very quickly came to be called Cephas (Aramaic: *Kēpā'*, "rock") or Peter (Greek: *Petros* from *petra*, "rock"), is always named first in the lists of the Twelve and was clearly the most important of that group during Jesus' lifetime. The unanimous Gospel tradition is that

SUMMARY OF BASIC INFORMATION

DATE: If written by Peter, 60–63; more likely 70–90.

TO: An area in northern Asia Minor (perhaps evangelized by missionaries from Jerusalem).

AUTHENTICITY: Possibly by Peter using a secretary; more likely by a disciple carrying on the heritage of Peter at Rome.

UNITY: Although the vast majority now opts for unity, some would see two documents joined: one (1:3–4:11) where "persecution" was only a possibility, and one (4:12–5:11) where the community was actually undergoing it.

INTEGRITY: Those who detect the presence of a confessional fragment and/or hymns usually think they were included by the writer.

FORMAL DIVISION:
- A. Opening Formula: 1:1–2
- B. Body: 1:3–5:11
  - 1:3–2:10: Affirmation of Christian identity and dignity
  - 2:11–3:12: Appropriate behavior for bearing good witness in a Pagan world
  - 3:13–5:11: Christian behavior in the face of hostility
- C. Concluding Formula: 5:12–14.

---

he denied Jesus and failed in loyalty during the arrest. Nevertheless, after the risen Jesus appeared to him (Luke 24:34; I Cor 15:5), he was restored to preeminence and exercised a leadership role among the followers of Jesus in Jerusalem in the first few years. He was the most active missionary among the Twelve, venturing to accept new groups into the Christian community (Acts 8:14–25; 9:32–11:18). Peter was a major figure at the Jerusalem meeting of AD 49 that decided on the acceptance of the Gentiles (Acts 15; Gal 2:1–10). Subsequently he functioned in the church of Antioch (where there was a controversy with Paul) and by the year 55 a group of Christians at Corinth regarded him as their patron (I Cor 1:12; 3:22). He was martyred in Rome sometime between 64 and 68 during Nero's persecution. I Clement 5, written from Rome, treats Peter and Paul as the most righteous pillars of the church who were persecuted unto death.

Peter's image remained extremely important after his death. In John 21 he is portrayed as the leading fisherman (missionary) among the Twelve, and then as the shepherd (pastor) commissioned to feed Jesus' sheep. In Matt 16:18 Peter, who has responded in faith to the Messiah, the Son of God, is the one on whom Jesus will build the church and to whom he will give the keys of the kingdom of heaven.

GENERAL ANALYSIS OF THE MESSAGE

OPENING FORMULA (1:1–2). I Pet uses the same type of Jewish letter greetings that Paul employed, although I Pet modifies the standard "grace and peace" by adding "be multiplied to you" from OT letter format (exemplified in Dan 4:1). The address is "To the exiles of the diaspora," a term used in the OT for Jews living outside Palestine. Yet it is reasonably clear from the contents of the letter that the recipients are Gentile Christians who are now the "chosen" people (1:1–2; 2:4,9) in the diaspora—scattered among pagans and perhaps also away from their heavenly home. The addressees are located in northern Asia Minor. Noteworthy in I Pet's formula is the triadic mention of God the Father, the Spirit, and Jesus Christ.

FIRST SECTION OF THE BODY (1:3–2:10): *Affirmation of Christian identity and dignity.* I Pet lacks a Thanksgiving. In its place the Body of the letter opens with a remarkably affirmative section stressing the dignity of the Christian believers. The description strongly echoes the imagery of the exodus from Egypt and the experience at Sinai. The demand of God at Sinai, "Be holy because I am holy," is repeated (Lev 11:44; I Pet 1:16); and there are echoes of other elements of the Exodus account. The addressees are reminded that they were ransomed not with silver and gold but with the precious blood of Christ as an unblemished lamb.

Since 3:18–22 is specific, "Baptism which corresponds to this now saves you," many scholars think that the writer was drawing his imagery from baptismal parlance: the language of a baptismal hymn or hymns (that can be reconstructed), a baptismal liturgy, or a baptismal homily. One covers the basic thrust of the section if one thinks of the writer evoking language and traditional Scripture passages heard at baptism by the addressees, who had been evangelized by missionaries with a very deep attachment to the traditions of Israel.

The climax of this section focuses on two sets of three OT texts: the set in 2:6–8 centers on Christ as the stone selected by God but rejected by some human beings; and the set in 2:9–10 centers on the Christian community, once no people but now the people of God. The privileges of Israel are now the privileges of Christians.

SECOND SECTION OF THE BODY (2:11–3:12): *Appropriate behavior for bearing witness in a Pagan world.* Given the dignity of the Christian people, there is a standard of conduct that can set an example for the surrounding Pagans in order to counteract their low estimate of Christians. This leads to the final of the five household codes (2:13–3:7) found in the NT. Attention is given here not on changing the existing order, but only on how to behave in the present situation in a way that exemplifies the patience and self-giving of Christ. The code addresses all Christians as a whole, then it speaks specifically to separate groups of slaves, wives, and husbands. As for details, being subject to the emperor and governors who punish evildoers will show that the Christians are not evildoers despite what people say. Slaves are to be patient when they are beaten unjustly, even as the sinless Christ left an example patiently accepting insults and suffering. Wives are to be subject to their husbands, in order to win them to obedience to the word; husbands are to be understanding and to honor their wives, "so that [the husbands'] prayers may not be hindered." This portion of I Pet concludes in 3:8–12 by addressing "all of you" with both five brief imperatives on how to treat one another as a truly Christian community, and the promise of a blessing from the Lord, quoted from Ps 34:13–17.

THIRD SECTION OF THE BODY (3:13–5:11): *Christian behavior in the face of harassment.* Christians are suffering, and whether it stems from persecution or alienation is debated. However it occurs, Christians have the example of Christ. His death was not the end, for he was made alive in the spirit, and then went to preach to "the spirits in prison" (3:18–19) who formerly disobeyed in the days of the flood. From that flood Noah and others, eight in all, were saved, just as Christians have been saved through the cleansing waters of baptism (3:20–21).

The Christians are alienated because they cannot live the way their Pagan neighbors do. I Pet 4:5–6 promises that a judgment by God will deal with those who malign Christians. This judgment of all things is coming soon because the end of all things is at hand (4:7). As for the present, amid the hostility of their neighbors they can survive if they love, support, and serve one another (4:8–11). Since Christ showed that suffering was the path to glory, Christians should not be surprised if "a fiery ordeal" and greater sufferings come (4:12–19). Judgment will begin with the Christian community. Therefore Peter encourages the presbyters to take care of the flock (5:1–4). The model for them is Christ the chief shepherd.

Closing the Body of the letter are a set of admonitions (5:5–9), piled one upon the other. The imagery portraying the situation, echoing Ps 22:14, is memorable: "Your adversary the devil is prowling around like a roaring lion looking [for someone] to devour." Offering consolation, the doxology (5:10–11) pledges that in this struggle Christ will confirm, strengthen, and establish the Christians after they have suffered a little.

CONCLUDING FORMULA (5:12–14). Peter now intervenes with personal greetings, perhaps added in his own hand. He mentions Silvanus, and greets his audience from both the church (of Rome) and Mark. He advocates a "kiss of love" and offers "peace to all."

I PET 3:19 AND 4:6 AND THE DESCENT OF CHRIST INTO HELL

Two texts in I Pet are of import for this issue: I Pet 3:18–20: (Christ was put to death in the flesh and made alive in the Spirit) "in which having gone he made proclamation to the spirits in prison. Formerly they had been disobedient when God's patience waited in the days of Noah"; and I Pet 4:6: "For this reason the gospel was preached also to the dead, in order that, having been judged in the flesh by human estimation [literally, 'according to men'], they might live in the Spirit in God's eyes ['according to God']."

A number of vague NT texts indicate that Christ, presumably after his death, descended beneath the earth (Rom 10:7; Eph 4:9), that he took up dead saints from below (Matt 27:52; Eph 4:8), and that he triumphed over the evil angelic powers (Phil 2:10; Col 2:15). The second-century apocrypha the *Ascension of Isaiah* (9:16; 10:14; 11:23), the *Odes of Solomon* (17:9; 42:15), Melito of Sardis (*On the Pasch* 102), and the *Gospel of Nicodemus* all handle this theme. From the fourth century through the sixth an article was making its way into the Apostle's Creed: "He descended into hell." Curiously, the church has never decided the exact purpose of that journey. Indeed, some modern churches have deleted the clause as meaningless for contemporary faith. That is an overreaction, for certainly it is a way of expressing figuratively that Christ's death affected those who had gone before. But in what way?

Two major explanations intertwined with interpretation of the I Pet texts have been offered:

For salvific purposes. This is the oldest interpretation, dating at least to early in the second century. In *Gospel of Peter* 10:41, as Christ is being brought forth from the tomb by two immense angels followed by the cross, a voice from heaven asks, "Have you made proclamation to the fallen-asleep?" The cross makes obeisance in answering, "Yes." The context suggests that the preaching would be beneficial, as clearly affirmed by Justin, *Dialogue* 72, written ca. 160. Clement of Alexandria (ca. 200) offers the first attested interpretation of I Pet 3:19 in this way, a view attractive to Origen, who held that hell was not eternal. A modification of the approach to avoid the implication about hell holds that Christ went to limbo in order to announce to the deceased *saints* that heaven was now open for them and/or to offer sinners a second chance if they accepted the proclamation.

For condemnatory purposes. If one interprets I Pet 3:19 in light of 4:6, the proclamation to the spirits in prison is the same as evangelizing the dead and has to have had a salvific intent. Some, however, have made a strong case that the two verses do not refer to the same event. I Pet 4:6 does not have Christ do the preaching; rather it refers to the preaching about Christ, which is the proclamation of the gospel. Christians who accepted the gospel and have since died are alive in God's eye. I Pet 3:19, on the other hand, does have (the risen) Christ do the preaching but to the spirits in prison, without any mention of the dead. In Semitic anthropology "spirits" (as distinct from "shades") would be an unusual way to refer to the dead; more likely it would refer to angels. The reference to disobedience in the days of Noah suggests that these are the angels or sons of God who did evil by having relations with earthly women (Gen 6:1–4), a wickedness that led God to send the great flood from which Noah was saved (6:5–8:22). In pre-NT Jewish mythology the story of these wicked angels is greatly elaborated; for example, God had the spirits rounded up and imprisoned in a great pit under the earth until the day when they would be judged (*I Enoch* 10:11–12; *Jubilees* 5:6). I Pet 3:19 has the risen Christ go down there to proclaim his victory and crush the Satanic forces (cf. John 16:11; Rev 12:5–13). This interpretation does most justice to the facts as known and seems to be the most plausible explanation of 3:19.

·✳·

34

Epistle (Letter) of James

Among the "Catholic Epistles" we now come to a work called by
Luther an epistle of straw ("right strawy epistle"), but which has come
into its own in our time as the most socially conscious writing in the
NT. After the *Background* and *General Analysis*, a subsection will treat *James
2:24 and Paul on Faith and Works*.

THE BACKGROUND

Who is the figure presented as the author? "James, servant of God
and of the Lord Jesus Christ." In the NT there are several men named
"James" (Greek *Iakōbos*, derived from the Hebrew for "Jacob," the pa-
triarch from whom descended the twelve tribes). At least two of them,
both members of the Twelve, may be dismissed as extremely unlikely
candidates for authorship: the brother of John and son of Zebedee,
James ("the Great") who died in the early 40s; and James (son?)
of Alphaeus, of whom we know nothing. A totally unknown James,
not mentioned elsewhere in the NT, has been suggested (to explain

SUMMARY OF BASIC INFORMATION

DATE: If pseudonymous, after the death of James ca. 62, in the range 70–110; most likely in the 80s or 90s.

TO: A homily employing diatribe, shaped in a letter format to "the twelve tribes in the dispersion," i.e., probably Christians outside Palestine quite conservative in their appreciation of Judaism.

AUTHENTICITY: Claimed author is James (the brother of the Lord); but most think it was written by someone (a disciple?) who admired the image of James as the Christian authority most loyal to Judaism.

UNITY AND INTEGRITY: Not seriously disputed today.

DIVISION ACCORDING TO CONTENTS (TOPICS):

1:1: Greetings (Opening Formula)
1:2–18: The role of trials and temptations
1:19–27: Words and deeds
2:1–9: Partiality toward the rich
2:10–13: Keeping the whole Law
2:14–26: Faith and works
3:1–12: Power of the tongue
3:13–18: Wisdom from above
4:1–10: Desires as the cause of division
4:11–12: Judging one another as judging the Law
4:13–17: Further arrogant behavior
5:1–6: Warning to the rich
5:7–11: Patience till the coming of the Lord
5:12–20: Admonitions on behavior within the community.

---

why the work failed to get wide acceptance); in later tradition, it is thought, he would have been confused with James the brother of the Lord.

A shortcut around the (imaginative) last suggestion brings us to the only truly plausible candidate: *James listed first among the "brothers" of Jesus in* Mark 6:3; Matt 13:55, not a member of the Twelve but an apostle in a broader sense of the term (I Cor 15:7; Gal 1:19). There is no evidence that he followed Jesus during the public ministry (Mark 3:21,31–32; 6:1–4); rather he stayed behind in Nazareth with the other relatives. Yet the risen Jesus appeared to him (I Cor 15:7), and seemingly from then on he was a prominent figure (Gal 1:19). That is reflected in the Coptic *Gospel of Thomas* 12, where Jesus tells the disciples that after his departure they should go to James the Just, "for whose sake heaven and earth have come to exist." Once the Jerusalem church was structured, James (accompanied by the elders) was portrayed as the presiding leader and spokesman. He was executed by stoning in the early 60s at the instigation of the high priest Ananus II, who, when the Roman prefect was absent, convened a Sanhedrin and accused James ("the brother of Jesus who was called the Messiah") of having transgressed the Law (Josephus, *Ant.* 20.9.1; #200). Several apocrypha bear the name of James, but none betrays knowledge of the letter being discussed.

For this letter the most important element of background is the imagery of James as a conservative Jewish Christian very loyal to observing the Law. He was not an extreme legalist, for he concluded that Gentile Christians did not need to be circumcised (Gal 2; Acts 15). Yet the speech that appears on his lips in Acts 15:13–21 offers the most traditional reason for that acceptance of Gentiles by applying to them elements of Lev 17–18 applicable to strangers living within Israel. He was given the sobriquet "the Just," which Eusebius (EH 2.23.4–7) explained in terms of his having lived as a Nazirite (an ascetic especially dedicated to God) and his praying so often in the Temple that his knees became as calloused as those of a camel. It is not surprising, then, that, whether or not written by James, the NT letter that bears his name echoes in many ways traditional Jewish belief and piety.

GENERAL ANALYSIS OF THE MESSAGE

OPENING FORMULA OR GREETING (1:1). Both OT and NT usage show that in Jas 1:1 the writer is designating himself modestly as "servant of God." Jas spends little time on christological reflection; some have even thought of it as a Jewish writing only slightly adapted for Christian use. Nevertheless, the coupling of "God" and "the Lord Jesus Christ" in the first line shows the traditional Christian faith of the writer. Scholars debate whether Jas was addressed to Jewish or Gentile Christians. Nevertheless, in Jas there is no correction of vices that in the eyes of Jews were characteristically Gentile (idolatry, sexual impurity); the "twelve tribes" is more Jewish than the I Pet address; the addressees meet in a "synagogue"; and the leading Jewish Christian authority is pictured as the author. We might be well advised, then, to think of the addressees as Christians strongly identified by the Jewish heritage.

TRIALS, TEMPTATION, WORDS, DEEDS (1:2–27). The "grace and peace" greeting of Paul's letters (also I Pet 1:1) is lacking in Jas, as is the Thanksgiving element in the letter format. Indeed, after 1:1 Jas bears little semblance to a regular letter, as the writer launches immediately into a series of exhortations. The attitude and subject matter strongly echo the late Wisdom books of the OT. Noticeable are the eschatological outlook, along with the emphases attributed to Jesus in his teaching in Q, the Sermon on the Mount (Matt 5–7), and Luke 6. On the other hand, the format resembles that of the Greco-Roman diatribe.

The alternating address (Jas 1:9–11) to those of low estate and of wealth, contrasting their fate, is striking. Here Jas is close to the Lucan form (6:20,24) of the beatitude for the poor with the accompanying woe for the rich. The poor/rich issue most likely reflects a social situation known to the writer in his own church. In dealing with the responsibility for evil, in the tradition of Sirach (15:11–13), Jas 1:13 is firm, "God tempts no one." But for God's will to be fruitful, Christians cannot simply be hearers of the word (the gospel); they must manifest its working in their lives. From the beginning, however, it is worth noting that the good works flow from the power of the gospel word that has been implanted. There is nothing theoretical about the religion advocated in Jas 1:27: a religion manifested in taking care of needy widows and orphans and keeping oneself undefiled by the world.

RICH AND POOR, AND THE WHOLE LAW (2:1–13). Although Wisdom Literature abounds in similes and metaphors introduced simply as illustrations, it is hard to think that the picture painted here in Jas is purely rhetorical. Jas and the addressees come together into what is still being called a synagogue (literal rendering of 2:2, often translated as "assembly"), and there rich members tend to be received with favor. Apparently the inevitable institutionalization of a gospel community has taken place, and Jas (2:5) is correctively calling on what they were taught in the past about the poor being heirs of the kingdom. Jas' accusations against the rich are so strong that one wonders whether they describe real conflict between the rich and the poor or are rhetorical echoes of OT language (Amos 8:4; Wisdom 2:10). As previously for Jesus (from Lev 19:18), so now for Jas 2:8–10, love of neighbor sums up the Law and the commandments. The stunning expression "law of liberty" in Jas 2:12 challenges a dichotomy between law and freedom.

FAITH AND WORKS (2:14–26). The writer begins in the style of Greco-Roman diatribe with an imaginative example of his own creation, illustrating the disastrous results of indifference to good works. He then (2:21–25) offers biblical examples of the importance of works: Abraham in Gen 15 and 22, and Rahab in Josh 2. Scholarly discussion of this passage has been dominated by the contrast between Jas' insistence on the insufficiency of faith without works and Paul's rejection of the salvific value of works (of the Mosaic Law). Jas is working out in practice Jesus' warning that not everyone who says, "Lord, Lord," will enter the kingdom of heaven. In any period outsiders would certainly judge Christians by the commonsense standard of 2:26 that faith without works is dead.

FAULTS THAT DIVIDE A CHRISTIAN COMMUNITY (3:1–5:6). In a series of paragraphs Jas treats one example after another of sins and shortcomings that are particularly threatening to the harmony required by the commandment to love one another. Like an OT wisdom teacher, the writer clusters examples (bit in horse's mouth, rudder on a ship, fire, poison, bitter water), eloquently describing the potential damage of a loose tongue. He states the irony that the tongue is used both to bless God and to destroy human beings in God's image. Here one is not far from the beatitudes, the Sermon on the Mount, or Paul's fruit of the Spirit in Gal 5:22.

This emphasis on how the wise should live leads to the quotation from Prov 3:34 in Jas 4:6: "God resists the proud but gives grace to the humble." In turn, the writer condemns judging one's brother or sister as arrogance over against the Law of God, the supreme lawgiver and judge. In a further attack on arrogance readers are reminded that they are not masters of their own lives. A blistering attack on the rich returns, denouncing their self-indulgent lives of luxury on the earth. Finally, in 5:7–9(11) the writer exhorts the community using clearly Christian eschatological language and images.

PARTICULAR ADMONITIONS ABOUT BEHAVIOR IN THE COMMUNITY (5:12–20).
Oaths, prayer, and correction of the wayward are the final subjects
treated, still seemingly in the context of the forthcoming final judgment. Given the strongly admonitory atmosphere of much of Jas, one
might think of the writer as stern and even unforgiving. The last lines
(5:19–20) come then as a surprise: he is very concerned with bringing back (and implicitly forgiving) those who have deviated. If for I Pet
4:8 love (Greek *agapē*) covers a multitude of sins, for Jas the activity of
seeking out the lost does that.

JAS 2:24 AND PAUL ON FAITH AND WORKS

One of the most, perhaps the most, famous issue related to the interpretation of Jas is the question of his often-perceived conflict with
Paul concerning "faith vs. works." In Gal 2:16 Paul affirmed: "A person is not justified by works of the Law but through faith in/of Jesus
Christ." Slightly later he stated in Rom 3:28, "A person is justified by
faith, apart from the works of the Law." By contrast Jas 2:24 claims,
"A person is justified by works and not by faith alone." The wording
is remarkably close, and in the context both writers appeal to the example of Abraham in Gen 15:6. Thus, it is very difficult to think that
the similarity is accidental; one of the views is a reaction to the other.
The faith/works issue is a major emphasis for Paul in Gal and Rom,
whereas it is more incidental in Jas, so it would seem that the writer
of Jas is correcting a Pauline formula. Or to be more precise, he is correcting a misunderstanding of a Pauline formula. Paul was arguing that
observance of ritual works prescribed by the Mosaic Law, particularly
circumcision, would not justify the Gentiles; faith in what God had
done in Christ was required—a faith that involved a commitment of
life. The writer of Jas is thinking of people who are already Christian
and intellectually believe in Jesus (even as the devil can believe: 2:19)
but have not translated that belief into life practice; and he is insisting
that their works (not ritual works prescribed by the Law but behavior that reflects love) must correspond to their faith—something with
which Paul would agree, as can be seen from the "imperative" sections
of his letters insisting on behavior. If the writer of Jas had read Rom,
he should have been able to see that Paul and he were not dealing

with the same issue: Paul was not proclaiming justification through a faith that did not involve living as Christ would have his followers live. For that reason it seems more logical to think that, when Jas was being written, a Pauline formula had been repeated out of context and given a misinterpretation that needed to be corrected. Thus, Jas and Paul were essentially using many of the same words, but they were using them quite differently and they were actually not speaking to the same concerns. In fact, as the writer of Jas discusses faith and works, his remarks seem to show that he does not really comprehend how anyone could advocate the position that he seems compelled to oppose. He really seems more baffled by the remark he contests than anything else. The juxtaposition of faith and works is clearly not a typical thought for the writer of Jas.

✴

35

Letter (Epistle) of Jude

Origen found Jude "packed with sound words of heavenly grace." Yet today, except for the memorable phrasing in Jude 3 "to contend for the faith once for all delivered to the saints," most people find this very brief work too negative, too dated, and too apocalyptic to be of much use. Although the difficulties are undeniable, Jude nevertheless does give us a look into how a church authority responded to dangers as Christians began to divide from within.

After the *Background* and *General Analysis*, a subsection will consider Jude's use of noncanonical literature.

THE BACKGROUND

Which figure was intended when the writer described himself as "Jude, the servant of Jesus Christ and the brother of James"? The same Greek name *Ioudas* (from the Hebrew for Judah) is rendered in the English NT as both Judas and Jude—the second rendering in order to avoid confusion with Iscariot, the one who gave Jesus over. If we leave

SUMMARY OF BASIC INFORMATION

DATE: Virtually impossible to tell. A few scholars place it in the 50s; many in 90–100.

FROM/TO: Probably *from* the Palestine area where the brothers of Jesus were major figures *to* Christians influenced by the Jerusalem/Palestinian church(es). Some scholars think Jude was written in Alexandria.

AUTHENTICITY: Very difficult to decide. If pseudepigraphical, by one for whom the brothers of Jesus were authoritative teachers.

UNITY AND INTEGRITY: Not seriously disputed.

FORMAL DIVISION:

  A. Opening Formula: 1–2

  B. Body: 3–23:

    3–4: Occasion: Contend for the faith because of certain ungodly intruders

    5–10: Three examples of the punishment of disobedience and their application

    11–13: Three more examples and a polemic description of the ungodly intruders

    14–19: Prophecies of Enoch and of the apostles about the coming of these ungodly people

    20–23: Reiterated appeal for faith; different kinds of judgment to be exercised

  C. Concluding Doxology: 24–25.

Iscariot aside, there are two minor figures, one in Luke (6:16) and the other in Acts (15:22,27–33), about whom we know nothing or very little. (Moreover, a few scholars argue that "brother" is metaphorical = Christian friend.)

The most common and plausible suggestion of why the writer identified himself through a relationship to James is that *the intended Jude was one of the four named brothers of Jesus* (Mark 6:3; Matt 13:55) and thus literally the brother of James. With such family status, although not an apostle this Jude presents himself as an authority with standing in the tradition. In the self-designation of v. 1, Jude would be identifying himself modestly as a servant in relation to Jesus (see Jas 1:1), but more specifically as brother of James of Jerusalem. Tradition would have it that members of that family were dominant forces among Christians in both Galilee and Jerusalem until Trajan (98–117). Thus, what follows is based on the assumption that this is a letter sent in the name of Jude, brother of Jesus and of James.

GENERAL ANALYSIS OF THE MESSAGE

OPENING FORMULA (vv. 1–2). For Jude Christians are those "called" and designated as was Israel, "the beloved of God."

THE BODY (vv. 3–23) is framed by references to faith in vv. 3 and 20. In the Body Opening *the occasion is expounded in vv.* 3–4. The writer speaks to the "beloved" addressees of "our common salvation," about which he had intended to write, but his plans were interrupted by "certain ungodly people" who creep in and turn the grace of God into licentiousness and deny the Lord Jesus Christ (v. 4). Yet this description is hostile, and those denounced may have considered themselves evangelizing missionaries.

Three Examples of the Punishment of Disobedience and Their Application (5–10). The writer offers in vv. 5–7 three examples from Israelite tradition in which God punished disobedience. During the exodus many showed their lack of faith and were destroyed by death (Num 14). Angels left heaven to lust after women (Gen 6:1–4), and God locked them up till judgment day (see the development of this theme in the extrabiblical writing I Enoch 10:4–6; chaps. 12–13). Sodom and Gomorrah practiced immorality and were punished by fire (Gen 19:1–28). These three examples are followed in vv. 8–10 by applicable commentary. In vv. 9–10 the derisive presumptuousness of the adversaries is contrasted with the modesty of the archangel Michael, who did not blaspheme when the devil tried to claim Moses' dead body, but only rebuked him (Clement of Alexandria identifies here the *Assumption of Moses,* a lost apocryphon).

Three More Examples and a Polemic Description of the Ungodly Intruders (11–13). In a "woe" against the adversaries, the writer bunches three examples of those who in rabbinic tradition (*'Aboth R. Nathan* 41.14) "have no share in the world to come": Cain (Gen 4:8; I John 3:2), Balaam (Num 31:8; Deut 23:5; Josh 24:9–10), and Korah (Num 16). The writer then (vv. 12–13) lets loose a torrent of colorful invective against the ungodly intruders.

Prophecies of Enoch and of the Apostles About the Coming of These Ungodly People (14–19). It is part of the style of warnings like that of Jude to recall that the coming of the impious was foretold for the last times. Jesus himself is recalled as giving such an apocalyptic notice (Mark 13:22). Jude 14–15 begins with a prophecy by Enoch from Jewish tradition (*I Enoch* 1:9) beyond Gen (5:23–24). The writer then turns to a prophecy of the apostles, though no such passage is preserved in the NT; and so the writer seemingly is drawing on a wider Christian tradition.

Reiterated Appeal for Faith; Different Kinds of Judgment To Be Exercised (20–23). Despite the polemic, these verses may represent both the purpose and the true climax of the letter. In vv. 20–21 the writer spells out how his addressees are to contend for the faith: by praying in the Holy Spirit and keeping themselves in God's love while waiting for mercy at the judgment by the Lord Jesus Christ. The audience themselves are to show mercy to those who doubt or hesitate; to save others by snatching them out of the fire; and with extreme caution to show mercy still to others, hating their corruption.

CONCLUDING DOXOLOGY (vv. 24–25). Jude concludes with a solemn doxology. Jude blesses the one and only (*monos* = monotheism) God who can keep them safe without failing and bring them exulting to judgment without stumbling. The Christian modification of this Jewish monotheistic praise is that it is through Jesus Christ our Lord.

JUDE'S USE OF NONCANONICAL LITERATURE

This use has been a problem: throughout the centuries theologians have contended that if the author was inspired, he should have been able to recognize what was inspired and what was not. Today most deem this a pseudoproblem that presupposes a simplistic understanding of inspiration and canonicity.

Yet the lack of a fixed canon may not be to the point. Seemingly Jews and early Christians used books as sacred and with authority without asking whether they were on the same level as the Law and the Prophets. Indeed, we cannot confine Jude's dependence on the noncanonical to the citation of *I Enoch* in vv. 14–15 and that of the *Assumption of Moses* in v. 9. In addition, the punishment of the angels in v. 6 is derived from *I Enoch*; and the polemic in v. 16 may draw on the *Assumption of Moses*. In the Cain and Balaam examples of v. 11, Jude is dependent on tradition that has been developed about the biblical characters far beyond the biblical account. Also in vv. 17–18 he cites words of the apostles not found in books that Christians would ultimately judge to be biblical. In other words, the writer accepts and feels free to cite a wide collection of Israelite and Christian traditions, and is not confined to a collection of written books ever deemed canonical by any group that we know. Thus canonicity may never have entered the writer's mind.

.·✦·.

36

Second Epistle (Letter) of Peter

In all likelihood this pseudonymous work was the last NT book to be written. After the *Background* and the *General Analysis*, a subsection will be devoted to *Canonicity* and *Early Catholicism*.

THE BACKGROUND

The writer used for this "apostle of Jesus Christ" a Greek form of his personal name close to the Hebrew original (not "Simōn" but "Symeōn") and highlighted his eyewitness presence at the transfiguration (2:16–18). The author alludes to I Pet by calling the present writing "the second letter I write to you" (3:1). He also speaks knowingly of what "our beloved brother Paul wrote to you." Indeed, a bit patronizingly he hints at his own superior teaching, since in Paul's letters there are "some things hard to understand." Without naming his source, he quotes large sections of Jude (in whole or in part nineteen of Jude's twenty-five verses). Gone are the struggles of the mid-first century between Paul, James, and Symeon Peter. II Pet is a bridge figure

SUMMARY OF BASIC INFORMATION

DATE: After Pauline letters; after I Pet and Jude; most likely AD 130, give or take a decade.

TO/FROM: Probably to a general audience of eastern Mediterranean (Asia Minor?) Christians who would have known Pauline writings and I Pet. Perhaps from Rome, but Alexandria and Asia Minor have been suggested.

AUTHENTICITY: Pseudonymous, by someone desiring to present a final message with advice from Peter.

UNITY AND INTEGRITY: No major dispute.

FORMAL DIVISION:

   A. Opening Formula: 1:1–2
   B. Body: 1:3–3:16
      1:3–21: Exhortation to progress in virtue
      2:1–22: Condemnation of false teachers (polemic from Jude)
      3:1–16: Delay of the second coming
   C. Concluding Exhortation and Doxology: 3:17–18.

---

seeking to hold together the various heritages. In that sense this is a very "Catholic Epistle."

GENERAL ANALYSIS OF THE MESSAGE

THE OPENING FORMULA (1:1–2) is II Pet's only substantial gesture toward a letter format. The addressees are "those who have received a faith of the same value as ours." In other words, there is only one Christian faith. The greeting is a copy from I Pet 1:2. The "knowledge of Jesus our Lord" (II Pet 1:2) is the antidote to false teaching.

THE BODY (1:3–3:16). *II Pet 1:3–21, an Exhortation to Progress in Virtue,* uses terms heaped on one another: faith, virtue, knowledge, self-control, perseverance, godliness, mutual affection, love. Christians who do not make progress become blind and forget that they were cleansed from their sins (II Pet 1:9).

Speaking as Peter facing death, the writer reminds the addressees that what he spoke about Christ was not "cleverly devised myths" but eyewitness testimony to God's own revelation from heaven at the transfiguration acknowledging Jesus as the beloved divine Son (1:16–19).

Prophecy also enters into the II Pet picture. According to 1:14 Jesus announced beforehand Peter's (forthcoming) death. This brings us to the most famous passage in II Pet (1:20–21): "All prophecy of Scripture is not a matter of one's own interpretation; for not ever is prophecy brought forth by human will; rather people who were carried along by the Holy Spirit spoke from God." Who is the "one" of "one's own"? The prophet? The recipient of prophecy? In pondering this matter we should not forget that the writer's primary intent was to support the veracity of the expected Parousia ("coming," sometimes "second coming") of Christ.

The Polemic Condemnation of the False Teachers (2:1–22) takes over the polemic en masse from Jude, with differences. The "noncanonical" examples in Jude are not used. Unlike Jude, II Pet (2:5–9) is interested in proof that God knows how to rescue the godly from the trial.

The false teachers had escaped the defilements of the world through knowledge of Christ, and now they have become entangled again, so that the final state is worse than the first. As illustration, 2:22 cites two proverbs: a biblical proverb about a dog (Prov 26:11), and another about a pig (Syriac Ahiqar 8:18 [the story of an Assyrian wise man], and others).

Delay of the Second Coming (3:1–16). The polemic continues. II Pet 3:4 becomes specific about false teachers. They are denying the promise of the Parousia because leading first-generation Christians have died and things remain unchanged. The writer offers refutation: predictions by apostles and prophets support the Parousia. Moreover, the God who flooded the world will judge the created heaven and earth with fire, destroying the ungodly and ensuring the Parousia. Furthermore, the author observes that divine "time" is not our time. If the Parousia is delayed, it is because the Lord is forbearing and wants to allow time for repentance. Eventually, the day of the Lord will come unexpectedly, like a thief. The delay reveals God's patience, and in 3:14–16 he adds the witness of "our dear brother Paul."

CONCLUDING EXHORTATION AND DOXOLOGY (3:17–18). This is an effective summation of what has gone before. Symeon Peter issues a warning. He wishes that they grow in the grace and knowledge of "our Lord and Savior Jesus Christ." The doxology gives glory both now and until the day of eternity.

CANONICITY AND EARLY CATHOLICISM

Of the twenty-seven NT books II Pet had the least support in antiquity. In the Western church II Pet was either unknown or ignored until ca. 350, and even after that Jerome reported that many rejected it because it differed in style from I Pet. In the Eastern church Origen acknowledged disputes about it. Bodmer P[72] (third century) shows that II Pet was being copied in Egypt; yet in the early fourth century Eusebius did not treat it as canonical, and most of the great church writers of Antioch ignored it. Nevertheless, during the fourth century II Pet was making its appearance in some Eastern and Western church lists (Athanasius, III Carthage); and by the early sixth century even the Syriac-speaking church was accepting it. Despite that checkered history Luther did not relegate II Pet to the back of his 1522 NT (as he did Jas, Jude, Heb, and Rev). In modern times, however, particularly among more radical Protestant scholars II Pet has been attacked; and the occasional voice has been raised for removing it from the canon because of a dislike of its "Early Catholicism."

"Early Catholic" is a label for features in II Pet, wherein some say that the writer of the epistle was stressing that faith was a body of beliefs. The prophetic Scriptures were not a matter of one's own interpretation but had to be interpreted by authoritative teachers (like Peter). A chain of apostolic authority from the eyewitnesses of Jesus' ministry was now assumed. Hellenistic philosophic terminology ("partakers of the divine nature") was substituted for the existential language of the early NT books. Critics contend that all this would eventually produce the kind of Christianity exemplified by Roman Catholicism and represented the wrong direction. A logical implication would be that the church made a mistake in canonizing II Pet, hence the call for deletion.

Disagreement with this approach has been expressed on two scores. First, a challenge has been mounted against the right of interpreters to decide that what favors their theology and their church inclination is the true message of the NT and that what does not is distortion. Second, some have questioned whether the analysis of the thought of II Pet as given above is correct. Many of the ideas at issue (faith as

believed truths, importance of apostolic authority, authoritative interpretations, danger of untraditional private teachers) are found widely
in the NT, including the undisputed Pauline letters. II Pet can provide
an opportunity to discuss the validity of those ideas, but the dialectic
isolation of them may not facilitate a valid exegesis of the writer's
intent.

.⋆.

37

The Book of Revelation (The Apocalypse)

Now comes the final book of the canonical NT even though it was not the last to be composed. Either of the two names in the title of this chapter may be used for the book, since both literally mean "unveiling" (but not Revelations—the whole book is one Revelation).

Rev is widely popular for the wrong reasons. Many people read it as a guide to how the world will end, assuming that Christ gave the author detailed knowledge of the future that is communicated in coded symbols. What follows below will challenge that view by providing a different kind of interpretation of the book. The study begins with the *Literary Genre of Apocalyptic*, after which comes the *General Analysis*, a bit longer than usual, because Rev is difficult to understand. Then a final section examines *Millenarianism* (20:4–6).

THE LITERARY GENRE OF APOCALYPTIC

Characteristic of biblical apocalypses is a narrative framework in which a revelatory vision is accorded to a human being, most often through the intervention of an otherworldly being—for example, an

SUMMARY OF BASIC INFORMATION

DATE: Probably between AD 92 and 96 at the end of the Emperor Domitian's reign.

TO: Churches in the western sector of Asia Minor.

AUTHENTICITY: Written by a Jewish Christian prophet named John who was neither John son of Zebedee nor the writer of the Johannine Gospel or of the Epistles.

UNITY: Only a few scholars contend that two apocalypses (from the same hand or school) have been joined—an attempt to explain the repetitious and seemingly different time perspectives.

INTEGRITY: The writer may have included visions and passages that were already part of Christian apocalyptic tradition, but overall the work is entirely his own.

DIVISION ACCORDING TO CONTENTS:

A. Prologue: 1:1–3

B. Letters to the Seven Churches: 1:4–3:22
   Opening Formula with attached praise, promise, and divine
      response (1:4–8)
   Inaugural Vision (1:9–20)
   Seven Letters (2:1–3:22)

C. Part I of the Revelatory Experience: 4:1–11:19
   Visions of the Heavenly Court: The One Enthroned and the Lamb
      (4:1–5:14)
   Seven Seals (6:1–8:1)
   Seven Trumpets (8:2–11:19)

D. Part II of the Revelatory Experience: 12:1–22:5
   Visions of the Dragon, the Beasts, and the Lamb (12:1–14:20)
   Seven Plagues and Seven Bowls (15:1–16:21)
   Judgment of Babylon, the Great Harlot (17:1–19:10)
   Victory of Christ and the End of History (19:11–22:5)

E. Epilogue (with Concluding Blessing): 22:6–21.

---

angel who takes someone to a heavenly vantage point to reveal the vision and/or to explain it. The vision of the supernatural world or of the future helps to interpret present circumstances on earth, which are almost always tragic. Apocalypses are most often addressed to those living in times of suffering and persecution. In apocalyptic, however, the visions of the otherworldly have become far more luxuriant, most often accompanied by vivid symbols and mysterious numbers.

The figurative language of apocalyptic raises hermeneutical issues. Rev is the most apocalyptic book in the NT. It reuses many of the elements from Ezek, Zech, the Isaian Apocalypse, and Dan; and it does so with remarkable creativity. Many times one can detect a historical referent in the description. Yet sometimes the symbols are polyvalent. The symbolism of apocalyptic compels imaginative participation on the part of the hearers/readers.

GENERAL ANALYSIS OF THE MESSAGE

PROLOGUE (1:1–3). The book is announced as the "revelation of Jesus Christ," that is, the revelation given by Christ about the divine meaning of the author's own times and about how God's people will soon be delivered. An angel confers this revelation on a seer named John, who is on the small island of Patmos in the Aegean Sea. The blessing in v. 3, the first of seven in Rev, indicates that this prophetic message is meant to be read aloud and heard in the churches addressed.

LETTERS TO THE SEVEN CHURCHES (1:4–3:22). This section begins with an *Opening Formula* (1:4–5a), as if the seven letters to come are part of one large letter. The Opening's triadic patterns are phrased in the symbolic style that pervades this book: God is the one who is and was and is to come. Similarly three phrases describe Jesus in terms of his passion (faithful witness), his resurrection (firstborn from the dead), and his exaltation (ruler of earthly kings).

The *doxology of Christ* in 1:5b–6 celebrates Christ's love and the liberation from sins that has been accomplished by his blood, and the resultant dignity of Christians stated in terms of kingdom and priesthood (Exod 19:6; I Pet 1:2,19; 2:9). An echo of Dan 7:13 and Zech 12:10 reminds the addressees of their identity and assures them Christ will come in judgment on all enemies. In 1:8 *the Lord God affirms* the triadic designation of 1:4 (who is, was, and is to come), prefacing that with "I am the Alpha and the Omega," and concluding with "the Almighty" (Greek *Pantokratōr*, the first of nine occurrences). Thus, God is the beginning and the end, the majestic, the all-powerful.

Inaugural Vision (1:9–20). John explains that he has been on Patmos "because of the word of God." Most interpret that to mean imprisonment or exile, a background that would explain the atmosphere of persecution in Rev. That he sees a voice (prophets saw words: Isa 2:1; Amos 1:1; etc.) and that a constant "like" governs the seer's descriptions warn that matters have moved beyond a realm confined to the external senses into one of spiritual experience and symbolism. The vision of Christ is resplendent with rich symbolism, much of it derived from Dan—for example, "one like a son of man" (Dan 7:13), but he is also described with attributes belonging to the Ancient of Days (Dan 7:9 = God). The seven golden lampstands prepare for the seven churches, and the seven stars in the right hand were the angels of the seven churches. The atmosphere is evocative of the Jerusalem Temple (I Chron 28:15, from Exod 25:37).

Letters to the Seven Churches (2:1–3:22). These letters are very important for understanding the whole book. They give more information about a group of churches in western Asia Minor than most other NT books do about their addressees. With regard to the great visions of chaps. 4–22, it is important to remember that these letters are reported in order to convey a message to the Christians of those cities. The meaning of the symbolism must be judged from the viewpoint of the first-century addressees.

In their arrangement, the letters are remarkably parallel in some ways, yet strikingly diverse in others. For instance, in terms of the judgment passed by the Son of Man who dictates the letters, nothing bad is said of Smyrna and Philadelphia; nothing good is said of Sardis and Laodicea. Three sorts of problems confront the seven churches: false teaching (Ephesus, Pergamum, Thyatira); persecution (Smyrna, Philadelphia); and complacency (Sardis, Laodicea). Most modern readers think of persecution as the only issue addressed and consequently reinterpret the book in light of threatening situations today. The struggle against complacency may be much more applicable to modern Christianity. The false teaching is conditioned by the first century in one way (eating meat offered to idols), and yet the underlying issue of Christians conforming in an unprincipled way to the surrounding society certainly remains a current problem.

There are abundant OT references in most of the letters, but few in those to Sardis and Laodicea. The titles or descriptions of Christ that begin the letters echo in varying degrees descriptions in chap. 1. Details in the rest of each letter show that the seer knew the area well. Some churches are strong; some are weak; but whether commending

Table 7. Letters to the angels of the churches (Rev 2–3)

ITEMS IN EACH LETTER	EPHESUS (2:1–7)	SMYRNA (2:8–11)	PERGAMUM (2:12–17)
Titles or description of the speaker (Christ):	The One holding the seven stars in right hand and walking among the seven golden lampstands	The First and the Last who died and came to life	The One having the two-edged sword
Status of the church: GOOD THINGS acknowledged by speaker: . . . . Status of the church: BAD THINGS speaker has against them	I know your deeds, labor, endurance; not tolerant for wicked; you tested would-be apostles, finding them false; you endure patiently for my name's sake; not weary . . . . Have abandoned first love	I know your tribulation; rich despite poverty; blasphemed by those calling themselves Jews who are only a synagogue of Satan . . . . NOTHING BAD SAID	I know you dwell where Satan's throne is; you hold fast my name; did not deny faith in me; Antipas my faithful witness was killed among you where Satan lives . . . . Some hold teachings of Balaam who seduced Israel to idol food and immorality; some hold teaching of Nicolaitans
Admonitions; encouragements:	Remember whence you have fallen; repent and do the former works; if not, I will come to remove your lampstand from its place; you hate the works of the Nicolaitans which I hate	Do not fear what you are about to suffer; the devil will throw some in prison to test you, and you will have tribulation ten days; be faithful unto death, and I will give you the crown of life	Repent; if not, I will come soon and war against them with the sword of my mouth
Promise to whoever has ears to hear what the Spirit says to the churches:	To the victor I will give to eat from the tree of life which is in the paradise (garden) of God	The victor will not be harmed by the second death	To the victor I will give the hidden manna and a white stone inscribed with a new name that no one knows except the recipient

THYATIRA (2:18–29)	SARDIS (3:1–6)	PHILADELPHIA (3:7–13)	LAODICEA (3:14–21)
The Son of God, having eyes like a blazing fire and feet like burnished bronze	The One having the seven spirits of God and the seven stars	The Holy and True One having the key of David; opens—none can shut; shuts—none can open	The Amen, faithful and true Witness; the *Archē* (ruler or beginning) of God's creation
I know your deeds, love, faith, service, endurance; your latter deeds exceed former . . . . You tolerate the woman Jezebel a "prophetess" whose teaching seduces to immorality and idol food; I gave her time but she refuses to repent	NOTHING GOOD SAID . . . . I know your deeds; you have the name of being alive but are dead	I know your deeds; I have opened before you a door that can't be shut; you have little power but have kept my word and not denied my name . . . . NOTHING BAD SAID	NOTHING GOOD SAID . . . . I know your deeds; you are neither cold nor hot, but lukewarm; am about to spit you out of my mouth. You claim to be rich, affluent, not needy; you do not know that you are wretched, pitiable, poor, blind, and naked
I will throw her into sickbed, and into great affliction those who commit adultery with her, unless they repent their works; I will put her children to death. All the churches will know I am the searcher of minds and hearts; I will give to each of you according to your works. But I lay no burden on the rest of you who do not hold this teaching, who have not known the deep things of Satan; but hold fast what you have till I come	Awake; strengthen what remains and is about to die; I have not found your works complete before my God. Remember and keep what you received and heard; repent; if you are not awake, I shall come as a thief at an hour you know not. But you have a few names who have not soiled their garments; they shall walk with me in white for they are worthy	I will make synagogue of Satan (not really Jews; they lie) come and bow before your feet. Because you kept my word of endurance, I will keep you from the hour of trial about to come on the whole world, to test those dwelling on earth. I will come soon; keep what you have so that no one can take your crown	I advise you to buy from me gold refined by fire in order to be rich, and white garments to be clothed in lest your naked shame be shown, and eyesalve in order to see. Those whom I love I reprove and chastise, so be zealous and repent. Behold I stand at the door and knock; if anyone hears my voice and opens the door, I will enter and we will eat together
To the victor who keeps my works to the end I will give power over the nations to rule them with a rod of iron as when earthen vessels are broken, even as I have received it from my Father; I will also give the morning star	Thus the victor will be clad in white garments; and I shall not erase his/her name from the book of life but confess it before my Father and before His angels	I will make the victor a pillar in the temple of my God, never to leave it; I will write on him/her the name of my God and of His city (the new Jerusalem descending from heaven, from my God), and my own new name	To the victor I will grant to sit with me on my throne, as I was victorious and sat with my Father on His throne

or reprimanding, the writer assumes common knowledge that later readers do not share. For example, there were imperial temples in all the cities addressed, except Thyatira. Nevertheless, the overarching message that spans the seven letters and matches the theme of the rest of the book is to stand firm and make no concession to what the author designates as evil. The optimistic promises to the victor in each letter fit the goal of encouragement that is characteristic of apocalyptic.

Part I of the Revelatory Experience (4:1–11:19). Beyond the letters to the churches, it is difficult to diagnose the author's overall organizational plan for the body of Rev. Yet many scholars detect two large subdivisions, one beginning with the open door in heaven seen in 4:1, the other, after the opened heavens in 11:19, beginning with the great sign seen there in 12:1.

Visions of the Heavenly Court: The One Enthroned and the Lamb (4:1–5:14). Just as the seer knows the local situation in Asia Minor, simultaneously he sees what is happening in heaven as part of his understanding that "what must take place after this" interweaves earth and heaven. Drawn from Ezek 1:26–28, precious gems are used to describe the Lord God seated on the heavenly throne. Moreover, the lightning and the four living creatures echo the vision of the cherubim in Ezek 1:4–13; 10:18–22. The hymn of worship to the enthroned God by the living creatures and twenty-four elders(?) reproduces the threefold "Holy" of the seraphim in Isa 6:3 and centers on creation.

A matching vision in Rev 5 centers on the Lamb, noting the Lamb's ability to open the scroll written within and on the back, sealed with seven seals. The Lamb, which stands as though slain, is identified as the Lion of the tribe of Judah, the Root of David, who has conquered. The hymn sung to Jesus (the Lamb), the victorious Davidic Messiah, has a refrain about being "worthy" similar to that in the hymn to God in the preceding chapter. Thus God and the Lamb are being put on virtually the same plane, with one being hailed as the creator and the other as the redeemer.

Seven Seals (6:1–8:1). The first four seals opened by the Lamb (6:1–8) are the four different colored horses, respectively white, red, black, and pale (green?), ridden by the famous four horsemen of the Apocalypse, representing respectively conquest, bloody strife, famine, and pestilence (Zech 1:8–11; 6:1–7), all part of the eschatological judgment of God. The selection of disasters may have been shaped by contemporary circumstances, such as the Parthian attacks against Rome. The fifth seal (6:9–11) depicts souls of the martyrs (killed by Nero in the 60s?) under the heavenly altar. The sixth seal (6:12–17) describes cosmic disturbances that are part of God's punishment (not to be taken literally) in traditional imagery and repeated again and again in apocalyptic. Even the great ones of the earth will not escape the wrath of the Lamb.

Before he describes the seventh seal (8:1), the seer narrates an intervening vision (7:1–17) wherein four angels who were at the four corners of the earth holding back the four winds (cf. I Enoch 76) are told not to wreak harm until God's servants have been sealed on their foreheads. The vision distinguishes two groups: the symbolic number of 144,000 Christians (12,000 from each tribe) and the innumerable multitude (of martyrs) from every nation, tribe, people, and tongue whose white garments have been washed in the blood of the Lamb. They cry out, "Salvation belongs to our God who sits on the throne, and to the Lamb." The peace brought by being in the presence of God is beautifully described in 7:16–17: no more hunger or thirst, no more burning or scorching heat, as the shepherding Lamb leads them to springs of living water.

Seven Trumpets (8:2–11:19). The opening of the seventh seal in 8:1 is climactic, but further sevens (seven angels with seven trumpets) are now unveiled. The seven trumpets are divided with an initial group of four; but now the background is the plagues of the exodus. As those plagues prepared for the liberation of God's people from Egypt, so these plagues prepare for the deliverance of God's people in the final days. That only one third is affected indicates that this is not the whole of God's judgment (cf. Ezek 5:2).

In Rev 8:13 an eagle cries out a triple woe (contrast Rev 4:8), anticipating the last three trumpet blasts of judgment. The vision of the fifth trumpet, scorpion-like locusts with the appearance of battle horses from the smoking bottomless pit (9:1–11), combines images from the Egyptian plagues (Exod 10:1–20) with Joel 1–2. The demonic is now being let loose, as the name of the king of the locusts indicates: "Destruction" in both Hebrew and Greek (9:11). This is the first of the three woes.

The sixth trumpet (9:13–21) has angels release an immense number of cavalry to kill a third of humankind. Despite these horrendous
punishments, the rest of humankind refuses to believe. After the sixth
trumpet the sequence is interrupted. In 10:1–2 a mighty angel comes
down from heaven with a little scroll. This angel is described in the
trappings of God, of the transfigured Jesus (Matt 17:2), and of Rev's
initial vision of the Son of Man (1:12–16). This immense angel warns
that when the seventh trumpet is sounded, the mysterious plan of God
promised by the prophets (Amos 3:7) will be fulfilled. The seer is told
to eat the little scroll, which is sweet in the mouth but bitter in the
stomach (see Ezek 2:8–3:3), and then to prophesy: of the victory of
the faithful and of the bitter news of the painful disaster coming on
the world.

The prophet was given a measuring rod and told to measure the
temple of God. By envisioning the actual arrangement of the Jerusalem
Temple, one is able to understand the visionary experience recounted
in chapter 11 of measuring the heavenly temple. A distinction is made
between the temple sanctuary area belonging to God and the court
outside the sanctuary. The measuring of the sanctuary of God and those
who worship there (11:1–2) is a sign of protection, whereas outside
is given over to the Gentiles to trample, which may represent the Jerusalem Temple destroyed by the Romans in AD 70. There are two prophetic witnesses, two olive trees, and two lampstands (11:3–4) who
prophesy with miraculous power for 1,260 days (equivalent to forty-
two months and the three-and-a-half times or years of 12:14), until
they are killed by the beast from the pit in the great city where the Lord
was killed. The various ways of calculating half-seven are related to Dan
7:25; 9:27; and 12:7. Their dead bodies lie in the street for three and a
half days. The two figures are raised up by God and made victorious by
being taken up into heaven. Are these purely eschatological figures, or
two historical martyrs? Some of the imagery here reflects OT accounts
in Zech 4:1–14. There are also echoes of OT accounts of Moses and
Elijah. "The great city" is meant as Jerusalem, but 14:8; 16:19; etc.,
use "the great city" for Rome. Is there double meaning, and is the martyrdom of Peter and Paul in Rome in the 60s in mind? Subsequently
an earthquake wreaks havoc on the city. That is the second of the three
woes (11:14).

The seventh trumpet is finally sounded in 11:15–19, signaling that the kingdom of the world has become the kingdom of our Lord and his Christ. This might give the impression that the end of the world has come. But there is much more to follow, as the opening of God's temple in heaven to show the ark of the covenant (11:19) introduces Part II.

PART II OF THE REVELATORY EXPERIENCE: 12:1–22:5. Part II begins with three chapters of inaugural visions. They introduce characters, the dragon and the two beasts, that will figure prominently in the rest of the book. Indeed these chapters have been looked on as the heart of Rev.

Visions of the Dragon, the Beasts, and the Lamb (12:1–14:20). Certainly some of the imagery of Gen 3:15–16 and the struggle between the serpent and the woman and her offspring are part of the background for chap. 12 (see 12:9). The woman clothed with the sun, having the moon under her feet and on her head the crown of twelve stars, represents Israel, echoing the dream of Joseph in Gen 37:9. There is also the mythic sea-serpent imagery, which is found in biblical poetry as Leviathan or Rahab (Isa 27:1; 51:9; Pss 74:14; 89:11; Job 26:12–13; etc.), and even outside Israel.

Metaphorical birth-giving of the people of God is an OT theme (Isa 26:17; 66:7–8; see also *IV Ezra* 9:43–46; 10:40–49). In Rev the woman brings forth her child the Messiah (Ps 2:9) in pain; this is an instance of Jewish expectations of birth pangs of the Messiah, meaning the wretchedness of the world situation that becomes a signal for the coming of God-sent deliverance (Micah 4:9–10). The dragon (the ancient serpent, Satan) tries to devour the child, who escapes by being taken up to God. This leads to a war in heaven; the dragon is cast down to earth where, in anger with the woman, he makes war on her offspring. There is reference here not to Jesus' physical birth or to Jesus as an infant, but to Jesus' birth as the Messiah through his death. The subsequent struggle between the dragon and the woman (now the church) and her children in the wilderness lasts 1,260 days and three-times-and-a-half, that is, the time of persecution that will lead to the end time; but she is protected by God (with eagle's wings; cf. Exod 19:4). Taking his stand on the sands of the sea, the dragon employs in his campaign on earth two great beasts, one from the sea, the other from the land.

The first beast, with ten horns and seven heads, rises from the sea (13:1–10). Dan 7 had illustrated the use of four chimerical beasts to represent world empires, with the ten horns on the fourth beast representing rulers. Accordingly the beast in Rev combines elements of Dan's four as a way of symbolizing that the Roman Empire is as evil as all the others combined. The seven heads are explained in 17:9–11 as the Seven Hills of Rome and also as seven kings, five of whom have fallen, the sixth is, and the seventh is yet to come; and then the passage adds an eighth, probably indicating Domitian. The one seemingly wounded head that heals may represent the legend of Nero redivivus (that is, come back to life; 13:3). In the imagery of Rev, as well as waging war against the holy ones, the Empire had caused people to worship the devil, and thus to be excluded from the book of life (13:4–8).

The second beast, the one from the earth (13:11–18), is an evil parody of Christ. It has two horns like a lamb but it speaks like a dragon; later it is associated with a false prophet (16:13; 19:20; 20:10); it works signs and wonders, like those of Elijah; it has people marked on the right hand or the forehead, even as the servants of God are sealed on their forehead (7:3; 14:1). This beast is emperor worship, which began very early in Asia Minor. The description in 13:18 ends with perhaps the most famous image in Rev: the number of the beast, a human number that calls for understanding, is 666. By somewhat complex gematria, the name Nero Caesar totals 666.

The Lamb and the symbolically numbered 144,000 (14:1–5) are a consoling picture, meant to assure Christians that they will survive the assaults of the dragon and the two beasts. Three angels (14:6–13) proclaim solemn admonitions: an eternal gospel directed to the whole world, stressing the need to glorify God because the hour of judgment has come; a woe to Babylon (a code word for Rome); and a severe warning that those who have worshiped the beast and bear its mark will undergo hell fire. A voice from heaven blesses those who die in the Lord. Then (14:14–20) the Son of Man, with a sickle in his hand, and more angels execute a bloody judgment, throwing the vintage of the earth into the winepress of God's fury.

Seven Plagues and Seven Bowls (15:1–16:21). Comparable to the seven seals and trumpets of Part I of Rev are seven plagues and seven bowls containing them that portend the final judgment. But before they are poured out, chap. 15 presents a scene in the heavenly court where the Song of Moses is sung, echoing the victory of the Hebrews crossing the Reed (Red) Sea (Exod 15:1–18). Once more the plagues preceding the exodus from Egypt (Exod 7–10) serve as background. The frogs from the mouth of the false prophet are three demonic spirits performing signs like the magicians of Egypt. A famous image appears in Rev 16:16: Armageddon as the place of the final battle with the forces of evil. The seventh bowl (16:17–21) marks the climax of God's action; its contents smash Rome into parts as a voice proclaims, "It is done." The results are devastating.

Judgment of Babylon, the Great Harlot (17:1–19:10). This fall of Rome is now described in vivid detail, following the OT convention of portraying cities marked by idolatry or godlessness (Tyre, Babylon, Ninevah) as harlots, and those who accept their authority as fornicators (Isa 23; 47; Nahum 3; Jer 50–51; Ezek 16; 23; 26–27). The doom of Babylon/Rome, drunk with the blood of the martyrs, is dramatically proclaimed in chap. 18 by angels in a great lament. Just as ancient Babylon was symbolically to be cast into the Euphrates (Jer 51:63–64), so Babylon/Rome is to be thrown into the sea. Counterpoised to the lament on earth is a chorus of joy in heaven (19:1–10). In that rejoicing we hear of the marriage of the Lamb and his bride that anticipates the final vision of the book. The OT theme of the marriage of God and the people of God (Hos 2:1–25; Isa 54:4–8; Ezek 16—sometimes in contexts of unfaithfulness) has been shifted to Christ and the believers.

Victory of Christ and the End of History (19:11–22:5). The seer describes Christ as a great warrior leading the armies of heaven, as the King of kings and the Lord of lords (19:16). The beast and the false prophet both are thrown into the lake of fire symbolizing eternal damnation. Chap. 20 describes the millennial reign of Christ (see the subsection below). Only the dragon (the devil/Satan) remains from the triad of opponents, and now it is shut up in a pit for a thousand years while Christ and the Christian martyr saints reign on earth. The saints who died once will live forever, for over them the second death (final destruction) has no power (20:6). After the thousand years Satan is let loose to gather Gog and Magog, all the nations of the earth; but fire comes down from heaven and consumes them, while the devil is thrown into the lake of fire where the others had been cast. Both death and hell yield up the deceased. And the dead are judged before the throne of God according to what is written in the book of life; and the second death takes place (20:11–15).

To replace the devastation of the first heaven and first earth, there is a new heaven and a new earth, and a new Jerusalem that comes down out of heaven from God (21:1–22:5), like a bride adorned for her husband (21:2). The dwelling of God with humanity is described lyrically, offering hope for all who live in the present world; no more tears, death, mourning, crying, or pain; a city as beautiful as a precious jewel built on the foundation walls bearing the names of the Twelve Apostles of the Lamb; a city perfectly cubic in shape, immense enough to contain all the saints. In that city there is no temple, for the Lord God the Almighty and the Lamb are its temple. The city has no need of sun or moon, for the glory of God gives it light and its lamp is the Lamb. Nothing unclean will ever be found within its perimeters. As in Paradise of old, a river of the water of life flows through the city watering the tree of life.

EPILOGUE (WITH CONCLUDING BLESSING) 22:6–21. John the seer is told not to seal up the words, for the time is near. As in the inaugural vision before the Seven Letters (1:9–20), the Alpha and the Omega who is now the Lord Jesus speaks, lending authority to the words of warning and of invitation heard by the seer. The audience is admonished not to add to or subtract from the prophetic words of the book. In response to Jesus' affirmation that he is coming soon, John the seer utters an impassioned "Amen. Come, Lord Jesus," an echo of one of the oldest prayers used by Christians (I Cor 16:22).

Having begun in letter format, Rev ends in the same way (22:21) with a very simple Concluding Blessing on "all the saints," that is, those who have not yielded to Satan or the beasts.

MILLENARIANISM (THE THOUSAND-YEAR REIGN: 20:4–6)

Rev states that at the end those who had been beheaded for their testimony to Jesus and for the word of God, who had not worshiped the beast, came to life and reigned with Christ a thousand years, while the rest of the dead did not come to life until the thousand years were ended. The origins of such belief may be found in a certain tension between prophetic and apocalyptic expectations. On the one hand, from a more "prophetic" viewpoint, an anticipation that survived the Babylonian exile was that one day God would restore the kingdom of David under a model anointed king, the Messiah; indeed, earlier Scripture was reread with this understanding (for example, Amos 9:11–12). This would be an earthly, historical kingdom. On the other hand, in a pessimistic view of history, some apocalyptic literature pictured God's direct final intervention without any mention of the restoration of the Davidic kingdom (Isa 24–27; Dan).

One way of combining the two expectations was to posit two divine interventions: first, a restoration of an earthly kingdom or period of blissful prosperity to be followed by the second intervention, God's end time victory and judgment. Various numbers were used to symbolize the duration of aspects of the expected periods: in I Enoch (third–second century BC) there are ten weeks of years; in IV Ezra (late first century AD) the Messiah will reign for 400 years. In Christian apocalyptic I Cor 15:23–28 offers this atemporal sequence: first the resurrection of Christ; then of those belonging to Christ, who reigns until he has put all his enemies under his feet; then the end when Christ delivers the kingdom to God after destroying every rule, authority, and power. Furthermore, in the late first century AD the Ascension of Isaiah has Beliar (the devil) ruling as an Antichrist for 1,332 days.

The variation of the numbers in these expectations should alert one that none of the writers had an exact knowledge about future time spans and (for the most part) probably never intended to convey exactness. The writer of Rev, then, would have used the thousand-year reign of Jesus on earth not to describe a historical kingdom but as a way of saying that eschatological expectations will be fulfilled.

Nevertheless, throughout Christian history some have taken the thousand years of Rev quite literally and speculated about it. (Only three verses mention the millennium; there has been extravagant growth from small beginnings.) Among the orthodox in the second and third centuries Papias, Justin, Tertullian, Hippolytus, and Lactantius believed in the millennium, as did the heterodox Cerinthus and Montanus. Further literalists arose over time; others rejected the concept altogether; and still others completely allegorized the idea and the texts related to it.

Especially in the subsequent Western church, from time to time millennial expectations have been revived in various forms. Some "leftwing" groups during the Reformation embraced it (for example, the Zwickau prophets, T. Münzer, and John of Leiden). In the United States during the nineteenth century millennialist groups proliferated, usually with one foot in Dan and the other in Rev, sometimes reinforced by private revelations. Prominent persons in the formation of Seventh-Day Adventists, Mormons, and Jehovah's Witnesses are examples. In some evangelical groups sharp divisions arose between Premillennialists and Postmillennialists: the former with the view that the golden age will come only after the evil present era is destroyed by the second coming; the latter, exhibiting optimistic liberalism, with the view that the present age will be gradually transformed into the millennium by natural progress in society and religious reform. A form of the premillennial movement features dispensationalism, which is identifying periods of time in world history. Usually the thesis is that this is the sixth dispensation, and the seventh (final) is about to come. The older, established churches remain convinced that, while the final stage in the divine plan will be accomplished through Jesus Christ, the thousand years are symbolic and no one knows when or how the end of the world will come. Acts 1:7 sets the tone: "It is not for you to know times and seasons that have been set by the Father's own authority."

APPENDIX I
THE HISTORICAL JESUS

A brief survey of scholarship on the historical Jesus is germane to this Introduction. The NT is a small library of books written within a hundred years of Jesus' death by those who believed he was the Messiah. Thus without him there would be no NT. A great deal of work takes place in this area. A brief overview can familiarize readers with some trends in scholarship.

OVER TWO HUNDRED YEARS
(1780–2015) OF THE MODERN QUEST

For some 1,800 years Christianity largely took for granted that the Gospel portrayal of Jesus with all its christological evaluations was a literally factual account of Jesus' lifetime. The "Enlightenment" of the eighteenth century led to a new approach to the Bible. The same historical principles used to study other ancient works first began to be applied to the NT by R. Simon, a Catholic priest (1690), and by a Protestant scholar, J. D. Michaelis (1750). H. S. Reimarus, whose work was published posthumously in 1778, was the first to develop a picture of Jesus distinct from the Christ described in the Gospels. The former was a Jewish revolutionary who attempted unsuccessfully to establish a messianic kingdom on earth, while the latter was the fictional projection of those who stole his body and pretended he had risen from the dead. Unfortunately, then, from the beginning, the application of systematic historical analysis to Jesus was mixed with a rationalism (touted as scientific but actually lacking in objectivity) that a priori denied the possibility of the supernatural. Often the search for the historical Jesus has been conducted with an overtone of freeing Jesus from the theological impositions of the later church, but in fact many of the searchers have imposed their own skepticism and anti-theological biases on the picture they claim to have "found." In 1835 D. F. Strauss, a student of F. C. Baur (1792–1860; a radical historical skeptic), published a *Life of Jesus* based on the principle that the Gospels had transformed and embellished by faith the picture of Jesus so that what resulted was mythical. The change was so profound that he judged it almost impossible to write a historical account of Jesus' life. From that (same) stance B. Bauer (1877) could argue that Jesus and Paul never existed, and E. Renan (1863) could portray a purely human Jesus. Soon the Fourth Gospel was dismissed as a theological creation and thus a totally unreliable historical source, while Mark (along with Q) was attentively studied as a key to the human Jesus. In 1901, however, W. Wrede (*The Messianic Secret*, Ger 1901; Eng 1971) argued that Mark was also the product of theology in which Jesus was presented as divine, and so not a reliable historical source. Behind the different exemplars of what has been called the "first quest" of the historical Jesus was the implication that modern theology ought to change according to what scholars now discerned about Jesus.

In *The Quest of the Historical Jesus* (*Von Reimarus zu Wrede*—Ger 1906; Eng 1910—since the 1913 edition it has been entitled *Geschichte der Leben-Jesu-Forschung*; revised Eng ed. 2000), A. Schweitzer passed judgment on more than a hundred years of such "historical Jesus" research. He contended that most of the investigation told us more about the investigators than about Jesus. Following the lead of J. Weiss (1863–1914), Schweitzer argued that the previous quest had overlooked Jesus' apocalyptic outlook in which he saw himself as the Messiah who by his death would bring about the end of the world. For Schweitzer, therefore, Jesus was a noble failure. In *The So-Called Historical Jesus and the Historic Biblical Christ* (Ger 1892; Eng 1964) M. Kähler presented another skeptical reaction to the "Jesus research" by arguing that it was impossible to separate out the historical Jesus from the Christ of faith, since the NT writings all focus on the latter. The Christ of faith is the one who has been proclaimed by Christians and the only one to be concerned with. R. Bultmann moved in the same direction. In *The History of the Synoptic Tradition* (Ger 1921; Eng 1963), he used form criticism not only to classify what was said about Jesus in the Synoptic Gospels but also to judge its historicity; and he attributed the highest percentage of the Jesus tradition to the creativity of the early Christians. Thus the quest for the historical Jesus was a virtual impossibility. Bultmann's pessimism about what can be known of Jesus historically corresponded to his theological principle (influenced by a Lutheran background) that one should not seek a historical basis for faith. Thus, if we may simplify, contrary to the "quest" Bultmann would not change theology according to "discoveries" about the historical Jesus, since they were irrelevant to belief. Paradoxically Bultmann did not wish to dispense with the exalted Gospel picture of Jesus, for the proclamation of that Gospel picture offers a challenge today for people to believe that is existentially similar to the challenge that Jesus offered to people in his lifetime. Those who respond by belief, God delivers from the hopeless incapacity of their own human abilities.

The reaction to Bultmann, largely led by his own students, constituted what some have called the "second quest" of the historical Jesus. In 1953 E. Käsemann gave a lecture published as "The Problem of the Historical Jesus" (see his *Essays on NT Themes*, 1964) in which he pointed out the danger of the gap Bultmann had opened up: if there is no traceable connection between the glorified Lord of the Gospels and the historical Jesus, Christianity becomes a myth. For Käsemann, faith, rather than being indifferent, requires an identity between the earthly Jesus and the exalted Lord. Recognizing that the Gospel sources are not coldly factual biography, he sought to develop criteria for determining what is historical in the Gospel tradition. Other "Post-Bultmannians" sought to determine historical features beneath the Gospel presentation; the results included various portrayals of Jesus of religious significance, for example, one who regarded himself as God's eschatological representative, exemplifying God's love and values by his actions, teachings, or authority and offering the possibility of an encounter with God. Bultmann's influence remains in that an existential touch dominates all such portrayals—a Jesus to whom one can relate but not one who offers explicit christological formulation, for that is the product of subsequent Christian reflection.

In roughly this same period, other scholars worked in their own ways in relation to the question of the historical Jesus. In *New Testament Theology: The Proclamation of Jesus* (Ger/Eng 1971), J. Jeremias studied the teaching of Jesus in its various forms in the Gospels in order to discern the historical source of that teaching in the actual life of the historical Jesus. In his teaching and mission, the historical Jesus saw himself inaugurating the kingdom of God, announcing the suddenness of the dawning of the last things, and articulating the claim of the kingdom on human lives. Ultimately Jeremias understood Jesus to have had a clear sense of his mission to die as the Suffering Servant of God. Similarly, in *The Founder of Christianity* (1970), C. H. Dodd went his own way in studying the historical Jesus, not falling into a pessimism but rather taking a positive approach of working toward a clear, trustworthy idea of the historical facts of the foundation of Christianity. In this endeavor, Dodd identified considerable historical material in the Synoptic Gospels. For Dodd, Jesus' parables proclaim the message that the kingdom of God is already evident in his mission. This viewpoint was part of Dodd's distinctive "realized eschatology," which eschewed the notion of a purely future cosmic judgment and emphasized the reality of "eschatology" already in the message and mission of Jesus.

THE CURRENT STATE OF "QUESTING" FOR JESUS

In the past few decades scholarly assessment of the historical Jesus has continued apace. Much work has been done, but as a whole it is hard to characterize. There is little new methodology, and one might say that there are few if any new conclusions. Perhaps some insights have been advanced or nuanced further than they had been before. But one cannot speak of a consensus, and the old methods ("criteria of authenticity," etc.) seem to be playing out for many scholars. The monumental comprehensive study by J. P. Meier (*A Marginal Jew*, 1991) approaches its end. And a few (quite diverse) scholars, for example, E. P. Sanders (*Jesus and Judaism*, 1985; *The Historical Figure of Jesus*, 1993),

J. D. G. Dunn, *Jesus Remembered*, 2003), and D. C. Allison Jr. (*Constructing Jesus: Memory, Imagination, and History*, 2010), have found ways to try new approaches. But there is no discernable unified direction in this work. Nevertheless, in order to give some form to this enterprise, what follows is a discussion of three notable current tendencies:

First, a willingness to attribute explicit christology to the lifetime of Jesus got new life in late twentieth-century scholarship, as once more it became respectable to hold that Jesus actually thought he had a unique relationship to God and reflected that outlook in his speech and attitudes. The scholarly practice of assigning the introduction of certain christological titles to specific post-Jesus stages in the geographical and temporal spread of Christianity is now seen to be too simple. Continuity between Jesus' lifetime and the Gospel portraits may be more inclusive than hitherto thought. Thus, operating with a hermeneutic of consent, certain scholars argue that the biblical texts themselves portray Jesus' being made aware through his own experiences of his true identity as "Son of Man—Messiah," titles that in the biblical portrait occur repeatedly as "Son of God," "Son of Man," and "Messiah"—three titles that do not represent alternatives but in a Jewish way jointly designate Jesus as the one mediator through whom God wills to accomplish redemption (for example, P. Stuhlmacher, *Jesus of Nazareth—Christ of Faith*, Ger 1988; Eng 1993).

Second, other scholars contend that Jesus was primarily a Jewish teacher of Wisdom whose followers probably misunderstood his parabolic/metaphorical teachings and, either deliberately or not, misrepresented his viewpoint, so that they re-presented him as an apocalyptic prophet. Applying standard scholarly criteria, these NT interpreters work to separate the original teaching of Jesus from that which is regarded as later layers of additional, often apocalyptic material. From working primarily with Jesus' parables and aphorisms, some of which have little or no explicit apocalyptic coloring, these scholars bolster their conclusion that Jesus was not an eschatological prophet. He may have, in his first-century context, healed and exorcized "demons," but he was basically a teacher of Wisdom. For some interpreters, Jesus' activities identify him with Hellenistic-Jewish-Cynic philosophers—freeing him from the discomfiting role of an eschatological prophet.

Third, moving along the line established by J. Weiss and A. Schweitzer, a majority of scholars argue that Jesus was an eschatological prophet who announced the imminent coming of the kingdom of God, which included an eschatological judgment. Thus, the right context for comprehending Jesus and his mission is first-century (and earlier) Jewish apocalyptic eschatology. These scholars argue that if Jesus did not issue eschatological proclamation, one is hard-pressed to fit him into his historical context. If JBap, his predecessor, was himself a prophetic figure who preached an eschatological message, and if Paul, one of Jesus' principal postresurrectional advocates, viewed the world through an apocalyptic eschatological frame, then how is one to understand Jesus in this mix? The chain of JBap-Jesus-Paul is difficult, if not impossible, to grasp if Jesus is thought to be devoid of eschatological features. But, understood as presented in NT writings, as an apocalyptic eschatological prophet, Jesus is at home in his own time. On the other hand, unlike an inspired, compassionate, egalitarian sage, he would not easily fit into the present day world. In fact, if one were to meet him, he probably would make that person more than a little uncomfortable.

APPENDIX II

JEWISH AND CHRISTIAN WRITINGS
PERTINENT TO THE NEW TESTAMENT

As Jewish background for the NT, besides the OT (including the Deuterocanonical Books), there are a series of extracanonical writings from the third century BC into the second century AD, including the DSS, the Apocrypha, and the works of Josephus. There are also Christian writings for the period AD 90–200, some of them considered apocryphal, some called "Apostolic Fathers," and (on opposite sides) gnostic and early patristic writings. The goal here is to supply in the briefest manner some useful information on the most important.

JEWISH WRITINGS

The Dead Sea Scrolls. The title "Qumran Literature" covers some ten scrolls and thousands of fragments found, beginning in 1947, in caves near Qumran on the NW shore of the Dead Sea. Written or copied between the late third century BC and the early first century AD, they consist of OT books, including many Deuterocanonical Books; Apocrypha; and compositions of the community of Jews who lived at the Qumran settlement. Most scholars identify this community as Essenes.

I (Ethiopic) Enoch. I Enoch is preserved partially (33 percent) in Greek, and completely in Ethiopic. Divided into five books, it contains imaginative expansions of Gen 6:1–4; apocalyptic descriptions, dream visions, and divisions of world eras; astronomical speculations; and elaborate materials describing a preexistent Son of Man.

Jubilees. This second-century BC rewriting of Gen 1–Exod 14 is related to other apocryphal Moses material. About one quarter of Jub is preserved in Latin; but the whole book has been preserved only in Ethiopic. The most notable characteristic is calendric interest, a solar calendar followed also by the Qumran community that protested against the Maccabean use of a lunar calendar in Temple observance.

(Letter of) Aristeas to Philocrates. Reflecting the large Jewish community in Alexandria, this small second-century BC book (not a letter) narrates the *(legendary)* origin of the translation of the Pentateuch from Hebrew into Greek. Seventy-two elders sent by the high priest in Jerusalem to Alexandria produced the LXX (Septuagint, from the Latin for the rounded number seventy), although that name is applied to the Greek translations and compositions of the *whole* OT.

Lives of the Prophets. There are numerous Greek mss., many of them with Christian additions. The best Greek ms., a sixth-century AD codex in the Vatican Library, treats twenty-three Jewish prophets without *obvious* Christian interpolations. The stated goal is to supply the name of the prophet, where he was from, where and how he died, and where he was buried. As background for the Gospels, the *Lives* attest a biographical interest in the prophetic figure, disproportionately concentrated on the death.

Testament (or Assumption) of Moses. Antiquity knew of both a *Testament of Moses* and an *Assumption of Moses.* An untitled Latin work that has survived, although entitled *Assumption* by its first editor, is Moses' final speech or testament (cf. Deut 31–34) to Joshua about the future history of Israel, concluding with the Roman intervention after Herod the Great's death. (Probably from before AD 30.)

IV Maccabees. This philosophical discourse or "diatribe" on the supremacy of Jewish religious reason over human passions and sufferings is illustrated by OT examples. Composed in Greek probably ca. AD 40, it embodies a theology of vicarious suffering in martyrdom that inspired Christian commemoration of martyrs.

IV Ezra, or the Apocalypse of Ezra. A work known as 2 Esdras (or IV Esdras in the Latin Vulgate) contains sixteen chapters, of which chaps. 1–2 and 15–16 are Christian compositions. Chaps. 3–14 constitute *IV Ezra*, a Jewish work of ca. AD 90–120, written in Hebrew or Aramaic but preserved most completely in Latin. It exemplifies Jewish apocalyptic literature contemporary with the later part of the NT.

II Baruch, or the *Syriac Apocalypse of Baruch*. Preserved in a Syriac translation from the (original?) Greek, this Jewish work from AD 95–120 is dependent on *IV Ezra* or a source common to both. Baruch, the secretary of Jeremiah, issued prophetic/apocalyptic warnings and encouragement.

Psalms of Solomon. Preserved in medieval Greek mss. and Syriac, these eighteen psalms were originally composed in Hebrew in Palestine (Jerusalem) 65–40 BC. They interpret the Roman invasion by Pompey as punishment of the corruption of the Sadducee high priests. Descriptions in Pss 17–18 of the anticipated Davidic Messiah are important background for the NT.

Flavius Josephus. Born in Palestine of a priestly clan in AD 37, Josephus ben Matthias died after 94, probably in Rome. Although he was a commander of Jewish forces in Galilee during the revolt against Rome (66–70), he surrendered to Vespasian, who set him free when he predicted that the Roman general would become emperor. In turn, Titus brought him to Rome and installed him in the imperial palace. There in the 70s he wrote *The Jewish War*. Ca. 94 he finished the *Jewish Antiquities* (*Ant.*) in twenty vols., a massive history of the Jews from patriarchal to Roman times. The famous *Testamonium Flavianum* (*Ant.* 18.3.3; # 63–64) is Josephus' witness to Jesus; shorn of later Christian additions it tells of Jesus' astonishing deeds and teaching and that Pilate condemned him to death upon the indictment of "the first-ranking men among us."

Testaments of the Twelve Patriarchs. If Jacob blesses his twelve sons in Gen 49, this work (preserved in late Greek mss. but composed before AD 200) contains the testament of each of those twelve to his own sons. Its witness to messianic expectations is important. There are Christian passages: were they additions to a Jewish original, or was the basic work a Jewish Christian composition drawing on earlier sources?

Sibylline Oracles. Jews and Christians imitated pagan oracles, and this Greek work in fourteen books represents a combination of two collections (150 BC to AD 650). It is not always possible to distinguish Jewish from Christian oracles.

CHRISTIAN (AND GNOSTIC) WRITINGS

Gospel of the Hebrews. This Jewish Christian gospel, apparently known to Papias (ca. 125), survives only in a few patristic quotations. It treats distinctively the preexistence, Spirit-endowment, and resurrection appearances of Jesus.

Secret Gospel of Mark (SGM). Passages from this work appear in an eighteenth-century copy of a mysterious, otherwise unknown letter of Clement of Alexandria (ca. 175–200) in which, according to Clement, Mark wrote canonical Mark in Rome; then, after Peter's martyrdom, Mark brought his notes to Alexandria and expanded the earlier work into "a more spiritual gospel" for the use of those being brought to perfection—a guide to the mysteries. Scholars debate the origin and purpose of this writing; most think of it as a conflated pastiche from the canonical Gospels used to support esoteric initiations.

Gospel of Peter (GPet). This Greek work was known in the second century and hesitantly rejected as unsound by Bishop Serapion of Antioch. It treats a segment of the passion from the final trial of Jesus to the resurrection. There are elements in it that are clearly not historical. Most scholars regard GPet as an imaginative expansion of the canonical Gospels. The work does, however, display an anti-Jewish disposition.

Protevangelium of James. This work, preserved in many Greek mss. beginning in the third century, was in circulation by mid-second century. Dealing with Mary's family and her upbringing and marriage to Joseph, as well as with the birth of Jesus, it claims James (likely "the brother of the Lord") as its author. Its incorrect knowledge of Judaism shows that it is not a historical account, even though it may contain some reliable items of earlier tradition. It has greatly influenced religious art and the development of Mariology.

Infancy Gospel of Thomas. The original Greek survives only in very late mss., although there are Latin and Syriac texts from the fifth century. It consists of a number of legendary episodes showing the miraculous powers of the boy Jesus from age five through twelve. Christologically it is meant to show that the boy Jesus had the same powers (and the same opposition) as the adult Jesus.

Odes of Solomon. It is uncertain whether the original composition (by a Jewish Christian in the early second century AD) was in Hebrew or Aramaic or Greek; but the most complete presentation of the forty-two *Odes* is in Syriac. Although some think of them as gnostic, they have parallels to Jewish apocalyptic and the DSS, as well as to certain aspects of the Fourth Gospel.

1 Clement. A letter-treatise from the church of Rome to the church of Corinth in order to support some Corinthian presbyters who had been deposed. Most date it ca. 96, although 96–120 would be a more certain time range. The letter stresses authority and has the (twofold) church structure of bishops and deacons stem from the apostles.

Didache. More fully known as *The Teaching (Didachē) of the Lord Through the Twelve Apostles to the Nations,* this is an instructional handbook on ethics and liturgical practices (baptism, eucharist). Whether it is a unified composition is uncertain. It is somewhat close to Matt. The picture of church organization (bishops and deacons replacing prophets and teachers) seems to imply a pre-Ignatius situation.

Letters of Ignatius of Antioch. The bishop of Antioch was arrested, condemned, brought to Rome as a criminal, and executed there ca. 110. During the journey Christian representatives visited him; and he wrote seven letters (six to churches and one to Polycarp). The letters attest to and support the threefold structure of one bishop, presbyters, and deacons. In *Smyrneans* 8.2 he uses the expression "the catholic church."

Letter of Polycarp (to the Philippians). This cover letter for a collection of Ignatius' letters may be composite, written before and after his martyrdom (AD 110–135). Polycarp seems to show knowledge of various Pauline writings, especially the Pastorals. In a chain of second-century church writers Polycarp was acquainted at the earlier end with Ignatius and at the later end with Irenaeus.

Shepherd of Hermas. Some in the early church elevated this vibrant call to conversion of heart, composed in Rome before AD 150, to the level of canonical Scripture; for instance, it was part of the fourth-century Codex Sinaiticus of the NT. Hermas seems to have been a manumitted slave who was a prophet who received revelations: *Visions, Mandates,* and *Similitudes.* The instructions on virtue in the Mandates suppose a spiritual anthropology in which good and bad spirits are active and have to be discerned. The *Similitudes* strongly stress the care of the poor. *Hermas* shows a strong Jewish bent in Roman Christianity.

The Epistle of Barnabas. This treatise was written in Greek by an unknown author (probably a Gentile) employing the allegorical style of OT interpretation in vogue in Alexandria. It was contained in Codex Sinaiticus. The ethical instruction involves the "two ways," that is, the way of light and the way of darkness. Although the author is heavily influenced by Jewish thought, he criticizes Jewish ritual.

Writings of Justin Martyr. A Gentile from Palestine, he spent time in Ephesus, and was martyred in Rome ca. 165. His writings are apologetic in nature, both explaining (to Emperor Antonius Pius) and defending (against Trypho, a Jew) Christianity.

Diatessaron of Tatian. Born in the East, Tatian came to Rome, was converted to Christianity, and became a pupil of Justin. He returned to Mesopotamia in 172. His *Diatessaron* was a harmony from the four Gospels and some noncanonical material. It had enormous influence and served in place of the canonical Gospels for centuries in the Syriac-speaking church. The original was lost, and so it had to be reconstructed from later writings.

Gospel of Thomas (GTh). From Nag Hammadi, GTh, a collection of 114 sayings of the living (risen) Jesus, is the most important treatise for NT purposes. It is actually a collection of sayings without a biographical framework, and so not exactly a gospel. Seventy-nine sayings have some parallel in the Synoptic tradition. Most scholars think that, although GTh may have preserved some original sayings of Jesus, as a whole the work is a composition of the second century and reflects at times incipient gnosticism.

Gospel of Truth. The original of this eloquent Nag Hammadi homiletic reflection on Jesus was composed in Greek in the second century AD and may have been written by the famous gnostic teacher Valentinus. The gnostic myth of the fall of Sophia from the divine realm to this world seems to underlie its picture of Jesus as the manifestation of the unknowable Father God.

BIBLIOGRAPHY

CHAPTER 1: THE NATURE AND ORIGIN
OF THE NEW TESTAMENT

The Anchor Bible Dictionary. Ed. D. N. Freedman et al. 6 vols. New York: Doubleday, 1992.

Eerdmans Dictionary of the Bible. Ed. D. N. Freedman et al. Grand Rapids: Eerdmans, 2000.

Exegetical Dictionary of the New Testament. Ed. H. Balz and G. Schneider. 3 vols. Grand Rapids: Eerdmans, 1993. German orig., 1980–83.

Koester, H. *Introduction to the New Testament.* 2 vols. Philadelphia: Fortress, 1982. 2nd ed. Vol. 1. New York: de Gruyter, 1995.

Kümmel, W. G. *Introduction to the New Testament.* Rev. enlarged ed. Nashville: Abingdon, 1986.

Metzger, B. M. *The Canon of the New Testament: Its Origin, Development, and Significance.* New York: Oxford University Press, 1987.

The New Interpreter's Dictionary of the Bible. Ed. K. D. Sakenfeld et al. 5 vols. Nashville: Abingdon, 2006–9.

The New Jerome Biblical Commentary. Ed. R. E. Brown et al. Englewood Cliffs, N.J.: Prentice Hall, 1990. References are to articles and sections, not page numbers.

CHAPTER 2: HOW TO READ THE NEW TESTAMENT

Barton, J., ed. *The Cambridge Companion to Biblical Interpretation*. Cambridge: Cambridge University Press, 1998.

Brown, R. E., and S. M. Schneiders. "Hermeneutics." NJBC 71:3–51.

Kselman, J. S., and R. D. Witherup. "Modern New Testament Criticism." NJBC 70:3–84.

The New Interpreter's Bible. Ed. L. E. Keck et al. Vol. 1. Nashville: Abingdon, 1994—contains specifically focused articles on "How the Bible Is Read, Interpreted, and Used" historically and in social locations.

CHAPTER 3: THE TEXT OF THE NEW TESTAMENT

Aland, K., and B. Aland. *The Text of the New Testament*. 2nd ed. Grand Rapids: Eerdmans, 1989.

Epp, E. J., and G. D. Fee. *Studies in the Theory and Method of New Testament Textual Criticism*. Studies and Documents 45. Grand Rapids: Eerdmans, 1993.

Marshall, I. H., ed. *New Testament Interpretation: Essays on Principles and Methods*. Grand Rapids: Eerdmans, 1977. Reprinted frequently.

Metzger, B. M., and B. D. Ehrman. *The Text of the New Testament*. 4th ed. New York: Oxford University Press, 2005.

CHAPTER 4: THE POLITICAL AND SOCIAL
WORLD OF NEW TESTAMENT TIMES

Boardman, J., et al., eds. *Greece and the Hellenistic World*. Vol. 1 of *The Oxford History of the Classical World*. New York: Oxford University Press, 1988.

Ferguson, E. *Backgrounds of Early Christianity*. 3rd ed. Grand Rapids: Eerdmans, 2003.

Hengel, M. *Judaism and Hellenism*. 2 vols. Philadelphia: Fortress, 1974; single-vol. ed., 1981.

Hornblower, S., and A. Spawforth, eds. *The Oxford Classical Dictionary*. 3rd rev. ed. New York: Oxford University Press, 2003.

Schürer, E. *The History of the Jewish People in the Age of Jesus Christ* (175 B.C.– A.D. 135). Rev. ed. (G. Vermes et al., eds.). 3 vols. in 4. Edinburgh: Clark, 1973–87.

Smallwood, E. M. *The Jews Under Roman Rule: From Pompey to Diocletian: A Study in Political Relations*. 2nd ed. Leiden: Brill, 2001—originally published 2nd ed., 1981.

Sordi, M. *The Christians and the Roman Empire*. Norman, Okla.: University of Oklahoma Press, 1986.

Stambaugh, J. E., and D. L. Balch. *The New Testament in Its Social Environment*. LEC 2. Philadelphia: Westminster, 1986.

CHAPTER 5: THE RELIGIOUS AND PHILOSOPHICAL WORLD OF NEW TESTAMENT TIMES

Collins, J. J., and D. C. Harlow, eds. *The Eerdmans Dictionary of Early Judaism*. Grand Rapids: Eerdmans, 2010.

Johnson, L. T. *Among the Gentiles: Greco-Roman Religion and Christianity*. AYBRL. New Haven: Yale University Press, 2009.

Klauck, H.-J. *The Religious Context of Early Christianity: A Guide to Graeco-Roman Religion*. Minneapolis: Fortress, 2003.

Koester, H. *Introduction to the New Testament*. 2nd ed. Vol. 1. New York: de Gruyter, 1995.

Nock, A. D. *Conversion: The Old and the New in Religion from Alexander the Great to Augustine of Hippo*. Oxford: Clarendon, 1933. Johns Hopkins Paperbacks ed., 1998.

Sanders, E. P. *Judaism: Practice and Belief 63 BCE–66 CE*. Philadelphia: Trinity, 1992.

CHAPTER 6: GOSPELS IN GENERAL; SYNOPTIC GOSPELS IN PARTICULAR

Bauckham, R. *Jesus and the Eyewitnesses: The Gospels as Eyewitness Testimony*. Edinburgh: Clark, 2006.

Hengel, M. *The Four Gospels and the One Gospel of Jesus Christ: An Investigation of the Collection and Origin of the Canonical Gospels*. Harrisburg, PA: Trinity, 2000.

Sanders, E. P., and M. Davies. *Studying the Synoptic Gospels*. Philadelphia: Trinity, 1989.

Talbert, C. H. *What Is a Gospel? The Genre of the Canonical Gospels*. Philadelphia: Fortress, 1971.

CHAPTER 7: THE GOSPEL ACCORDING TO MARK

Best, E. *Mark: The Gospel as Story.* Edinburgh: Clark, 1983.

Collins, A. Y. *The Beginning of the Gospel: Probings of Mark in Context.* Minneapolis: Fortress, 1992.

Collins, A. Y. *Mark: A Commentary.* Hermeneia. Minneapolis: Fortress, 2007.

Culpepper, R. A. *Mark.* Smyth and Helwys Bible Commentary 20. Macon, Ga.: Smyth and Helwys, 2007.

Marcus, J. *Mark 1–8.* AB 27. New York: Doubleday, 2000.

———. *Mark 8–16.* AYB 27A. New Haven: Yale University Press, 2009.

Rhoads, D. M., et al. *Mark as Story: An Introduction to the Narrative of a Gospel.* Rev. ed. Minneapolis: Fortress, 1999.

CHAPTER 8: THE GOSPEL ACCORDING TO MATTHEW

Schnackenburg, R. *The Gospel of Matthew.* Grand Rapids: Eerdmans, 2002. German original, 1985/87.

Stanton, G. N. *A Gospel for a New People: Studies in Matthew.* Louisville: W/JK, 1992.

Talbert, C. H. *Reading the Sermon on the Mount: Character Formation and Ethical Decision Making in Matthew 5–7.* Grand Rapids: Baker Academic, 2004.

Witherup, R. D. *Matthew: God with Us.* Hyde Park, N.Y.: New City, 2000.

CHAPTER 9: THE GOSPEL ACCORDING TO LUKE

Bock, D. L., and A. J. Köstenberger, eds. *A Theology of Luke and Acts: God's Promised Program Realized for All Nations.* Biblical Theology of the New Testament Series. Grand Rapids: Zondervan, 2012.

Fitzmyer, J. A. *Luke the Theologian.* New York: Paulist, 1989.

Shillington, V. G. *An Introduction to the Study of Luke-Acts.* New York: Clark, 2007.

Talbert, C. H. *Reading Luke: A Literary and Theological Commentary.* Rev. ed. Macon, Ga.: Smyth and Helwys, 2002.

CHAPTER 10: THE ACTS OF THE APOSTLES

Becker, J., ed. *Christian Beginnings: Word and Community from Jesus to Post-Apostolic Times.* Louisville: W/JK, 1993. German original, 1987.

The Book of Acts in Its First Century Setting. Ed. B. W. Winter et al. 6 vols. Grand Rapids: Eerdmans, 1993–97.

Dibelius, M. *Studies in the Acts of the Apostles.* Ed. H. Greeven. London: SCM, 1956. Rev. ed. reissued as *The Book of Acts: Form, Style, and Theology.* Ed. K. C. Hanson. Minneapolis: Fortress, 2004. A classic.

Hengel, M. *Acts and the History of Earliest Christianity.* Philadelphia: Fortress, 1979. Reissued by Wipf and Stock, 2003.

Soards, M. L. *The Speeches in Acts: Their Content, Context, and Concerns.* Louisville: W/JK, 1994.

CHAPTER 11: THE GOSPEL ACCORDING TO JOHN

Brown, R. E. *An Introduction to the Gospel of John.* Rev. and ed. by F. J. Moloney. ABRL. New York: Doubleday, 2003.

Brown, R. E. *The Gospel According to John.* AB 29. Garden City, N.Y.: Doubleday, 1966.

Brown, R. E. *The Gospel According to John.* AB 29A. Garden City, N.Y.: Doubleday, 1970.

Culpepper, R. A. *Anatomy of the Fourth Gospel: A Study in Literary Design.* Philadelphia: Fortress, 1983.

Donahue, J. R., ed. *Life in Abundance: Studies of John's Gospel in Tribute to Raymond E. Brown, S.S.* Collegeville, Minn.: Liturgical, 2005.

Martyn, J. L. *History and Theology in the Fourth Gospel.* 3rd ed. NTL. Louisville: W/JK, 2003.

CHAPTER 12: FIRST EPISTLE (LETTER) OF JOHN

Some of the Bibliography of Chapter 11, for example, on Johannine theology and community history, may treat the Johannine Epistles alongside the Gospel.

Brown, R. E. *The Community of the Beloved Disciple. The Life, Loves, and Hates of an Individual Church in New Testament Times.* New York: Paulist, 1979.

Brown, R. E. *The Epistles of John.* AB 30. Garden City, N.Y.: Doubleday, 1982.

Schnackenburg, R. *The Johannine Epistles.* New York: Crossroad, 1992. German original, 1975.

Westcott, B. F. *The Epistles of St. John*. Grand Rapids: Eerdmans, 1966. Original ed., 1883. A classic.

CHAPTER 13: SECOND LETTER OF JOHN

The *Bibliography* of Chapter 12 is pertinent to all three of the Johannine Epistles.

Culpepper, R. A. *The Johannine School*. SBLDS 26. Missoula, Mont.: Scholars, 1975.

Lieu, J. *The Second and Third Epistles of John*. Edinburgh: Clark, 1986.

CHAPTER 14: THIRD LETTER OF JOHN

Fry, V. R. L. "Diotrephes." ABD 2.204.

Kysar, R. "John, Epistles of." ABD 3.900–912.

Malherbe, A. J. "The Inhospitality of Diotrephes." GCHP 222–32.

CHAPTER 15: CLASSIFICATION AND FORMAT
OF NEW TESTAMENT LETTERS

Klauck, H.-J. *Ancient Letters and the New Testament: A Guide to Context and Exegesis*. Waco, TX: Baylor University Press, 2006.

Murphy-O'Connor, J. *Paul the Letter-Writer*. GNS 41. Collegeville: Liturgical, 1995.

Puskas, C. B., and M. Reasoner. *The Letters of Paul: An Introduction*. 2nd ed. Collegeville: Liturgical, 2013.

White, J. L. *Light from Ancient Letters*. Philadelphia: Fortress, 1986.

CHAPTER 16: GENERAL ISSUES IN PAUL'S LIFE AND THOUGHT

Beker, J. C. *Paul the Apostle*. 2nd ed. Philadelphia: Fortress, 1984.

Bruce, F. F. *Paul: Apostle of the Heart Set Free*. Grand Rapids: Eerdmans, 1984.

Fitzmyer, J. A. *According to Paul*. New York: Paulist, 1993.

Gorman, M. J. *Apostle of the Crucified Lord: A Theological Introduction to Paul and His Letters*. Grand Rapids: Eerdmans, 2004.

Knox, J. *Chapters in a Life of Paul*. Nashville: Abingdon, 1950. Rev. ed. by Mercer University Press, 1987.

Sanders, E. P. *Paul: A Very Short Introduction.* Oxford: Oxford University Press, 1991.

———. *Paul and Palestinian Judaism: A Comparison of Patterns of Religion.* Philadelphia: Fortress, 1977.

Schnelle, U. *Apostle Paul: His Life and Theology.* Grand Rapids: Baker, 2012.

Soards, M. L. *The Apostle Paul: An Introduction to His Writings and Teaching.* New York: Paulist, 1987.

Wright, N. T. *Paul and the Faithfulness of God.* Vol. 4 of *Christian Origins and the Question of God.* In 2 parts. Minneapolis: Fortress, 2013.

CHAPTER 18: FIRST LETTER TO THE THESSALONIANS

Best, E. *A Commentary on the First and Second Epistles to the Thessalonians.* BNTC. London: Black, 1972.

Donfried, K. P. *Paul, Thessalonica, and Early Christianity.* Grand Rapids: Eerdmans, 2002.

Donfried, K. P. *The Thessalonian Debate: Methodological Discord or Methodological Synthesis?* Grand Rapids: Eerdmans, 2000.

Horsley, R. A. *Paul and Empire: Religion and Power in Roman Imperial Society.* Harrisburg, Pa.: Trinity, 1997.

Malherbe, A. J. *Paul and the Thessalonians: The Philosophic Tradition of Pastoral Care.* Philadelphia: Fortress, 1987.

CHAPTER 19: LETTER TO THE GALATIANS

Barclay, J. M. G. *Obeying the Truth: A Study of Paul's Ethics in Galatians.* Edinburgh: Clark, 1988.

Barrett, C. K. *Freedom and Obligation: A Study of the Epistle to the Galatians.* Philadelphia: Westminster, 1985.

Braxton, B. R. *No Longer Slaves: Galatians and African American Experience.* Collegeville: Liturgical, 2002.

Martyn, J. L. "Galatians." TBOB 2.271–84. This essay anticipated the following item.

Martyn, J. L. *Galatians.* AB 33A. New York: Doubleday, 1997.

Soards, M. L., and D. J. Pursiful. *Galatians.* Smyth and Helwys Bible Commentary 26A. Macon, Ga.: Smyth and Helwys, 2015.

CHAPTER 20: LETTER TO THE PHILIPPIANS

Cassidy, R. J. *Christians and Roman Rule in the New Testament. New Perspectives.* Companions to the New Testament. New York: Crossroad, 2001.

Collange, J.-F. *The Epistle of Saint Paul to the Philippians.* London: Epworth, 1979.

Meeks, W. A. *The First Urban Christians: The Social World of the Apostle Paul.* New Haven: Yale University Press, 1983.

Osiek, C. *Philippians, Philemon.* ANTC. Nashville: Abingdon, 2000.

CHAPTER 21: LETTER TO PHILEMON

Barclay, J. M. G. *Colossians and Philemon.* NTG. Sheffield: Sheffield Academic, 1997.

Brogdon, L. *Not a Slave but a Brother: An African American Reading of Paul's Letter to Philemon.* Saarbrucken, Ger.: Scholar's Press, 2013.

Petersen, N. R. *Rediscovering Paul: Philemon and the Sociology of Paul's Narrative World.* Philadelphia: Fortress, 1985.

Thompson, M. M. *Colossians and Philemon.* Two Horizons New Testament Commentary. Grand Rapids: Eerdmans, 2005.

CHAPTER 22: FIRST LETTER TO THE CORINTHIANS

Brown, A. R. *The Cross and Human Transformation: Paul's Apocalyptic Word in 1 Corinthians.* Minneapolis: Augsburg/Fortress, 1995.

Fee, G. D. *God's Empowering Presence: The Holy Spirit in the Letters of Paul.* Peabody, Mass.: Hendrickson, 1994.

Keener, C. S. *1–2 Corinthians.* New Cambridge Bible Commentary. New York: Cambridge University Press, 2005.

Martin, D. B. *The Corinthian Body.* New Haven: Yale University Press, 1995.

CHAPTER 23: SECOND LETTER TO THE CORINTHIANS

Collins, R. F. *The Power of Images in Paul.* Collegeville, Minn.: Liturgical, 2008.

Matera, F. J. *II Corinthians: A Commentary.* NTL. Louisville: W/JK, 2003.

Murphy-O'Connor, J. *The Theology of the Second Letter to the Corinthians.* New Testament Theology. New York: Cambridge University Press, 1991.

Wan, S.-k. *Power in Weakness: Conflict and Rhetoric in Paul's Second Letter to the Corinthians*. New Testament in Context. Harrisburg, Pa.: Trinity, 2000.

CHAPTER 24: LETTER TO THE ROMANS

Donfried, K. P. *The Romans Debate*. Rev. ed. Peabody, Mass.: Hendrickson, 1991.

Keck, L. E. *Romans*. ANTC. Nashville: Abingdon, 2005.

Watson, F. *Paul, Judaism, and the Gentiles: Beyond the New Perspective*. Rev. ed. Grand Rapids: Eerdmans, 2007.

Westerholm, S. *Perspectives Old and New on Paul: The "Lutheran" Paul and His Critics*. Grand Rapids: Eerdmans, 2003.

CHAPTER 25: PSEUDONYMITY AND
THE DEUTERO-PAULINE WRITINGS

Collins, R. F. *Letters That Paul Did Not Write: The Epistle to the Hebrews and the Pauline Pseudepigrapha*. GNS 28. Wilmington, Del.: Glazier, 1988. Reissued by Wipf and Stock, 2005.

Murphy-O'Connor, J. *St. Paul the Letter Writer: His World, His Options, His Skill*. Collegeville, Minn.: Liturgical, 1995.

CHAPTER 26: SECOND LETTER TO THE THESSALONIANS

Ascough, R. S. "Thessalonians, Second Letter to the." *The New Interpreter's Dictionary of the Bible*. 5.574–79.

Collins, R. F. *The Thessalonians Correspondence*. BETL 87. Leuven: Leuven University Press, 1990.

Donfried, K. P. *Paul, Thessalonica, and Early Christianity*. Grand Rapids: Eerdmans, 2002.

Furnish, V. P. *1 Thessalonians, 2 Thessalonians*. ANTC. Nashville: Abingdon, 2004.

CHAPTER 27: LETTER TO THE COLOSSIANS

Arnold, C. E. *The Colossian Syncretism: The Interface Between Christianity and Folk Belief at Colossae*. Grand Rapids: Baker, 1996.

Balla, P. *The Child-Parent Relationship in the New Testament and Its Environment*. WUNT 2/155. Tübingen: Mohr Siebeck, 2003.

Brown, R. E. *The Churches the Apostles Left Behind*. New York: Paulist, 1984.

Francis, F. O., and W. A. Meeks, eds. *Conflict at Colossae*. SBLSBS 4. Rev. ed. Missoula, Mont.: Scholars Press, 1975.

CHAPTER 28: EPISTLE (LETTER) TO THE EPHESIANS

Arnold, C. E. *Ephesians, Power and Magic: The Concept of Power in Ephesians in Light of Its Historical Setting*. SNTSMS 63. New York: Cambridge University Press, 1989.

Best, E. *Essays on Ephesians*. Edinburgh: Clark, 1997.

Dahl, N. A. *Studies in Ephesians*. Ed. D. Hellholm et al. WUNT 131. Tübingen: Siebeck, 2000.

Martin, R. P. *Reconciliation: A Study of Paul's Theology*. Rev. ed. Grand Rapids: Academie, 1989.

PASTORAL LETTERS

Brown, R. E. *The Churches the Apostles Left Behind*. New York: Paulist, 1984.

Collins, R. F. *Letters That Paul Did Not Write: The Epistle to the Hebrews and the Pauline Pseudepigrapha*. GNS 28. Wilmington, Del.: Glazier, 1988. Reissued by Wipf and Stock, 2005.

Donelson, L. R. *Pseudepigraphy and Ethical Argument in the Pastoral Epistles*. HUT 22. Tübingen: J. C. B. Mohr, 1986.

Harding, M. *What Are They Saying About the Pastoral Epistles?* New York: Paulist: 2001.

CHAPTER 32: LETTER (EPISTLE) TO THE HEBREWS

Attridge, H. W. *Hebrews*. Hermeneia. Philadelphia: Fortress, 1989.

Harrington, D. J. *What Are They Saying About the Letter to the Hebrews?* New York: Paulist, 2005.

Hurst, L. D. *The Epistle to the Hebrews: Its Background of Thought*. SNTSMS 65. New York: Cambridge University Press, 1990.

Koester, C. R. *Hebrews*. AB 36. New York: Doubleday, 2001.

Thompson, J. W. *The Beginnings of Christian Philosophy: The Epistle to the Hebrews*. CBQMS 13. Washington, D.C.: 1982.

Vanhoye, A. *Structure and Message of the Epistle to the Hebrews.* Rome: Pontifical Biblical Institute Press, 1989.

CHAPTER 33: FIRST LETTER OF PETER

Brown, R. E., et al., eds. *Peter in the New Testament.* Minneapolis/New York: Augsburg/Paulist, 1973.

Elliott, J. H. *A Home for the Homeless: A Sociological Exegesis of 1 Peter, Its Situation and Strategy.* Philadelphia: Fortress, 1981.

Goppelt, L. *A Commentary on I Peter.* Grand Rapids: Eerdmans, 1993. German original, 1978.

Harner, P. B. *What Are They Saying About the Catholic Epistles?* New York: Paulist, 2004.

CHAPTER 34: EPISTLE (LETTER) OF JAMES

Batten, A. J. *What Are They Saying About the Letter of James?* New York: Paulist, 2009.

Bauckham, R. *James: Wisdom of James, Disciple of Jesus the Sage.* New Testament Readings. New York: Routledge, 1999.

Johnson, L. T. *Brother of Jesus, Friend of God: Studies in the Letter of James.* Grand Rapids: Eerdmans, 2004.

Tamez, E. *The Scandalous Message of James: Faith Without Works Is Dead.* New York: Crossroad, 1992.

CHAPTER 36: SECOND EPISTLE (LETTER) OF PETER

Bauckham, R. *Jude and the Relatives of Jesus in the Early Church.* Edinburgh: Clark, 1990.

Chester, A., and R. P. Martin. *The Theology of James, Peter, and Jude.* New Testament Theology. New York: Cambridge University Press, 1994.

Knight, J. *2 Peter and Jude.* NTG. Sheffield: Sheffield Academic, 1995.

Kraftchick, S. J. *Jude, 2 Peter.* ANTC. Nashville: Abingdon, 2002.

Reese, R. A. *2 Peter and Jude.* Two Horizons New Testament Commentary. Grand Rapids: Eerdmans, 2007.

Richard, E. J. *Reading 1 Peter, Jude, and 2 Peter: A Literary and Theological Commentary.* Reading the New Testament Series. Macon, Ga.: Smyth and Helwys, 2000.

CHAPTER 37: THE BOOK OF REVELATION (THE APOCALYPSE)

Bauckham, R. *The Climax of Prophecy: Studies in the Book of Revelation*. Edinburgh: Clark, 1992.

Koester, C. R. *Revelation*. AYB 38. New Haven: Yale University Press, 2014.

———. *Revelation and the End of All Things*. Grand Rapids: Eerdmans, 2001.

Malina, B. J. *On the Genre and Message of Revelation*. Peabody, Mass.: Hendrickson, 1995.

Roloff, J. *The Revelation of John*. CC. Minneapolis: Fortress, 1993. German original 2nd ed., 1987.

APPENDIX I: THE HISTORICAL JESUS

This topic is tangential to the main purpose of this Introduction, which is concerned with the books of the NT; and so here only a very limited list is offered, indicating possibilities for further study.

Allison, D. C., Jr. *Constructing Jesus: Memory, Imagination, and History*. Grand Rapids: Baker Academic, 2010. This is but one of several important works by Allison that deal with the historical Jesus.

Dunn, J. D. G., and S. McKnight, eds. *The Historical Jesus in Recent Research*. Sources for Biblical and Theological Study. Lake Winona, Ind.: Eisenbrauns, 2005.

Evans, C. A. *Encyclopedia of the Historical Jesus*. New York: Routledge, 2008.

Meier, J. P. *A Marginal Jew*. 5 vols. ABRL/AYBRL. New York/New Haven: Doubleday/Yale University Press, 1991, 1994, 2001, 2009, 2016.

Theissen, G., and A. Merz. *The Historical Jesus: A Comprehensive Guide*. Minneapolis: Fortress, 1998. German original, 1996.

APPENDIX II: JEWISH AND CHRISTIAN WRITINGS
PERTINENT TO THE NEW TESTAMENT

Evans, C. A. *Noncanonical Writings and New Testament Interpretation*. Peabody, Mass.: Hendrickson, 1992. Very brief information on all noncanonical works, Jewish and Christian.

JEWISH WRITINGS

Dead Sea Scrolls

Fitzmyer, J. A. *Responses to 101 Questions on the Dead Sea Scrolls*. New York: Paulist, 1992. Very useful in correcting sensationalist nonsense about the Scrolls.

Galor, K., J.-B. Humbert, and J. Zangenberg. *Qumran: The Site of the Dead Sea Scrolls: Archaeological Interpretations and Debates*. Leiden: Brill, 2006.

García Martínez, F. *The Dead Sea Scrolls Translated: The Qumran Texts in English*. 2nd ed. Leiden: Brill; Grand Rapids, Mich.: Eerdmans, 1996. The best collection.

Pseudepigrapha

Charlesworth, J. H., ed. *The Old Testament Pseudepigrapha*. 2 vols. Garden City, N.Y.: Doubleday, 1983–85. The most complete collection.

Josephus

Loeb Classical Library: Nine vols. (Greek text with English translation).

Philo

Loeb Classical Library: Ten vols. (Greek text with English translation).

CHRISTIAN (AND GNOSTIC) WRITINGS

Apocrypha (NT)

Hennecke, E., W. Schneemelcher, and R. McL. Wilson, eds. *New Testament Apocrypha*. Rev. ed. 2 vols. Louisville: W/JK, 1991–92. German original, 1989–90. The most complete collection.

Early Church Writers

Holmes, M. W., ed. *The Apostolic Fathers. Greek Texts and English Translations*. Rev. 3rd ed. Grand Rapids: Baker, 2007. After the work of J. B. Lightfoot and J. R. Harmer.

Gnostics

Jonas, H. *The Gnostic Religion*. 2nd ed. Boston: Beacon, 1963. A classic.

Robinson, J. M. *The Nag Hammadi Library*. 3rd ed. San Francisco: Harper and Row, 1988. The complete corpus in English translation.

Rudolph, K. *Gnosis: The Nature and History of Gnosticism*. San Francisco: Harper and Row, 1983.

·✦·

INDEX

Page ranges in **bold** indicate main discussion (chapter.)

Paul (Saul) (continued)
145, 161, 171–72, 196–97;
and Ephesus, 96–97, 112, 150,
154, 156, 187, 194–95, 196,
238–39, 244 (see also Ephesians,
Epistle to the; Timothy: First Letter to); eschatological message,
304; evangelizing missions,
xx–xxi, 108–14, 149, 154–57,
163–66, 168–70, 174–76,
186–87, 202–3, 208, 237–38
(see also specific locations); hardships
suffered, 108, 157, 159–60,
168, 196–97, 198, 199, 250 (see
also Paul: arrested/imprisoned);
healing by, 108; heritage, 161–
62; historicity, 300; in Jerusalem, 105, 109–10, 150, 152,
153, 154, 155; and Mosaic Law,
109–10, 155, 161, 167, 171,
204, 205, 207, 209; origins and
background, 25, 29, 151–52;
and Philippi, 111, 149, 156,
163–64, 174–78 (see also Philippians, Letter to); righteousness, 152, 197, 203–6, 208–9,
243, 250; and Rome (church),
201–3, 208 (see also Romans,
Letter to; Rome); "second
career," 233, 239, 243, 245,
247–49; sermons/speeches,
108, 111, 112, 113; sources of
knowledge about, 148–51; and
Timothy, 149–50, 161, 163,
165, 174, 213, 237–39 (see also
Timothy). See also Pastoral Letters
of Paul; Paul, Letters of; Pauline
letter writing; and specific letters/
epistles and topics

Paul, Letters of, 161; author(s) and
dating, 3, 4, 5, 144, 164, 169,
175, 181–82, 186, 194–95,
202; classification, 145;
deutero-Pauline letters, 210–12
(see also specific letters); early mss.,
16; and events in Paul's life,
148–51; format, 146–47; inclusion in NT canon, 4–6; order,
144; purpose, 145; referred to
in II Pet, 279; school of Pauline
writing, 161–62; significance,
148. See also Letters/Epistles; and
specific letters
Pauline letter writing, 161–62. See
also Pastoral Letters of Paul; Paul,
Letters of; and specific letters
Pentecost, 100–101
Pergamum (church), xxvi, 287,
288–90
permissibility of all things, 189,
193
persecution: of Christians, 4, 21,
22, 23–24, 105, 152, 296 (see
also specific individuals); in Rev, 293
(see also judgment)
Peter (Cephas, Simon): as apostle,
66; arrested/imprisoned, xx,
104, 107; called, 80; confession of Jesus by, 50, 59, 66,
71, 82; death, xxi, 3, 21, 158,
261, 292; faith of, 65, 66, 262;
and Gentiles, 106–7, 108, 155,
261; healings by, 102–3, 106–7;
after Jesus' death/resurrection,
98, 103, 106–7, 260–62; Jesus
denied, 54, 70–71, 89, 125,
127, 261; and the Last Supper,
88; as missionary, 261; mother-